A COLLECTION OF TELUGU PROVERBS

A COLLECTION OF TELUGU PROVERBS

TRANSLATED, ILLUSTRATED, AND EXPLAINED;

TOGRHER WITH SOME

SANSCRIT PROVERBS

PRINTED IN THE DEVANAGARI AND TELUGU CHARACTERS.

BY

CAPTAIN M. W. CARR,

Madras Staff Corps

GYAN

Published by

Gyan Publishing House
5, Ansari Road
Daryaganj, New Delhi-110002
Phone: 011-47034999, 9811692060
E-mail: books@gyanbooks.com

Distribution Network
gyanbooks.com
India, USA, Canada, UK, Australia, France

ISBN : 978-81-212-4265-3 (PB)
First Published, 1868

2nd Impression 2020

Printed at: Gyan Press, Delhi.

A
Collection or Telugu Proverbs
Author: Captain M. W. Carr

ఆంధ్రలోకోక్తిచంద్రిక.

A

COLLECTION

OF

TELUGU PROVERBS

TRANSLATED, ILLUSTRATED, AND EXPLAINED;

TOGETHER WITH SOME

SANSCRIT PROVERBS

PRINTED IN THE DEVANÂGARÎ AND TELUGU CHARACTERS.

BY

CAPTAIN M. W. ÇARR,
Madras Staff Corps.

MADRAS:
PRINTED AND SOLD AT THE CHRISTIAN KNOWLEDGE SOCIETY'S PRESS,
18, CHURCH STREET, VEPERY.

LONDON:
SOLD BY TRÜBNER AND CO. 60, PATERNOSTER ROW.
1868.

PREFACE.

THE collection of Telugu Proverbs contained in this volume was commenced several years ago, at the request of the translator, by Râvipâṭi Guruvayya Gâru, the able Munshî to the Telugu Translator to the Government of Madras, who has up to within a late date perseveringly laboured in adding to the small beginning at first made. To him therefore the public are indebted for this gathering of the 'household words,' and homely maxims of his countrymen and countrywomen—the property specially of the latter for, as among other nations so among the Hindûs, "the women of the family retain a larger number of such household words in their memories, than any other class of the community."*

That Proverbial phrases give an insight into the minds and sentiments of a people that cannot otherwise be easily obtained, will generally be admitted. It is hoped that the present addition to the numerous collections of "people's words"† may not be altogether profitless.

In the translation, escape from the accusation *Translators, traitors*‡ by the preservation as far as possible of the idea contained in the original, has been aimed at, and to this end, the rendering has been made as literal as could be, leaving it to the English reader to transfer the sentiment into epigrammatic language of his own.

The difficulty of transferring proverbs—intertwined as they are with the peculiar thoughts, manners, and customs of a people—from their own language to another tongue will be acknowledged, and the defects of the present work in that respect, will, it is hoped, be pardoned. As has been well said, "Transport them under other skies, or, which is still more fatal, empty them from vessel to vessel, and their strength

* *Friend of India*, June 18, 1868.

† लोकोक्तिः

‡ Traduttori, traditori.

and flavour will in great part have disappeared in the process."* The translator is under obligation to R. Guruvayya Gâru for his valuable assistance.

In the hope of making this collection of their sayings more acceptable to Telugu readers who have had an English education, European proverbs exactly or approximately corresponding to some of the Telugu Proverbs, have been quoted by way of illustration. The similarity in many instances is striking. These European Proverbs have been culled from the useful volumes in Bohn's Antiquarian and Classical Libraries, and from Kelly's Proverbs of all Nations.

In respect to the few Sanscrit Proverbs which are appended, it is scarcely necessary to state that no pretension is here made to present a collection of proverbial sayings and Aphorisms found in the literature of that language. For such the reader must go to the Indische Sprüche of Professor Böhtlingk. (St. Petersburgh, 1863-65.) Some Sanscrit phrases were collected promiscuously with Telugu proverbs, and it was thought expedient to separate them. To these others were added from the *Kavitâratnâkara* and other sources. For the convenience of Telugu readers, unacquainted with the Devanâgârî character, these proverbs have also been printed in the Telugu character. In the translation of the Sanscrit portion, material assistance has been rendered by Śrîrekam Râmânuja Sûri, Head Telugu Munshî in the Madras Presidency College.

In the Supplement will be found additional Telugu proverbs, an Index Verborum, and an Index to the European Proverbs.

The translator has to thank the Rev. P. Percival, Professor of Vernacular literature, Madras Presidency College, for kindly placing at his disposal a MS., containing a large number of Telugu Proverbs.

His acknowledgments are also due to the printers for their pains and labour.

MADRAS, *July*, 1868.

* Archbishop Trench.

*** As this collection is doubtless very far from complete, the translator will feel obliged by the communication of Telugu proverbs not found herein.

CONTENTS.

ఆంధ్రలోకోక్తిచంద్రిక.

TELUGU PROVERBS.

అ

1. అంగటివీథిలో అబ్బా అంటే, యెవరికి పుట్టినావురా కొడకా అన్నట్టు.

When addressed [by his son] in the bazar as "Father," he replied, "Son! unto whom wert thou born?"

(See Nos. 412, 1610.)

Want of natural affection. Selfish indifference.

2. అంగట్లో అన్నీ వున్నవి, అల్లుని నోట్లో శని వున్నది.

There is every thing in the bazar, but Saturn is in the mouth of the son-in-law.

Some unfortunate circumstance prevented a son-in-law from availing himself of the good fare of his father-in-law.

Evil fate.

3. అంగట్లో బెల్లము గుళ్లో లింగానికి నైవేద్యము.

Offering the molasses in the bazar to the idol in the temple.

(See Nos. 910, 1396, 1560.)

Naivêdyam is the ordinary oblation.

Willing to be liberal at the expense of others.

4. అంగిట బెల్లము, ఆత్మలో విషము.

Molasses in the roof of the mouth, and poison in the heart.

(See Nos. 5, 834, 839.)

Honey in his mouth, words of milk;
Gall in his heart, fraud in his deeds. (Latin.)*

5. అంగిట విషము, మున్నాలికను తియ్యదనము.

Poison in the palate, sweetness on the tip of the tongue.

(See Nos. 4, 834, 839.)

Full of courtesy, full of craft.

6. అంటా ముట్టరాని అగ్రహారము.

An Agrahâram which should not be touched or felt.

An *Agrahâram* is a Brahman village or quarter.

Said of any thing that should scrupulously be avoided.

7. అంటూ సంటూ ఆసాదివానిది, రట్టూ రవ్వా గంగానమ్మది.

All the offerings go to the priest, the noise to Gangânamma.

(See No. 1545.)

Gangânamma is a certain village goddess.

8. అంటూ సంటూ లేని కోడలి దాని మేనమామ కొడుకు చిక్కుడు చెట్టుకిందికి పోయి పక్కలు యెగరవేశినాడట.

The wife's maternal uncle's son, who had nothing to do with ceremonial uncleanness, went and sobbed under the bean tree.

Chikkuḍu Cheṭṭu is the Lablab Cultratus, often grown over a shed in the yard of a Hindu's house.

Claiming relationship.

9. అంతమాత్రమా కొడకా చెవులు పట్టుకొని తడవేవు అన్నట్టు.

Am I so well off, my son, that you should feel my ears?

(See No. 819.)

Said by an old woman to a thief.

---

* Mel in ore, verba lactis,
Fel in corde, fraus in factis.

10. అంత్య నిష్ఠురముకన్నా ఆది నిష్ఠురమే మేలు.

Annoyance at the beginning is better than annoyance at the end.

(See No. 246.)

A prompt denial causes less annoyance than compliance with a request and disappointment in the end.

Better a friendly denial than an unwilling compliance. (German.)*

11. అందము చిందినట్టు, నాగరికము నష్టమయినట్టు.

His beauty has overflowed and his politeness has gone.

(See Nos. 12, 16.)

Said ironically of an ugly ruffian.

12. అందములో పుట్టిన గంధపుచెక్క, ఆముదములో పుట్టిన మడ్డి.

A piece of sandal wood born of beauty, and the dregs of castor oil.

(See Nos. 11, 16.)

13. అందని మాని పండ్లకు ఆశ పడ్డట్టు.

Like wishing for fruit which cannot be reached.

14. అందరికీ నేను లోకువ, నాకు నంబి రామాయ లోకువ.

I am below all, but Nambi Râmâya is below me.

15. అందరూ వకయెత్తు, అగస్త్యుడు వకయెత్తు, అతని కమండలం వకయెత్తు.

The whole people [of the earth], the sage Agastya, and his jar are all of equal weight.

The legend is that when all the great men of the earth had, on one occasion, assembled at Kailâsa, their weight was so great that the earth began to topple over. On this, Agastya was sent to weigh down the other side which he accordingly did, but his presence being afterwards required at Kailâsa, he transferred his virtue to his jar of holy waters, left it to balance the earth, and obeyed the summons.

* Besser freundlich versagen, als unwilling gewähren.

16. అందానికి రెండు బొందలు, ఆటకు రెండు తాళాలు.

Two holes in beauty; two cymbals in a dance.

(See Nos. 11, 12.)

Said of an ugly and bad dancer.

17. అందులో పసలేదు, గంజిలో వార్చుమన్నట్టు.

There is no substance in that, strain the rice water.

Equivalent to the English "there's nothing in him" or "there's nothing in it."

18. అంధునకు అద్దము చూపినట్టు.

Like giving a blind man a looking glass.

A blind man will not thank you for a looking glass.

19. అంబటి యేరు వచ్చినది అత్తగారూ అంటే, కొలబుర్ర నాచేతిలో వున్నది కోడలా అన్నదట.

"A river of porridge has come, mother-in-law!" she cried. "But *I* have the measure, daughter-in-law," replied the dame.

(See Nos. 165, 161.)

20. అంబలి తాగేవారికి మీసాలు యెగబట్టేవారు కొందరా.

Do people that live on porridge keep men to hold up their mustaches?

(See Nos. 856, 1608, 1792.)

Said of a poor man trying to appear grand.

A proud mind and a poor purse are ill met.

21. అకట వికటపు రాజుకు అవివేకి ప్రధాని, చాదస్తపు పరివారము.

A foolish minister, and a clumsy retinue, to a perverse king.

22. అక్కన్న మాదన్నగారు అందలమెక్కితే, సాటికి సరప్ప చెరువు కట్ట యెక్కినాడట.

When Akkanna and Mâdanna mounted their state palankin, Sarappa got on the bund of the tank to make himself equal.

(See No. 1857.)

Envying and mocking the wealthy.

Puppies imitating their mistresses. (Latin.)*

23. అగడ్తలో పడ్డ పిల్లికి అదే వైకుంఠం.

The moat is heaven to the cat that falls into it.

It cannot possibly escape, and dies.

An inextricable difficulty.

24. అగస్త్య భ్రాత.

The brother of Agastya.

Agastya was a great sage, who was not known to have any brother.

Applied to a new-comer, attempting to make himself out a great personage.

25. అగ్గువ అయితే అంగడికి వస్తున్నది.

When it is cheap, it comes to the bazar.

(See No. 857.)

26. అగ్గువ అయితే అందరూ కొంటారు.

When it is cheap, all will buy.

27. అగ్నిలో మిడత పడ్డట్టు.

Like a grass-hopper jumping into the fire (flame).

(See No. 177.)

To try, they say, to extinguish it.

Applied to rash acts.

---

* Catulæ dominas imitantes.

28. అగ్నిహోత్రముకు పోయిన సోమిదేవమ్మ ఆరునెలల గర్భముతో వచ్చినది.

Sômidêvamma went for fire (for the sacrifice) and came back six months in pregnancy.

Sômidêvamma is an honorific title given to the wife of a sacrificing priest; she is supposed to be very pious.

29. అగ్నిహోత్రములో ఆజ్యము పోసినట్టు.

Like ghee poured on fire.

To cast oil in the fire is not the way to quench it.

30. అచ్చం తిరుమణిధారి అయితే పుల్ల పట్టడంలోనే తెలుసును.

You can tell whether he is really a Vaishṇava or not by the way in which he holds the pencil.

***Tirumaṇi* is the clay used for the Sectarian mark worn on the forehead by Vaishṇavas, and *Pulla* is a bit of grass with which the mark is made.**

Halt not before a cripple.

31. అచ్చివచ్చిన భూమి అడిగెడే చాలును.

If the ground is lucky, a foot of it is enough.

Luck is all.

32. అటయితే కందిపప్పు, యిటయితే పెసరపప్పు.

In the one case Kandi, in the other Pesara.

(See No. 33.)

***Kandi* is the Cajanus Indicus; *Pesara* is the Phaseolus Mungo.**

Said by a Brahman quack referring to the recovery or death of his patient. In either case he is feasted.

33. అటయితే వైద్యకట్నము, యిటయితే వైతరణిగోదానము.

In the one case, Medical fees; in the other, the gift of a Vaitaraṇi cow.

(See No. 32.)

A cow is presented at funerals to a Brahman to enable the soul of the deceased to get across the burning river Vaitaraṇi which is said to separate heaven from earth.

Said by a Brahman priest and doctor.

34. అట్లువండే ఆబిడకు ఆరుగురు అమర్చవలెను.

A Hopper-woman requiring six people to assist her.

" Hopper" is a kind of cake (*Tamil* அப்பம்).

Said of a person giving himself airs.

35. అడకత్తులోని పోక.

Like a nut in the nippers.

Aḍakattu are nippers used for breaking Areca nuts.

To be between the hammer and the anvil. (French.)*

36. అడగనేరను, పూడ్చి పెట్టుమన్నట్టు.

I cannot ask, sweep the whole [into my dish].

Feigned modesty.

I don't want it, I don't want it, but put it into my hood. (Spanish.)†

37. అడిగేవానికి చెప్పేవాడు లోకువ.

He who has to answer is inferior to him who questions.

It is one thing to put questions, another to answer them.

38. అడియాశ పోడియాశ దుఃఖానకు కారణము.

Vain hopes are a source of grief.

Hope and expectation are a fool's income. (Danish.)‡

---

* Etre entre le marteau et l'enclume.
† No lo quiero, no lo quiero, mas échadme lo en la capilla.
‡ Haabe og vente er Giekerente.

39. అడవి కాచిన వెన్నెల.

Like moon-light in the jungle.

(See Nos. 1618, 1619.)

Wasted on a spot where it is not appreciated.

40. అడవి నక్కలకు కొత్వాలు దురాయా.

What does a wild Jackal care for the threats of a Police Officer?

(See No. 1094.)

What does the moon care if the dogs bark at her? (German.)*

41. అడివి వుశిరికకాయ, సముద్రపు వుప్పు కలిసినట్టు.

Like salt from the sea being mixed with Emblic Myrobalan grown in the [distant] jungle.

Usirikakâya is the Emblica Officinalis.

Used with reference to an advantage gained by an unlooked for coincidence.

42. అడుగులోనే హంసపాదా.

What! a caret in the commencement?

Said by a man to an ignorant scribe who, in writing the customary invocation "*Srî Râmajaya*" at the heading of a letter, omitted a syllable.

Blundering at the very beginning of any business.

He who begins ill finishes worse. (Italian.)†

Well begun is half done.

43. అడుసులో నాటిన స్తంభము.

A post fixed in the mire [swinging to and fro].

(See No. 44.)

Said of a time server.

To sit on two stools. (Latin.)‡

---

* Was Kümmert's den Mond, wenn ihn die Hunde anbellen.
† Chi mal comincia, peggio finisce.
‡ Duabus sellis sedere.

44. అడ్డగోడమీఁది పిల్లి.

Like the cat on the cross wall.

(See No. 43.)

It can jump down either side.

Applied to an unprincipled, double-dealing person.

Jack o' both sides.

45. అడ్డెడు తవ్వెడు బియ్యము యిచ్చి అమ్మా నీ ప్రసాదము అన్నట్లు.

Like giving [a cook] two and a half measures of rice and saying, " Madam, this is your gift."

The cook gets four-fifths of the rice for herself, and yet she must be coaxed to cook the food. The allusion is to a traveller endeavouring to get some person to cook for him.

46. అతడు వుంటే మంగలవాణ్ని అయినా పిలుచును.

[Like a widow saying] " if he were alive, he would at least call the barber."

This is a reproach to the husband as being a useless fellow only fit to be employed as a messenger, and is also a joke, as the widow only, and not the wife, requires the services of a barber, to shave her head.

47. అతిరహస్యం బట్టబయలు.

The great secret is laid bare to all.

(See Nos. 525, 635, 1521.)

Tom Noddy's secret.

48. అత్త కొట్టిన కుండ అడుగోటి కుండ, కోడలు కొట్టిన కుండ కొత్త కుండ.

The pot broken by the mother-in-law was a cracked pot, the pot broken by the daughter-in-law was a new pot.

(See No. 51.)

49. అత్తగారి సాధింపు.

The rancour of a mother-in-law.

(See Nos. 54, 67, 632.)

Among Hindus the husband's mother, when living, rules the house, and to her the wife is subject.

The husband's mother is the wife's devil. (German.)*

---

* Des Mannes Mutter ist der Frau Teufel.

50. అత్త చస్తే కోడలు యేడ్చినట్టు.

Like the daughter-in-law lamenting the death of her mother-in-law.

Feigned sorrow.

Crocodile tears.

51. అత్తచేశిన పనులకు ఆరళ్లు లేవు.

There is no one to blame the mother-in-law.

(See No. 48.)

52. అత్తతో చెప్పి అషు అనిపించలేడుగాని, లంభించడానకు బ్రహ్మకొడుకు.

He was not able to get the consent of my mother-in-law [to give me my wife,] but he is a very son of Brahmâ in reviling.

53. అత్తపేరు బెట్టి కూతురిని కుంపట్లో వేశినట్టు.

Giving her child her mother-in-law's name, she threw it into the fire.

(See Nos. 386, 407, 1562.)

Cutting off one's nose to spite one's face.

54. అత్త మంచీ, వేముల తీపూ లేదు.

There is no goodness in a mother-in-law nor sweetness in Margosa trees.

(See Nos. 49, 57, 531.)

Vêmu is the Azadirachta Indica.

She is well married who has neither mother-in-law nor sister-in-law. (Spanish.)*

55. అత్తలేని కోడలు వుత్తమురాలు, కోడలులేని అత్త గుణవంతురాలు.

Where there is no mother-in-law, the daughter-in-law is perfect; where there is no daughter-in-law, the mother-in-law is good tempered.

As long I was a daughter-in-law I never had a good mother-in-law, and as long as I was a mother-in-law I never had a good daughter-in-law. (Spanish.)†

---

* Aquella es bien casada, que no tiene suegra ni cuñada.

† En quanto fue nuera, nunca tuve buena suegra, y en quanto fue suegra, nunca tuve buena nuera.

56. అత్తవల్ల దొంగతనమున్ను, మగనివల్ల రంకున్ను నేర్చుకొన్నట్టు.

Deceitfulness is learnt from a mother-in-law, adultery is learnt from a husband.

Jealous watching leads to unfaithfulness.

At the gate where suspicion enters, love goes out.

If the wife sins, the husband is not innocent. (Italian.)*

57. అత్తవారింటి సుఖము మోచేతి దెబ్బవంటిది.

The pleasure felt in a mother-in-law's house is like a blow on the elbow.

(See Nos. 49, 54, 532.)

Happy is the wife who is married to a motherless son.

58. అత్తా వకరింటి కోడలే.

The mother-in-law was herself once a daughter-in-law.

The mother-in-law forgets that she was a daughter-in-law. (Spanish.)†

59. అత్తి పూచినట్టు.

Like the fig blossoming.

(See No. 1963.)

This tree (Ficus Glomerata) bears no apparent blossoms.

That is as likely as to see a hog fly.

60. అదంత్రునికి ఆశపెట్టరాదు, బలవంతునికి చోటివ్వరాదు.

You should not encourage vain hopes in a helpless dependant, nor give place to a powerful man.

61. అదికుమ్ము, యిదిదుమ్ము, పదరా పందిట్లోకి.

There are smouldering ashes there, and dust here; let us go out into the Pandili.

(See No. 102.)

Pandili is a verandah thatched with leaves.

---

* Se la moglie pecca, non è il marito innocente.

† No se acuerda la suegra que fue nuera.

62. అదుగో అంటే ఆరునెలలు.

When he says, "here you are," it means six months.

(See No. 2091.)

One "Take it" is better than two "You shall have its." (French.)*

63. అదే పతకమయితే మనము బ్రతకమా.

If this were a brooch, might we not be made rich ?

Patakam (Sans. *Padaka*) is a valuable ornament attached to the *Kanṭhasara* (necklace). The allusion is to one made of false gold, and set with false gems.

Disappointment.

The treasure turned out charcoal. (Latin.)†

64. అదేమి రెడ్డీ వంగి వంగి నడుస్తావంటే, యెప్పటికాలు అట్టెట్టే అన్నాడట.

"What is it that makes you limp, Reḍḍi?" asked one. "My old leg is the same as ever," he replied.

Habit.

65. అద్దము మీద పెసరగింజ పడ్డట్టు.

Like a Pesara seed on a looking glass.

(For *Pesara* see No. 32.)

Used with reference to a remark aimed at a particular person, but conveyed in such general terms that he is unable to take notice of it.

He said devil, but meant you. (Dutch.)‡

66. అద్దములోని ముడుపు.

Like a bag of money in a looking glass.

Visionary prospects.

67. అద్దెకు వచ్చిన గుర్రాలు అగడ్తలు దాటుతవా.

Will hired horses leap over ditches ?

---

* Mieux vaut un tenez que deux vous l'aurez.
† Thesaurus carbones erant.
‡ Hij zegt duivel en meent u.

68. అద్దె పేరంటము, శిద్దె మురికి.

[Going to] an entertainment on hire is [to get] the dirt off a leathern ghî bottle.

Pêranṭam is an invitation given to married women on the occasion of any domestic festival. Family priests sometimes hire married women to attend on such occasions, the condition being that all presents received go to the priest. The food set before these substitutes is often bad.

Come uncalled sit unserved.

Go neither to a wedding nor a christening without invitation.

69. అధమునికి ఆలయ్యేటంతకంటె, బలవంతునికి బానిసె అయ్యేది మేలు.

Better be the hand-maid of a great man than the wife of a low fellow.

Better fare hard with good men than feast with bad.

70. అధిక ఆషాఢం.

An intercalary Âshâḍha.

The month Âshâḍha corresponds with June—July.

Said by a man when excusing himself for not observing the rules of the house in which he was staying.

71. అధికాశ లోకదారిద్ర్యము.

Excessive cupidity leads to excessive poverty.

Avarice bursts the bag. (French.) *

72. అని అనిపించుకోవలెనా అత్తగారా.

O mother-in-law, should you accuse me and bring a reproach on yourself in return?

(See No. 780.)

Those who live in glass houses should not throw stones.

73. అన్న చొరవేగాని, అక్షర చొరవలేదు.

Clever at his meals, but stupid at his books.

(See Nos. 518, 1070, 1381, 1385.)

Well fed, but ill taught. (French.) †

He has two stomachs to eat, and one to work.

* L' avarice rompt le sac.
† Bien nourri et mal appris.

74. అన్నము పెట్టితే అరిగిపోతుంది, చీరయిస్తే చిరిగిపోతుంది, వాత పెట్టితే కలకాలము వుంటుంది.

If I give you rice, you will eat it up; if I give you a cloth, it will wear out; but if I brand you, it will last for ever.

Said by a stingy person to a beggar.

75. అన్నము లేకపోతే వరి అన్నము, బట్ట లేకపోతే పట్టుబట్ట.

If you have no common food, [give me] the best; if you have no common cloth, [give me] a silk one.

(See No. 1607.)

Said by an impertinent beggar when refused assistance by a stingy person.

76. అన్నరసముకన్నా ఆదరణరసము మేలు.

A kind reception is better than a feast.

Welcome is the best cheer.

In hospitality it is the spirit that is the chief thing. (Greek.)*

77. అన్నిబొండాల నీళ్లూ నీవే తాగరా అయ్యల్లా.

Alas! my son, drink the water of all the cocoanuts.

(See Nos. 507, 508, 1169.)

The father had refused to give his son a single cocoanut while alive, but offered him the whole after he had died of thirst.

To lock the stable door when the steed is stolen.

78. అన్నీ వున్నవి, అయిదువతనము లేదు.

I lack nothing, but I am a widow.

79. అన్యాయపురిలో ఆలూ మొగుడికి రంకు.

In the " city of injustice," husband and wife even are accused of adultery.

80. అపకారికయినా వుపకారమే చెయ్యవలెను.

You should do good even to him who has done you evil.

" *If thine enemy be hungry, give him bread to eat; and if he be thirsty, give him water to drink.*" Proverbs xxv. 21.

---

* Ξενίων δέ τε Θυμος ἄριστος.

81. అప్పటిమాటలకు దుప్పటి యిచ్చినానుగాని, కలకాలము కప్పుకో నిచ్చినానా.

I presented you with the robe in return for the compliments you then paid me, but did I intend you to wear it for ever?

(See No. [illegible].)

A liberal gift regretted and withdrawn.

Give a thing and take again,
And you shall ride in hell's wain.

82. అప్పువంక బావచుట్టము, ఆళ్లవంక తిరగలి చుట్టము.

He is nothing to me but my sister's husband; the millstone is only valued for the grain it grinds.

Âḷḷu is the plural of *Âruga* (Paspalum Scrobiculatum).

83. అప్పు ఆకటికి వచ్చునా.

Will a debt be repaid when you are hungry?

Can you ever get a debt repaid when you are in want?

84. అప్పు దొరికితే పప్పుకూడు.

If I could raise a loan, [I should be able to live on] dâl and rice.

An excuse made by a host for treating his guest with poor fare.

85. అప్పు ముప్పు.

Debt is misfortune.

Debt is the worst poverty.

86. అప్పు యిచ్చినవాడు బాగుకోరును, తీసుకొన్నవాడు చెడగోరును.

Your creditor will wish you well, your debtor will wish you ill.

He that doth lend doth lose his friend.
Money lent, an enemy made. (Portuguese.)*

* Dinheiro emprestaste, inimigo ganhaste.

87. అప్పు లేకపోతే వుప్పుగంజే మేలు.

Rice water and salt without debt are good.

(See No. 88.)

Without debt, without care. (Italian.) *

He is rich enough who owes nothing. (French.) †

88. అప్పులేని గంజి దొప్పెడే చాలును.

A cupful of rice water without debt is enough.

(See No. 87.)

Out of debt, out of danger.

Happy is he who owes nothing. (Greek.) ‡

89. అబద్ధాలకు అర్థములేదు.

No meaning can be given to erroneous expressions.

Applied to discrepancies in a statement.

90. అబద్ధాల పంచాంగముకు అరవైగడియలు త్యాజ్యము.

A bad almanack makes all the hours of the day unpropitious.

Applied to unreasonable objections.

There are 60 *Gaḍiyas* in a day; a *Gaḍiya* therefore equals 24 minutes.

91. అబ్బిగాడు చస్తే ఆ పంచె నాది.

If the boy dies, that cloth is mine.

Want of feeling.

92. అబ్బితే శిగ, అబ్బకపోతే కాళ్లు.

If possible, [he seizes] the tuft; if not, the feet.

Applied to a base fellow who tries to ruin others, and, when he fails, cringes at their feet.

Anoint a villain and he will prick you, prick a villain and he will anoint you. (French.) §

---

* Est assez riche qui ne doit rien.

† Senza debiti, senza pensieri.

‡ Εὐδαίμων ὁ μηδὲν ὀφείλων.

§ Oignez vilain il vous poindra, poignez vilain il vous oindra.

93. అబ్బురాన బిడ్డ పుట్టెను, గడ్డపార తేరా చెవులు కుట్టుతాను.

The long desired child has been born, fetch a crow-bar and I will bore its ears.

(See No. 1778.)

Ridiculing unusual and extraordinary care being taken of any thing not worthy of it.

94. అభ్యాసము కూసు విద్య.

Practice [makes] art easy.

(See No. 1117.)

Practice makes perfect.
Custom makes all things easy.

95. అభ్యాసములేని రెడ్డి అందలమెక్కితే అటూ యిటూ అయినదట.

When the unpractised Reḍḍi got into a palankin, it swung from side to side.

(See Nos. 184, 896, 474.)

96. అమర్చినదాంట్లో అత్తగారు వేలు పెట్టినది.

The mother-in-law put her finger in every dish prepared [by the daughter-in-law].

No work and all the credit.

One man knocks in the nail, and another hangs his hat on it. (German.)*

97. అమావాస్య ప్రొద్దుకు వంగలు కాచునా.

Will the new-moon bring out the brinjals?

Vanga (called by Europeans "brinjal") is the Solanam Melongena.

98. అమ్మగా మిగిలిన మేక.

The only goat remaining unsold.

A wretched fate.

* Der Eine schlagt den Nagel ein, der Andere hängt den Hut daran.

99. అమ్మ గృహప్రవేశము, అయ్య శ్మశానప్రవేశము.

The bride enters her husband's house, and the bridegroom enters the tomb.

(See No. 711.)

Regarding *Gṛihapravêśa* ("house-entering") see No. 803.

Applied to a great calamity happening when most unlooked for. Also to a luckless woman.

After a dream of a wedding comes a corpse.

100. అమ్మ చెడ్డ చేటుకు ముసుకు వకటా.

Is this miserable wretched woman to wear a veil?

101. అమ్మ తానూ పెట్టదు, తిరుచుకోనీ తిననివ్వదు.

The mother neither gives food herself [to her child,] nor allows it to beg.

102. అమ్మదగ్గిర కింద పడుకొన్నా వకటే, అబ్బదగ్గిర నేల పడుకొన్నా వకటే.

It is all one whether [the child] sleep on the ground with its mother, or on the floor with its father.

(See No. 61.)

Equally bad.

Where bad is the best, naught must be the choice.

Whatever way you take there is a league of bad road. (Spanish.)*

103. అమ్మ పెట్టేవి నాలుగూ అప్పుడే పెట్టితే చెయ్యనా.

If you had beaten me as my mother used to do, would I not have done [the work]?

Said by a daughter-in-law to her mother-in-law.

Applied to a person with whom mild measures are of no avail, with whom

There is no argument like that of the stick. (Spanish.)†

---

* Por do quiera hay su legua de mal camino.
† No hay tal razon como la del baston.

104. అమ్మబోతే అడివి, కొనబోతే కొరివి.

When he went to sell, his bargains were [as ruinous as] a jungle; when he went to buy [his purchases were as bad as] firebrands.

Losing on both sides.

Buy and sell and live by the loss.

105. అయితంపూడి వుద్యోగము అయితే గియితే, ఆరావుల పాడిచేస్తే గీస్తే, పెరుగూ పాలూ మీవారికి పోస్తావా మావారికి పోస్తావా.

"Were I to be employed in Aithampûḍi, and possess six milch cows, would you supply milk and curds to your relations or to mine?"

The story is, that the wife being asked this foolish question by her husband answered "to my people," on which she was beaten.

106. అయితే అతడి ఆలాయె, కాకపోతే దాసురాలాయె.

"If we succeed, she shall be his wife; if not, she shall be a recluse."

Said by the parents of a girl, who had set their hearts upon getting her married to a certain man.

Either Cæsar or nobody. (Latin.)*

107. అయితే ఆరుగ, కాకుంటే కంది.

If the Âruga fails, we shall have Kandi.

(For *Âruga* see No. 92. For *Kandi* see No. 32.)

These are both sown together. The *Âruga* crop sometimes perishes.

To have two strings to one's bow.

Good riding at two anchors men have told;
For if one break, the other may hold.

* Aut Cæsar aut nullus.

108. అయినవారందరు ఆ దోవను పోగా, జంగాన్ని పట్టుకొని జాము యేడ్చినాడు.

When all his friends went away, he caught hold of a Jangam and cried for three hours.

Taking an unconcerned person into your counsels.

Jâmu is a watch of three hours, the day from sunrise to sunset being divided into four *Jâmus.*

109. అయ్యకు రెండో పెండ్లి అని సంతోషమేకాని, అమ్మకు సవితిపోరు అని యెరగడు.

[The son] is glad that his father has taken a second wife, but he little knows what quarrels there will be between her and his mother.

110. అయ్యకు విద్యా లేదు, అమ్మకు గర్వమూ లేదు.

When the husband has no learning, the wife has no pride.

111. అయ్య దాసండ్లకు పెట్టితే, అమ్మ జంగాలకు పెట్టినది.

When the master fed the Dâsaris (devotees of Vishṇu), the mistress fed the Jangams (devotees of Śiva).

Applied to a spirit of contradiction.

112. అయ్యనీటు అడిగితీరదు, అమ్మ దమ్మయపాలెంలో దంచుకొని తాగుతున్నది.

The foppish husband gives himself great airs, while his wife is living by pounding rice in Dammayapâlem.

113. అయ్య రాకుంటే అమావాస్య అట్టె వుంటుందా.

If the priest does not come, will the new moon wait for him?

Time and tide wait for no man.

114. అయ్య వాతబెట్టినా బఱ్ఱె బ్రతకనా.

When his lordship brands the buffalo, will she get over it?

Said of a clumsy fellow, who makes a mess of every thing.

I meant to cross myself and put out one of my eyes. (Portuguese.)*

115. అయ్యవారిని చెయ్యబోతే కోతి అయినది.

His attempt to make [an image of] Gaṇêśa ended in [the moulding of] a monkey.

Mud images of Gaṇêśa are made and worshipped on the 4th day of the light fortnight in the month Bhâdrapada (August—September).

A ridiculous failure.

116. అయ్యవారు అటికంత, అయ్యవారి పెండ్లాము పుటికంత.

The Brâhman is like a small pot, and his wife is like a basket.

Spoken of things which do not match.

117. అయ్య సవాశేరు, లింగము అరవీశెడు.

The man [weighs] a seer and a quarter, the lingam [round his neck] two and a half.

(See Nos. 2070, 2074.)

118. అరచేత వెన్న పెట్టుకొని నేతికి యేడ్చినట్టు.

Like a man with butter in the palm of his hand, calling out for ghî.

(See No. 2002.)

119. అరచేతి రేగుబంటికి అద్దము కావలెనా.

Do you require a glass to look at a berry in the palm of your hand?

(See No. 1741.)

The berry spoken of is the fruit of the Zisyphus Jujuba.

As clear as crystal.

As plain as a pike-staff.

---

* Fui para me benzer, e quebrei hum olho.

120. అరచేతిలో ఉప్పు పెట్టితే ఆరునెలలు తలుచుకో వలెను.

If he puts a little salt in the palm of your hand, you should think of it for six months.

The duty of gratitude.

121. అరచేతిలో వైకుంఠము చూపుతాడు.

He offers heaven in the palm of his hand.

Deceiving by false hopes.

122. అరణ్య రోదనము.

Lamentations in the jungle.

Of no avail.

123. అరవ యేడుపు.

Like a Tamil mourning.

Among the Tamilians, women are sometimes hired to mourn over a deceased person.

Applied to an unwilling performance of any duty.

124. అరవై యేండ్లయితే అరులు మరులు.

When sixty years have passed, dotage.

125. అరవై యేండ్లయిన తర్వాత అమ్మా అన్నాడట.

After sixty years had passed, he cried Ammâ (mother).

Second childhood.

Old men are twice children. (Latin.)*

126. అరవై యేండ్లయినవి, చదువుకోకుండా మొత్తుకొంచానా అన్నాడట.

Sixty years have passed; am I to do without learning?

An ironical speech.

An old dog will learn no tricks.

* Bis pueri senes.

127. అరవై వరహాలు యిచ్చినా అత్తవంటి బానిసె దొరకదు.

Although you pay sixty Pagodas, you cannot obtain as good a handmaid as your mother-in-law.

Said jokingly of a mother-in-law not allowed to have the management of the house, but kept in subjection to her daughter-in-law.

128. అరిచే కుక్క కరవ నేరదు.

A barking dog never bites.

Great barkers are nae biters. (Scotch.)

A barking cur does not bite. (Italian.)*

129. అరిటాకు వచ్చి ముంటిమీద పడ్డా అరిటాకుదే కష్టము, ముల్లు వచ్చి అరిటాకుమీద పడ్డా అరిటాకుదే కష్టము.

The plantain leaf alike suffers, whether it falls on the thorn, or the thorn falls on it.

(See No. 419.)

130. ఆరటిపండు వలిచి చేత వుంచినట్టు.

Like placing peeled plantain in one's hand.

(See No. 2004.)

Applied to any thing made perfectly easy.

131. అరుంధతీ కనపడదు, అధ్వాన్నమూ కనపడదు, అరవై వరహాల అప్పు మాత్రము కనపడుతున్నది.

I can't see the star Arundhati, botheration take it! I can see nothing but a debt of sixty pagodas.

Said by a man who had got over head and ears in debt for his marriage, when the priest pointed out the propitious star.

132. అర్తి దుఃఖం ఆరునెలలు, కడుపు దుఃఖం కలకాలం.

The grief of the neck [lasts] six months; the grief of the womb, for ever.

The "grief of the neck" signifies widowhood, when the marriage cord is broken. (See No. 878). The "grief of the womb" signifies the loss of a child.

---

* Can ch'abbaia non morde.

133. అర్థమూ ప్రాణమూ ఆచార్యాధీనము, తాళమూ దేహమూ నా ఆధీనము.

The money [in the box] and the soul [within the body] are made over to the spiritual guide, but the key and the body are retained by me.

Applied to giving a person only the form of authority, but no real power.

134. అలవాటులేని ఔపాసనం చెయ్యబోతే మీసాలన్నీ తెగకాలినవి.

The man unaccustomed to burnt-offerings burnt off his mustaches in the attempt.

(See Nos. 95, 398, 474.)

135. అలివిగాని ఆలిని కట్టుకొని మురిగిచచ్చెరా ముండా కొడుకు.

The miserable fellow is ruined by his wretched marriage.

The folly of being headstrong.

Marry in haste and repent at leisure.

136. అల్పునకు ఐశ్వర్యము వస్తే, అర్ధరాత్రివేళ గొడుగు తెమ్మన్నాడట.

When fortune smiled on a mean person, he ordered an umbrella to be brought at midnight.

An umbrella is a sign of rank and authority.

Set a beggar on horseback, he'll ride to the devil.

There is no pride like that of a beggar grown rich. (French.)*

137. అల్లి అడిగినది, యిల్లి యిచ్చినది, మల్లి మాయము చేసినది.

Alli asked for it, Illi gave it, Malli made away with it.

---

* Il n'est orgueil que de pauvre enrichi.

138. అల్లుడలిగితే కూతురిని తీసుకొని పోతాడు.

If the son-in-law gets in a huff, he will [only] take away the daughter.

Said by a father-in-law or mother-in-law.

139. అల్లుడికి నెయ్యి లేదు, అల్లుడితోటి కూడా వచ్చినవారికి నూనే లేదు.

There is neither ghî for the son-in-law, nor oil for his friends.

Said of inability in a person to do that which his duty imperatively requires of him.

140. అల్లుడికి వండిన అన్నము కొడుకుకు పెట్టి కొట్టుకొన్నదట.

She grudgingly gave to her son the food prepared for her son-in-law.

The affection of a mother-in-law for her son-in-law.

141. అల్లులలో మల్లు పెద్ద.

Mallu is a great man among the weavers.

Great among low people.

Among the common people Scoggin is a doctor.

142. అవలక్షణము గలవానికి అక్షతలు యిస్తే, అవతలికి పోయి నోట్లో వేసుకొన్నాడట.

When sacred grain was given to a luckless fellow, he went away and ate it up (instead of placing it on his head).

The term *Avalakshaṇa* is applied to a man who bears unlucky marks on his person, or whose manners are inauspicious.

143. అవసరగానికి ఆకులో పెట్టు, నాకు నేలను పెట్టు.

Give the man who is in a hurry his food on a leaf, but give me mine on the floor.

The food of Hindus is ordinarily served on a large leaf or several small leaves sewn together.

Applied to a person wishing to have something done for himself in great haste, before others are attended to.

144. అవివేకితో స్నేహముకన్నా వివేకితో విరోధము మేలు.

Enmity with a wise man is better than friendship with a fool.

145. అవ్వను పట్టుకొని వసంతాలాడినట్టు.

Like playing games with your grand-mother.

Lit. "Throwing scarlet water over her," a sport among young people at marriages, &c.

(See No. 1041.)

Disrespectful and unseemly conduct towards elderly people.

146. అవ్వ వడికిన నూలు తాత మొలతాటికి సరి.

The thread spun by the grand-mother is only sufficient for the waist cord of the grand-father.

Waste of that gained by another's industry.

147. అవ్వా కావలెను, బువ్వా కావలెను.

I want grand-mother and I want food.

Said by a child who did not wish to leave its grand-mother, but who had to do so to get its dinner.

You cannot drink and whistle at the same time. (Danish.)*

---

* Man kan ikke drikke og pibe paa eengang.

148. అశుద్ధముమీద రాయివేస్తే ముఖాన పడుతుంది.

If you throw a stone into filth, it will fly into your face.

(See No. 336.)

If you will stir up the mire, you must bear the smell. (Danish.)*

Meddle with dirt, and some of it will stick to you. (Danish.)†

149. అశ్రద్ధపితాళ్లకు యేతాం తర్పణము.

The water drawn with the Picota is the drink offering of disregarded ancestors.

Tarpaṇa is a drink offering to the manes of deceased ancestors (*Pitṛis*).

An irreverent fellow, when pressed by his friends to perform the ceremony, offered the water he was drawing for other purposes.

An unwilling action, done to satisfy others.

150. అసలు సోమిదేవమ్మ, అందులో వేవిళ్లు.

She is not only the wife of a priest, but is also in an interesting condition.

(See Nos. 483, 1214, 1829, 2034.)

A double excuse. Applied to idle persons.

Sick of the idles.

A large sheep thinks its wool heavy.

ఆ.

151. ఆ అంటే అపశబ్దము, నారాయణా అంటే బూతుమాట.

If I say "Â" (yes), it's wrong; if I say "Nârâyaṇâ," it's obscene.

(See Nos. 199, 365.)

Faults are thick where love is thin. (Welsh.)

152. ఆకలి ఆకాశమంత, గొంతుక సూది బెజ్జమంత.

The appetite is as great as the sky, but the throat is as small as the eye of a needle.

Applied to great ambition, but small abilities.

---

* Hvo som vil röre i Skarn, faaer og lugte det.

† Man bliver ei snarere skiden end af Skarn.

153. ఆకలి కాని భోజనము, ఆలిమీద లంజరికము.

Eating when the appetite is satisfied; unfaithfulness to a wife.

Both bad.

154. ఆకలిగొన్న కరణము పాతకవిలె తీసినాడు.

The hungry Karaṇam looked into his old accounts.

A *Karaṇam* is a village accountant.

155. ఆకలి యెత్తుతుంది అత్తగారా అంటే, రోకలి మింగవే కోడలా అన్నదట.

When the daughter-in-law said she was hungry, her mother-in-law told her to swallow the pestle.

(See Nos. 19, 161.)

Rôkali is a wooden pestle, five or six feet long, used for pounding rice.

156. ఆకలి రుచి యెరగదు, నిద్ర సుఖమెరగదు, వలపు శిగ్గు యెరగదు.

Hunger knows not taste, sleep knows not comfort, lust knows not shame.

(See Nos. 217, 806.)

Hunger is the best sauce.

157. ఆకాశ పంచాంగము.

A sky calendar.

(See Nos. 1006, 1786.)

A fanciful tale.

158. ఆకాశ వర్తకుడు.

A trader in the air.

A swindler. An impostor.

159. ఆకును అందదు, పోకను పొందదు.

It reaches not the leaf, it suits not the nut.

Quite inadequate.

160. ఆకుపోయి నూతపడితే, వెతకపోయి యేడుగురు పడ్డారట.

When the leaf went and fell into the well, seven men went in search and fell in after it.

The gain is not worth the candle. (French.)*

161. ఆగడపలు వేశినవి అత్తగారా అంటే, కొలబుర్ర నాచేతిలోనే వున్నది కోడలా అన్నదట.

"See! The signs of rain appear!" cried the daughter-in-law "What of that?" said the mother-in-law "*I* have the measure."

(See Nos. 19, 155.)

162. ఆగభోగాలు అక్క కుడిస్తే, అంబటి పరకలు బావ కుడిచినాడు.

While my sister enjoyed every luxury, my brother-in-law had nothing to eat but the scum of the porridge.

Said of a man who is poorly treated in his father-in-law's house while his wife fares well.

163. ఆగ్రహాన ఆనపెట్టుకొన్నట్టు.

Like taking an oath in a fit of passion.

164. ఆచారం అదిరిపడ్డది, ధూపార్తి తుల్లిపడ్డది, కొత్త కుండ తేరా నెత్తాళ్లు వండుకొందాము.

Let our sanctity be scandalized, let the censer be shocked bring a new pot and let us cook sprats.

---

* Le jeu ne vaut pas la chandelle.

165. ఆచారం ఆచారం అన్నంభొట్లూ అంటే, పెద్ద చెరువు కుక్క ముట్టుకొన్నది అన్నట్టు.

[Seeing a hypocrite] they cried out, "O Annambhotlu! purity! purity!" He answered "Alas! a dog has touched the big tank."

166. ఆచారానకు అంతమూ లేదు, అనాచారానకు ఆదీ లేదు.

There is no limit to purity, nor any beginning to impurity.

Man is sinful from his birth, and never attains to perfect purity.

167. ఆచార్యుని తలచి నిప్పులో చెయ్యిపెట్టితే కాలదా?

If you think of your spiritual guide and put your hand in the fire, will it not be burnt ?

(See No. 781.)

168. ఆటా తీరె, పాటా తీరె, కోటలో రామరాజ్యము.

The dancing is over, the song is finished, and every one is as free as in the kingdom of Râma.

(See Nos. 278, 1644, 1867.)

169. ఆడదానిచేతి అర్థమూ, మొగవానిచేతి బిడ్డా బ్రతకదు.

Money left in the hands of a woman wont last ; a child left in the hands of a man wont live.

170. ఆడదాని మాట, నీళ్ల మూట.

A woman's word, a bundle of water.

A woman's mind and winter wind change oft.

171. ఆడది బొంకితే గోడ పెట్టినట్టు, మొగవాడు బొంకితే తడిక కట్టినట్టు.

If a woman lies, it's like building a wall ; if a man lies, it's like putting up a mat (easily seen through.)

172. ఆడ నేరక మద్దెలమీఁద తప్పు చెప్పినట్లు.

Not being able to dance, she abused the drum.

A bad workman complains of his tools.
An ill shearer never got a hook. (Scotch.)

173. ఆడపెత్తనము, తంబళి దొరతనము.

Woman's rule, a Tambaḷi's government.

A *Tambaḷi* is a Śaiva priest of low origin, who wears the sacred thread, and endeavours to observe Brahminical customs.

174. ఆడబోయిన తీర్థము యెదురుగా వచ్చినది.

The sacred water in which the man was going to bathe came to meet him.

(See No. 1920.)

A thing sought for to come to hand without trouble.

175. ఆడి తప్పరాదు, పలికి బొంకరాదు.

Having promised, you should not fail; having spoken, you should not lie (retract).

176. ఆ తండ్రికి కొడుకు కాడా.

Is he not the son of that father?

(See Nos. 185, 1019, 1977.)

Like father, like son.
Such a father, such a son. (Portuguese.)*
He is his father's son. (Latin.)†

177. ఆతురగానికి తెలివి మట్టు.

A hasty man is not wise.

(See Nos. 27, 858.)

He that is hasty of spirit exalteth folly. Proverbs xiv. 29.
A hasty man never wants woe.

---

* Qual o pai tal o filho.
† Patris est filius.

178. ఆ తుష్టికీ యీ నష్టికీ సరి.

That profit and this loss are equal.

179. ఆత్మస్తుతీ, పరనిందా, అర్థాపేక్షా, లేని మహానుభావుడికి నాకూ డబ్బు, శుద్ధశుంఠకు వాడికీ డబ్బా.

Am I, an upright man, not a boaster, a fault finder, nor covetous, to have one pice, and is this great fool to have a pice also ?

(See No. 788.)

In this speech a man committed the very three faults from which he boasted he was free.

180. ఆత్మా రావే నూతపడుదాము అంటే, ఆదివారము రోజున అందరమూ పడుదాము అన్నదట.

When he thought of putting an end to himself, his soul said within him " Let us wait until Sunday and all drown together."

The word " All" refers to the elements of which man is composed. Sunday is a propitious day.

Judge well before you act.

Consideration is the parent of wisdom.

181. ఆదాయములేకనే శెట్టి వరదబోడు.

Without [the hope of] gain, a Śeṭṭi will not venture into the flood.

(See No. 1902 .)

The *Śeṭṭis* (merchants) are very greedy and very cowardly.

182. ఆపతి మొక్కులు, సంపతి కుంట్లు.

Vows in times of trouble, carping [at the gods] in times of prosperity.

(See No. 1578.)

The devil was sick, the devil a monk would be;
The devil grew well, the devil a monk was he. (Latin.)*

---

* Aegrotat daemon, monachus tunc esse volebat;
Daemon convaluit, daemon ut ante fuit.

183. ఆ పప్పు యీ నీళ్లకు వుడకదు.

That pulse cannot be cooked with this water.

The pulse alluded to is the Cajanus Indicus (See No. 32) commonly called *Dâl* (Hind.) It requires to be boiled in good sweet water to make it soft and fit for eating.

A phrase similar to "That game won't pay," "That cock won't fight."

184. ఆపస్తంబులా ఆశ్వలాయనులా అంటే, ఆపస్తంబులమూ కాము, ఆశ్వలాయనులమూ కాము, అప్పారావుగారి హర్కారాలము అన్నారట.

When asked whether they belonged to the Âpastamba or Âśvalâyana sect, they replied " We are neither the one nor the other, we are messengers of Appâ Râu."

Utter ignorance of religion.

185. ఆ బుర్రలో విత్తనాలే.

They are seeds out of the same bowl.

(See Nos. 176, 1019, 1977.)

Coming from the same bad stock.

186. ఆమడలు దూరమయితే, అంతఃకరణాలు దూరమా.

If the leagues are long, are the hearts far distant ?

An *Âmaḍa* (4 *Kôs*) is a distance varying from 8 to 10 miles.

Distance cannot alter true friendship.

187. ఆముదపు చేటేగాని, బిడ్డ బ్రతకడము లేదు.

Only waste of castor oil, but not [saving] the child's life.

Useless endeavours.

188. ఆముదములో ముంచిన యేకువలె వున్నాడు.

He is like a flock of cotton dipped in castor oil.

To look like a drowned mouse.

189. ఆయం తప్పితే గాయమంత సుఖము లేదు.

If the vital parts escape, there is no comfort like that which follows a wound.

An invalid receives every attention from his friends.

190. ఆయన ముందర పోవలె.

He must die first, *or*
I must die before him.

An ambiguous phrase used by a bad wife.

191. ఆరగించగా లేనిది అడిగితే వస్తున్నదా.

Will a man get by begging, what was wanting in the feast?

(See No. 696.)

192. ఆరాటపు కదురు యే రాటాన బెట్టినా బర బర.

The restless spindle, to whatever spinning wheel it may be attached, rattles.

193. ఆరుగ కోసిన ముహూర్తాననే కంది కూడా కొయ్యండి.

Reap the Âruga and Kandi together in the same propitious hour.

(For *Âruga* see No. 82, and for *Kandi* see No. 88.)

Applied to hasty actions.

194. ఆరు నెలలనుంచి వాయించిన మద్దెల వోటిదా గట్టిదా అని అడిగినట్టు.

Like asking if the drum is cracked or strong, after using it for six months.

195. ఆరెల మానుకింద బూరెల మాను విరగబడ్డట్టు.

Like a tree loaded with cakes falling below an Âre tree.

(See Nos. 1362, 1425, 1430, 1886.)

Âre is the Bauhinia Racemosa; it bears fruit like cranberries.

Great luck.

196. ఆర్చేవా, తీర్చేవా, అక్కర వస్తే మునిగేవా.

Would you comfort me, or remove my grief, or if necessary would you plunge [into the water to save me] ?

Asking proofs of professed friendship.

A friend in need is a friend indeed.

197. ఆర్చేవారే గాని, తీర్చేవారు లేరు.

There are comforters but no real helpers.

198. ఆలికి అన్నము పెట్టడము వూరికి వుపకారమా.

Is feeding one's wife a benefit to the village ?

(See No. 350.)

199. ఆలిని వల్లని వానికి యీలకూరలో వుప్పు చాలదు.

For the husband who does not love his wife, there is not enough salt in the Îlakûra.

(See Nos. 151, 365.)

This herb (Salsola Indica) is occasionally used as a vegetable, and is naturally very salt.

Where there is no love, all are faults.

If you want a pretence to whip a dog, it is enough to say he ate up the frying pan.

200. ఆలి వంకవారు ఆత్మబంధువులు, తల్లి వంకవారు తగినవారు, తండ్రి వంకవారు దాయాదులు.

Your wife's people are your own relations; your mother's people are distant relations; your father's people are enemies (because they are co-heirs).

(See Vêmana Book II, 32.)

201. ఆలు కాదు, అది వ్రాలు.

She is not his mate but his fate.

(See Vêmana Book II, 16.)

202. ఆలు వల్లక అరవై యేండ్లు, మొగుడు వల్లక ముప్ఫయి యేండ్లు, బాలప్రాయము పది యేండ్లు.

For ten years they were children, for thirty years the husband disliked the wife, and for sixty years the wife disliked the husband.

Applied to an unprofitable and unhappy life.

203. ఆలూ మొగునిసందు పోట్లాట అద్దముమీద పెసరగింజ వేశినంత సేపు.

A quarrel between man and wife only lasts as long as a Pesara seed stays on a looking glass.

(For *Pesara* see No. 92.)

204. ఆలూ లేదు, చూలూ లేదు, కొడుకు పేరు సోమలింగం.

There is neither wife nor conception, but the son's name is to be Sômalingam.

(See Nos. 526, 936, 1470, 1471.)

We have no son and yet are giving him a name. (Spanish.)*

Count not your chickens before they are hatched.

---

* Hijo no tenemos, y nombre le ponemos.

205. ఆవగింజకు సందువుంటే, అరవై గారెలు అప్పుడే తిననా.

Had there been room for a mustard seed, would I not have eaten sixty more cakes?

A glutton suffering from indigestion after a feast was recommended to eat some mustard, when he replied as above.

206. ఆవ తిన్న అమ్మకు యేవ పారినదట.

The woman who fed on mustard grew strong.

Fattening on poor fare.

207. ఆవలింతకు అన్నదమ్ములున్నారుగాని, తుమ్ముకు తమ్ముడయినా లేదు.

Yawning has elder and younger brothers, sneezing has not even a younger brother.

Yawning is sympathetic, sneezing is not.

A good gaper makes two gapers. (French.)*

208. ఆవాలు ముద్ద చేశినట్టు.

Making mustard seed into a ball.

An impossible combination.

209. ఆవు చేనిలో మేస్తే, దూడ గట్టున మేసునా.

If the cow grazes in the field, will the calf graze on the bank?

Intimate friends, or near relatives, will follow in the same path.

---

* Un bon bailleur en fait bailler deux.

210. ఆవు పాడి యెన్నాళ్లు ఐశ్వర్యం యెన్నాళ్లు, బర్రె పాడి యెన్నాళ్లు భాగ్యం యెన్నాళ్లు.

How long will you have the cow's milk, and how long will you have your fortune? How long will your buffaloe's milk last, and how long will your riches endure?

(See Nos. 341, 873.)

Said to a man proud of his good fortune.

Riches have wings.

211. ఆవుల మళ్లించినవాడు అర్జునుడు.

Arjuna was the man who brought back the cows [of Virâṭa].

(See *Virâṭaparva* of the *Mahâbhârata.*)

Used when speaking of a man to whom the credit of any successful undertaking is really due.

212. ఆవులూ ఆవులూ పోట్లాడితే, లేగల కాళ్లు విరుగుతవి.

When the cows fight, the sucking calves' legs are broken.

When the great fall out, the poor suffer.

213. ఆశకు అంతము లేదు.

There is no limit to desire.

Much would have more.

No one is content with his lot. (Portuguese.)*

The more one has the more one wants. (Spanish.)†

214. ఆశపడి ఆరు లంఖణాలుచేస్తే, ఆవేళా జొన్న మెతుకేనా.

After fasting for six days, with the desire [of being fed with rice (i. e. dainty food given to an invalid)], am I only to have millet?

Failure of a foolish scheme.

---

* Ninguem se contenta com sua sórte.
† Quien mastiene, masquiere.

215. ఆశ బోధిస్తున్నది, అవమానము బాధిస్తున్నది.

Desire incites, the fear of shame prevents.

Shame may restrain what the law does not prohibit.

216. ఆశలేని కూటికి ఆకలి లేదు.

There is no appetite for food unhoped for.

217. ఆశ శిగ్గు ఎఱగదు, నిద్ర సుఖమెఱగదు.

Avarice knows not shame; sleep knows not comfort.

(See No. 156.)

When sleep overpowers, comfort is not thought of.

218. ఆశా పాతక బాపడు గోచిపాతలో తూమెడు కట్టుకొన్నాడట.

The avaricious Brahman tied up a tûmu [of grain] in his clout.

(For *Tûmu* see No. 619.)

219. ఆసోది మాటలకు అర్థమూ లేదు, గుడ్డి కంటికి చూపూ లేదు.

There is no sense in words of condolence nor sight in a blind eye.

220. ఆహారమందూ వ్యవహారమందూ శిగ్గు పడకూడదు.

In eating and in business you should not be modest.

(See Nos. 241, 2012.)

A bashful dog never fattens. (German.)*

A modest man at Court is the silliest wight breathing.

---

* Es wird kein blöder Hund feit.

ఇ.

221. ఇంగువ కట్టిన గుడ్డ.

A rag which had held assafœtida.

(See No. 1861.)

Said of a man who is respected on account of his connection with the family of some famous person, no longer living ; or on account of his own greatness, now passed away.

222. ఇంటింటికి మట్టి పొయ్యి.

Every house has an earthen fire-place.

(See No. 997.)

Every man has his faults.

223. ఇంటింటికి ఒక మట్టిపొయ్యి అయితే, మాయింట మరి ఒకటి.

Every house has an earthen fire-place, my house is still worse off.

Acknowledging one's failings.

224. ఇంటికన్నా గుడి పదిలము.

The temple is stronger than the house.

Said by a ruined man who had been obliged to take refuge in a temple, but pretended that he had gone there for the safety of his property.

Make a virtue of necessity.

225. ఇంటికి జ్యేష్ఠాదేవి, పొరుగుకు లక్ష్మీదేవి.

The goddess of misfortune at home, the goddess of fortune abroad.

Bad to his own, but good to others.

226. ఇంటిదీపమని ముద్దు పెట్టుకొంటే, మూతిమీసాలన్నీ తెగగాలినవట.

When he kissed the lamp belonging to his own house, all his mustaches were burnt off.

Undue familiarity. Extravagant demonstration.

A man may love his weel, and no ride on the riggin o't. (Scotch.)

227. ఇంటిదేవర యాఁగి చస్తే, పొలందేవర గంపజాతర అడిగినదట.

When the household deity was dying of hunger, the goddess of the field demanded a basket procession.

(See Nos. 799, 969, 1781, 1798.)

After an abundant harvest, an earthen image of the goddess of the field is placed in a basket, and carried in procession, with musical instruments and much rejoicing.

To be asked to give to others when badly off one's self.

228. ఇంటిదొంగను యీశ్వరుడూ పట్టలేడు.

Even Śiva himself cannot find out a thief amongst the household.

229. ఇంటినిండా కోళ్లు వున్నవిగాని, కూశేటందుకు కోడి లేదు.

The house is full of fowls, but there's not a cock to crow.

(See No. 343.)

Said of useless people.

230. ఇంటిపేరు కస్తూరివారు, యిల్లు గబ్బిలాలవాసన.

His house name is Kastûri (musk), his house smells of bats.

(See Nos. 240, 276, 613, 1250, 1542, 1796.)

The "house name" is the gentilitious or family name; it precedes the proper name.

A fine name, but a paltry fellow.

231. ఇంటిమీఁద రాయి వేశి వీపు వొగ్గేవాడు.

Having thrown a stone on the top of the house, he stoops to catch it on his back.

232. ఇంటివాడు గొడ్డుగేదె అంటే, పొరుగువాడు పాడిగేదె అన్నట్టు.

When the owner said his she-buffalo was barren, the neighbour said it was milch.

(See Nos. 111, 486.)

Applied to a spirit of contradiction.

233. ఇంటివాణ్ని లేపి దొంగచేతికి కఱ్ఱ యిచ్చినట్టు.

Like waking the master, and giving the thief a stick.

To hold with the hare, and hunt with the hounds.

234. ఇంటివారు వేలు చూపితే, బయిటివారు కాలు చూపుతారు.

If the members of your family point their fingers at you, the outsiders will point their legs.

235. ఇంటివెనకాలకు వెళ్లి యిల్లు ముందుకు తెచ్చినట్టు.

He brought the house forward by going behind it.

Said jokingly of a man who professed to have improved the family prospects.

236. ఇంటిసొమ్ము యిప్పపిండి, పొరిగింటిసొమ్ము పాడిబెల్లము.

His own property is like Ippapiṇḍi, his neighbour's like fine molasses.

Ippapiṇḍi is the refuse of the nuts of the *Ippa* tree (Bassia Latifolia) and is remarkably bitter.

Applied to a niggard.

237. ఇంట్లో పాయసమున్ను మందలో పాలుకూడానా.

What! milk pudding in the house and milk also in the field?

(See No. 838.)

Greediness.

238. ఇంట్లో పెండ్లి అయితే, వూళ్లో కుక్కలకు అడావుడీ.

A marriage in the house is a fine thing for the village dogs.

(See No. 271.)

Men crowd to enjoy that for which they don't pay.

239. ఇంట్లో యీగపులి, బయిట పెద్దపులి.

At home he is a spider, abroad he is a tiger.

Demure at home, a ruffian abroad.

He looks as if butter would not melt in his mouth.

240. ఇంట్లో యీగలమోత, బయిట సవారీలమోత.

In the house a buzzing of flies, outside the hum of palankin bearers.

(See Nos. 230, 276, 613, 1250, 1542, 1796.)

Outward show, but poverty at home.

241. ఇంతమంది దొరలు చావకపోతే నేను మాత్రము చస్తానా, నాకూ అక్కరలేదు అన్నాడట.

If so many great people don't die, shall I alone die? I don't want it.

(See Nos. 220, 2012.)

Said by a man when unwillingly refusing to eat something because Velamas did the same.

Never be ashamed to eat your meat.

He that is ashamed to eat is ashamed to live. (French.)*

242. ఇక్కడ అక్కడ వుంటే యీడేరి పోతావు, నాయింటికి రావే నవిశి పోతువుగాని అన్నాడట.

If you stay here and there you will thrive, come to my house and pine away.

Said jokingly by a poor man to a young girl.

---

* Qui a honte de manger a honte de vivre.

243. ఇచ్చినవాడు దాత, యివ్వనివాడు పాత.

He who gives is a donor, he who does not give is a clout.

(See Nos. 75, 264, 1510, 1607.)

The impertinent speech of a beggar.

244. ఇచ్చినవాడే మెచ్చినవాడు, చచ్చినవాడే అచ్చినవాడు.

The over liberal man is ruined; when a man dies, his debts go with him.

245. ఇచ్చి పుచ్చుకొని మొగుడి వీపెల్లా తడివినట్టు.

She gave it, took it back again, and looked on her husband's back for it.

246. ఇచ్చి వచ్చే నిష్ఠురముకన్నా, యివ్వక వచ్చే నిష్ఠురము నయము.

The offence given by not lending is to be preferred to the annoyance caused after lending.

By anger on account of some damage done to the article lent.

(See No. 10.)

247. ఇచ్చుడుకాడూ గాడు, చచ్చుడుకాడూ గాడు, పూట పూటకూ కూటికి వచ్చుడుగాడు.

He doesn't pay, hang him, but he comes for every meal.

Said by a cateress, of a customer who was more regular in his attendance than in his payments.

248. ఇచ్చేవాణ్ని చూస్తే, చచ్చేవాడైనా లేచును.

Even a dying man will rise up when he sees a liberal person.

With the hope of receiving something from him.

249. ఇచ్చేవానికి పత్రమూ వద్దు, చచ్చేవానికి మందూ వద్దు.

You need not take a bond from a man who is willing to pay, nor administer medicine to one who has made up his mind to die.

250. ఇత్యర్థలు యిగురు, యితిభావలు పులుసు.

For sweet vegetable [take your] " plain significations," and for acid [take your] " deep meanings."

The reply of the wife of a logician (who would pay no attention to household matters and had given her no means of providing food) when he grumbled at the bad fare.

251. ఇది చలమో ఫలమో.

Is this done wantonly or with an object ?

252. ఇదుగో పులి అంటే, అదుగో తోక అన్నట్టు.

When one said " Here's a tiger !" the other said " And there's his tail !"

Rivaling each other in exaggeration. Capping *a long-bow man.*

253. ఇనప గుగ్గిళ్లు గాని, మినప గుగ్గిళ్లు కావు.

Grains of iron, not of black gram.

(See Nos. 737, 1233, 1729, 1757.)

The pulse spoken of is the Phaseolus Roxburghii.

Said of a puzzling passage or a jawbreaking verse.

254. ఇనుము కరిగేచోట యీగలకేమి వున్నది.

What is there for flies in the place where iron is melted ?

A place where nothing is to be got.

255. ఇనుము, తీట, పేము, పట్టిన చెయ్యి వూరకుండదు.

The hand which has a bit of iron, the itch, or a bit of cane in it, never remains quiet.

256. ఇనుమునగూర్చి అగ్నికి సమ్మెటపెట్లు.

The fire suffers the blows of the sledge-hammer for the sake of the hot iron.

(See Nos. 1240, 1840.)

Being drawn into difficulties by one's associates.

257. ఇనుము విరిగితే అతక వచ్చునుగాని, మనసు విరిగితే అతక కూడదు.

If iron be broken it may be united, but if friendship be broken it cannot be healed.

Broken friendship may be soldered, but never made sound. (Spanish.)*

258. ఇన్నాళ్లు బ్రతికి యింటివెనక చచ్చినట్లు.

After living so long he died at the back of his house.

A miserable end.

259. ఇప్పపూలకు వాసన వెతక వలెనా.

Must we search for the smell of the Ippa flower?

(See Nos. 371, 515, 571, 573, 632, 894, 1475, 1494.)

The flowers of the *Ippa* tree (see No. 236) have a very strong smell.

260. ఇరుపోటీల యిల్లు చెడును, వాతనొప్పుల వొళ్లు చెడును.

By rivalry a house is ruined, by rheumatic pains the body is worn out.

261. ఇల్లలకగానే పండగ అవుతున్నదా.

Is smearing the house always the sign of a feast?

---

* Amigo quebrado soldado, mas nunca sano.

262. ఇల్లాలు గుడ్డిదయితే, యింటి కుండలకు చేటు.

If the mistress of the house be blind, all the pots will be broken.

Without supervision things will go to ruin.

When the gude wife's awa', the keys are tint. (Scotch.)

263. ఇల్లు కట్టి చూడు, పెండ్లి చేసి చూడు.

Try building a house, try making a marriage.

An expense greater than contemplated.

Building and the marrying of children are great wasters.

264. ఇల్లు కాలినది జంగమయ్యా అంటే, నా జోలే కప్పరా నావద్దనే వున్నవి అన్నాడట.

When the Jangam was told that the house had caught fire, he replied "I have my bag and bowl with me."

(For *Jangam* see No. 111.)

Selfish indifference.

265. ఇల్లు కాలుచుండగా వాసాలు దూసుకొన్నట్టు.

Like pulling the rafters out of a burning house.

A clumsy expedient.

266. ఇల్లు గెలవలేనివాడు రచ్చ గెలుచునా.

Will he who cannot rule his own house, rule in the council?

He who has no voice in the valley, will have none in the council. (Spanish.)*

---

* Quien no apriata en vallejo, no aprieta en consejo.

267. ఇల్లు చొరబడి యింటివాసాలు లెక్కపెట్టినాడట.

He got into the house and counted the rafters.

Preparatory to laying a false claim to it, and adducing his intimate knowledge as a proof that the building was his own.

(See Nos. 636, 665, 1077, 1078, 1079, 1850.)

Swindling.

268. ఇల్లు తిరిగి రమ్మంటే, యిలారం తిరిగి వచ్చినట్టు.

When he was asked to walk round the house he walked round the shed.

269. ఇల్లు మింగే అత్తగారికి యుగము మింగే కోడలు.

A daughter-in-law who swallows the age (Yuga) to a mother-in-law who swallows the house.

(See No. 703.)

270. ఇల్లు యిర్కటం, ఆలు మర్కటం.

The house is small, and the wife like a monkey.

A double difficulty.

271. ఇల్లు యేడ్చే అమావాస్య, యిరుగూ పొరుగూ యేడ్చే తద్దినం, వూరుయేడ్చే పెండ్లి లేదు.

There is no new moon which the household regrets; nor annual ceremony, the neighbours; nor marriage, the whole village.

(See No. 236.)

At the new moon the Hindus abstain from eating rice in the evening, but take care to make up for it with other good things ; at the *Taddina* (ceremony on the anniversary of a deceased relative's death) the neighbours are feasted ; and to a marriage the whole village is invited.

272. ఇల్లు విప్పి పందిలి వేశినట్టు.

He pulled his house to pieces and built a Pandili [with the materials].

(For *Pandili* see No. 61.)

Said of an arrant fool.

273. ఇల్లు వెళ్లగొట్టగా విడుపుల శృంగారము, మొగుడు వెళ్లగొట్టగా మొత్తల శృంగారము.

Putting on fine clothes when turned out of the house; adorning the threshold when driven out by the husband.

Trying to please when too late.

274. ఇల్లు వెళ్లిపోరా నంబీ అంటే, నా మాన్యము యెక్కడ అని అడిగినాడట.

When a Nambi was told to get out of the house, he asked for his glebe-land.

(See Nos. 360, 1304, 1821.)

Nambi is a priest in a Vishṇu temple.

Effrontery.

275. ఇల్లెక్కి కొరివి తిప్పినట్లు.

Getting on the roof [of a thatched house] and whirling a firebrand.

276. ఇల్లెల్లా కొట్టితే, తట్టెడు పెంకులు లేవు.

When the whole house was knocked down, the tiles did not fill a basket.

(See Nos. 230, 613, 1250, 1542, 1796.)

Appearances are deceitful.

277. ఇల్లే తీర్థం, వాకిలే వారణాశి, కడుపే కైలాసం.

My house is my holy place; my threshold is Benares; my belly is my heaven.

Said by an irreligious man.

"*Whose God is their belly.*" Philippians iii. 18.

278. ఇవతల చెర, అవతల సొర, నడమ రామరాజ్యము.

On this side is capture, on that side is sorrow, in the middle is the kingdom of Râma.

(See Nos. 168, 1644, 1867.)

279. ఇవ్వని మొండికి విడవని చండి.

One obstinate man who wouldn't give and another who wouldn't take a refusal.

280. ఇషుంట రమ్మంటే, యిల్లంతా చేకొన్నట్టు.

Like taking possession of the whole house, when asked to come in for a while.

(See No. 923.)

Give a rogue an inch and he will take an cll. (Danish.)*

281. ఇసుక తక్కిడి, పేడ తక్కిడి.

Cheating with sand, cheating with cowdung.

(See No. 1744.)

Two travellers met: one had a bundle of sand, the other a bundle of cowdung; one said his bundle contained raw rice, the other that his contained boiled rice. They agreed to exchange, and immediately ran off in different directions, each to find himself outwitted by the other. (See story 54, in *Telugu Selections*).

One trick is met by another. (Spanish.)†

282. ఇస్తి వాయనము, పుచ్చుకొంటి వాయనము.

I gave cakes and took cakes.

(See No. 290.)

Vâyanam is a gift of cakes, &c., to a Brahman.

Taking as much as you give.

To one who has a pie in the oven you may give a bit of your cake. (French.)‡

283. ఇస్తే చెడేది లేదు, చస్తే వచ్చేది లేదు.

If a man gives, he will not be ruined; when a man dies, he carries nothing with him.

Give and spend, and God will send.

The charitable give out at the door, and God puts in at the window.

"*When he dieth he shall carry nothing away.*" Psalm xlix. 17.

---

* Giv Skalken et Spand, han tager vel heel Alen.

† Con una cautela otra se quiebra.

‡ A celui qui a son paté au four on peut donner de son gâteau.

284. ఇస్తే పెండ్లి, యివ్వకపోతే పెటాకులు.

If you give, [I shall consider there is] a marriage [in your house] and if you don't give, a funeral.

(See Nos. 243, 1510.)

The impertinent speech of a beggar.

ఈ.

285. ఈ కంటికి యీ రెప్పలు దూరమా.

Are these eyelids distant from this eye ?

(See Nos. 119, 1741.)

Applied to any thing which can easily be tested by actual observation.

286. ఈగకు యిలి, పాముకు బలి పుట్టదు.

No food for a fly nor offering for a snake.

(See Nos. 864, 1968, 2027.)

Said of a miser's house.

Ye'll brak your neck as soon as your fast i' his house. (Scotch.)

287. ఈ చేత చేసి ఆ చేత అనుభవించినట్టు.

Doing with this hand, and receiving the reward with that.

Said of the certain result of either a good or bad deed.

As you sow you shall reap.

As you make your bed, so you must lie on it.

288. ఈతకంటే మించిన లోతు లేదు.

When a man has to swim it matters not what the depth is.

When a man determines to face his difficulties nothing daunts him.

(See No. 289.)

Over shoes, over boots.

It is all the same whether a man has both legs in the stocks or one. (German.)*

---

* Mit beiden Beinen im Stock, oder mit Einem, ist gleichviel.

289. ఈతకు మించిన లోతూ, గోచికి మించిన దారిద్ర్యమూ లేదు.

There is no greater depth to the man who is obliged to swim, nor poverty to him who is reduced to a clout.

(See No. 288.)

Reduced to the last extremity.

290. ఈతగింజ యిచ్చి తాటిగింజ లాగేవాడు.

A man who gives a date stone and takes a palmyra nut.

(See No. 292.)

Îta is the wild date (Phoenix Sylvestris). *Tâḍu* is the Palmyra (Borassus Flabelliformis).

Offering a gift of slight value for the purpose of gaining a rich present.

Throw in a sprat to catch a salmon.

291. ఈతచెట్టుకింద పాలు తాగినా, కల్లే అంటారు.

If you even drink milk under a date tree they will say it's toddy.

(For *Îta* see No. 290.)

People are judged by the company they keep.

Tell me the company you keep, and I'll tell you what you are.

From a clear spring clear water flows. (Latin.)*

292. ఈతముల్లు విరగ దొక్కే కాలము.

He is at the age when he can tread on and break a date-thorn.

(For *Îta* see No. 290.)

Said of an unruly scamp.

293. ఈదబోతే తాగ నీళ్లు లేవు.

When he went to swim, there was not enough water to drink.

Disappointed hopes.

---

* A fonte puro pura defluit aqua.

294. ఈనగాచి నక్కలపాలు చేసెను.

He watched [the field] until the harvest, and then let it go to the jackals.

295. ఈ వూరికి ఆ వూరెంతో, ఆ వూరికి యీ వూరంతే.

The distance between that village and this village is the same as that between this village and that village.

(See No. 1306.)

Six of one and half a dozen of the other.

296. ఈ వూళ్లో పెద్దలు యెవరంటే తాళ్లు, దాతలు యెవరంటే చాకళ్లు.

When asked who were the great (men) in the village, he said "The Palmyras;" when asked who were the givers (of presents), he replied "The washermen."

A joke. The Palmyras (see No. 290) are the tallest trees, and the washermen give people back their clothes.

ఉ.

297. ఉంగరాల చేతితో మొట్టితే, నొప్పి వుండదు.

A rap with ringed fingers will cause no pain.

A man who wears rings is generally well off, and therefore pays handsome damages for injuries inflicted.

298. ఉంటే వూరు, పోతే పాడు.

If [the people] stay, it is a village; if [the people] go, it is a ruin.

299. ఉండనిస్తే పండుతుంది, వూడదీసివేస్తే యెండుతుంది.

If you leave it alone, it will bear fruit; if you pull it up, it will wither away.

300. ఉండి చూడు వూరు అందం, నానాటికి చూడు నా అందం.

Wait and see the beauty of the village, but examine my beauty day by day.

Said by an ugly man in a dirty village.

301. ఉండేది గట్టి, పోయినది పొట్టు.

What remains is solid, what has gone is empty husk.

(See No. 1568.)

302. ఉండేవెల్లా వుండగా, వుపాధ్యాయుల భార్యకు దడిబియ్యము.

[To perform the ceremony of] Daḍi Biyyam to the priest's wife when there are many other things to be done.

Daḍi Biyyam is a ceremony performed before the consummation of marriage.

Going out of your way to do something for others, and neglecting much that you have to do of your own.

303. ఉండ్రాళ్లు పిండివంటా కాదు, వూద ధాన్యమూ కాదు.

Gaṇêśa's rice-balls are not cakes, Ûda is not grain.

Ûda is the Panicum Flavidum.

304. ఉట్టికి యెక్కలేనమ్మ స్వర్గానకు యెక్కునా.

Will the lady who cannot get up into the sling get up into heaven ?

(See Nos. 486, 2021.)

Uṭṭi is a net work sling hung up in Hindu houses at a height of seven or eight feet, to keep earthen pots containing food in.

He that can't ride a gentle horse, must not attempt to back a mad colt.

305. ఉడకకే వుడకకే వో వుల్లిగడ్డ, నీవెంత వుడికినా నీ కంపుపోదు.

Don't boil, don't boil, O garlick! However much you boil, your smell will not go.

Said to an envious person, who is said to burn inwardly.

306. ఉడకవే కూడా వుగాది దాకా అంటే, నాకేమి పనిలేదు యేరువా కదాకా అన్నాడట.

[The host said] "Boil, boil away, O food, until new year's day!" [the guest added] "My business will not take me away until the ploughing-season."

(See No. 367.)

During the Pongal feast in January a stingy man tried by a broad hint to avoid giving a visitor food, but the latter was not to be done out of his dinner. The Telugu New year's day falls in April, and cultivation commences in July.

Eat and welcome; fast and heartily welcome.

Let the guest go before the storm bursts. (German.)*

307. ఉడతకు వుడతా భక్తి.

A squirrel performs a squirrel's service.

The squirrels are said to have assisted Râma in building the bridge at Râmêśvaram by dipping themselves into the water and then rolling in sand, which they brought for the mortar.

Willingly doing what one can.

308. ఉడతకేలరా వూళ్లో పెత్తనము.

What has the squirrel to do with the management of the village?

(See Nos. 732, 1338, 1360, 1363, 1498.)

Presumptuous interference. Impertinent meddling.

---

* Lass den Gast ziehen eh das Gewitter ausbricht.

309. ఉడుముకు రెండు నాలికలు.

The Guana has two tongues.

Said of a man that breaks his word.

" *A sinner that hath a double tongue.*" Ecclesiasticus vi. 1.

310. ఉడుమును చంక పెట్టుకొని వూళ్లో ప్రవేశించినట్టు.

Going into a village with a guana in one's arms.

(See No. 1459.)

Eccentric conduct.

311. ఉడుము పోయినా చెయ్యి వస్తే చాలును.

Never mind if I lose the guana, if I get my hand out it's enough.

(See No. 1805.)

Said by a man whose hand had been caught by a guana in a hole.

Catching a Tartar.

312. ఉత్తచెవికన్నా తాటాకుచెవి మేలు.

An ear with a palmyra leaf in it is better than a bare ear.

(See Nos. 314, 1906.)

Half a loaf is better than no bread.

313. ఉత్త చేతులు మూర వేసినట్టు.

Like measuring the air.

(See No. 96.)

Idle dreams.

314. ఉత్తముండకన్నా అత్తముండ మేలు.

A wretch of a mother-in-law is better than a strange slut.

(See Nos. 312, 1906.)

A bad bush is better than the open field.

Better a lean jade than an empty halter.

315. ఉత్తర కుమార ప్రజ్ఞలు.

The boastings of Uttara Kumâra.

(See No. 547.)

Uttara, the son of king Virâṭa, volunteered to attack the Kurus, but his courage failed him and he turned tail at the sight of the enemy (see Virâṭaparva of the Mahâbhârata).

Bragging. Bombast.

316. ఉత్తర చూచి యెత్తర గంప.

Take up your basket [of seed] when you see [the sun in] Uttara.

Uttara is one of the twenty-seven lunar mansions. When the sun is in Uttara there is invariably rain, and seed is then sown.

Make hay while the sun shines.

Know your opportunity. (Latin.)*

317. ఉత్తర ఉరిమి కురిశినా, పాము తరిమి కరిచినా తిరగదు.

If there be rain with thunder when the sun is in Uttara, there will be no drought; if a snake pursues and bites you, the bite will be fatal.

(For *Uttara* see No. 316.)

318. ఉద్యోగం పురుషలక్షణం, అది పోతే అవలక్షణం.

Employment makes the man; he is a luckless fellow if he lose it.

319. ఉద్యోగం పురుషలక్షణం అన్నాడు, గొడ్డలి తేరా నిట్రాడు నరుకుదాము.

They say "endeavour makes the man," so bring an axe, and let us cut down the centre post.

(See Nos. 1387, 1388, 1389.)

---

* Nosce tempus.

320. ఉన్నమాట అంటే, వులికేసుకొని వస్తున్నది.

A man starts with anger when the truth is told of him.

It is truth that makes a man angry. (Italian.)*

321. ఉన్నమాట చెప్పితే, వూరు అచ్చి రాదు.

If a man speaks the truth he will find the village too hot for him.

(See No. 1275.)

Truth produces hatred. (Latin.)†

322. ఉన్నవాడు వూరికి పెద్ద, చచ్చినవాడు కాటికి పెద్ద.

He that is alive is the head man of the village, and he that is dead is the head man of the burial ground.

A taunt used to one who tries to make out that he is very highly connected.

323. ఉపకారముకు పోతే అపకారము వెంటనే వచ్చినది.

Immediately after doing good, I received an ill return.

Base ingratitude.

324. ఉపాధ్యాయులవారూ ఉక్తం ఉక్తం.

O teacher, uktam! uktam!

Said by a school-boy when he saw a board about to fall on his master's head. He had been taught to render the Sanscrit word *Uktam* by *Palaka baddadi* ("it was said"). These words also signify "the board has fallen," which the boy took to be the correct meaning of the Sanscrit word.

Applied to an ignorant blunder.

---

* Del vero s'adira l'uomo.
† Veritas odium parit.

325. ఉపాధ్యాయులు యేమి చేస్తున్నాడంటే, అబద్ధాలు వ్రాసి దిద్దుకొంటున్నాడు అన్నాడట.

When asked what the school master was doing, one replied "he is correcting the mistakes he has made."

A bad workman.

326. ఉపాయము యెరగనివాణ్ని వూళ్లో వుండనివ్వ కూడదు.

A witless fellow should not be allowed to remain in the village.

327. ఉప్పు తిన్నవాడు నీళ్లు తాగుతాడు.

The man that has eaten salt drinks water.

(See No. 1092.)

328. ఉప్పువాడూ చెడె, పప్పువాడూ చెడె, తమలపాకులవాడు తమాం చెడె.

The salt seller is ruined, the pulse vender is ruined, and the betel seller is entirely ruined.

329. ఉభయపవిత్రాలూ తిని వుద్ధరిణెడు నీళ్లూ తాగి వూహూ అంటావా వుత్తమాశ్వమా.

Dost thou neigh after eating two grass rings and a tea spoonful of water, O excellent steed?

Said by a poor Brahman priest to his miserable pony which he had only fed with two rings (made of sacred grass and worn on his ring fingers), and had given him water out of the small spoon used in sipping water in ceremonies.

Giving little pay and expecting much work to be done.

330. ఉభయ భ్రష్టుత్వం, వుప్పర సన్న్యాసిత్వం.

Ruined in both ways like a well-digger who turns Sanyâsi.

He is neither employed in his old trade nor supported in his new character.

331. ఉమ్మడిగొర్రె పుచ్చి చచ్చినది.

The sheep which was the joint property of two persons, was deserted and died.

(See No. 1556.)

The ass of many owners is eaten by wolves. (Spanish.)*

Between two stools fall to the bottom.

332. ఉయ్యాలలో పిల్లను వుంచి వూరెల్లా వెతికినట్టు.

Putting a child in a cradle and looking for it all over the village.

He looks for his ass and sits on its back. (French.)†

333. ఉరుకు వురుకుమనే నా సవతేకాని, తోడు వురికే నా సవతి యొకతె యున్నా లేదు.

All these wretched women say to me "run, run" [on to the pile], but not one comes with me.

Said by a widow when pressed to become *Satî.*

334. ఉల్లి పది తల్లుల పెట్టు.

Garlick is as good as ten mothers.

(See No. 345.)

335. ఉల్లిపాయంత బలిజవుంటే, వూరంతా చెరుస్తాడు.

If there be a Balija man as small as a clove of garlick, he will ruin the whole village.

(See No. 1748.)

Balija is a caste among Telugu and Canarese Śûdras.

One scabbed sheep will mar a whole flock.

One ill weed mars a whole pot of pottage.

---

* Asno de muchos, lobos le comen.
† Il cherche son âne et il est monté dessus.

336. ఉల్లి ముట్టనిదీ వాసనరాదు.

Unless you had touched the garlick [your fingers] would not have smelt.

(See No. 148.)

If you had not meddled with a bad business you would not have got a bad name.

He who touches pitch defiles himself. (Italian.)*

337. ఉల్లి వుంటే మల్లి వంటలక్క.

When there are onions Malli is a fine cook.

Onions make up for bad cooking.

338. ఉసురు వుంటే వుప్పు అమ్ముకొని బ్రతకవచ్చును.

If you preserve your life, you can at least live by selling salt.

Used as an argument not to risk life for the sake of gain.

339. ఉస్తెకాయ వూరనెంత, నంజ పెట్టనెంత.

How long does it take to salt an Ustekâya ? How much is there of it to put on a dish ?

(See No. 1417.)

Ustekâya (Solanum Trilobatum) is a small fruit.

Applied to something very insignificant.

ఊ.

340. ఊడుగ విత్తనము వంటివాడు.

He is like an Ûḍuga seed.

The seed of the *Ûḍuga* (Alangium Decapetalum) after falling from the tree, is said to attach itself again to the trunk when the rain falls.

To stick to a man like a leech in spite of all rebuffs.

---

* Chi tocca la pece, s'imbratta.

341. ఊదకూడు యెన్నాళ్లు, వుద్యోగము యెన్నాళ్లు.

How long will the Ûda food last? How long will your employment continue?

(See Nos. 310, 373.—*For Ûda see No. 306.*)

342. ఊపిరి పట్టితే బొజ్జ నిండునా.

Can the belly be filled by holding in the breath?

(See Nos. 1636, 2022.)

Inadequate measures. Idleness.

Idleness must thank itself if it go barefoot.

343. ఊరంతా చుట్టాలు, వుట్టికట్ట తావులేదు.

The village is full of relations, but there is no place to hang up the sling (i. e. no shelter).

(See No. 229.—*For Uṭṭi see No. 304.*)

Give out that you have many friends, and believe that you have but few. (French.)*

344. ఊరంతా వడ్లు యెండబెట్టుకొంటే, నక్క తోక యెండబెట్టుకొన్నదట.

When the whole village put their rice in the sun to dry, the jackal put his tail to dry.

Foolish imitation.

345. ఊరంతా వుల్లి, నీవెందుకే తల్లి.

The village is full of garlick, what do I want with thee O mother?

(See No. 334.)

* Il faut se dire beaucoup d'amis, et s'en croire peu.

346. ఊరకుంటు, అడివిలేడి.

Lame in the village and an antelope in the jungle.

A skulk.

347. ఊరికంతా వకదోవ, వులిపికట్టెకు వకదోవ.

All the village has one way, and the prig another.

348. ఊరికి పొయ్యేవానికి లేకపోయినా, బహిర్భూమికి పొయ్యేవానికి బత్యము కట్టుమన్నట్టు.

Never mind giving provisions to the man setting out on a journey, but supply them to the man going to the rear of the village.

349. ఊరికి వక బోగముది, యెవరివద్ద ఆడును.

There is but one dancing girl in the village; before whom is she to dance?

350. ఊరికి వుపకారముగా ఆలికి కోక కొని పెట్టుతాను, యింటింటికీ డబ్బు యివ్వండి అన్నాడట.

As a public benefaction, I will buy a cloth for my wife; give me a pice from each house.

(See No. 198.)

351. ఊరికె వస్తే మావాడు మరివకడు వున్నాడు.

If they are to be had for nothing, I have a relative here.

Wishing to get two shares.

Greediness.

352. ఊరికె వుండలేక పోతే, వురి పెట్టుకో.

If you can't be quiet, hang yourself.

353. ఊరి పిడుగు వచ్చి వీరిశెట్టిని కొట్టుకొని పోయినది.

The misfortune of the village has carried off Vîriśeṭṭi.

The story is as follows: A burglar in digging through the wall of a house was killed by the wall falling upon him; his wife prosecuted the owner of the house for having badly built walls; the house owner blamed the builder; the builder blamed a woman who had distracted his attention while at his work, by passing by that way; the woman blamed a goldsmith to whom she was going to get certain jewels which he had not finished for her; the goldsmith blamed the banker for not letting him have gold in time; the banker was sentenced accordingly to be impaled, but on the point of being put to death he suggested that the size of the instruments would be much better suited to fat Vîriśeṭṭi (to whom he owed a grudge); fat Vîriśeṭṭi was executed accordingly. This happened at *Anyâyapura* (the city of injustice).

The innocent suffering for the guilty.

354. ఊరి మీద నూరు పడ్డా, కరణము మీద కాసు పడదు.

Though a hundred [pagodas] be levied from the village, not a cash will be paid by the Karaṇam.

(See Nos. 579, 2045.—For *Karaṇam* see No. 154.)

A cash (కాసు) is 1-60th of an Anna.

The instrument of oppression does not himself suffer.

355. ఊరివాడికి కాటిభయం, పొరుగూరివాడికి నీటిభయం.

The inhabitant of the village is afraid of the cemetery; the stranger is afraid of the water.

The inhabitant of the village has a superstitious dread of the burial or burning ground, and avoids it; but the stranger does not know its situation and walks through it. On the other hand, the villager knows the depth of the tank, and does not fear going into it, but the stranger is afraid to venture.

No safe wading in an unknown water.

356. ఊరివారి బిడ్డను నగరివారు కొట్టితే, నగరివారి బిడ్డను నారాయణుడు కొట్టును.

If one of the royal family strike a villager's child, Nârâyaṇa will strike his child.

" [*The LORD*] *will avenge the blood of his servants.*" Deuteronomy xxxii. 43.

357. ఊరు పొమ్మంటుంది, కాడు రమ్మంటుంది.

The village says "go," the cemetery says "come."

(See Nos. 1966, 1967.)

About to die.

He is burnt to the socket.

358. ఊరు విడిచి పొరుగూరికి వెళ్లినా, పూనిన కర్మము మానదు.

Although you leave the village and go to another, your evil destiny will still attend you.

(See Nos. 1149, 1871.)

359. ఊరు వుస్తెకాయంత, సిద్ధాంతము తాటికాయంత.

The village is like the Ustekâya and the religious duties are like the Tâṭikâya.

The *Ustekâya* (No. 339) is a small fruit, and the *Tâṭikâya* (No. 390) a large fruit.

Applied to exactions imposed upon people for religious purposes greater than they can bear.

360. ఊరే చేరవద్దు రౌతా అంటే, గుర్రాన్ని యెక్కడ కట్టేది అన్నాడట.

When a trooper was told not to come into the village, he asked where he was to put up his horse.

(See Nos. 274, 1304, 1921.)

361. ఊళ్లు యేలే కొమారుడికన్నా వుపాదానమెత్తే పెనిమిటి నయము.

A husband that begs is better than a son that rules over villages.

The one clings to his wife, the other despises his mother.

ఋ.

362. ఋణశేషము, వ్రణశేషము, అగ్నిశేషము వుంచకూడదు.

Remains of a debt, of a sore, or of a fire should not be left.

363. ఋషిమూలము, నదీమూలము, స్త్రీమూలము విచారించకూడదు.

Enquire not into the origin of a Ṛishi, a river, or a woman.

Ṛishi is a saint. (See Wilson's Sans. Dict.)

ఎ.

364. ఎంగిలిచేత్తో కాకికయినా మెతుకు విదపడు.

He will not even throw his leavings to the crows.

(See Nos. 296, 1963, 2027.)

Said of a great miser.

365. ఎంచబోతే మంచమెల్లా కంతలే.

If you begin to count, you will find the whole cot full of holes.

(See Nos. 151, 199.)

Referring to a bed made of plaited rope.

When a man wishes to find fault, he loses no opportunities.

When love fails we espy all faults.

366. ఎంచివేస్తే ఆరి తరుగునా.

Will the *number* decrease by drying ?

A reply given to a cheat who thus attempted to account for a deficiency in the *quantity* of vegetables.

367. ఎండబడితే వుండబడుతుంది, వుండబడితే వండబడుతుంది, వండబడితే తిండబడుతుంది, తిండబడితే పండబడుతుంది.

If the sun gets hot, he will have to stay; if he stays, dinner will have to be cooked for him; if it is cooked, it will have to be eaten; and if he eats it, he will have to lie down.

(See No. 306.)

The muttered grumblings of a stingy host.

368. ఎంతదయో నరకడికి చేంత్రాడు వెతుకుతున్నాడు.

How kind the scamp is, searching for the well-rope!

(See No. 1141.)

Said scoffingly by the wife whose husband was looking for the well-rope, not to draw water for her, but to chastise her with.

369. ఎంతప్రొద్దు వుండగా లేచినా, తుమ్మగుంట వద్దనే తెల్లవారినది.

However early he rose the day always dawned while he was at the Tumma tank.

Tumma is the Acacia Arabica. Tanks are often named from the trees planted around them. The earlier the man got up the more he dilly-dallied on the strength of it, so the sun always found him at the tank, in the way to his work.

Early up, and never the nearer.

370. ఎంతమంచి గొల్లకయినా, నిమ్మకాయంత వెఱ్ఱి లేకపోదు.

However good a man a shepherd may be, he will not be entirely free from foolishness.

371. ఎంతమంచి పంది అయినా, అమేధ్యము తినక మానదు.

However good the pig may be, it will never cease to eat filth.

(See Nos. 259, 515, 571, 573, 622, 924, 1475, 1494.)

A hog in armour is still but a hog.

372. ఎందుకు యేడుస్తావురా పిల్లవాడా అంటే, యెల్లుండి మావాండ్లు కొట్టుతారన్నాడట.

A lad when asked "Why are you crying my boy?" answered "They say my people are going to beat me the day after tomorrow."

(See No. 691.)

Anticipating evils.

You cry out before you are hurt.

373. ఎక్కడ కట్టితే నేమి, మనమందలో యీనితే సరి.

What matters it whose the bull was? If the cow calves in our herd, it's all right.

Applied to an unprincipled action.

374. ఎక్కడనయినా బావా అనవచ్చునుగాని, వంగతోట వద్ద బావా అనగూడదు.

Call me brother-in-law any where but at the Brinjal garden.

(For *Vanga* see No. 97.)

Unwillingness to acknowledge relationship when it would cost anything.

375. ఎక్కడ వున్నావే కంబళీ అంటే, వేశిన చోటనే వున్నాను వెంగళీ అన్నదట.

"O blanket where are you?" said he "Where you left me, you madman," it replied.

A smart repartee.

376. ఎక్కడికి పోతావు విధమ్మా అంటే, వెంటనే వస్తాను పదమ్మా అన్నదట.

"Where are you going to Madam Fate?" asked one "I'll follow you, go on" she replied.

The evil results of mixing with bad company.

377. ఎక్కితే గుర్రపు రౌతు, దిగితే కాలి బంటు.

If I ride I shall be a trooper, if I dismount I shall be a foot soldier.

A man who makes himself useful in any position.

378. ఎక్కిన వానికి యేనుగ లోజ్జు.

The elephant is subject to the man who has mounted it.

379. ఎక్కిపోయి పట్టిచూచి దిగివచ్చి రాళ్ల రువ్వినట్టు.

Having mounted [the tree] and felt [the fruit], he came down again and threw stones at it.

380. ఎక్కిరించబోయి వెల్లకిత్తలా పడ్డాడట.

He went to mock, and fell on his back.

He went out shearing and he came home shorn.

The biter bit.

381. ఎగదీస్తే బ్రహ్మత్య, దిగదీస్తే గోహత్య.

If I say this, it will be killing a Brahman; if I say that, it will be killing a cow.

Said by a reluctant witness to himself, when called to give evidence regarding a complaint made by a Brahman that another man's cow had grazed in his field.

Being placed in a dilemma by having to give evidence in a quarrel between two friends.

382. ఎత్తుకొని తిన్నబోలె యెదురుగా వస్తే, చంకన వున్నబోలె సలాం చేసినదట.

When he was met by the bowl that he used to collect alms in and eat out of, the bowl under his arm made salâm to it.

A begging impostor paying a visit on one occasion to a village where he thought he was not known, kept his alms-bowl under his arm, but when he met a man carrying an old bowl that had once belonged to him, the one under his arm is said to have betrayed its owner by claiming acquaintance with its predecessor.

383. ఎత్తుపడ్డ గొడ్డు పులికి జడుస్తున్నదా.

Is a bullock which has fallen down from fatigue afraid of a tiger?

Resignation to one's fate through utter helplessness.

384. ఎదట అన్నది మాట, యెదాన పెట్టింది వాత.

Reprove a man to his face; brand a man on his chest.

Don't abuse a man behind his back.

He who praises in praesentia, *and abuses in* absentia, *have with him* pestilentia. (German.)*

385. ఎదట వున్నవాడు పెండ్లికొడుకు.

The man in front is the bridegroom.

386. ఎదటి పొయ్యి మండితే తన పొయ్యిలో నీళ్లు పోసుకొన్నట్టు.

When the fire was lighted in the opposite house, he threw water on his own.

(See Nos. 53, 1592.)

An envious man waxes lean with the fatness of his neighbour.

Envy is its own torturer. (Danish.)†

---

* Wer einen lobt in Praesentia und schimpft in Absentia, den hole die Pestilentia.

† Avindsyg er sin egen Böddel.

387. ఎదురు పడ్డమ్మ యెండిపోయినదట.

The woman who was met wasted away.

(See No. 514.)

One woman met another out of whom a spirit had been driven, and fancied she was possessed.

Unreasonable fears.

388. ఎద్దు దున్నగా పిఱుఁజు ఘ్రుగిరించినది.

While the bullock was ploughing, the tick puffed and blew.

(See No. 491.)

Applied to a person who does little in assisting others but makes much of it.

What a dust have I raised! quoth the fly upon the coach.

389. ఎద్దు పుండు కాకికి ముద్దా.

Is the bullock's sore tender to the crow ?

Said of one devoid of sympathy for others.

390. ఎద్దు యీనెనంటే, కొట్టాన కట్టుమన్నట్టు.

" The bullock has calved" [said one] " Then tie it up in the shed" [replied the other].

(See No. 1172.)

Applied to a foolish speech.

391. ఎద్దు యెండకు లాగ, దున్నపోతు నీడకు లాగ.

The bullock pulled towards the sun, and the buffalo towards the shade.

A bad match.

Every couple is not a pair.

392. ఎద్దుల వెంబడే తాళ్లు.

Ropes after bullocks.

Taken to tie them up with.

Providing one's self with what is necessary.

393. ఎద్దేమి యెరుగురా అటుకులచవి, గాద్దేమి యెరుగురా గంధపొడి వాసన.

What does a bullock know of the taste of parched grain? what does an ass know of the smell of perfume?

To throw pearls before swine.

Strew no roses before swine. (Dutch.)*

394. ఎనుబోతుమీద వాన కురిశినట్టు.

As rain falls on a male buffalo.

Apathetic indifference.

395. ఎనుము తన్నునని గుర్రమువెనక్కు పోయినట్టు.

Fearing the buffalo would kick, he went behind the horse.

396. ఎన్నడూ యెరగని రెడ్డి గుర్రము యెక్కితే, ముందూ వెనక ఆయెను.

The Reḍḍi who had never mounted a horse before, sat with his face to the tail.

(See Nos. 95, 134, 474.)

397. ఎన్ని బూతులయినా పిడికెడు కొర్రలు కావు.

Abuse me as much as you like, I've got my handful of grain out of you.

Said by a beggar who had received alms and abuse together.

When you have given me roast meat, you beat me with the spit.

---

* Strooit geen rosen voer varkens.

398. ఎన్నో రణాలు కోశినానుగాని, నారణమంత తీపు లేదన్నట్టు.

I have cut many boils, but there was never such pain as in my own.

Said by a Surgeon.

To cut into another man's ear is like cutting into a felt hat. (Danish.)*

He laughs at scars who never felt a wound. (German.)†

399. ఎప్పటి మేలు అప్పటికే.

When a good deed [is done,] then only [is it thought of].

(See No. 81.)

Eaten bread is soon forgotten.

400. ఎరగని వూళ్లో మెప్మెలు చేస్తే, యేకులు నీ మొగుడు వడుకుతాడా.

If you give yourself airs in the village where you are a stranger, will your husband spin the cotton?

401. ఎరుక పిడికెడు ధనము.

Acquaintance is a handful of money.

402. ఎరువుల సొమ్ములు బరువుకు చేటు, తియ్యా పెట్టా తీపుల చేటు, వాటిలో వొకటి పోతే అప్పులచేటు.

Borrowed ornaments cause inconvenience by their weight, pain by taking them off and putting them on, and debt if one of them is lost.

He that goes a borrowing goes a sorrowing.

403. ఎర్రను చూపి చేపను పట్టినట్టు.

Like catching a fish with a worm.

Fish follow the bait.

---

* At skaere i fremmed Ore er ikke anderledes end i Filtehat.
† Der Narben lacht, wer Wünden nie gefühlt.

404. ఎలుకకు పిల్లి పొంచు వేసినట్లు.

Like a cat crouching for a mouse.

405. ఎలుకకు పిల్లి సాక్షి.

The cat a witness in the rat's case.

Interested evidence.

A fox should not be of the jury at a goose trial.

406. ఎలుక చావుకు పిల్లి మూర్ఛపోనా.

Will the cat faint at the death of the rat?

Indifference.

407. ఎలుకమీఁది కోపాన యింటికి చిచ్చు పెట్టుకొన్నట్లు.

Like getting angry with a rat and setting fire to one's house.

(See No. 53.)

Burn not your house to fright away the mice.

408. ఎలుగు వెంటికి తండసము తీసినట్లు.

Like pulling a bear's hairs out with tweezers.

An endless business.

A cask that will never fill. (Greek.) *

409. ఎల్లవారమ్మల బ్రతుకు తెల్లవారితే తెలుస్తుంది.

When it dawns, we shall know whose mother is alive.

Said by a man to his wife, at whose instigation he had agreed that they should kill his mother. The mothers of the pair slept together and the wife's mother was murdered instead of the husband's, with the latter's knowledge. The wife, having an inkling of the truth, endeavoured to persuade her husband to go and see which of the two they had spared, and he replied as above.

---

* Ἄπληστος πίθος.

410. ఎల్లిశెట్టి లెక్క యేక లెక్క.

Elli Śeṭṭi's account is a single account.

Receipts and disbursements, profits and loss, all muddled up together.

411. ఎవరి అబ్బ సొమ్మురా యెక్కెక్కి యేడ్చేవు.

Whose father's property are you sobbing for?

Said to a man who is disappointed at not getting what he has no right to expect.

He has a good estate, but the right owner keeps it from him.

412. ఎవరికి పుట్టిన బిడ్డవురా యెక్కెక్కి యేడ్చేవు.

Whose child are you, that you cry and weep so bitterly?

(See Nos. 1, 1610.)

413. ఎవరికి వారే యమునా తీరే.

Every man to his own way on the banks of the Yamunâ (Jumna).

There every man is free to do what he has a fancy for.

414. ఎవరి నీళ్లలో వారు మునగ వలె.

Every man must dip in his own waters.

Every one must bear his own troubles.

Each cross hath its inscription.

Every one bears his cross. (French.)*

415. ఎవరి ప్రాణము వారికి తీపు.

Every man's life is sweet to himself.

Life is sweet.

---

* Chacun porte sa croix.

416. ఎవరి వెఱ్ఱి వారికి ఆనందము.

Every man's folly is pleasure to himself.

Fools are pleased with their own blunders.

417. ఎవరు యేమి చేసినా, యింటికి ఆలు అవుతుందా, దొంతికి కడవ అవుతుందా.

Will any service rendered by another be as a wife to the house or a pot for the pile ?

Said by a man whose wife has died or gone astray.

ఏ.

418. ఏకాదశా బ్రాహ్మణుడా అంటే, కాలే కొరివి మొగసన తోస్తావా అన్నాడట—ద్వాదశా బ్రాహ్మణుడా అంటే, ఆపదలు కాపురాలు చేస్తావా అన్నాడట.

"Is it the fast O Brahman ?" [asked one] "Will you stir up the fire ?" [replied the Brahman already irritated by fasting]. "Is it the festival ?" [said the first]. "Do troubles last for ever ?" [answered the Brahman, delighted at the prospect of being fed.]

Welcome and unwelcome intelligence.

419. ఏ కాలు జారినా, పిల్లకే మోసము.

Whichever leg slips there is danger to the child.

(See No. 129.)

420. ఏకుల వంటి మెతుకులు వేసుకొని యెనప పెరుగు పోసుకొని యమరాలిని గనుక తింటూ వున్నాను గాని, దగ్గిరికి రాకండి పిల్లల్లాలా జడుసుకొనేరు.

I am a terrible woman eating grains of rice like flocks of cotton mixed with buffalo curds, so don't come near me children, you'll take fright!

Said by a greedy woman to keep her children off.

421. ఏకులు వుంచితే బుట్ట చిరుగుతున్నదా.

Will a basket be broken by being filled with flocks of cotton?

(See Nos. 1665, 2023, 2077.)

Ineffectual measures.

422. ఏ గాలికి ఆచాప యెత్తినట్టు.

Like setting the sail according to the wind.

(See No. 455.)

Set your sail according to the wind. (French.)*.

423. ఏటి ఆవలి ముత్యములు తాటికాయలంతేశి అన్నట్టు.

The pearls on the other side of the river are as large as palmyra fruits.

(See Nos. 534, 841, 1622.)

Exaggeration in describing things not present.

424. ఏటికి యెప్పుడు పోయినావు యిసక యెప్పుడు తెచ్చినావు అంటే, ఆడవారు తలిస్తే అది యెంతసేపు అన్నదట—మొగవారు తలిస్తే యిది యెంతసేపు అని నాలుగు బాదినాడట.

"When did you go to the river, when did you bring the sand?" [asked the husband] "If women like, how long will that take?" [saucily replied the wife] "If men like, how long will this take?" [said the husband] giving her four double-handers.

The husband's question was caused by finding sand in his food.

---

* Il faut tendre voile selon le vent.

425. ఏటిదరి మానికి యెప్పుడూ చలనము.

A tree on the river bank always totters.

(See No. 428.)

Said of a man in an insecure position.

426. ఏటి యీతకూ లంక మేతకూ సరి.

The grazing on the island is not worth the swim across the river.

427. ఏటివద్ది నక్క కాగానే, పాటిరేవు యెరుగునా.

Although the jackal lives near the river, will it know where the ford is ?

Applied to ignorant persons in high position.

428. ఏటి వొడ్డు చేను.

A field on the bank of the river.

(See No. 425.)

A dangerous situation.

429. ఏట్లో వంకాయలు కాస్తవా అంటే కాస్తవి అన్నట్టు.

Like saying "yes" when asked whether brinjals grow in the river.

(For *Brinjal* see No. 97.)

A time server.

430. ఏట్లో వేశినా యెంచి వెయ్య వలెను.

Although you throw [things] into the river, take an account of them.

Keep your expenditure within bounds.

431. ఏడిచేదాని మొగుడు వస్తే, నా మొగుడూ వస్తాడు.

If the weeping widow's husband returns, mine will come also.

Stolid indifference. Want of feeling.

432. ఏడిచే బిడ్డకు అరిటిపండు చూపినట్టు.

Like shewing a plantain to a crying child.

433. ఏడుపులో యేడుపు యెడమ చెయ్యి బయిట పెట్టుమన్నట్టు.

Show your [withered] left hand and add to their grief.

The story is that after a marriage the bridegroom was found to be a fool, which caused much regret to the family of the bride. The bridegroom's friends then told him to show the withered state of his left hand which he had hitherto concealed.

Making bad matters worse.

434. ఏడుస్తూ యేరువాక సాగితే, కాడి మోకులు దొంగలు యెత్తుకొని పోయినారట.

While the man was sluggishly ploughing, thieves stole the rope collars.

435. ఏతి అంటే ప్రేతి అంటాడు.

When one says he's going, the other says he's dying.

(See No. [illegible].)

Spirit of contradiction.

436. ఏదుకు పెడతల బుద్ధి.

The porcupine has sense in the back of its head.

Said of a man without brains.

437. ఏనుగకు కాలు విరగడమూ, దోమకు రెక్క విరగడమూ సమము.

The loss of a wing is the same to a mosquito as the loss of a leg to an elephant.

Proportionate losses.

438. ఏనుగకు వక శీమ, గుర్రానికి వక వూరు, బర్రెకు వక బానిసె.

To keep an elephant [a man requires] a country, to keep a horse a village, and to keep a she-buffalo a maid.

439. ఏనుగకు వెలక్కాయలు లొటా లొటా.

A wood apple is very small in an elephant's throat.

A very easy matter.

440. ఏనుగ దాహముకు చూరు నీళ్లా.

Will the thirst of an elephant [be quenched] by the water which drops from the eaves?

441. ఏనుగను చూచి కుక్కలు మొరిగినట్టు.

Like dogs barking at an elephant.

(See No. 692.)

442. ఏనుగను తెచ్చి యేకుల బుట్టలో వుంచి అది తననెత్తిన పెట్టి తన్ను యెత్తుకో అంటాడు.

He tells me to put the elephant into the cotton basket, to place the basket on his head, and to lift him up.

Êkulabuṭṭa is a very small hand basket.

Being asked to do an utter impossibility.

443. ఏనుగనెక్కినవాడు కుక్క కూతకు జడియడు.

The man who has mounted an elephant will not be afraid at the bark of a dog.

He who is in favor with the great will not fear the enmity of the mean.

444. ఏనుగ పడుకొన్నా గుర్రమంత యెత్తు.

Even when the elephant lies down he is as high as the horse.

(See No. 1805.)

A man much superior to another.

445. ఏనుగ మింగిన వెలగ పండు వత్తు.

Like a wood-apple swallowed by the elephant.

(See No. 798.)

It is swallowed whole, and is said to be found afterwards empty though unbroken.

Said of a person in an influential position who does not benefit others.

446. ఏనుగమీద పొయ్యేవాణ్ని సున్నము అడిగినట్టు.

Like asking a man on an elephant for some chunam.

His hand cannot be reached. (For *chunam* see No. 2114.)

447. ఏనుగలు తినేవాడికి పీనుగలు పిండివంట వత్తు.

To the man that eats elephants, corpses are as pastry.

(See Nos. 694, 778, 1006.)

A thoroughly bad man won't stick at trifles.

448. ఏ పాటు తప్పినా సాపాటు తప్పదు.

Whatever work is neglected, eating is not forgotten.

449. ఏ పుట్టలో యే పాము వున్నదో తెలియదు.

What snake it is, and what hole it lives in, we don't know.

Said of persons whose abilities are not yet known.

450. ఏమి అప్పాజీ అంటే, కాలం కొద్దీ రాయజీ అన్నాడట.

"What, O Appâji! [is to be done?" said the king] "As occasion requires, O king!" replied [the minister].

(See Nos. 422, 455.)

451. ఏమి పోలిశెట్టీ అంటే, యెప్పటి మొత్తుకోళ్లే అన్నాడట.

When Pôliśeṭṭi was asked how he was getting on, he replied "I am in trouble as usual."

452. ఏమీ తోచకపోతే, యెక్కిరించినాడట.

Not knowing what to do, he began to mimic others.

453. ఏమీ లేనమ్మకు యేడ్పుల శృంగారము, కలిగినమ్మకు కడుపుల శృంగారము.

Weeping is the ornament of a poor woman, *embonpoint* is the ornament of a rich woman.

454. ఏమీ లేని ఆకులు యెగసి పడితే, అన్నీ వున్న ఆకులు అణిగి వుండినవి.

The leaf dishes which were empty rose up high; those that were full remained steady.

(See Nos. 508, 1274.)

The conceit of little knowledge, the humility of true learning.

Shaal waters mak the maist din. (Scotch.)

455. ఏ యెండకు ఆ గొడుగు పట్ట వలెను.

The umbrella must suit the hour of the day.

(See Nos. 422, 450.)

Suitable to the occasion.

456. ఏరుకొని తినే పక్షి ముక్కున ముల్లు విరిగినట్టు.

Like a thorn piercing the beak of a bird that was picking up food.

Losing the only means of support.

457. ఏరు తీశినట్టు.

Like the flood subsiding.

Perfect stillness after a tumult.

After a storm comes a calm.

458. ఏరు నిద్ర పోయినట్టు.

As the river sleeps.

Smooth waters run deep.

There is no worse water than that which sleeps. (French.)*

459. ఏరు మూరెడు తీస్తే, కయ్య బారెడు తీస్తుంది.

When the river goes down a cubit, the water in the field goes down a fathom.

If you lose a little in the favor of the great, you sink four times as much in the estimation of the people.

460. ఏరు యెంత పారినా కుక్కకు కతుకు నీళ్లే.

Let the river flow ever so abundantly, the dog only gets what it can lap up.

A servant neglected by a master liberal to strangers.

---

* Il n'y a pire eau que l'eau qui dort.

461. ఏరు యేడామడ వుండగానే, చీర విప్పి చంక పెట్టుకొని పోయినట్టు.

She took off her cloth and put it under her arm, while the river was still seventy miles off.

(See Nos. 1206, 1696.)

Do not strip before bed time. (French.)*

462. ఏలిన వానికి రేయుం బగులు వకటే.

Day and night are one to the [Supreme] Ruler.

"The darkness and the light are both alike to Thee." Psalm cxxxix. 12.

463. ఏలుకోవడానకు వూళ్లు లేవుగాని, యెత్తుకొని తినడానకు వూళ్లు లేవా.

There are no villages to rule over, but are there not villages to beg in?

Said by a beggar refused alms.

464. ఏలేవాని యెద్దు పోతేనేమి, కాచేవాని కన్ను పోతేనేమి.

If the master's ox be lost what is it [to the servant?]. If the watchman's eye be lost what is it [to the master?].

ఐ.

465. ఐశ్వర్యానికి అంతము లేదు.

There is no limit to riches.

466. ఐసా ఫయిసా.

Either one way or the other.

(See No. 472.)

(Corrupted from the Hindustani.)

* Il ne faut point se dépouiller avant de se coucher.

ఒ.

467. ఒంటికి లేని వ్యాధి కొని తెచ్చుకొన్నట్టు.

Like buying and bringing a disease with which the body is not troubled.

Wilfully bringing trouble on one's self.

468. ఒంటికి ఓర్వలేనమ్మ రెంటికి ఓర్చునా.

Will the woman who cannot bear one [trouble] bear two?

(See Nos. 1158, 1394.)

469. ఒక కంచాన తిని ఒక మంచాన పడుకొనేవారు.

They eat of one dish and sleep on one bed.

(See Nos. 1283, 1949.)

Extreme intimacy.

They are hand and glove.

470. ఒక కన్ను కన్నూ కాదు, ఒక కొడుకు కొడుకూ కాదు.

One eye is no eye, one son is no son.

471. ఒక కలగంటే తెల్లవారుతున్నదా.

Will the morning dawn after dreaming one dream?

After one trouble, think not that you have passed through all.

472. ఒకటే దెబ్బ రెండే ముక్కలు.

One blow and two pieces.

(See No. 455.)

To give a direct answer and settle a matter one way or the other.

473. ఒకటొకటిగా నూరా వకటే మాటు నూరా.

A hundred one by one, or a hundred at once?

Said in doubt of a person's liberality, as the "hundred" promised would probably turn out to mean only one.

474. ఒకనాటి భాగవతములో మూతి మీసాలన్నీ తెగకాలినవి.

With one day's acting, all his mustaches were burnt off.

By standing too near the torches which are used to light up the figures of the performers, and on which powdered resin is thrown.

(See Nos. 95, 134, 896.

Said of a clumsy novice.

475. ఒకనాడు ధారణ, వకనాడు పారణ.

One day holding (fasting); one day breaking fast.

(See No. 476.)

A precarious subsistence.

Change of fortune is the lot of life.

To-day a king, to-morrow nothing. (French.)*

476. ఒకనాడు విందు, వకనాడు మందు.

One day a feast, one day medicine.

(See No. 475.)

One day favor, one day disfavor.

To-day in finery, to-morrow in filth. (German.)†

477. ఒకరి కలిమికి యేడిస్తే వక కన్ను పోయినది, తనలేమికి యేడిస్తే మరి వక కన్నూ పోయినది.

By weeping at the good fortune of another he lost one eye, and by weeping at his own ill fortune he lost the other.

---

* Aujourd'hui roi, demain rien.

† Heut' im Putz, morgen im Schmutz.

478. ఒకరిని యిద్దరిని చంపితేనేగాని, వైద్యుడు కాడు.

A man is no Doctor until he has killed one or two [patients.]

(See No. 1259.)

Said to a bungling tyro.

If the doctor cures, the sun sees it; if he kills, the earth hides it.

479. ఒక వూరికి వెయ్యి దోవలు.

There are a thousand ways to a village.

Every man in his way.

There are more ways to the wood than one.

480. ఒక్క చెయ్యి తట్టితే, చప్పుడు అవునా.

If you clap with one hand will there be any sound?

Nothing can be done successfully by a single person.

One man is no man. (Latin.)*

Two heads are better than one.

Hand washes hand, and finger finger. (Greek.)†

481. ఒక్కొక్కరాయి తీస్తూ వుంటే, కొండయినా తరుగుతుంది.

If you remove stone by stone, even a mountain will be levelled.

You must pluck out the hairs of a horse's tail one by one. (Latin.)‡

Drop by drop the lake is drained.

482. ఒరగబెట్టి తాగేది చెరిచెరా కంచరవాడు.

The brazier has spoilt the dish which before I ate out of slantingly (on account of the hole in it).

(See Nos. 681, 846, 1567.)

---

* Unus vir nullus vir.

† Χεὶρ χεῖρα νίπτει, δάκτυλός τε δάκτυλον.

‡ Caudae pilos equino paulatim oportet evellere.

483. ఒళ్లు వంగనమ్మ కాలి మెట్టెలను కందిపోయినదట.

The lazy woman complained that her toe-rings pinched her.

(See Nos. 150, 1314, 1829, 2034.)

Idle folks lack no excuses.

484. ఒళ్లు వాచిన రెడ్డీ వడ్లు యేమిధర అని అడిగితే, అవి లేకనే నా వొళ్లంతా వాచినది అన్నాడట.

"Well, swollen-bodied Reḍḍi! how do you sell your paddy?" "The want of it alone has made my whole body swell," he replied.

_ The Hindus believe that longing for any desired object causes the legs and face to swell.

485. ఒళ్లెరుగని శివము, మనసెరగని కల్ల వున్నదా.

Is there any inspiration which makes a man unaware of his own actions? Is there any lie not known to him that utters it?

ఓ.

486. ఓకారము రానివాడు వడ్లు గుణించినట్టు.

Like one who does not know the alphabet attempting multiplication.

(See Nos. 304, 2021.)

487. ఓడలు బండ్లా వస్తున్నవి, బండ్లు వోడలా వస్తున్నవి.

Ships come on carts; carts come on ships.

When ships are broken up, the pieces are carried on carts.

Good and ill fortune follow each other.

488. ఓడు ఓడంటే, కంచం ఓడన్నట్టు.

One said " Loss, loss !" the other replied " A hole in the dish."

A pun on the word *Ôḍu.*

489. ఓపనివాడు కోరనిదీ, ఒంటనివాడు ఆడనిదీ లేదు.

There is nothing which an invalid will not ask for; and there is nothing which an envious man will not say.

490. ఓపనివారికి వద్దన్నవారే తల్లి తండ్రులు.

The lazy man looks upon those as his parents who say " Don't [work]."

An idler is delighted at every interruption.

491. ఓబీ ఓబీ నీవు వడ్లు దంచు, నేను పక్కలు యెగర వేస్తాను.

Ôbi, Ôbi, you pound the rice, and I'll shake my sides.

(i. e. imitate the action of pounding).

(See No. 388.)

Applied to an idle skulk, who pretends to be always busy.

Lazy folks take the most pains.

492. ఓరిస్తే ఓరుగల్లు పట్నమవుతుంది.

With patience, Ôrugallu will become a city.

(For Ôrugallu see No. 1971.)

Rome was not built in a day.

493. ఓర్వలేనమ్మ వడిని నిప్పులు కట్టుకొంటే, వడీ దడీ కూడా కాలినది.

When the envious woman put fire in her waist, her clothes were burnt and the mat screen also.

(See Nos. 53, 386, 1562.)

Causing one's own ruin through envy.

494. ఓర్వలేని రెడ్డి వుండీ చెరిచెను, చచ్చీ చెరిచెను.

The envious Reḍḍi ruined the village while living, and was a curse to it when dead.

A Reḍḍi who had oppressed the people of his village all his life, requested them, when dying, to burn his body in a certain spot. This they willingly acceded to, and took the Reḍḍi's corpse there for that purpose, when they were attacked by the inhabitants of the neighbouring village, within the limit of which the Reḍḍi had desired to be burned, and this became an everlasting cause of contention. (See Tâtâchâri's Tales Page 5.)

495. ఓలి తక్కువ అని గుడ్డిదాన్ని పెండ్లాడితే, దొంతి కుండలన్నీ పగల గొట్టినదట.

When a man married a blind woman, on account of the smallness of the jointure, she broke all the pots in the pile.

(See No. 496.)

496. ఓలి తక్కువ అని గుడ్డిదాన్ని పెండ్లాడితే నెలకు మూడు ఆవాలు.

When he married a blind woman, because of the small jointure, [she broke] three kilns of pots a month.

(See No. 495.)

False economy.

497. ఓహో కనుక్కోలేక పోతిరిగదా అన్నట్టు.

Aha ! so you were not able to find me !

Said by a jackass of a bridegroom who had hidden himself on the top of the shed at the time of the marriage, and looked on while the bride was married to another man.

ఔ.

498. ఔషధానకు అవపథ్యానకు చెల్లు, రోగము పై పెచ్చు.

[The benefit derived from] the medicine is to be deducted from [the harm done by] carelessness in diet, and the balance remaining is an increase of the disease.

Diet cures more than the lancet.

The best physicians are Dr. Diet, Dr. Quiet, and Dr. Merryman.

క.

499. కంకణముల చెయ్యి ఆడితే, కడియముల చెయ్యి ఆడును.

If the hand with Kankaṇamulu moves, the hand with Kaḍiyamulu moves also.

Kankaṇamulu are bracelets worn by women. *Kaḍiyamulu* are those worn by men.

Where woman leads man follows.

500. కంచము అమ్మి మెట్టెలు కొన్నట్టు.

Selling the dish and buying toe-rings.

He has given the hen for the egg. (German.)*

501. కంచి అంత కాపరము గడ్డలు చేసినది.

She made the family as large as Kanchi into clods.

Said of a woman who by going astray brings disgrace upon the whole family.

Kanchi is the celebrated town of Conjeveram.

---

* Er hat die Henne für das Ei gegeben.

502. కంచు మోగినట్టు కనకము మోగునా.

Does gold ever ring like bell metal ?

(See Nos. 454, 1974.)

A wise man is sparing of his words, but a fool likes the sound of his own voice.

A deluge of words and a drop of sense.

" It is not the hen which cackles most that lays most eggs." (Dutch.)*

503. కంటికి యింపయితే, కడుపుకు యింపు.

What is pleasant to the eye is good for the stomach.

504. కంఠగత ప్రాణముగా వున్నది.

The life has reached the throat, (i. e. all but departed).

Being placed in a most difficult position.

505. కండ్లకు దూరమయితే చెవులకు దూరమా.

If out of sight, is it out of hearing also ?

506. కండ్లు చెరిపిన దేవుడు మతి యిచ్చినట్టు.

The God who destroyed the eyes, gave understanding.

When God deprives a man of sight, He increases his intellectual powers.

507. కండ్లు పోయిన తర్వాత సూర్య నమస్కారములా.

Will you worship the sun after losing your eyes ?

(See Nos. 77, 508, 1169.)

If their sight begins to fail, Hindus worship the sun for their recovery.

Persisting in that which has become of no avail.

---

* Het hoen, dat het meest kakelt, geeft de meeste eijers niet.

508. కండ్లు వుండగానే కాటుక.

[Apply] collyrium to your eyes while you have them.

(See Nos. 77, 507, 1169.)

Make use of your opportunities before they pass from you.

509. కందకు లేదు, చేమకు లేదు, తోటకూరకు వచ్చెనా దురద.

No acridity in Kanda or Chêma, how can there be any in Tôṭakûra?

(See No. 510.)

Kanda is the Arum Campanulatum; *Chêma* is the Colocasia Antiquorum; *Tôṭakûra* is applied to the Amaranthus Oleraceus, and other herbs.

When a man's relatives and friends won't assist him, why should help be expected from a mere acquaintance?

510. కందకు లేని దురద బచ్చలికేమి.

If the Kanda possess no acridity, why should it be looked for in the Bachchali?

(See No. 509.)

Bachchali is Basella Cordifolia (the Indian spinach).

511. కక్కిన కుక్కవద్దికీ కన్న కుక్కవద్దికీ కానివాణ్ని అయినా పంపవద్దు.

Don't send even your enemy near a dog which has vomited, or a bitch which has pupped.

512. కట్టిన యింటికి వంకలు చెప్పేవారు వెయ్యమంది.

Those who criticize the design of a built house are a thousand.

He that buildeth upon the highway hath many advisers. (Dutch.)*

Every fool can find faults that a great many wise men can't remedy.

* Die aan den weg timmert, heeft veel berechts.

513. కట్టినవానికి వకయిల్లు అయితే కట్టనివానికి వెయ్యిండ్లు.

A man that has built a house has one house, a man that has built no house has a thousand houses.

A man without a house can change his residence as often as he pleases.

He who has no house of his own is every where at home. (Spanish.)*

514. కట్టుకొన్న ఆపె పెట్టుకొన్న ఆపె వుండగా, యెదురుపడ్డ ఆపె యొండిపోయినదట.

When the woman who had worn the cloth, and the woman who had the cloth in her possession met another woman, she began to pine away.

(See No. 387.)

The cloth spoken of is the కాటేరికోక worn by pregnant women to propitiate the goddess కాటేరి (Kāṭēri). If a pregnant woman who has neglected the worship of this goddess, sees one of these garments, she takes fright.

515. కట్టెవంక పొయ్యి తీరుస్తున్నది.

The fire place takes the crookedness out of the stick.

(See Nos. 259, 371, 571, 573, 632, 924, 1479, 1494.)

A bad man's evil qualities only disappear in the funeral pile.

The wolf loses his teeth but not his inclination. (Spanish.)†

516. కడగా పొయ్యే శనైశ్చరుడా మా యింటిదాకా వచ్చి పొమ్మన్నట్టు.

O Saturn! who art passing by, pay my house a visit.

Saturn is the god of misfortune.

He that courts injury will obtain it. (Danish.)‡

---

* El que no tiene casa de suyo, vecino es de todo el mundo.
† El lobo pierde los dientes, mas no los mientes.
‡ Han mase have Skaden, som har sögt den.

517. కడవంత గుమ్మడికాయ అయినా కత్తిపీటకు లోకువ.

Although the pumpkin be as big as a large pot, yet it is subject to the kitchen knife.

Gummaḍi kâya is the Cucurbita Maxima.

However great a family a wife may come from, she must still be subject to her husband.

518. కడి అంటే నోరు తెరచి, కళ్లెమంటే నోరు మూశినట్టు.

Like [a horse] which opens its mouth for a morsel, and shuts it for the bridle.

(See Nos. 73, 1070, 1381, 1385.)

519. కడి గండము గాచును.

A lump of food [given in charity] will save you from trouble.

He who lends to the poor, gets his interest from God. (German.)*

520. కడుపు కూటికి యేడిస్తే, కొప్పు పూలకు యేడ్చినది.

When the belly cried for food, the hair cried for flowers.

(See Nos. 1033, 1798.)

521. కడుపుతో వున్నమ్మ కనక మానునా, వండినమ్మ తినక మానునా.

Will the woman with child refrain from bringing forth? will the woman who cooked not help herself?

One is as certain as the other.

He is a poor cook that cannot lick his own fingers.

---

* Werden Armen leihet, dem zahlet Gott die Zinsen.

522. కడుపునిండా గారెలు తింటే, వంటినిండా జ్వరము.

If you eat a bellyful of cakes, [you will get] a bodyful of fever.

523. కడుపు నిండిన బేరము.

A bargain [with a man] with his belly full.

A person in easy circumstances will drive a hard bargain.

524. కడుపు నిండినవానికి గారెలు చేదు.

Cakes are bitter to a man with his belly full.

A rich man will not care for trifling gains.

525. కడుపులోని మాట అంటే, వూరంతా అవుతున్నది.

If you let out your secret, it will get all over the village.

(See Nos. 47, 685, 1521.)

Three know it, all know it. (Italian.)*

The secret of two is God's secret; the secret of three is all the world's. (French.)†

526. కడుపులో బిడ్డ కడుపులోనే వుండగా, కొడుకు పేరు సోమలింగం.

While the child is still in the womb, the son is named Sômalingam.

(See Nos. 204, 986, 1470, 1471.)

Boil not the pap before the child is born.

---

* Tre lo sanno, tutti lo sanno.
† Secret de deux, secret de Dieux; secret de trois, secret de tous.

527. కడుపులో లేనిది కౌగిలించుకొంటే వస్తున్నదా.

Will [affection] that does not exist in the heart be caused by embracing [the body] ?

528. కడుపు వస్తే కనే తీర వలెను.

After conception there's nothing for it but to bring forth.

(See No. 1003.)

A work undertaken must be completed.

529. కతికితే అతకదు.

If he laps, it wont answer.

If a person goes to get a wife for another, and eats in the house before the matter is arranged, it is sure to fall through.

530. కత్తి తీసి కంపలో వేసి యేకు తీసి పొడుచుకొంటానన్నట్టు.

Like a man throwing away the knife and threatening to kill himself with a flock of cotton.

Saying and doing are two things.

531. కత్తిపోటు తప్పినా కలంపోటు తప్పదు.

Though the stab of the sword may fail, the stab of the pen will not fail.

(See No. 533.)

532. కత్తి మెత్తనా అత్త మంచీ లేదు.

There is no softness in a sword, nor goodness in a mother-in-law.

(See No. 54.)

533. కత్తివాడా కలంవాడా.

Is the sword sharp or the pen ?

(See No. 531.)

The pen in the hand of the strong is more powerful than the sword.

A goose-quill is more dangerous than a lion's claw.

534. కథకు కాళ్లు లేవు ముంతకు చెవులు లేవు.

No legs to the tale, no ears to the pot.

Said of a story that one cannot make head or tail of.

A story without a head. (Greek.)*

535. కననిది బిడ్డ కాదు, కట్టనిది చీర కాదు.

That which has not been brought forth is not a child ; that which is not worn is not a garment.

Nothing belonging to others can make up for the want of one's own.

536. కని గుడ్డు విని చెవుడు.

Seeing, blind ; hearing, deaf.

" Eyes have they, but they see not : they have ears, but they hear not." Psalm cxv. 5, 6.

537. కనుక్కొని రారా అంటే కాల్చి వచ్చేవాడు.

When told to go and look, he goes and burns.

Alluding to the story of Hanumân setting fire to Lankâ, when sent to look for Sîtâ.

538. కన్న తల్లికయినా కను మరుగుండ వలెను.

Some things must be hidden even from the mother that bore you.

---

* *Ἀκέφαλος μῦθος.*

539. కన్ను తగిలే పుల్లను కనిపెట్ట వద్దా.

Should you not be careful of that which may stick into your eye?

Keep an eye on your enemies.

540. కన్ను పొయ్యేటంత కాటుక పెట్టుకొందురా.

Will you put so much collyrium on your eye, as to destroy it?

Little sticks kindle a fire, but great ones put it out.

541. కన్ను మెరగకున్నా కడుపు మెరుగుతుంది.

Although the eye does not see, the belly finds.

A man's want leads him to seek and find a livelihood.

A hungry man sees far.

A hungry man discovers more than a hundred lawyers. (Spanish.)*

542. కన్ను ఎఱ్ఱనయినా మిన్ను ఎఱ్ఱనయినా కారక మానదు.

When the eye is red, or the sky is red, (at sunset) there will surely be a dropping.

543. కన్నేల పోయెనోయి కనకలింగమా అంటే, చేసుకొన్న కర్మమోయి శంభులింగమా అన్నాడట.

"O Kanakalingam! how did you lose your eyes?" asked one; "The result of my deeds, O Śambhulingam!" replied the other.

An evasive answer.

544. కప్పకు కాటూ, బ్రాహ్మణునికి పోటూ లేదు.

A frog never bites, a Brahman never fights.

Said of a cowardly person.

---

* Mas descubre un hambriento que cien letrados.

545. కమ్మ నీచు కడిగినా పోదు, కాకిచిప్ప పెట్టి గోకినా పోదు.

The smell of Kammavâru cannot be got rid of by washing, or scraping with a shell.

Kammavâru are a class of Telugu Śûdras, whose occupation is farming. They are proverbially dirty people.

546. కరేపాకు కోసేవాడు వాగినట్టు.

Muttering like a man plucking Kari Vêpa leaves.

Kari Vêpa is the Bergera Koenigii and is used in making curries. There is an idea that the leaves lose their flavour if plucked silently.

547. కర్ణ ప్రతాపము.

The valour of Karṇa.

A blusterer.

548. కర్మములుగల మగణ్ని కంబట్లో కట్టి బుజముమీద వేసుకోంటే జారి వీథిలో పడ్డట్టు.

Like the guilty husband who slipped out of the blanket and fell into the street when his wife was carrying him on her shoulder (to save him from punishment).

549. కర్ర లేనివాణ్ని గొర్రె అయినా కరుస్తుంది.

Even a sheep will bite a man without a stick.

Every man should be prepared to defend himself.

550. కర్రికుక్క కపిలగోవు అవునా.

Will a black bitch become a Kapila cow ?

The *Kapila* is a tawny cow worshipped by the Hindus.

551. కలకాలపు దొంగ ఒకనాడు దొరుకుతాడు.

The everlasting thief is one day caught.

The old fox is caught at last.

The old ape is taken at last. (Latin.)*

552. కలబంద యెండూ, కోడలి కొత్తా లేదు.

There is no dryness in the aloe, nor newness in a daughter-in-law.

(See No. 1587.)

A daughter-in-law is never a stranger.

553. కలలో పాలు తాగడానకు కంచుదయితేనేమి కనకపుదయితేనేమి.

What matters it whether one drinks milk in a dream out of bell metal or gold?

Building castles in the air.

554. కలలో భోగము.

Enjoyment in a dream.

555. కలవారింటి ఆడపడుచుకు కాకరకాయ కానరాదు.

A girl who has come from a rich man's house cannot even look at a Kâkarakâya.

Kâkarakâya is the Memordica Charantia.

Puffed up with pride.

556. కలిగితే కాళ్లముయ్య, లేకపోతే మోకాళ్లముయ్య.

If you can afford it, [your dress] should cover your feet; if not, it should cover your knees.

Living according to one's means.

Cut your coat according to your cloth.

---

* Anus simia sero quidem.

557. కలిగినయ్య గాదె తీసేటప్పటికి పేదవానికి ప్రాణము పోయినది.

By the time the rich man opened his corn bin, the poor man had died.

558. కలిగినయ్య కలిగినయ్యకే పెట్టును, లేనయ్య కలిగినయ్యకే పెట్టును.

The rich man will feed the rich man and the poor man will feed the rich man.

(See No. 560.)

Who has, is—(Italian.)*

559. కలిపోశి కలిపి పెట్టినా వుట్టివంక చూస్తాడు.

Although they give him food mixed with rice washings, he looks towards the net.

(For Uṭṭi see No. 304.)

The guest disbelieved the poor state of the house.

560. కలిమి కులాల మిండడు.

Wealth is the paramour of all castes.

(See No. 558.)

A rich man is sought after by all.

Rich people are every where at home. (German.)†

561. కలిమిలేములు కావటి కుండలు.

Having and not having are the pots in a Kâvaḍi.

Equally balanced.

(See No. 563.)

Fortune and misfortune are two buckets in a well. (German.)‡

Every day hath its night, every weal its woe.

---

* Chi ha, è.
† Reiche Leute sind überall daheim.
‡ Glück und Unglück sind zwei Eimer im Galgenbrunnen.

562. కలియుగము రెండు రోజులు పోవలెను.

The few days remaining in the Iron age must pass away.

The *Kali Yuga* is said to contain 432,000 years of which the 4968th year commenced in A. D. 1866.

An ironical phrase applied to procrastination.

563. కలియుగ రావణాసురుడు.

A Râvaṇa of the Iron age.

Applied to a man as bad in this, the Iron age, as Râvaṇa was in the Golden.

564. కల్పవృక్షము కింద గచ్చపొద వున్నట్టు.

Like the Gachcha bush growing round the Kalpa tree.

The *Gachcha* is a thorny bush, (Guilandina Bonducella); the *Kalpa* is the celestial tree of desire.

Applied to a benevolent man surrounded by evil persons, who do not suffer others to approach him.

565. కల్ల పయిడికి గరుకులు మెండు.

False gold is very rough.

566. కల్ల పసిడికి కాంతి మెండు.

False gold is very bright.

All is not gold that glitters.

567. కళ్యాణము వచ్చినా కక్కు వచ్చినా ఆగదు.

When marriage comes, or vomiting, it cannot be stopped.

568. కష్ట సుఖాలు రెండూ కావటి కుండల వంటివి.

Sorrow and joy are like two pots on a Kâvaḍi.

(See No. 561.)

Kâvaḍi is the yoke made of a split bamboo, used by Indian coolies. To the ends are slung loads of equal weight.

Joy and sorrow are to-day and to-morrow.

569. కాకి కర్రుమంటే గుండె ఝల్లుమంటుంది.

When the crow cawed, she started.

Feigned sensitiveness.

570. కాకి గండాగుండిగాని కోకిల పిరికి.

The crow is plucky, the cuckoo is cowardly.

571. కాకిని తెచ్చి పంజరములో పెట్టితే చిలుకవలె పలుకునా.

If you put a crow in a cage will it talk like a parrot?

(See Nos. 259, 371, 515, 573, 839, 994, 1475, 1494.)

Wash a dog, comb a dog, still a dog is but a dog. (French.)*

572. కాకి పిల్ల కాకికి ముద్దు.

The crow's chick is dear to the crow.

The crow thinks her own bird the fairest.

573. కాకి పుట్టీ నలుపే పెరిగీ నలుపే.

The crow is black when it is born, and black when it is grown.

(See Nos. 259, 371, 515, 571, 839, 994, 1475, 1494.)

What's bred in the bone will never be out of the flesh.

The wolf changes his hair but not his nature. (Latin.)†

574. కాకి ముక్కున దొండపండు కరుచుకొన్నట్లు.

Like a Doṇḍa fruit in a crow's beak.

(See Nos. 718, 720.)

Doṇḍa is a bright red fruit (Coccinea Indica).

A beautiful thing possessed by a person who is unworthy of it.

---

* Lavez chien, peignez chien, toujours n'est chien que chien.
† Lupus pilum mutat, non mentem.

575. కాకులకు కాని నెమ్మలు కాస్తేనేమి పూస్తేనేమి.

What is it to the crows if the Nemmi trees, which they don't like, grow or blossom?

Nemmi chettu is the Dalbergia Oojeinensis.

576. కాకులను కొట్టి గద్దలకు వేసినట్టు.

To kill crows and throw them to the kites.

(See No. 829.)

He robs Peter to pay Paul.

577. కాగల కార్యములు గంధర్వులే తీరుస్తారు.

Predestined events will be accomplished by Gandharvas.

In allusion to the death of Kîchaka whom Draupadî declared to have been killed by her husbands the Gandharvas. (See *Virâṭa Parva* of the *Mahâbhârata.*) *Gandharvas* are celestial musicians.

The judgments of God are fulfilled by unseen instruments.

The feet of the avenging deities are shod with wool. (Latin.)*

578. కాటికి కాళ్లు చాచుకొని తిండికి చెయ్యి చాచేవాడు.

He stretches out his legs towards the cemetery, and stretches out his hand for food.

Greedy to the last.

579. కాటికి పోయినా కరణాన్ని నమ్మ రాదు.

Don't trust a Karaṇam even when he is being taken to the cemetery.

(See Nos. 354, 2045.)

580. కాటిలో పండినవి కాకులు తిన్నవి.

The crows ate up the fruit which grew in the forest.

Property common to all.

---

* Dii irati laneos pedes habent.

581. కాదు అంటే అరవవాడి చెవ్వి.

If you say Kâdu, it is a Tamilian's ear.

(See No. 582.)

582. కాదు కాదు అంటే నాది నాది అన్నాడట.

When one said "Kâdu, Kâdu" the other said "Nâdi, Nâdi."

(See No. 581.)

Kâdu in Telugu means "it is not," "no;" in Tamil it signifies "the ear." A Telugu man on one occasion accidentally stuck the barb of his spear into a Tamilian's ear, on which the latter cried out "*Kâdu! Kâdu!*" (My ear! my ear!) The Telugu man thinking he meant to say "Not yours, not yours" pulled at the spear all the harder, saying "*Nâdi! Nâdi!*" (It's mine! it's mine!).

Said to a man who is obstinate in argument.

583. కానకుండా కట్టిడిచ్చేను కాని వినకుండా వీరణాలు వాయించేవా.

I will give you a bundle of grain without any one else seeing me, but will you play on the double drum without any one else hearing it?

A silly request made by a female, who was not allowed to indulge her taste for music.

584. కానని వారి పాయసము గంపలాది అన్నట్టు.

Speaking of people who are not known, as having distributed rice-milk by baskets full.

(See Nos. 429, 841, 1622.)

Exaggerating the bounty of absent persons.

585. కాని కాలముకు కర్రే పాము అవుతుంది.

In your evil hour your own stick will become a snake.

i. e. your own friends will turn against you.

586. కాని మందం కోటి దుఃఖం.

One sixty-fourth part of folly will bring ten millions of sorrows.

A little neglect may breed great mischief.

587. కానివాడు లేనివాడితో జత.

An unfriendly person is equal to one that is not.

588. కాని వేళకు కందులు గుగ్గిళ్లు అయినట్టు.

In an unlucky time his Kandi wouldn't boil soft.

(For *Kandi* see No. 32.)

589. కాపు వచ్చిన యేడే కరువూ వచ్చినది.

The famine came in the very year that the cultivator came to the village.

An unfortunate coincidence.

590. కారణము లేకనే కార్యము పుట్టదు.

There is no effect without a cause.

Every why has a wherefore.

There is a cause for all things. (Italian.)*

591. కార్తెముందర వురిమినా, కార్యము ముందర పదిరినా, చెడుతుంది.

If it thunders before the Kârte, if you are hasty in a business, it will be spoilt.

Kârte is "the particular constellation of the 27 in which the sun happens to be." The *Kârte* here spoken of is that in which rain should fall. If it thunders before the time, the rain will be insufficient.

* Ogni cosa ha cagione.

592. కార్యం గొప్పా వీర్యం గొప్పా.

Is the business of importance or are the means ?

593. కాలము నాటి కందిగింజ, పెద్దల నాటి పెసరగింజ.

In the ages past he was Kandi and in the time of his forefathers he was Pesara.

(For *Kandi* and *Pesara* see No. 32.)

Said of a prosy old fellow who spins long yarns.

594. కాలనేమి జపము.

Kâlanêmi's prayers.

Kâlanêmi was a pretended sage. (See the *Râmâyaṇa.—Yuddha Kâṇḍa.*)

Applied to hypocrisy.

595. కాలబెట్టి నేల రాచినట్టు.

Burning and rubbing on the ground.

Annoying and ill-treating another.

596. కాలమొక్క రీతి గడప వలెను.

Time must be spent in one way.

Change of circumstances should not change the man.

597. కాలానికి కడగండ్లూ దేశానికి తిప్పలూ వచ్చినవి.

Time is afflicted, and the country is wandering [in trouble].

Said jokingly by a person when asked whether he was in trouble. *Dêśamu* here means literally the country and not the inhabitants of it.

598. కాలికి వేస్తే మెడకు, మెడకు వేస్తే కాలికి.

He removes the rope from the leg to the neck, and from the neck to the leg.

Attempting to entrap a person by unfair questions.

599. కాలితో చూపితే తలతో చెయ్య వలెను.

If he points with the foot, it must be done with the head.

Said of the obsequiousness necessary to a dependant.

Cringing is a gainful accomplishment.

600. కాలిన మన్నూ కాలని మన్నూ అంటవు.

Burnt earth will not adhere to unburnt.

People in different positions in life cannot be very intimate.

601. కాలీ కాలని మొండి కట్టె.

A half-burnt log.

Said of a mean spirited creature who resents no affront.

602. కాలు కాలిన పిల్లవలె తిరుగుతాడు.

He hops about like a cat with a burnt paw.

603. కాలు జారితే తీసుకో వచ్చునుగాని, నోరు జారితే తీసుకో కూడదు.

If your foot slips you may recover your balance, but if your mouth slips you cannot recall your words.

A slip of the foot may be soon recovered; but that of the tongue perhaps never.

Better a slip of the foot than of the tongue. (French.)*

A word and a stone once let go cannot be recalled. (Spanish.)†

* Mieux vaut glisser du pied que de la langue.
† Palabra y piedra suelta no tiene vuelta.

604. కాలు జారి నేలనుపడి భూమి అచ్చి వచ్చినది కాదన్నట్టు.

He slipped and fell, and then said the ground was unlucky.

Attributing events to a wrong cause.

605. కాలు పట్టుకొని లాగితే చూరు పట్టుకొని వేలాడేవాడు.

When you pull him out by the leg, he holds on by the eaves.

(See Nos. 340, 2017.)

A man of no delicacy of feeling, not to be got rid of easily. A toady.

606. కాలే కడుపుకు మండే గంజి.

Scalding rice water to a burning (hungry) stomach.

(See No. 156.)

Anything is acceptable to one who is in want.

Beggars must not be choosers.

Hungry dogs will eat dirty puddings.

A hungry ass eats any straw. (Italian.)*

607. కాళ్లను చుట్టుకొన్న పాము కరవక మానునా.

Will a snake coiled round your leg not bite you ?

Said of a helpless dependant who must be supported.

608. కావడి యెన్ని వంకలు పోతేనేమి యిల్లు చేరితే సరి.

What if the Kâvaḍi bends ever so much ! If it reaches the house, it is enough.

(For Kâvaḍi see No. 568.)

All's well that ends well.

---

* Asino che ha fame mangia d'ogni strame.

609. కాశికి పోగానే కర్రి కుక్క గంగి గోవు అవునా.

Will a black dog become a holy cow by merely going to Benares?

(See No. 1086.)

Formal observances cannot make a sinful man holy.

He that goes a beast to Rome, a beast returns. (Italian.)*

Send a fool to the market, and a fool he'll return.

610. కాశికి పోయి కుక్క బొచ్చు తెచ్చినట్టు.

Like going to Benares, and bringing back dog's hair.

(See Nos. 612, 1667.)

Great labour and small results.

611. కాశికి పోవడము వకటి, కావడి తేవడము వకటి.

Going to Benares is one thing; bringing back a Kâvaḍi (of Ganges water) is another.

(For *Kâvaḍi* see No. 568.)

Two great things to be done. Applied to keeping one great object in view.

612. కాశికి వెళ్లి గాడిద గుడ్డు తెచ్చినట్టు.

Like going to Benares and bringing back an ass's egg.

(See Nos. 610, 1667.)

An absurd exploit.

---

* Chi bestia va à Roma bestia retorna.

613. కాసుకు గతిలేదు, కోటికి కొడి వేసినాడు.

He was without a cash, but raised his banner for a crore.

(See Nos. 230, 240, 278, 1250, 1542, 1796.)

A cash (*Kâsu*) equals about one fortieth of a penny.

Penniless, but bragging of having a plum.

614. కాసుకు దోవలేదు, నూటికి పరవా లేదు.

He has not the means of [getting] one cash, but thinks nothing of [spending] a hundred [pagodas].

(For *cash* see No. 613.) A pagoda = 3½ Rupees.

Wanton extravagance.

He is able to buy an abbey.

615. కాసు గొడ్డుకు రూక బందె.

A fine of a fanam for [the trespass of] a cow worth a cash.

(See Nos. 820, 889, 1439.)

A fanam = 80 cash. (For *cash* see No. 613.)

Expense disproportionate to the value of an article.

616. కిం అంటే కం అనలేడు.

When asked "what?" he cannot say "whom?"

(See No. 960.)

He cannot say bo to a goose.

617. కీడెంచి మేలెంచ వలెను.

Count the disadvantages first, then the advantages.

(See No. 1052.)

Measure twice, cut but once.

Don't buy a pig in a poke.

618. కుంచములో కదుళ్లు పోశినట్టు.

Like pouring spindles into a corn measure.

A noiseless operation.

619. కుంచెడు గింజలకు కూలికి పోతే, తూమెడు గింజలు దూడ తిన్నట్టు.

While she was out working for a kuncham of grain, the calf [at home] ate a tûmu.

(See Nos. 1104, 1794.)

A *tûmu* is a measure equal to 4 *kunchams.*

One step forwards and two backwards.

620. కుంటి కులాసం, యింటికి మోసం.

What's the cripple's delight is harm to the house.

Such a man is said always to be in mischief.

621. కుంటి గాడిదెకు జారినదే సాకు.

A slip of the leg is the excuse of a lame donkey.

622. కుంటెద్దు రానిదీ దూలమెత్తరు.

Until the lame bullock comes, they won't lift the beam.

623. కుండలో కూడు కూడుగానే వుండ వలె, పిల్లలు మొద్దులలాగున వుండ వలె.

The food must remain undiminished in the pot, and the children must be fat and strong.

(See No. 692.)

To wish for two things opposed to each other.

You can't eat your cake and have it too.

624. కుండల్లో గుర్రాలు తోలేవాడు.

A driver of horses among the pots.

A man that sticks at home. A mollycoddle.

625. కుంపట్లో తామర మొలిచినట్టు.

Like a lotus springing up in a chafing dish.

Utterly incredible.

626. కుక్క అమేధ్యము తిన్నది.

The dog ate filth.

(See Nos. 628, 630, 632.)

The nature of the animal.

627. కుక్క కాటుకు చెప్పు దెబ్బ మందు.

For the bite of a dog, a slap with a slipper is the cure.

The proper punishment for a slanderer.

628. కుక్కకు వచ్చేవి అన్నీ గొగ్గి పండ్లు.

All the teeth that a dog gets are crooked.

(See Nos. 626, 630.)

Said of a man who spoils every thing he meddles with.

629. కుక్క తీసిన కొయ్య నక్క తీసిన కొయ్య.

A stick taken by a dog, a stick taken by a jackal.

No one agreeing with his neighbour.

All at sixes and sevens.

630. కుక్క తెచ్చేవి అన్నీ గొడ్డెలు.

All that a dog brings is filth.

(See Nos. 626, 628.)

'Tis the nature of the beast.

631. కుక్కతోక పట్టుకొని గోదావరి యీద వచ్చునా.

Could you swim over the Gôdâvari, by catching hold of a dog's tail?

Reliance upon mean persons for great things.

Trust not to a broken staff.

632. కుక్కను అందలములో కూర్చుండ పెట్టితే, అమేధ్యము చూచి దిగ వురికినది.

When they seated the dog in a palanquin, it saw filth and jumped down and ran to it.

(See Nos. 259, 371, 515, 571, 573, 924, 1475, 1494.)

Mean persons although exalted will not give up their low habits.

Crooked by nature is never made straight by education.

"Set a frog on a golden stool, and off it hops again into the pool." (German.)*

633. కుక్కను కొట్ట బచ్చెన కొయ్య కావలెనా.

Do you require a painted stick to strike a dog with?

634. కుక్కను కొట్టితే యిల్లంతా పారుతున్నది.

If you beat the dog, it fouls the whole house.

---

* Setz einen Frosch auf golden Stuhl,
Er hupft doch wieder in den Pfuhl.

635. కుక్కను చంపిన పాపము గుడి కట్టినా పోదు.

The sin of killing a dog cannot be expiated even by building a temple.

636. కుక్కను పెంచితే, గండాయె కూటి కుండలకెల్లా చేటాయె.

If you rear up a dog, when it becomes big it will empty all your dishes.

(See Nos. 367, 665, 1077, 1078, 1079, 1850.)

Put a snake into your bosom and when it is warm it will sting you.

637. కుక్కను ముద్దు పెట్టుకొంటే, మూతెల్లా తెగ నాకుతున్నది.

If you kiss a dog, it licks your whole face.

The result of encouraging low people.

638. కుక్క నోట్లో కఱ్ర పెట్టితే లొళ్లుమంటున్నది.

If you poke a stick into a dog's mouth, it will snap.

A man may make his own dog bite him.

639. కుక్క వేషము వేస్తే, మొరగకుండా వల్ల కాదు.

If you assume the disguise of a dog, you must bark.

In for a penny, in for a pound.

640. కుక్క సంతకు పోయి తునకోల దెబ్బలు తిన్నట్టు.

When the dog went to the fair he was beaten with the scale-beam.

A vain fellow will be ignominiously treated.

641. కుట్టిన తేలు గుణవంతురాలు, కూశినమ్మ కుక్క ముండ.

The scorpion which stung is a good tempered creature, the [stung] woman who bawled out is a wretched slut.

A mischief maker often escapes blame.

642. కుడవబోతూ కూరాకు రుచి అడిగినట్టు.

Like enquiring the flavour of the vegetables when on the point of eating them.

Want of patience.

643. కుడుములు వండలేని ఆడదీ, కూనరాగము తియ్యలేని మొగవాడూ లేరు.

There is no woman who cannot cook kuḍumus, nor man who cannot hum a tune.

Kuḍumu is a common kind of cake.

Applied to things which are very common.

644. కుప్ప తగలబెట్టి పేలాలు వేయించుకొని తినేవాడు.

A man who sets fire to the whole heap and begins to eat parched grain.

The work of a fool.

645. కుప్పలో మాణిక్యము.

A diamond in a dunghill.

One worthy amongst many worthless.

A diamond is valuable though it lie on a dunghill.

646. కుమ్మర ఆవములో గచ్చకాయ వేసినట్టు.

Like throwing a Gachcha nut into a potter's kiln.

(See No. 586.—*For Gachcha see No. 584.*)

If the nut of this tree be thrown into a kiln, it will burst, and break the pots.

A great injury done by a slight action.

647. కుమ్మర ఆవములో యిత్తడి ముంత దొరుకునా.

Will a brass pot be found in a potter's kiln?

A worthy person is not to be found amongst the worthless.

648. కుమ్మరపురుగావటము.

The manner of the mole-cricket.

Never resting from doing mischief.

649. కుమ్మరపురుగుకు మన్ను వెంట అంటదు.

Earth does not adhere to the mole-cricket.

Engaging in a business but keeping clear of all responsibility.

650. కుమ్మరికి వక యేడు, గుదియకు వక పెట్టు.

One year to the potter, one blow to the cudgel.

The cudgel destroys in one blow what has cost the potter a year's labour.

The sudden loss of that gained by much labour.

651. కుమ్మ చెప్పుకొనేటందుకు గూడూరు పోతే, యేడు వూళ్ల కుమ్మ యెదురుగా వచ్చినది.

When he went to Gûḍûr to tell of his misfortune, the misfortune of seven villages met him.

Whither goest thou, Misfortune? To where there is more. (Spanish.)*

652. కురూపి యేమి చేస్తున్నాడంటే, సురూపాలన్నీ లెక్కపెట్టుతున్నాడు.

When one enquired what the ugly man was doing, [he was told that] he was counting all the good looking people.

An ugly person finds fault with the looks of others.

The kiln calls the oven burnt house.

The shovel makes game of the poker. (French.)†

The pan says to the pot "keep off or you'll smutch me." (Italian.)‡

---

* Adonde vas, mal? Adonde mas hay.
† La pêle se moque du fourgon.
‡ La padella dice al pajuolo, Fatti in la che tu me tigni.

653. కులమింటి కోతి అయినా మేలు.

A monkey [-like wife] of good family is better [than a pretty wife of low origin].

654. కులమెరిగి చుట్టము, స్థలమెరిగి వాసము.

[Form] your connexions when you know the caste, [choose] your residence when you know the place.

655. కులహీనమయినా, వరహీనము కారాదు.

Though [a husband] be low in rank, he should not be younger than his wife. (Or, *she should not be without one*?)

656. కూచమ్మ కూడ బెట్టితే, మాచమ్మ మాయము చేశినది.

Mâchamma made away with what Kûchamma gathered.

657. కూటికి పేదయితే, కులానికి పేదా.

Though a man be poor, will he lose caste?

658. కూడూ గుడ్డా అడగక పోతే, బిడ్డను సాకినట్టు సాకుతాను అన్నాడట.

If you don't ask me for food and raiment I will care for you as my own child.

(See Nos. 1349, 1711, 1936.)

Good words and no deeds are rushes and reeds.

Fair words butter no parsnips.

659. కూడైతే కద్దుగాని కులస్థులకు వెరచి వచ్చినాను.

As for food I have it, but I came here from fear of the caste people.

Said by an idle beggar, as an excuse for asking alms.

660. కూత కరణము.

A karaṇam to talk.

(See Nos. 1811, 2042.—For *Karaṇam* see No. 154.)

A great talker but not good at his work.

661. కూత లాభాటాలేగాని కుప్పలో గింజ లేదు.

Great cries, but not a grain in the heap.

(See Nos. 1704, 1708.)

A great noise of threshing, but no grain to thresh.

" Great cry and little wool" as the fellow said when he sheared the pig.

662. కూతుండ్ల కన్నమ్మకు కురిచీపీటలు, కొడుకుల కన్నమ్మకు గోడ పంచలు.

The lady who has daughters is given a chair, but the lady who has sons has to lean against the wall.

663. కూతురని కుంచెడిస్తే, తల్లియని కంచెడు బెట్టినదట.

When the mother gave her daughter a kuncham of grain, the daughter set before her mother a dishful of food.

(See No. 1739.)

Kindness returned.

One never loseth by doing good turns.

Kindness produces kindness. (Latin.)*

664. కూతురికి మంగళవారం శుక్రవారం, కోడలికి దియ్యాలు దియ్యాలు.

[I only anoint] my daughter on Tuesdays and Fridays, but [I anoint] my daughter-in-law every Diyyalu.

A catch. *Diyyalu* or *Dîpâvaḷi* is a feast held on the 14th day of the dark fortnight in the month *Âśvayuja* (October-November) on which occasion anointing the body with oil is indispensable. The "every Dîpâvaḷi" of the mother-in-law therefore only amounted to once a year, but she took better care of her own daughter.

---

* Gratia gratiam parit.

665. కూన అని పెంచితే, గండు అయి కరవ వచ్చినది.

He petted it as a kitten, but when it grew into a big cat it tried to bite him.

(See Nos. 267, 636, 1077, 1078, 1079, 1860.)

Evil men will injure their protectors.

Foster a raven and it will peck out your eyes. (Spanish.)*

666. కూన పులికి లేడి దీటా.

Is an antelope equal to a tiger's cub ?

667. కూనలమ్మ సంగీతము వింటే పుణ్యము లేదు, వినకుంటే పాపము లేదు.

If you listen to the song [in praise] of Kûnalamma, there is no merit; and if you don't listen to it, there is no sin.

Kûnalamma is the goddess said to preside over children.

668. కూర్చుండి పడుకో వలెను.

One must sit first, and then lie down.

Said to a man inclined to do a thing hastily.

First creep, then go.

669. కూర్చుండి లేవలేడు గాని, ఎగసి తాటికాయలు తన్నుతానన్నాడట.

He could not stand up, yet he talked of jumping up and kicking down a palmyra fruit.

(See No. 670.)

Vain boasting.

670. కూర్చుండి లేవలేడుగాని, వంగుండి తీర్థం వెళ్లుతానన్నాడట.

He could not rise from his seat and yet he proposed to crawl to the holy place.

(See No. 669.)

Offering to do that which is difficult, when unable to do that which is easy.

---

* Crea el cuervo, y sacarte ha los ojos.

671. కూలికి వచ్చి పాలికి మాట్లాడినట్టు.

He came for hire, and asked for a share [in the business].

A cool request.

672. కూశే గాడిదె వచ్చి మేశే గాడిదెను చెరిపినది.

The braying donkey came and spoiled the grazing donkey's business.

When the one that was outside brayed, the other that was inside answered and was consequently discovered and driven out of the field.

673. కృతఘ్నునికి చేశిన మేలు.

Good done to an ungrateful person.

674. కొండంత దూదికి కొండంత నిప్పు యేల.

Why a mountain of fire to [burn down] a mountain of cotton?

A little fire burns up a great deal of corn.

675. కొండంత దేవుణ్ని కొండంత పత్రితో పూజ చేస్తారా.

Do they offer to a god as great as a mountain, leaves and flowers as much as a mountain?

A worshipper is accepted according to his faith, not according to greatness of his offering.

676. కొండంత రెడ్డి పోగా పిడికెడు బొచ్చుకు యేడ్చినట్టు.

When the big Reḍḍi died they wept only for the handful of his hair.

Indifferent to a great loss, but lamenting over some trifle that went with it.

Fear not the loss of the bell more than the loss of the steeple.

677. కొండకు వొక వెంట్రుక ముడి వేస్తే, వస్తే కొండే వస్తున్నది, పోతే వెంట్రుకే పోతున్నది.

If you tie a hair to a mountain, the mountain will come or the hair only go.

The possibility of great gain with the risk of little loss.

678. కొండ తలకింద పెట్టుకొని రాళ్లు వెతికినట్టు.

Like putting a mountain under one's head and searching for stones.

(See Nos. 118, 2002.)

679. కొండ తవ్వి యెలుకను పట్టినట్టు.

Digging up a mountain to catch a rat.

680. కొండతో తగరు పోట్లాడినట్టు.

Like a ram butting a mountain.

Great conceit.

681. కొండనాలికకు మందు వేస్తే, వున్ననాలుక వూడిపోయినట్టు.

When he applied medicine to the uvula, it took out the whole tongue.

(See Nos. 483, 846, 1567.)

The remedy is worse than the disease.

682. కొండను చూచి కుక్కలు మొరిగినట్టు.

Like dogs barking at a mountain.

(See No. 441.)

683. కొండమంగలి గొరిగినట్లు.

As the hill-barber shaves.

(See No. 1087.)

The pilgrims who visit the sacred hill of Tirupati have to be shaved before entering the temple. The barbers in their greediness to secure customers are said to keep numbers round them half shaven, leaving off one to commence another.

Dabbling in many things, but completing none.

684. కొండ మింగే వానికి గోపురము అడ్డమా.

Will a man that swallows a mountain care for a Gôpuram?

(See Nos. 447, 773, 1006.)

Gôpuram is the tower over the gate of a Hindu temple.

685. కొండ మీద దెబగుబలేమంటే, కోమట్ల రహస్యాలు అన్నట్లు.

When asked what the row on the hill was, they said "The Kômaṭis' secrets."

(See Nos. 47, 595, 1591.)

The secret of Anchuelos. (Spanish.)*

686. కొండమీదినుంచి పడ్డ వానికి గాయములు యెన్ని.

How many are the wounds of a man who has fallen from the top of a hill?

A man inured to difficulties.

687. కొండ యెక్కే వాని మొలను కొడవలి చెక్కినట్లు.

Like a sickle carried in the waist of a man climbing up a hill.

An additional danger and difficulty.

---

* El secreto de Anchuelos. (See Kelly's "Proverbs of all Nations" p. 178.)

688. కొండ వలె వచ్చి మంచు వలె తేలినట్టు.

Coming like a mountain, and melting away like dew.

(See No. 2118.)

Said of a difficulty which appears great when distant but is easily overcome when grappled with.

689. కొండవీటి చేంత్రాడు.

Like a well-rope at Kondavîdu.

Where water is very scarce and the wells very deep.

Said of a long-winded story.

690. కొంప తీస్తివా రామన్నా అంటే, అందుకు సందేహమా అన్నట్టు.

"Have you ruined me Râmanna?" [said a man to his parrot] "Is there any doubt of that?" it replied.

A man was duped into buying a parrot by the seller pretending it had power to discover hidden treasure. He pointed to a place where money had been previously buried and enquired of the parrot, which answered "Is there any doubt of that?" the only sentence it had been taught to repeat. The purchaser having bought the parrot for a large sum, in vain endeavoured to cause it to discover treasure. At last in his disappointment he cried "Have you ruined me Râmanna?" when he received the same answer "Is there any doubt of that?"

Applied to a person who knowingly gives bad advice to others, and then laughs at their misfortunes.

691. కొట్టకమునుపే యేడుస్తావేమంటే, ముందు కొట్టబోతావని యేడుస్తానన్నట్టు.

"Why do you cry before being beaten?" he asked, "you are going to beat me in future" replied [the boy].

(See No. 372.)

Never yowl till you're hit.

Let your trouble tarry till its own day comes.

Sufficient for the day is the evil thereof.

692. కొడుకు బాగుండ వలె, కోడలు ముండ మొయ్య వలె.

The son must flourish, and the daughter-in-law must become a widow.

(See No. [illegible].)

693. కొత్తకుండలో జోరీగ చొచ్చినట్టు.

Like a gad-fly flying into a new pot.

The pot contains nothing, and the mouth being narrow, the fly has some difficulty in getting out again.

694. కొత్త నీరు వచ్చి పాత నీరు కొట్టుకొని పోయినది.

The new water came and washed away the old water.

A little gain once was the cause of all being lost eventually.

695. కొత్త నీళ్లకు చేపలెదురెక్కినట్టు.

Like fish going against the stream.

Undertaking a difficult task.

It is hard to swim against the stream. (Dutch.)*

696. కొత్త బిచ్చపువాడు ప్రొద్దెరగడు.

A new beggar knows not the time [to ask for alms].

697. కొత్త వింత, పాత రోత.

Fresh [news is heard with] pleasure, stale [news with] disgust.

698. కొనగా తీరనిది కొసరగా తీరునా.

Will the bad bargain be improved by receiving something over?

(See No. 191.)

---

* Tegen stroom is kwaad zwemmen.

699. కొన్నవాడి కన్న తిన్నవాడే మేలు.

The man that ate, was better off than the man that bought the things [and did not use them].

700. కొన్నవాడే తిన్నవాడు.

He that ate is he that bought.

If you want any thing, you must pay for it.

Nothing is had for nothing. (French.)*

701. కొబ్బరి చెట్టు యెందుకు యెక్కుతావురా అంటే, దూడ గడ్డికోసరము యెక్కుతానన్నట్టు.

Like a man saying, when asked why he was getting up the cocoanut tree, that he wanted grass for his calf.

An absurd reason.

702. కొరివితో కొప్పు గోకుకొన్నట్టు.

Like scratching one's head with a firebrand.

Applied to the use of bad agents.

703. కొర్రకు నక్కకొర్ర.

Nakkakorra to Korra.

(See No. 269.)

Nakkakorra is the Panicum Helvolum, an inferior grain produced in the hill countries. *Korra* is the Setaria Italica, a "farinaceous grain of the millet kind" (Shakespear's Hind. Dicty. under کورا).

Thwarting the evil designs of a bad man by means of a worse.

Devils must be driven out with devils. (German.)†

---

* On n'a rien pour rien.
† Teufel muss man mit Teufeln austreiben.

704. కొలిచేవాడూ గుడ్డి, కొలిపించుకొనేవాడూ గుడ్డి.

The man who measures [the grain] is blind, and the man who has had it measured is blind also (i. e., the buyer and the seller.)

Defects on both sides.

705. కొల్లు మునిగిన కొన్నాళ్లకు కోనా మునిగినది.

Soon after the destruction of Kollu by a flood, Kôna also was swept away.

Kollu and Kôna are the names of two villages on either side of a river. The calamity which happened to one was a source of rejoicing to the other, which soon however suffered the same fate.

Tauntingly used by a person towards those who took delight in his misfortune but have now been overtaken by a calamity themselves.

706. కొల్లేట్లో పండే పంటేగాని, చచ్చే దున్నపోతులకు లెక్క లేదు.

[They look at] the crops which grow in Kollêru, but there is no account of the buffaloes which die there.

Counting profit, but not loss.

707. కొసరిన కూరలోగాని పసలేదు.

There is no taste in the greens unless some are received over.

Said by Hindu women, who are never satisfied unless they obtain something over and above their money's worth.

708. కోటి విద్యలూ కూటి కొరకే.

Ten million arts are only for [getting] food.

(See No. 2036.)

All professions are only so many means of livelihood.

709. కోడలికి బుద్ధి చెప్పి అత్త రంకుపోయినది.

The mother-in-law gave good counsel to her daughter-in-law and went astray herself.

710. కోడలు కొడుకును కంటానంటే, వద్దనే అత్తగారు వున్నదా.

When a daughter-in-law says that she is about to bring forth a son, is there any mother-in-law who says "Don't"?

i. e. wish the child to be a daughter.

Will any one refuse to receive a benefit?

711. కోడలు గృహప్రవేశము, అత్త గంగాప్రవేశము.

The daughter-in-law enters the house (as a bride) and the mother-in-law enters the Ganges (dies).

(See No. 99.)

Death at the tae door an' heirship at the tither. (Scotch.)

712. కోడికి కులాసం లేదు, కోమటికి విశ్వాసం లేదు.

A fowl has no happiness and a Kômaṭi has no feeling.

The *Kômaṭis* are a class of shopkeepers.

713. కోడిగుడ్డు పగలగొట్ట గుండ్రాయి కావలెనా.

Do you want a stone roller to break an egg with?

714. కోడిపిల్లమీద పందిపిల్ల బలాదూరు.

Sacrificing a pig to save a chicken.

715. కోడి పోయి కొమ్మ యెక్కినట్టు.

When the fowl flew, it only mounted a branch.

(See No. 733.)

716. కోతికి అద్దము చూపినట్టు.

Like showing a looking glass to a monkey.

Persistently offering that which is disliked.

717. కోతికి కొబ్బరికాయ దొరికినట్టు.

Like a monkey with a cocoanut.

(See No. 728.)

Cannot use it, but won't give it up.

Like the dog in the manger, he will neither do nor let do.

718. కోతికి జల్తారు కుళ్లాయి పెట్టినట్టు.

Like putting a gold-laced cap on a monkey's head.

(See Nos. 674, 720.)

719. కోతి చేతి పామువలె.

Like a snake in a monkey's paw.

Jacko is afraid of it, but won't let it go.

720. కోతి చేతి పూల దండ.

A garland of flowers in a monkey's paw.

(See Nos. 674, 718.)

A good thing thrown away on a stupid person.

721. కోతి పిడికిలి.

A monkey's fist.

Not letting go any thing in its grasp.

Applied to obstinacy.

722. కోతి పుండు బ్రహ్మరాక్షసి.

A sore is a she-demon to a monkey.

Making a great fuss about nothing.

723. కోతి గురువింద సామ్యము.

Like the monkey and the Guruvinda.

(See No. 717.)

The seed of the *Guruviṇda* (Abrus Precatorius) is a small pretty black and red seed.

724. కోన కావలి.

[Placing] a guard over a forest.

Attempting impossibilities.

725. కోమటి నిజము.

A Kômaṭi's truth.

(See No. 728—For *Kômaṭi* see No. 712.)

726. కోమటి పిరికి, కొట్టితే వురికి.

A Kômaṭi is a coward; if you hit him, he runs away.

(For *Kômaṭi* see No. 712.)

727. కోమటి యిల్లు కాలినట్టు.

Like the burning of a Kômaṭi's house.

A heavy loss.

728. కోమటి విశ్వాసము.

The faith of a Kômaṭi.

(See No. 725— For *Kômaṭi* see No. 712.)

Faithlessness.

729. కోమటి సాక్ష్యము.

A Kômaṭi's evidence.

A story is told of a *Kômaṭi* who, when asked to identify a horse about which a Musalman and Hindu were quarrelling, said the forepart of it looked like the Musalman's horse and the hindpart like the Hindu's.

730. కోలలేని పెట్టు, తాడులేని కట్టు.

A blow without a rod, a bond without a rope.

(See No. 775.)

A sudden and unaccountable calamity.

731. కోళ్లకు రెక్కలూ తాళ్లకు చండ్లూ వున్నట్టు.

Like the wings of fowls, and the flower-stalks of palmyra trees.

(See No. 1063.)

Domestic fowls make no use of their wings, and the flower-stalk (spadix) of the palmyra (See No. 290.) bears no fruit.

Useless possessions.

732. కోళ్ల బేరానకు వెళ్లి కోటలో కబుర్లు అడిగినట్టు.

Going to sell fowls and asking the news in the fort.

(See Nos. 908, 1386, 1390, 1398, 1496.)

A meddling rascal.

733. కోవెల పోయి కొమ్మ యెక్కినట్టు.

When the cuckoo flew it only mounted a branch.

(See No. 715.)

ఖ.

734. ఖాజీని ఫాజీగా ఫాజీని ఖాజీగా చేస్తాడు.

He makes the great, mean; and the mean, great.

The power of God.

గ.

735. గంతకు తగిన బొంత.

Like packsaddle, like quilt.

(See Nos. 1281, 1668, 1698, 1846, 1969.)

Like pot, like cover. (Dutch.)*

736. గంధపొడిలో బూరగ పట్టినట్టు.

Like blowing a horn into perfumed powder.

Gandhapoḍi is thrown over one another by the relations of the bride and bridegroom at Hindu marriages.

737. గంప శిడి కాదు, గాలపు శిడి.

It is not the basket, but the hook.

(See Nos. 253, 1233, 1729, 1757.)

Gâlapu Śiḍi is the hook used in the swinging festival (Charak Pûja) and *Gampa Śiḍi* is a basket sometimes used instead of the hook.

Applied to a very difficult task.

738. గచ్చ పొద మీద యిసుక వేశి కయ్యానికి పిలుస్తున్నది.

Throwing sand on a thorn bush and asking it to fight.

(For *Gachcha* see No. 564.)

Done by a Xantippe who could get no one to quarrel with.

---

* Zoo pot, Zoo deksel.

739. గజ కచ్ఛప పోరు చందము.

Like a fight between an elephant and a tortoise.

740. గట్టివాడే గాని, కడుపు మాత్రము గుల్ల.

He is a clever man no doubt, but his belly is hollow.

An ironical phrase.

The word rendered *clever* also means "solid." The expression *his belly is hollow* is equivalent to "empty-headed."

741. గట్టి విడిచి పెట్టి పొట్టుకు పోరాడినట్టు.

Like leaving the grain, and fighting for the husk.

742. గట్టు చేరిన వెనక పుట్టివానితో పోట్లాడినట్టు.

Like fighting with the ferry-man after getting over the river.

The river past, the saint forgotten. (Spanish.)*

The peril past, the saint mocked. (Italian.)†

743. గడ్డం వపనముచ్యతే.

My beard will be fit for shaving.

Said by a goat to a lion which he threatened to devour to fulfil a vow.

744. గడ్డ తిన్నా కంపే, పాయ తిన్నా కంపే.

If you eat the root [of garlick] there is a smell, if you eat a clove of it there is a smell.

Whether you do a little evil or much, it is alike bad.

* El rio passado, el santo olvidado.
† Passato il punto, gabbato il santo.

745. గడ్డపలుగులు గాలికి కొట్టుకొనిపోతూ వుంటే, పుల్లాకు నా పని యేమి అన్నదట.

When the crowbars were blown about by the wind, the leaf-platter said "What is to become of me?"

Pullâku is a cast away leaf-dish which has been once used.

A mean person thinking of his own loss when his superiors are suffering.

746. గడ్డపలుగులు మింగి శొంఠి కషాయాలు తాగినట్లు.

Swallowing crowbars and taking ginger draughts.

An insufficient remedy.

747. గడ్డము కాలి వొకడు యేడుస్తూ వుంటే, చుట్టకు నిప్పు యిమ్మని వొకడు వెంబడించినట్టు.

When one man was crying out that his beard was on fire another followed him asking him for a light for his cigar.

If my beard is burnt, others try to light their pipes at it. (Turkish.)

748. గతిలేనమ్మకు గంజే పానకము.

Rice water is a rich drink to a poor lady.

Pânakam is a rich beverage made of expensive materials.

749. గతిలేనమ్మకు మతిలేని మొగుడు.

A helpless woman will get a foolish husband.

750. గబ్బిలము ఆకాశము పడకుండా పట్టుకొంటాననుకొన్నట్టు.

Like the bat which thinks it holds up the sky and keeps it from falling.

(See No. 1255.)

Said of a man who thinks everything depends on himself.

751. గరుడాయ లెస్సా అంటే, శేషాయ లెస్సా అన్నట్టు.

"How are you Garuḍa ?" said the snake Śêsha, "How are you Śêsha ?" replied the kite.

Śêsha took advantage of his position on the wrist of Śiva to address Garuḍa, the sacred kite of Vishṇu, in an impertinently familiar manner, to which Garuḍa was compelled to submit.

A mean person taking advantage of his influence with a great man, to treat his betters with insolence.

752. గాండ్లవాని ఆశ గోతమున్ను పట్టదు.

The oil-crusher's greediness cannot be contained even in a sack.

But little oil is extracted from a large quantity of seed.

753. గాజుల గుదికి రోకలి పూనినట్లు.

Like using a rice-pounder for [carrying] a bunch of glass bracelets.

When put down, the weight of the stick would break the bracelets.

A foolish action.

754. గాజుల బేరము భోజనానకు సరి.

By trading in glass bracelets a bare subsistence only can be obtained.

Because so many break.

Applied to any business which is attended with heavy losses.

755. గాడిదె గంపెడు వూక తిన్నది అన్నట్టు.

Like saying that a donkey has eaten a basketful of husk.

Nothing wonderful.

756. గాడిదె గత్తర.

A donkey's row.

A noisy brawl.

Nothing passes between asses but kicks. (Italian.)*

757. గాడిదెపిల్ల కోమలము.

The mildness of a young donkey.

Seemingly good but really useless.

758. గాడిదె పుండుకు బూడిదె మందు.

Ashes are the remedy for a deep ulcer.

Severe measures must be used with the incorrigible.

Desperate ills require desperate remedies. (French.)†

759. గాదెకింది యెలుక గాదెకింద బ్రతుక వలెనుగాని, మరియెక్కడ బ్రతుకుతుంది.

The rat below the corn bin must live below the corn bin, where else can it live?

Said of an idle parasite.

---

* Tra asino e asino, non corron se non calci.
† Aux grands maux les grands remèdes.

760. గాదెనిండా బియ్యము వుంటే, కరువునా కాలానా నా భార్యనూ పిల్లలనూ నేనే రక్షిస్తానన్నాడట.

He said that he himself would support his wife and family in dearth and in plenty, so long as the bin was full of corn.

761. గానుగ రోట్లో చెయ్యి పెట్టి పెరుమాళ్ల కృప అన్నట్టు.

Putting your hand into an oil press, and saying "The favour of Perumâḷ (Vishṇu) be upon me."

(See No. 767.)

Tempting Providence.

Put your finger in the fire, and say 'twas your ill fortune.

762. గానుగాపే గానుగాపే నీవు కూర్చున్న పసేగదా నూనె పొయ్యడము.

O oil-woman! oil-woman! you pour out the oil as finely as you sit.

Said to a cheat.

763. గాము సోకినట్టు.

As though possessed of a devil.

764. గారాబము గార్లెకు యేడిస్తే, వీపు దెబ్బలకు యేడుస్తున్నది.

You are teazing me and crying for cakes and your back is crying for a whipping.

Said by a father.

765. గాలికి పుట్టి ధూళికి పెరిగినట్టు.

Born of the wind, and reared up by the dust.

Said by parents to an ungrateful son, or by a benefactor to an ungrateful dependant.

766. గాలికి పోయిన పేలపిండి భగవదర్పితమన్నట్టు.

Offering to God the flour which had been blown away by the wind.

Let that which is lost be for God.

What the abbot of Bamba cannot eat, he gives away for the good of his soul. (Spanish.)*

767. గాలిలో దీపము బెట్టి దేవుడా నీ మహిమ చూపుమన్నట్టు.

Having put the lamp in the wind, he prays "O God! show thy power."

(See No. 761.)

768. గాలీ వానా వస్తే కథే మానుతుంది.

When a storm comes, the story ceases.

A sudden stop to anything.

769. గింజలు ముత్తుము, పిట్టలు పన్నిద్దుము.

Three bushels of grain for twelve bushels of birds.

770. గుండ్రాయి దాస్తే, కూతురి పెండ్లి నిలుచునా.

If you hide the grinding stone will the daughter's marriage be stopped?

A round grinding stone or pestle is used in marriage ceremonies.

A trifling hindrance put in a man's way will not divert him from his purpose.

771. గుండ్లు తేలి బెండ్లు మునిగినట్టు.

Bullets floating, Beṇḍu sinking.

Beṇḍu is the Æschynomene Indica from which pith hats, models, &c. are made.

The order of nature reversed.

---

* El abad de Bamba, lo que no puede comer, dalo por su alma.

772. గుడి పాము కరిచినట్టు, గంగిగోవు పొడిచినట్టు.

The bite of the temple-snake, the goring of the sacred cow.

An injury is none the less, though it be inflicted by a relation or friend.

773. గుడిమింగే వానికి గుళ్లో లింగము వుట్రవడియము.

To him who swallows the temple, the lingam in it is a sugar-plum.

(See Nos. 447, 684, 1006.)

774. గుడిలో గంట పోతే, నంబికేమి లోటు.

If the temple bell be lost what does it matter to the priestling?

A hireling cares not for the property of his master.

775. గుడి వచ్చి మీఁద పడ్డట్టు.

Like a temple coming and falling on you.

(See No. 730.)

An unexpected calamity.

776. గుడ్డి కన్నా మెల్ల మేలు.

A squint eye is better than a blind eye.

(See Nos. 312, 314, 1906.)

Of two evils choose the least.

777. గుడ్డి కన్ను మూసినా వకటే తెరిచినా వకటే.

It matters not whether the blind eye is open or shut.

A useless man's absence is as good as his presence.

778. గుడ్డి గుఱ్ఱానకు పండ్లు తోముతున్నాడు.

He is cleaning the teeth of a blind horse.

Unprofitable employment.

He is teaching a pig to play on a flute.

779. గుడ్డి నక్క వురిన పడ్డట్టు.

Like the blind jackal falling into the snare.

780. గుడ్డి మామగారా నమస్కారమయ్యా అంటే, రంధికి మూలమా రంకుల కోడలా అన్నాడట.

When she said "I salute you, O blind father-in-law!" he replied "Is this the commencement of strife? O adulterous daughter-in-law!"

(See No. 72.)

Let him that has a glass skull not take to stone throwing. (Italian.)*

781. గుడ్డి యెద్దు జొన్న చేన పడ్డట్టు.

Like a blind bullock going into a field of millet.

Not able to get much out of it.

782. గుడ్డివాడెరుగునా కుందనపు చాయ.

Can a blind man discern the colour of pure gold?

An uneducated man cannot judge of the attainments of the learned.

A blind man is no judge of colours. (Italian.)†

A pebble and a diamond are alike to a blind man.

783. గుడ్డు వచ్చి పిల్లను వెక్కిరించినది.

The egg made faces at the chicken.

(See No. 790.)

Mocking and mimicking a superior.

784. గుణము మానవే గూటాల పోలీ అంటే, నా మనువయినా మాను తానుగాని నా గుణము మానను అన్నదట.

When Gûṭâla Pôli was told to amend her ways, she said she would rather break off the match.

Obstinate behaviour. Stubborn conduct.

---

* Chi ha testa di vetro non faccia a' sassi.
† Il cieco non dee giudicar dei colori.

785. గుమ్మడికాయ పొయ్యే దారి యెరగడు, ఆవగింజ పొయ్యే దారి అట్టే పట్టి చూస్తాడు.

He does not know the way the pumpkin goes, but troubles himself to find the way the mustard seed goes.

(See No. 741.)

786. గుమ్మడి కాయల దొంగ అంటే, తన బుజాలు తానే పట్టి చూచుకొన్నాడట.

When the thief who stole the pumpkin was spoken of, he felt his shoulders.

Thinking some mark might have been left.

(See No. 1467.)

A guilty conscience needs no accuser.

He that has a muckle nose thinks ilka ane is speaking o't. (Scotch.)

787. గుమ్మళ్లు కుళ్లినవి ఆవాలు అల్లినవి.

The pumpkins have become rotten, the mustard plants have spread.

Said when the base and wicked rise in power and the great and good disappear.

788. గురువింద గింజ తన యెరుపేగాని ముడ్డి కింది నలుపు యెరగదు.

The Guruvinda seed knows its redness, but not the blackness of its lower part.

(See No. 179.—For *Guruvinda* see No. 723.)

A man values himself highly, but does not know his own defects.

No one sees his own faults. (German.)*

789. గురువుకు పంగనామాలు పెట్టినట్టు.

To put Panganâmams on your Guru.

To outwit him.

Panganâmam is a very large *Nâmam*, the sectarial mark worn on the forehead by Vaishṇavas.

---

* Niemand sieht seine eigene Fehler.

790. గురువుకు మించిన శిష్యుడు.

A disciple greater than his Guru.

(See No. 783.)

Said of an insolent fellow.

791. గురువుతో గుద్దులాటా.

May a man fight with his Guru?

792. గురువు మాట మీఱరాదు, గడ్డపార మింగరాదు.

You should not transgress the commandment of your Guru, nor swallow a crowbar.

The first is as bad for you as the second.

793. గుఱ్ఱము గుడ్డిదయినా దాణాలో తక్కువ వుండదు.

Although the horse be blind, he won't eat less corn.

Supporting a useless person.

A bad horse eats as much as a good one. (Danish.)*

794. గుఱ్ఱము చచ్చినదిగాక గుంట తవ్వ వైక రూక.

In addition to the horse's death, a fanam [must be paid] for digging a pit [to bury it in].

(For *Fanam* see No. 615.)

Loss upon loss.

After one loss come many. (French.)†

795. గుఱ్ఱమును తిన్న కుక్క అదేమి బ్రతుకును.

How can a dog which has eaten a horse live?

796. గుఱ్ఱము వలె కుక్కను పెంచి రెడ్డి తానే మొరిగినాడట.

The Reḍḍi fed his dog like a horse, and barked himself.

To pay a servant extravagantly and do his work yourself.

---

* En ond Hest aeder saa meget som en god.
† Après perdre perd on bien.

797. గుఱ్ఱానికి గుగ్గిళ్లు తిన నేర్పవలెనా.

Must one teach a horse to eat boiled gram ?

(See No. 936.)

Teach your grandmother to suck eggs.

798. గుఱ్ఱానికి తోక వుంటే తానే విసురుకొంటుందిగాని, సావిట్లో వుండే
గుఱ్ఱాలకన్నిటికీ విసురుతున్నదా.

If the horse has a tail, it drives away its own flies ; does it drive away the flies from all the horses in the stable ?

(See No. 445.)

Said when a selfish person is exalted.

An ill man in office is a mischief to the public.

799. గుళ్లో దేవునికి నైవేద్యము లేకుంటే, పూజారి పులిహోరకు యేడ్చి
నాడట.

While the idol in the temple was in want of Naivêdyam, the priest cried for Puḷihôra.

(See Nos. 227, 989, 1781, 1798.—For *Naivêdyam* see No. 3.)

Puḷihôra is a more expensive offering prepared with acid.

800. గువ్వ గూడెక్కెను, అవ్వ మంచమెక్కెను.

The owl took to its nest, the grandmother took to her bed.

801. గూనికి తోడు గుఱ్రపు వాయువు.

A humpbacked man with convulsions.

(See Nos. 1755, 1630.)

802. గూనివాడు పడుకొనేవల్ల గూనివానికే తెలుసును.

The humpback alone knows how he can lie comfortably.

(See No. 1419.)

Every man kens best where his own shoe pinches. (Scotch.)

803. గృహప్రవేశముకు వెళ్లుతూ గుడ్ల గూబను తోడుతీసుకొని పోయి నట్టు.

Like taking an owl with you to the ceremony of entering a a new house.

(See Nos. 310, 1459.)

Gṛihapravēśa is a ceremony only to be performed at an auspicious hour and in the absence of every bad omen. The owl is a peculiarly bad omen.

Keeping company with your ill-wishers.

804. గొంతు కోసేవాడు కత్తి యేమారునా.

Will a cut-throat forget his knife?

805. గొడారివాని వద్ద తోలు కొన్నట్టు.

Like buying leather from a shoemaker.

Purchasing at unreasonable prices. The shoemaker buys his leather to make up, not to retail to others.

806. గొడ్ల కాచేవాణ్ని కొట్టనివాడున్ను, గొర్రెల కాచేవాణ్ని తిట్టని వాడున్ను లేడు.

There is no person who has not struck a herdsman, or abused a shepherd.

Despised people.

807. గొడ్రాలికి యేమి తెలుసును బిడ్డ నొప్పులు.

What does the barren woman know of the pains of child-birth?

808. గొడ్డుపోతు యేమి యెరుగురా బిడ్డ చవి.

What does the barren woman know of the pleasure of having children?

He who has no children knows not what is love. (Italian.)*

---

* Chi non ha figliuoli, non sa che cosa sia amore.

809. గొడ్డువాడు గొడ్డుకు యేడిస్తే, గొడారివాడు తోలుకు యేడ్చినాడు.

When the owner cried for the cow [he had lost,] the shoemaker cried for the hide.

(See Nos. 990, 1482.)

It is an ill wind that blows nobody good.

810. గొరగగా మిగిలినది జుట్టు.

After shaving, all that is left is the top-lock.

To sponge on another until he has nothing left.

After shaving there is nothing to shear. (Italian.)*

811. గొఱ్ఱె కొవ్వితే గొల్లవాడికే లాభము.

If the sheep gets fat, it is for the benefit of the shepherd.

If the servant does in a huff more work than he is told, it is for the benefit of his master. The term translated *gets fat* also signifies "becomes proud."

812. గొఱ్ఱె కోసేవాణ్ణిగాని నమ్మదు.

The sheep only trusts him who cuts its throat.

The simple and unwary only trust their deceivers.

813. గొఱ్ఱెను తినేవాడు పోతే, బఱ్ఱెను తినేవాడు వచ్చినట్టు.

When the man who ate sheep went, a man who ate buffalos came.

Parting with one rascal and getting a greater scoundrel in his place.

814. గొఱ్ఱెలలో తోడేలు జొరబడ్డట్టు.

Like a wolf rushing in among sheep.

Easy prey.

---

* Dopo il radere non ci è più che tosare.

815. గొల్లవాడి కొమ్ము యెచ్చనూ యెచ్చదు, తగ్గనూ తగ్గదు.

The shepherd's Kâvaḍi neither rises nor sinks.

Because he does not swing his pots on each end.

(For *Kâvaḍi* see No. 568.)

The fortunes of a sheep-farmer are subject to sudden reverses.

Applied to a precarious mode of living.

816. గొల్లవారింటి పెండ్లి తెల్లవారింది.

The morning dawns before the shepherds' marriage is begun.

They have so many disputes that nothing can be settled.

817. గోంగూరలో చింతకాయ వేసినట్టు.

Like mixing unripe tamarinds with Gôgu greens.

Gôgu or *Gôngûra* is the Hibiscus Cannabinus.

A combination of evil persons.

818. గోచికి పెద్ద, అంగవస్త్రముకు చిన్న.

Too big for a clout, too small for a body-cloth.

Neither one thing nor the other.

Too little and too much spoils everything. (Danish.)*

Not too little, not too much. (German.)†

819. గోచి పాతల రాయడు దొంగల మిండడు.

Mr. Clout-Ragamuffin is the robbers' master.

(See No. 9.)

He that has nothing is frighted at nothing.

There is no stripping a naked man. (German.)‡

---

* For meget og for lidt fordaerver alting.
† Nicht zu wenig, nicht zu viel.
‡ Einen Nackten kann man nicht ausziehen.

820. గోట మీటితే పొయ్యే పనికి గొడ్డలి యెందుకు.

Why an axe for that which can be done with a fillip of the nail?

(See Nos. 815, 839, 1439.)

Unnecessary labour.

821. గోడకు పెట్టిన సున్నమూ, లంజకు పెట్టిన సొమ్మూ.

Lime put on a wall, money given to a harlot.

No return.

822. గోడ పెట్టూ, చెంప పెట్టూ.

A slap in the face for knocking one's head against the wall.

(See Nos. 898, 966.)

Misfortunes seldom come alone.

823. గోడ మీది సున్నము విడెయములోకి పనికి వచ్చునా.

Will the chunam on the wall be fit for betel leaf?

A little fine chunam (lime) is commonly eaten with betel.

Said of a man who does not serve his friends.

824. గోడ వుంటే చిత్రము వ్రాయ వచ్చును.

If there is a wall you can draw on it.

825. గోనెలకంటే గోతాలు మెండు.

There are more small sacks than big ones.

826. గోరంత వుంటే, కొండంత చేస్తాడు.

When it is as small as a finger nail, he makes a mountain of it.

To make a mountain of a mole-hill.

827. గోరీకాడి నక్కవత్తు.

Like a jackal at a tomb.

A tantalizing position, as he cannot get into it.

Like a cat round hot milk.

828. గోరుచుట్టు పయిన రోకటి పోటు.

A blow with a pestle on a whitlow.

(See Nos. 893, 966.)

829. గోవులను కోశి చెప్పులు దానము చేశినట్టు.

Like killing cows and giving away sandals [made of the hide.]

(See No. 578.)

Steal the goose, and give the giblets in alms.

830. గోవులేని వూళ్లో గొడ్డుగేదె శ్రీ మహాలక్ష్మి.

A barren buffalo is the emblem of Mahâ Lakshmî, in a village where there are no cows.

(See Nos. 1412, 1413.)

Mahâ Lakshmî is the goddess of fortune.

The one-eyed is a king in the land of the blind.

831. గ్రామశాంతికి బోడితల.

[Shaving] a bald head, to [propitiate] the village goddess.

No other will submit to the ignominy.

832. గ్రాసము లేని కొలువు.

Work without pay.

Work not paid for is ill done.

Work done expects money. (Portuguese.)*

---

* Obra feita dinheiro espera.

ఘ.

833. ఘంటాకర్ణునికి అష్టాక్షరీవుపదేశం చెయ్యబోయినట్టు.

Like attempting to teach Ghanṭâkarṇa the Ashṭâksharî.

Ghanṭâkarṇa (Bell-eared) is the name of an attendant on Śiva.

Ashṭâksharî is a sacred formula used in the worship of Vishṇu, composed, as the word denotes, of eight syllables (ఓం నమోనారాయణాయ.)

చ.

834. చంకపిల్ల జారిపడేటట్టు మాట్లాడుతాడు.

He speaks so as [to cause one] to let the child drop from the arms and fall.

(See Nos. 4, 5, 839.)

A deceiver.

A honey tongue, a heart of gall.

Bees that have honey in their mouths have stings in their tails.

835. చంట్లో యెముకలు యేరినట్టు.

Looking for bones in a woman's breast.

(See No. 2123.)

A minute investigation.

836. చక్కగా కూర్చోరా చాకలనాయడా అంటే, విన్నావటోయి యీడిగనాయడా మంగలనాయడి సరసము అన్నాడట.

"Sit properly Mr. Washerman" said one, "Mr. Toddy-drawer, do you hear Mr. Barber's joke ?" said the other.

Chaffing between *Sâtânis*, who are Vaishṇava converts from all castes.

837. చక్కదనానకు లొటిపిట, సంగీతానకు గాడిదె.

For beauty, a camel; for singing, an ass.

838. చక్కిలాలు తింటావా, చల్ది తింటావా అంటే, చక్కిలాలూ తింటాను, చల్దీ తింటాను, అయ్యతోటి వేడీ తింటాను అన్నాడట.

When [the guest] was asked whether he would take biscuits, or cold breakfast, he replied that he would take both, and hot breakfast too with the good man of the house.

Applied to an ill mannered glutton.

The first cut, and all the loaf besides.

839. చక్కెర పూత పూశిన విషము.

Poison covered with sugar.

(See Nos. 4, 5, 884.)

A flattering speech is honied poison. (Latin.)*

Sugared words generally prove bitter. (Spanish.)†

840. చచ్చిన చారమేకపాలు పోయిన బోశిముంతెడు.

The milk given by the streaked goat which is dead filled the lost pot with a piece out.

(See Nos. 841, 1631.)

841. చచ్చినవాని కండ్లు చేరెడు.

A dead man's eyes are very broad.

(See Nos. 840, 1631.)

Lavishing praises on the dead which were not bestowed on the living.

---

* Mellitum venenum, blanda oratio.

† Palabras azucaradas por mas son amargas.

842. చచ్చినవాని పెండ్లికి వచ్చినంత కట్నము.

Any quantity of presents must suffice at a dead man's marriage.

When a marriage takes place, presents of cloths are sent to the bride and bridegroom by their relations. Return gifts of about equal value are made shortly after the marriage. Should the bridegroom, however, die during the ceremonies, no presents are returned, and no complaints are therefore made regarding the value of those received.

843. చచ్చేదాకా బ్రతికి వుంటే పెండ్లి చేస్తానన్నట్టు.

If you live until I die, I'll get you married.

A jocular saying.

844. చచ్చేవానికి సముద్రము మోకాలి బంటి.

The sea to a desperate man is as [shallow water only up to] his knees.

Men in despair fear nothing.

Despair gives courage to a coward.

845. చదవ నేర్తువా వ్రాయ నేర్తువా అంటే, చదవా వ్రాయా నేరనుగాని చించ నేర్తును అన్నాడట.

When asked whether he could read and write, he said, "I can't read or write, but I can tear."

846. చదవ వేస్తే, వున్న మతి పోయినది.

When set to read, the [little] sense he had left him.

(See Nos. 482, 691, 1567.)

Making bad worse.

John has been to school to learn to be a fool. (French.)*

---

* Jean a étudié pour être bête.

847. చదివినవాని కన్నా చాకలవాడు నయము.

A washerman is better than an educated person.

The washerman, though illiterate, invariably distinguishes the clothes belonging to different people by putting certain marks on them, but many of the educated cannot discern between good and evil.

848. చదివేది రామాయణము, పడగొట్టేవి దేవస్థలాలు.

He reads the Râmâyaṇa, and knocks down temples.

(See No. 941.)

Much religion, but no goodness.

849. చదువు మా యింట లేదు, సంధ్య మా వంశాన లేదు.

There is no learning in my house, nor performance of Sandhya in my family.

Said by an uneducated and irreligious Brahman.

850. చద్దికంటే వూరగాయ ఘనము.

The best part of the cold food is the pickle.

851. చద్దికూడు తిన్నమ్మ మొగుడి ఆకలి యెరగదు.

The wife who has eaten breakfast [at home] does not think of her husband's hunger.

Little knows the fat sow what the lean one means.

The full belly does not believe in hunger. (Italian.)*

852. చద్ది తెచ్చుకొన్న బ్రాహ్మణుడా భోజనము చెయ్యి.

O Brahman ! if you have brought food, eat it.

Said to a selfish man who bores others by talking everlastingly of his own concerns.

---

* Corpo satollo non crede al digiuno.

853. చన్నీళ్లయినా చల్లార్చుకొని తాగ వలెను.

Even cold water should be drunk slowly.

(See No. 177.)

There is a pun here on the word చల్లార్చుకొని which also means "having cooled."

Nothing should be done hastily.

Good and quickly seldom meet.

Haste trips up its own heels.

854. చలిపందిటి కుండలకు తూట్లు పొడిచినట్లు.

Like making holes in the pots in a water-shed.

The water-shed in India corresponds to the drinking-fountain in Europe.

A despicable trick.

855. చలిపందిటి కుండలలో రాళ్లు వేసినట్లు.

Like throwing stones at the pots in a water-shed.

(See No. 854.)

856. చల్లకు వచ్చి ముంత దాచుకొన్నట్లు.

Coming to beg buttermilk and hiding the cup.

(See Nos. 90, 1608, 1782.)

Pride with poverty.

Pride and poverty are ill met yet often together.

857. చవక అయితే బాజారుకు వస్తున్నది.

When cheap it comes to the bazar.

(See No. 95.)

858. చవక దూబరదిండికి కారణము.

Cheapness causes extravagance.

A good bargain is a pick purse.

What is not needed is dear at a farthing. (Latin.)*

859. చస్తానని చద్ది అన్నము తింటే, చల్లగా నిద్ర వచ్చినదట.

Saying she would die (kill herself) she made a great breakfast and had a fine sleep.

A trick to get a good meal, as she said it was to be her last.

860. చా అంటే, తూ అనలేదు.

When one says "cha" (and), he cannot answer "tu" (but).

(See No. 618.)

861. చాకల అత్తా, మంగల మామ.

A washerwoman of a mother-in-law, a barber of a father-in-law.

A man abusing his wife's parents.

862. చాకలవాని భార్యకు మంగలవాడు విడాకు యిచ్చినట్టు.

Like the barber's giving a written divorcement to the washerwoman's wife.

863. చాప చిరిగితే చదరంత అయినా వుండకపోతున్నదా.

Although the mat be torn, will there not be found in it as much as a school boy's mat?

Çadaru is a very small square mat.

Every thing can be brought to some account.

Nothing so bad as not to be good for something.

---

* Quod non opus est, asse carum est.

864. చాలీ చాలనందుకు చాకింట గుడ్డలు శానా వున్నవి.

If you have not quite clothes enough, there are plenty at the washerman's.

Alluding to the habit which obtains among the natives of India of hiring other people's clothes from the washermen.

865. చావటి ముందరి కొంప కదపా పుల్లలకు సరి.

A thatched hut opposite a Court-house, is used up for bonds.

Bonds were formerly always written on Palmyra leaves, such as are used for thatching.

866. చావా చావడు, మంచమూ వదలడు.

He would neither die nor give up his bed.

867. చావా చావనివ్వడు, బ్రతకా బ్రతకనివ్వడు.

He will neither allow me to die nor to live.

Perpetual worrying.

868. చావుకు పెట్టితే గాని, లంఖణాలకు తెగడు.

He won't fast unless told that his life is in danger.

869. చావుకు మళ్లీ చావు వస్తుందా.

Does death come more than once?

870. చావు తప్పి కన్ను లొట్టపోయినట్టు.

Escaping death, but losing an eye.

871. చింత చచ్చినా, చింత పులుసు చావదు.

The tamarind may be dried, but it loses not its acidity.

Retaining vigour of mind though weakened in body.

872. చింతా చిగిరింత యేపు.

The growth of the tamarind and the burgrass.

The tamarind grows slowly, the *Chigirinta* (Panicum Verticillatum) shoots up very rapidly and soon withers.

(See No. 873.)

Slow and sure.

873. చికిలింత ఐశ్వర్యం.

Grass-like prosperity.

(See Nos. 210, 341.)

(For *Chikilinta* see *Chigirinta* in No. 872.)

874. చిక్కి శిగిలించేటంతకన్నా, వెళ్లి వెక్కిరించేది మేలు.

It is better to go and mock another, than to whine when you are caught.

875. చిచ్చాయ చిచ్చాయ అంటే, సందాయె సందాయె అన్నట్టు.

One cried out "Fire! Fire!" and another "Now's the time! Now's the time!"

The cry of Dvârapûḍi robbers on a certain occasion when they had set fire to a village, which they had long been unable to plunder on account of the wariness of the inhabitants.

876. చిత్త చిత్తగించి స్వాతి దయచేశి విశాఖ విశిరి కొట్టకుంటే, వీసానికి పుట్టెడు పండుతాను అన్నదట.

"If Chitta is kind, if Svâti shows favor, and if Viśâkha does not blow too much, I will produce a Puṭṭi [of corn] to a Vîsam [of land]" said [the field].

Chitta and *Svâti* are the 14th and 15th lunar mansions, in which rain is expected. *Viśâkha* is the 16th lunar mansion in which high winds are common.—*Puṭṭi* is a corn measure of 500lbs. *Vîsam* is the fraction $\frac{1}{16}$ —here the 16th part of a *Gunṭa*, a land measure equal to $\frac{1}{40}$ of an acre.

Calm weather in June sets corn in tune.

A shower in July, when the corn begins to fill,
Is worth a plough of oxen, and all belongs there till.

Dry August and warm doth harvest no harm.

877. చిత్తము శివునిమీఁద, భక్తి చెప్పులమీఁద.

He has a mind to worship Śiva, but his thoughts are on his shoes (left outside the temple).

878. చినపేరితాడు తెగితే, పెదపేరితాడు అప్పుడే తెగుతుంది.

If China Pêri's marriage-cord be broken, Peda Pêri's will be broken at the same time.

The *Tâḍu* is the cord tied round a bride's neck. To it is attached the gold *Tâliboṭṭu*, answering to the wedding ring. When a woman becomes a widow the cord is broken.

Said by one fellow wife to the other.

Both in the same boat.

879. చిన్నక్క చిలక, పెద్దక్క గిలక, చూస్తే చుక్క, రేగితే కుక్క.

The younger sister is a parrot, the elder sister is a rattle; when you look at them they are like stars; when angry they are like dogs.

880. చిన్నపామునయినా, పెద్ద కఱ్ఱతో కొట్ట వలెను.

Though the snake be small, you must hit him with a big stick.

881. చిన్నమూ కావలె, చిదరా కావలె, మేలిమీ కావలె, మెడ తిరగవలె.

The ornament must be one Chinnam or less in weight, of pure gold, and must go round the neck.

A *Chinnam* is a weight equal to the ninth part of a pagoda (No. 614).

Wishing to get a good thing and to pay little for it.

882. చిలక తన ముద్దేగాని ఎదటి ముద్దు కోరదు.

A parrot likes to be petted itself, but not to see others petted.

Applied to a selfish person.

883. చిలక ముక్కున దొండపండు వున్నట్టు.

Like a Donḍa fruit in a parrot's beak.

The reverse of No. 574 q. v.

884. చిలుము వదిలితే, ఛిద్రం వదులుతుంది.

When the "tin" goes, household broils disappear.

Chilumu is properly rust on other metals than iron; it is a slang term for money.

885. చిల్లిపేరే తూటు.

The name of a hole is a hole.

Said of persons contradicting each other, though really driving at the same end.

886. చీకట్లో జీవరత్నము.

A brilliant gem in the darkness.

(See No. 645.)

A bright exception among a bad lot.

887. చీపరకట్టకు పట్టుకుచ్చు కట్టినట్టు.

A silk tassel to a broom.

(See No. 1628.)

The grand appearance of a worthless person.

A leaden sword in an ivory scabbard.

888. చీర కట్టినమ్మ శృంగారము చూడు, గుడ్డ కట్టినమ్మ కులుకు చూడు.

Look at the finery of the well dressed and the strut of the poorly dressed woman.

889. చీర పిట్టకు దొమ్మ తెగులు.

A white louse with the staggers.

(See Nos. 615, 890, 1439.)

The Hindus' cure for the staggers is branding the flanks and legs with a ploughshare.

Applied to measures quite out of proportion to the necessities of the case.

890. చీర సింగారించేటప్పటికి పట్నమంతా చూరబోయినట్టు.

By the time he had finished equipping himself, the whole town was plundered.

(See No. 2069.)

Procrastination on the part of a boaster to conceal his cowardice or ignorance.

891. చుట్టమని చూడవస్తే, యింటివారంతా దయ్యాలై పట్టుకొన్నారట.

When he paid a visit to his relations, they all caught hold of him like devils.

To get something out of him.

892. చుట్టూ చూరుమంగళం, నడమ జయమంగళం.

The eaves are all in good order, and there is a joyful song in the court.

Expressive of prosperity.

893. చూచినది పాము, కరిచినది మామిడి టెంక.

What he saw was a snake, that which bit him was a mango stone.

After seeing the snake, he had trodden on a split mango stone which nipped his toe.

Flabbergasted with fright.

894. చూచినదెల్లా సుంకము, పాశినదెల్లా పంకము.

Every thing that is seen [is subjected to the payment of] duty; and every thing that is rotten [is thrown away in the] mud.

Excessive demands.

895. చూడగా చూడగా గుఱ్ఱము గాడిదె అయినది.

As he looked and looked the horse turned out a donkey.

(See No. 1030.)

By close inspection the true state is known.

896. చూడ చుంచెలుక, గోడలుతవ్వ పందికొక్కు.

To look at, it is like a musk rat, but to dig into walls it is like a bandicoot.

Insignificant in appearance, but having the power of doing much harm.

Little enemies and little wounds are not to be despised. (German.)*

897. చూడ చుట్టమూ, మొక్క దైవమూ లేదు.

No relation to visit or god to worship.

(See No. 1289.)

Utterly destitute.

898. చూడబోతే చుట్టాలు, రమ్మంటే కోపాలు.

If you visit them they are relatives, if you invite them to visit you they are angry.

---

* Kleine Feinde und kleine Wunden sind nicht zu verachten.

899. చూడ వచ్చిన వారికి శుక్రవారమేమి.

What is Friday to visitors?

If a married woman goes away from a house on Friday, the Hindus say that the goddess of fortune quits the house with her. The above is an excuse made by a casual visitor, who wished to get away.

Lame excuses.

900. చెంబూ కంచమూ పోతే, ముఖము మీద కొట్టినట్టు ముంతా మూకుడూ తెచ్చుకో లేనా.

If I lose my brass pot and bell metal dish, can I not beat you by getting others made of earth?

A determined man will not be discouraged by difficulties.

901. చెట్టు అయి వంగనిది మాను అయి వంగునా.

If a tree won't bend when it is young, will it bend when it is full grown?

If a man is not humble in his youth, will he grow meek in his old age?

Bend the tree while it is young. (Italian.)*

The old branch breaks if bent. (Danish.)†

"*Bow down his neck while he is young.*" *Ecclesiasticus* xxx. 12.

902. చెట్టుకొట్టి పయికి తెచ్చుకొన్నట్టు.

Cutting a tree and letting it fall on one's self.

Bringing trouble on one's own head.

The fool hunts for misfortune. (French.)‡

---

* Piega l'albero quando è giovane.
† Gammel Green bryder naar den skal böies.
‡ Le fou cherche son malheur.

903. చెట్టు చెడే కాలానకు కుక్క మూతి పిందెలు పుట్టుతున్నవి.

When the tree is about to perish, it brings forth blasted fruit.

Applied to the first signs of the coming ruin of a bad man.

Coming events cast their shadows before them.

904. చెట్టు పెట్టిన వాడు నీళ్లు పొయ్యడా.

Will he who planted the tree not water it?

(See No. 1478.)

Will God not support the creatures of his hand?

Said by a man who has lost his means of support.

God never sends mouths but he sends meat.

905. చెట్టు ముందా, విత్తు ముందా అన్నట్టు.

Like asking whether the tree was first or the seed.

(See No. 2118.)

A problem that cannot be solved.

Ask which was born first, the hen or the egg. (Italian.)*

906. చెట్టు యెక్కించి నిచ్చెన తీశినట్టు.

Making a man mount a tree and then taking away the ladder.

Treachery. Breach of faith.

907. చెట్టు యెక్కేవాణ్ని యెందాకా తొయ్య వచ్చును.

How far can you push a man up a tree?

How long is a man to be assisted?

---

* Domandar chi nacque prima, l' uovo o la gallina.

908. చెడిపోయిన బ్రాహ్మణుడికి చచ్చిపోయిన ఆవును దానము చేశినట్టు.

Like offering a dead cow to an outcast Brahman.

Knock a man down, and kick him for falling.

Him that falls all the world run over. (German.)*

All bite the bitten dog. (Portuguese.)†

909. చెడి స్నేహితుని యింటికి వెళ్లవచ్చునుగాని, చెల్లెలి యింటికి వెళ్ల కూడదు.

When you are ruined, you may go to your friend's house, but not to your sister's.

Friends are better in adversity than relations who envied you in prosperity.

Friends are the nearest relations.

Relationship gives rise to envy. (Latin.)‡

910. చెడేవాడు అబ్బడున్నాడు, మరీ పిడికెడు తేరా దానము చేస్తాను అన్నాడట.

It is Abbaḍu who will be ruined, bring me another handful [of money,] I will give it in alms.

(See Nos. 3, 1396, 1560.)

Abbaḍu is a familiar term applied to a lad.

Hens are ay free o' horse corn. (Scotch.)

911. చెడ్డ చేనికి మూడు మంచెలా.

Will a field of withered corn require three watcher's sheds?

To drive off the birds.

(See No. 912.)

---

* Wer da fallt, über ihm laufen alle Welt.
† Ao cao mordido, todos o mordem.
‡ Cognatio movet invidiam.

912. చెడ్డ చేనికి యింటి వడ్లు పొంగలా.

What! Offering the house-rice to a spoilt field?

(See No. 911.)

Pongali is a preparation of rice offered to the fields after the harvest. In this case the crop had failed and the offering had to be made from the old store. It was therefore a needless ceremony.

913. చెప్పినంత చేశేవారు శివునికన్నా వేరే యెవరూ లేరు.

Besides Śiva, there is no other who is as good as his word.

914. చెప్పిన బుద్ధీ, కట్టిన చద్దీ నిలవదు.

Advice given [will be forgotten]; and stale food tied up [in a bundle] will not keep.

Advice whispered in the ear is worth a jeer.

915. చెప్పుకింది తేలు.

A scorpion under a shoe.

A ruffian under restraint.

916. చెప్పుడు మాటలకన్నా తప్పుడు మాటలు నయము.

Lies are better than backbiting.

917. చెప్పులు తొడుగుకొన్న వానికి లోకమంతా తోలుతో కప్పబడ్డట్టు తోస్తున్నది.

To a man who wears sandals the whole earth seems to be covered with leather.

A man in comfortable circumstances does not realize the wants of others.

918. చెప్పే వాడికి శిగ్గు లేకపోతే, వినేవాడికయినా వివేకము వద్దా.

When the slanderer has no shame should not the hearer at least use discrimination?

Should he not swallow it *cum grano salis?*

Though the speaker be a fool let the hearer be wise. (Spanish.)*

Hear the other side, and believe little. (Italian.)†

Every man's tale is gude till anither's be tauld. (Scotch.)

919. చెయ్యి చూపి అవలక్షణము అనిపించుకొన్నట్టు.

Pointing with the hand, and being called a luckless fellow.

(For *Avalakshaṇam* see No. 142.)

Indiscreetly accusing a person openly of something which you are not able to prove.

A fool's tongue is long enough to cut his own throat.

Hear, see, and say nothing, if you wish to live in peace. (Italian.)‡

920. చెరపకురా చెడేవు, వురకకురా పడేవు.

Ruin not others, lest thou be ruined thyself; run not, lest thou fall.

He falls into the pit who leads another into it. (Spanish.)§

921. చెరుకా బెల్లము పెట్టుమంటే పెట్టునా.

If you ask the sugar-cane to give you molasses will it do so?

Strong measures must be used with stubborn folk.

922. చెరుకు తినడానకు కూలి యివ్వ వలెనా.

Is hire to be paid for eating sugar-cane?

---

* Aunque el decidor sea loco, el escuchador sea cuerdo.
† Odi l'altra parte, e credi poco.
‡ Odi, vedi, e taci, se vuoi viver in pace.
§ Cae en la cueva el que otro á ella lleva.

923. చెరుకు తీపి అని వేళ్లతో నమలవచ్చునా.

Because the sugar-cane is sweet are you to chew it with the roots?

(See No. 290.)

Said of a greedy, grasping person.

Milk the cow, but don't pull off the udder. (Dutch.)*

Give him an inch and he'll take an ell.

Give a clown your finger and he will take your whole hand.

924. చెరుకు వంకబోతే తీపు చెడునా.

Though the sugar-cane is crooked, will it lose its sweetness?

(See Nos. 259, 371, 515, 571, 573, 632, 1475, 1494.)

Good blood cannot lie. (French.)†

925. చెరువు మీాద అలిగి కాళ్లు కడుక్కోక పోయినట్టు.

Getting into a pet with the tank, he would not wash his feet in it.

(See No. 53.)

When a man grows angry, his reason rides out.

926. చెల్లీ చెల్లడములకు శెట్టిగారు వున్నారు.

The Śeṭṭi is here to test the genuineness.

(See No. 368.)

A fool travelling with a Śeṭṭi [merchant] was plundered. On the robbers' questioning the genuineness of the coin, the man referred to his rich friend who had up to that time escaped their observation.

To injure a friend unwittingly, from stupidity.

* Men moet de koe wel melken maar de spenen niet aftrekken.
† Bon sang ne peut mentir.

927. చెవిటి పెద్దమ్మా చేంత్రాడు తేవే అంటే, చెవుల పోగులు నా జన్మానా యెరగనన్నదట.

When the deaf old lady was asked to bring the well-rope, she replied "I have never seen earrings in all my life."

(See Nos. 928, 929, 2050.)

Applied to a stupid person not doing what he is told.

928. చెవిటి వాడికి శంఖము వూదితే, అది కొరకడానకు నీ తండ్రి తాతల తరము కాదన్నాడట.

When a horn was sounded in the ears of a deaf man, he said "to bite that is more than your fathers before you could do."

(See Nos. 927, 929, 2050.)

Applied to a stubborn person.

929. చెవుడు చెవుడూ అంటే, తవుడు తవుడూ అంటాడు.

When they call out "Deaf man! Deaf man!" he answers "[I've got] Bran, Bran!"

(See Nos. 927, 928, 2050.)

The jingle of the Telugu words is similar to that of the English equivalents.

930. చెవ్వాకు పోయినమ్మకు యెంత వ్యసనమో, దొరికినమ్మకు అంత సంతోషము.

The lady who found the ear-ornament was as glad as the lady who lost it was sorry.

(See Nos. 809, 1452.)

Ill-luck is good for something. (French.)*

* A quelque chose malheur est bon.

931. చేదు తింటారా చెట్లు కొట్టుతారా.

Are you eating bitter or cutting down trees?

Said of anything easy, or profitable.

932. చేనిపంట కొయ్యగాలే చెప్పుతుంది.

The stubble tells the produce of the field.

(See No. 1780.)

A slight acquaintance suffices to tell what a man is made of.

933. చేనిలో పుట్టిన బీడు యెక్కడికి పోను.

Can the waste land be taken out of the field?

You must take the fat with the lean.

934. చేనూ కొడవలీ నీ చేత యిచ్చినాను.

I have given the field and the sickle into your hands.

To hand anything over entirely to another. To give another full powers.

935. చేప పిల్లకు యీత నేర్ప వలెనా.

Must you teach a young fish to swim?

(See Nos. 797, 1041.)

Don't teach fish to swim. (French.)*

936. చేలోపత్తి చేలో వుండగానే, పోలికి మూడు మూళ్లు నాకు అరు మూళ్లు అన్నట్టు.

While the cotton crop was still in the field, he said "Three cubits [of the cloth] for Pôli and six for me."

(See Nos. 204, 598, 1470, 1471.)

Pôli is a female name and here represents a cousin.

Sune enough to cry "chick" when it's out of the shell. (Scotch.)

---

* Il ne faut pas enseigner les poissons à nager.

937. చేసిన పాపము చెప్పితే మానును.

Sin is removed by confession.

Confession of a fault makes half amends.

A sin confessed is half forgiven. (Italian.)*

938. చేసుకొన్న వారికి చేసుకొన్నంత మహాదేవ.

O Mahâdêva! what a man does, that does he in full receive.

(See Nos. 287, 964, 867.)

939. చేసేది బీద కాపరము, వచ్చేవి రాజ రోగాలు.

A man living in poor style, attacked by king's diseases.

A poor man having to meet great expenses quite beyond his means—The cure of the disease alluded to costs much money.

940. చేసేవి నాయకాలు, అడిగేవి తిరిపాలు, పెట్టకుంటే కోపాలు.

He gives himself the airs of a great man, but begs for alms, and is angry if he gets none.

941. చేసేవి శివపూజలు, చెప్పేవి అబద్ధాలు.

His employment is the worship of Śiva, but his words are lies.

(See No. 848.)

A hypocrite.

Much praying, but no piety.

Beads about the neck and the devil in the heart.

ఛ.

942. ఛిద్రమునకు చీరపేలు, దరిద్రమునకు తలపేలు.

A louse in the clothes is a sign of coming household broils, a louse in the head is a sign of coming poverty.

---

* Peccato confessato è mezzo perdonato.

జ.

943. జంగానికి బిడ్డలు పుట్టితే, వూరికి వుపాధి.

If children are born to a Jangam they are only an annoyance to the village.

Because they will add to the number of beggars. The Jangams are the Vîra Śaivas or followers of the Hindu reformer Basava.

Beggars breed, and rich men feed.

944. జగమెరిగిన బ్రాహ్మణునికి జంధ్యమెందుకు.

What is the use of the sacred thread to a well known Brahman?

That which is well known need not be published.

945. జడ్డిగములో మిడతపోటు.

A grasshopper eating the seed in the drilling machine.

Premature ruin.

946. జయము వుండే వరకు భయము లేదు.

As long as fortune favours you, you have nothing to fear.

947. జాతికొద్దీ బుద్ధి, కులముకొద్దీ ఆచారము.

Wisdom according to your birth, religious observances according to your caste.

948. జానెడు యింట్లో మూరెడు కర్ర.

A staff a cubic long in a house a span wide.

An impossibility.

949. జీతగాణ్ని తెచ్చుకొంటే, యింటికి ఖావందు అయినాడు.

The hireling has become the master of the house.

Applied to a forward person, who does not know his place.

950. జీతములేని నవకరు, కోపములేని దొర.

[Where] the servant [is] without pay the master [must be] without anger.

951. జీతమూ బత్యమూ లేకుండా తోడేలు మేకలు కాస్తాననన్నట్టు.

"I'll watch the sheep without wages," said the wolf.

A man offering to serve without pay for the sake of dishonest gains.

952. జీవన్మృతుడు, మృత జీవుడు.

Dead while living, living while dead.

A bad man is, in the estimate of his fellow men, as little valued as if he were dead, but the good man's deeds live after he himself has left the world.

"*The memory of the just is blessed.*" Proverbs x. 7.

953. జీవరత్నము యిత్తడిని పొదిగితే, రత్నానికి యేమి లోపము.

What does a fine ruby suffer by being set in brass?

The disgrace of putting a talented man in a mean situation attaches to the employer not to the employé.

954. జోగీ జోగీ రాచుకొంటే బూడిదె రాలినది.

When two Jôgis jostled against each other ashes fell [from their bodies].

Nothing is to be got out of the quarrels of the poor.

955. జ్ఞాతిగుర్రు అరిటికర్రు వదలవు.

The stain of plantain [can never be effaced], the grumbling of cousins never ceases.

డ.

956. డబ్బు యివ్వనివాడు ముందు పడవ యెక్కినట్టు.

The man that did not pay his fare, got into the boat first.

957. డబ్బులేని వానికి బోగముది తల్లి వరస.

A harlot is as a mother to a man without money.

Something beyond the reach of a man's means.

958. డొంకలో షరాఫు వున్నాడు, నాణెము చూపుకో వచ్చును.

The banker is in the thicket, you may get him to test the coin.

(See No. 966.)

త.

959. తంగేడు పూచినట్టు.

As the Tangêḍu blossoms.

(See No. 1882.)

Tangêḍu is the Cassia Auriculata.

960. తంటల మారి గుర్రముకు తాటిపట్టె గోరపం.

A vicious horse requires a comb made of Palmyra wood.

Full of splinters.

961. తండ్రి తవ్విన నుయ్యి అని అందులోపడి చావ వచ్చునా.

Will you drown yourself in the well because your father dug it?

962. తంబళి అనుమానము.

The scrupulosity of a Ṡaiva priest.

The Tambaḷas are a class of Sûdra priests who wear the sacred thread, and endeavour to observe Brahminical customs.

Applied to foolish scruples.

963. తంబళి తన లొటలొటేగాని, యెదటి లొటలొట యెరగడు.

A Tambaḷi prates, but does not listen to what others say.

964. తక్కువ నోములు నోచి యెక్కువ ఫలము రమ్మంటే వచ్చునా.

If you expect much fruit from few offerings will it be obtained?

(See Nos. 287, 986, 987.)

965. తగినట్టే కూర్చెరా తాకట్లమారి బ్రహ్మ.

That makebate Brahmâ has made a pretty match of it!

Said by one of an unhappy pair.

966. తగిలిన కాలే తగులుతుంది.

A wounded foot is always striking against something.

(See Nos. 822, 828.)

967. తగు దాసరికీ మెడ పూసలకూ, అమ్మకన్న కాన్పుకూ అయ్య యిచ్చిన మనుముకూ.

Like Dâsari, like beads; like the bringing forth of the mother, is the match made by the father.

Said by a miserable daughter, who had been married to a bad husband.

968. తడకలేని యింట్లోకి కుక్క దూరినట్టు.

As a dog enters into a house with an open door.

Applied to property not watched.

969. తడిగుడ్డలతో గొంతుక తెగకోస్తాడు.

He cuts a [man's] throat with a wet cloth.

Smooth words, but hidden malice.

They scratch you with one hand and strike you with the other. (Latin.)*

970. తడిశిగాని గుడిశె కట్టడు, తాకిగాని మొగ్గడు.

A man will not build a hut until he has been drenched, nor stoop until he has hit his head.

971. తడిశిన కుక్క బిగిశినట్టు.

When the cot was wet, it became tight.

The cots used by the poorest classes are plaited with the fibres of the Cannabis Sativa which shrink when wet.

A bad man is puffed up when flattered.

972. తడిశి ముప్పందుం మోశినట్టు.

Like carrying 30 Tûms (750 lbs.) when you're wet.

973. తణుకుకు పోయి మాచవరం వెళ్లినట్టు.

Like going to Mâçavaram round about by Taṇuku.

To do things in a roundabout way.

974. తద్దినము కొని తెచ్చుకొన్నట్టు.

Buying a Taddinam.

(See No. 1151—For *Taddinam* See No. 271.)

Bringing difficulties upon one's own head.

---

* Alterâ manu scabunt, alterâ feriunt.

975. తనకంపు తనకింపు, పరులకంపు తనకు వోకిలింపు.

The smell of a man is pleasant to himself, but the smell of others is disgusting.

People do not find fault with their own actions.

976. తన కలిమి యింద్రభోగము, తనలేమి లోకదారిద్ర్యము.

A man's having is the wealth of Indra, his not having is the poverty of the world.

In prosperity a man thinks himself the wealthiest of all, and in adversity the poorest.

977. తన కాళ్లకు బందాలు తానే తెచ్చుకొన్నట్టు.

He brought fetters for his own legs.

He brings a staff to brak his ain head. (Scotch.)

978. తనకు అని తవ్వెడు తవుడు వుంటే, ఆకటి వేళకు ఆరగించవచ్చును.

If you have even a Tavva (1 lb.) of bran of your own, you can eat it when you are hungry.

(See No. [illegible].)

Store is no sore.

979. తనకు కానిది గూడులంజ.

[He called] the woman whom he could not get [as a wife] a harlot.

Sour grapes as the fox said when he could not reach them.

What you can't have, abuse. (Italian.)*

---

* Qual che non puoi aver, biasima.

980. తనకు కాని రాజ్యము పండితేనేమి పడట కలిస్తేనేమి.

What does it matter whether the kingdom he has not possession of prospers or decays?

981. తనకు చెప్ప తడికెలచాటు ప్రకరికి చెప్ప ప్రెప్పుల కుప్ప.

When [the priest] applies [the law] to himself he screens himself [from its penalty]; but in laying down [the law] for others he is a beauty.*

Justice, but not in my own house. (Spanish.)†

No one likes justice brought home to his own door. (Italian.)‡

982. తనకు మాలిన ధర్మము, మొదలు చెడ్డ బేరము.

To give that in charity which a man himself needs to receive from others is like trading after the loss of one's principal.

983. తన కొంగున వున్న రూకా తన కడుపున పుట్టిన బిడ్డా పనికి వస్తవి.

The money tied up in your skirt and the child you have begotten will be of use to you.

(See No. 978.)

984. తన చెయ్యి కాలుతుందని సవితి బిడ్డ చేతితో కలియపెట్టినదట.

To save her own hand from being burnt, she stirred up the food with the hand of her fellow wife's child.

Cat's paw.

To draw the snake out of the hole with another's hand. (Spanish.)§

---

* Morton (*Bengali and Sanscrit Proverbs*) thus renders a Bengali epigram—

" Said a clown to a Brahmin, ' Sir, tell me, I pray
For crushing a spider what fine must I pay?'
' Why friend,' he replied, ' 'tis a grievous offence,
And demands an atonement of serious expence.'—
' Indeed— then alas, with deep sorrow I'm filled;
Your son, Sir, a poor little spider has killed.'—
' Out, fool,' cries the Brahmin, in anger—' away!
For killing a spider there's nothing to pay!' "

† Justicia, mas no por mi casa.
‡ A nessuno piace la giustizia à casa sua.
§ Con agena mano sacar la culebra del horado.

985. తన తలుపు తీశి పొరుగింటికి పెట్టి రాత్రి అంతా కుక్కలు తోలుతూ కూర్చున్నట్టు.

Having taken his own door and put it on his neighbour's house, he spent the whole night in driving away the dogs.

Over generous.

Charity begins at home.

986. తన తల్లి చావుకన్నా పిన తల్లి చావు మేలు.

The death of an aunt is better than the death of a mother.

987. తన నీడ తనతోనే వుంటున్నది.

A man's shadow remains with himself.

(See Nos. 267, 938, 964.)

The fruits of a man's actions go with him whether good or evil.

988. తనను పొడిచిన గంగిగోవునయినా పొడిస్తే పాపములేదు.

Killing a sacred cow that gores you is not sin.

989. తన పిల్ల తవిటికి యేడిస్తే, లంజ పిల్ల రావిరేకకు యేడ్చినది.

When the legitimate child cried for bran (the poorest food) the illegitimate child asked for an ornament.

(See Nos. 237, 799, 1781, 1798.)

An unreasonable request at an inopportune time.

990. తన పుట్టి పిచ్చగా వుంటే, పొరుగు పందుం పరా కొలిచినాడట.

When his Puṭṭi was found to be of short measure, he tested the Pandum and Para of his neighbour.

Puṭṭi, Pandum and *Para* are measures of capacity.

When a man was found cheating with a false measure, he tried to prove that his neighbour's measures were too large.

991. తన బలిమి కన్నా స్థాన బలిమి మేలు.

The power of the place is greater than the power of the man.

Every man is powerful in his own house.

Every one is a king in his own house. (Portuguese.)*

992. తన ముడ్డి కాకపోతే గంగదాకా దేకుమన్నట్టు.

If not on my posteriors, crawl as far as Kâśi (Benares).

993. తనవారు లోతుకు తీతురు, కానివారు కడకు తీతురు.

His own people will pull him into the depth, his enemies will pull him to the bank.

(See No. 999.)

Even an enemy is to be preferred to a relative in a time of danger.

994. తన వాశి తప్పితే, ఓక వన్నె తరుగును.

If virtue fails, honor decreases with it.

995. తన్నేకాలికి రోలు అడ్డమయినట్టు.

The mortar came in the way of the foot which kicked.

A fortunate hindrance in the commission of an act of violence.

996. తప్పులు వెతికేవాడు తండ్రి, ఒప్పులు వెతికేవాడు ఓర్వలేనివాడు.

The man who seeks out your faults is a father, but he that seeks for what is good in you is an envious person.

(See No. 1245.)

You may be more thankful to the fault finder than to the good natured.

997. తప్పులేని వారు ధరణిలో లేరు.

There is not a blameless man in the world.

(See No. 223.)

There's nane without a faut. (Scotch.)

Lifeless, faultless.

---

* Cada hum em sua casa he Rei.

998. తప్పూ ఒప్పూ దైవమెరుగును, పప్పూ కూడూ బాపడెరుగును.

God knows right and wrong; the Brahman knows Dâl and rice.

(For *Dâl* see No. 183.)

999. తలక్రింది కొరివి.

A brand under one's head.

(See Nos. 1002, 1368.)

A dangerous companion.

1000. తలకు మించిన ఆజ్ఞ లేదు.

There is no sentence beyond the head.

Do your worst, you can but cut my head off.

1001. తల కోసి ముందర పెట్టితే, గారడీ విద్య అన్నట్టు.

Though you cut off your head and place it before him he would call it magic.

Incredulity.

1002. తలగడ క్రింది పాము.

A snake under the pillow.

(See Nos. 999, 1368.)

1003. తల తడిపిన మట్టుకు గొరిగే తీరవలెను.

When the head has been wet, the shaving must be completed.

When a man has commenced a business he must finish it himself.

1004. తల ప్రాణము తోకకు వచ్చినది.

The life in a man's head went into his tail.

Applied to strenuous exertions made to accomplish a difficult task.

1005. తలలు బోడులయితే తలపులు బోడులా.

Their heads are clean shaven, but are their thoughts clean also?

(See Vêmana Book III. 875.)

1006. తలా తోకా లేని కథ, ముక్కూ ముఖము లేని పిల్ల.

A story without head or tail, a child without nose or face.

(See Nos. 157, 1785.)

A story without a head. (Greek.)*

1007. తలారి పగ తలతో తీరుతుంది.

A Talâri's hate ends with one's head.

Talâri is a village watchman.

1008. తలుపులు మింగే వానికి అప్పడాలు లోట లోటలు.

Cakes are trifles to a man that swallows doors.

(See Nos. 447, 684, 778.)

1009. తల్లి అయినా యేడవనిదీ పాలివ్వదు.

Unless the child cries, even the mother will not give it suck.

Nothing is got without asking.

Lose nothing for asking.

Asking costs little. (Italian.)†

1010. తల్లి కడుపు చూచును, పెండ్లాము వీపు చూచును.

The mother will look at his belly the wife at his back.

The mother will look to see how her son fares, the wife to see what her husband has brought home for her.

Come but come stooping.

---

* Ἀκέφαλος μῦθος.

† Il domandar costa poco.

1011. తల్లి కడుపులో చొరకముందు దయ్యాలదేవత, భూమిలో పుట్టిన తర్వాత యమదేవత.

Before he entered his mother's womb he was the prince of devils; after he was born into the world he became the god of death.

Said of a exceedingly wicked and relentlessly cruel man.

1012. తల్లికి కానివాడు దాదికవునా.

Will he who is disliked by his mother, be liked by his nurse?

(See No. 1027.)

1013. తల్లికి కూడు పెట్టనివాడు తగుదు తగుదునని తగువు తీర్చ వచ్చినట్టు.

Like a man who neglects his mother coming with a bold face to settle a dispute between others.

Shamefacedness.

1014. తల్లికి కొట్టరా వసంతము.

Throw scarlet water over your mother.

(See No. 145.)

1015. తల్లికి తగిన బిడ్డా, యింటికి తగిన పందిలి.

A child worthy of its mother, a Pandili fit for the house.

(See Nos. 176, 185, 1019, 1977—For *Pandili* see No. 61.)

1016. తల్లిగండము పిల్లగండము వున్నదిగాని మంత్రసాని గండము వున్నదా.

Evil may be predicted to the mother or to the child, but will any harm come to the midwife?

1017. తల్లి చనిపోతే తండ్రి పినతండ్రితో సమానము.

When the mother dies, the father is equal to an uncle.

He is not so affectionate as before.

1018. తల్లిచస్తే కడుపు పెద్ద, తలమాస్తే కొప్పు పెద్ద.

When the mother dies, a man's gluttony is seen; when the head is dirty, [a woman's] top-knot is large [and untidy].

As long as the mother lives her son's greediness is concealed.

1019. తల్లిచాలు పిల్లకు తప్పుతున్నదా.

Will the child (daughter) fail to follow in its mother's track ?

(See Nos. 176, 185, 1015, 1977.)

She hath a mark after her mother.

As the old cock crows, so crows the young.

"*As is the mother so is her daughter.*" Ezekiel xvi. 44.

1020. తల్లి చెవులకన్నా పినతల్లి చెవులే మేలు.

The ears of the aunt are better than those of the mother.

They are better supplied with ornaments.

To neglect one having great claims, for another whose claims are inferior.

1021. తల్లి చెవుల మద్దికాయలు దండగలకు, భార్య మెళ్లో పూసలు బోగాలవారికి.

His mother's ear-ornaments went to pay fines, and his wife's necklace of beads to pay harlots.

1022. తల్లిచెవులు తెంచిన వాడికి ముత్తవతల్లి చెవులు వెంట్రుక మాత్రము.

The man who tears [the ornaments out of] his mother's ears, will not care a rush for the ears of his great-grandmother.

1023. తల్లిదే వలపక్షము, ధరణీదేవిదే వలపక్షము.

Partiality belongs to a mother and to the earth.

A mother is partial to some of her children, and the earth is unequal in its favors, bringing forth more for one than for another.

1024. తల్లి దైవము, తండ్రి ధనము.

A mother is a divinity, a father a treasure.

1025. తల్లిని చూచి పిల్లనూ పాడిని చూచి బఱ్ఱెనూ తీసుకోవలెను.

Look at the mother before you take the daughter; see how much milk the buffalo gives before you buy her.

1026. తల్లి పుట్టిల్లు మేనమామ వద్ద పొగడినట్లు.

Will you boast of your mother's family before your maternal uncle?

1027. తల్లి రోశిన పిల్లను దాది రోయదా.

Will not the nurse hate the child which is hated by its mother?

(See No. 1012.)

1028. తల్లి లేని పిల్ల ఉల్లి లేని కూర.

A motherless child is like a curry without onions.

1029. తవుడు తింటూ వయ్యారమా.

Should a man strut who lives on bran?

1030. తవ్వగా తవ్వగా తథ్యం తేలుతున్నది.

By digging and digging the truth is discovered.

(See No. 996.)

1031. తవ్వి మీద తోసుకొన్నట్టు.

He dug and threw [the earth] on his own head.

1032. తాగనేరని పిల్లి బోర్ల దోసుకొన్నదట.

The cat which could not drink, upset the pot.

1033. తాగబోతే దప్పికి లేదు, తలకు అటకలి.

Not a morsel to eat, but Aṭakali for his head.

(See Nos. 520, 1728.)

Aṭakali is an expensive preparation used for cleansing the head.

1034. తాగేది దమ్మిడీ గంజాయి, యిల్లంతా చెడు వుమ్ములు.

He smokes half a farthing's worth of Ganjâyi, and fouls the whole house with spittle.

Ganjâyi (Hind. *Gânjhâ*) is the hemp plant (Cannabis Sativa) the leaves or young leaf-buds of which are bruised and smoked to produce intoxication. In its liquid form it is called *Bhang.*—A *Dammiḍi* is the twelfth of an *aṇâ* (anna).

Great injury caused by a little evil.

1035. తా చెడ్డ కోతి వనమెల్లా చెరిచినది.

The monkey ruined himself, and all the forest after him.

1036. తాటాకు చప్పుళ్లకు కుందేళ్లు బెదురునా.

Will hares be frightened by the rustling of palmyra leaves ?

1037. తాటి చెట్లలో ప్రొద్దు గూకినట్టు.

Like the sun setting in a palmyra grove.

Left in great difficulty.

1038. తాటి పట్టెకు యెదురు దేకినట్టు.

Like sliding on a palmyra beam, against the grain.

The bark of the Palmyra (See No. 290) is scaly and rugged.

Injuring one's self by perverse conduct.

1039. తాడు చాలకపోతే నుయ్యి పూడ్చుమన్నట్టు.

Like ordering the well to be filled up when the rope was found too short.

1040. తాడెక్కేవాణ్ని యెందాకా యెగసన తొయ్యను.

How far can you help the man who is climbing up a palmyra tree ?

(See No 907.)

A clumsy person must be helped to the end.

1041. తాతకు దగ్గ నేర్పవలెనా.

Must you teach your grandfather how to cough ?

(See Nos. 797, 935.)

1042. తాతాచార్యుల ముద్ర భుజము తప్పినా వీపు తప్పదు.

If Tâtâchâri's brand misses your shoulder, you'll catch it on the back.

Tâtâchâri was a wandering priest who branded his converts. If a man slipped away his shoulder, the seal caught him in the back.

Not being able to evade something disagreeable.

1043. తాతా పెండ్లాడుతావా అంటే, నాకెవడిస్తాడురా అబ్బా అన్నాడట.

When the grandfather was asked whether he would like to be married, he said, "Who will give me [a daughter,] my boy?"

1044. తాతా సంక్రాంతి పట్టు పట్టు.

O grandfather! Sankrânti [has arrived] catch it! catch it!

Sankrânti is the transit of the sun from Sagittarius to Capricornus, when the Hindus celebrate the Pongal feast.—This is chaff; old people observe the feast very scrupulously.

1045. తాదిన తవుడు లేదు, వారానికి వక పందిపిల్ల.

He has not even bran to eat, but he wants a pig every week.

1046. తానుండేది దాలిగుంట పట్టు, తలచేవి మేడా మాళిగెలు.

He lives in a pit, but dreams of castles.

His ideas are far above his position.

1047. తానుచేశిన పాపం తనువుతోఁ, తల్లిచేశిన పాపం ధరణితోఁ.

The sin which a man commits goes with his body, the sin which his mother commits goes with the earth.

This is interpreted to mean that if a man commits the sin of adultery, his crime may be expiated by a punishment equal to loss of life, but if a woman is guilty of the same offence, it clings to her descendants as long as the world endures.

1048. తాను పట్టిన కుందేటికి మూడే కాళ్లు.

The hare he caught had only three legs.

(See No. 1678.)

Said of a pertinaceous person.

1049. తాను పట్టిన కోడికి నాలుగు కాళ్లు.

The hen he has caught has four legs.

Exaggeration.

All his geese are swans.

1050. తాను పెంచిన పొట్టేలు తన చేతనే చంపబడ్డట్టు.

Like the ram reared by one's self being killed by one's own hand.

1051. తానుబోను దోవలేదు డోలు వకటి మెడను.

When there is no room for him to pass himself, he hangs a big drum round his neck.

Said of a man who tries to provide for another, when he has difficulty in managing for himself.

1052. తాను మింగేది తనను మింగేది చూచుకోవలశినది.

You should look what you can swallow, and what can swallow you.

(See No. 617.)

Look before you leap.

1053. తానూ గాక పిల్లి కూడానా.

Is a cat to come as well as himself?

Said when a man who is already a burden upon others, brings some one else with him. Amongst the Hindus a cat is an evil omen.

1054. తానూ వక మనిషేనా తవుడూ వక రొట్టేనా.

He calls himself a man, and the bran he eats, bread.

A vulgar person taking airs.

1055. తానే తుమ్మి తానే శతాయుస్సు అనుకొన్నట్టు.

After sneezing he blessed himself saying "May you live a hundred years!"

(See No. 1251.)

A joke. The blessing ought to come from another.

1056. తానొకటి తలిస్తే దైవమొకటి తలిచినది.

When he planned one thing, God planned another.

Man proposes, God disposes.

1057. తాపుల గొడ్డుకు రోలడ్డము.

A mortar is a [sure] check to a runaway cow.

When tied to its neck.

Applied to measures which to check the progress of crime.

1058. తాబెట్టినది ముషిణిమొక్క అయినా చేపట్టవలెను.

What he has planted although it be Strychnine he must cherish.

Mushiṇi Mokka is the Strychnos Nux-Vomica.

A patron must not forsake his dependent under any circumstances.

1059. తాబోతూ బొల్లి యెద్దుకు కుడితి.

When about to go off herself, [she ordered] the white ox [to be fed with] rice washings.

Applied to the absurdity of a person troubling himself with affairs in which he has no longer any interest.

1060. తాబోతే మజ్జిగలేదంటే, పెరుగుకు చీటివ్రాయుమన్నట్టు.

After being refused butter-milk, when he went himself, he ordered his servant to write for curds.

After being refused a trifling request, to demand authoritatively something much greater.

1061. తామరాకులో నీళ్లు తల్లడించినట్టు.

Like a drop of water on a lotus leaf.

A very unsettled state.

1062. తాళిమి తన్నూ కాచును యెదిరినీ కాచును.

Patience will save you and your neighbour.

1063. తాళ్లకు తలను చండ్లు మేకలకు మెడను చండ్లు.

The Palmyra trees have teats on their heads, the goats have teats (wattles) on their necks.

(See No. 731.)

The Hindus call the flower stalk (spadix) of the Palmyra a teat.

Useless appendages.

1064. తాళ్లపాకవారి కవిత్వము కొంత, తన పైత్యము కొంత.

Part [of the book] is the poetry of Tâḷḷapâkavâru, the rest is his own rubbish.

Said of a man who has spoilt the good work of another.

1065. తాళ్లు తన్నేవారి తలలు తన్నేవాడు.

A man that kicks the heads of people who kick the tops of Palmyra trees.

More wicked than the other.

1066. తావలచినది రంభ, తాములిగినది గంగ.

He thinks the woman he loves to be Rambhâ and the water he bathes in, the Ganges.

Rambhâ is the most beautiful of all the Apsarases or courtezans of Svarga, the Hindu elysium.

1067. తింటే కదలలేను, తినకపోతే మెదలలేను.

If I eat I can't move, if I don't eat I can't stir.

1068. తింటేగాని రుచి తెలియదు, దిగితేగాని లోతు తెలియదు.

Without eating you can't tell the taste; without going down [into the water] you can't know the depth.

The proof of a pudding is in the eating.

1069. తిండికి చేటూ నేలకు బరువూ.

He's not worth his food, and is a burden on the earth.

(See No. 1366.)

He is not worth his salt.

1070. తిండికి తిమ్మరాజు, పనికి పోతరాజు.

He is a Timma Râzu (monkey-king) at eating; and a Pôta Râzu (buffalo-king) at work.

(See Nos. 73, 518, 1381, 1385.)

As greedy as a monkey and as lazy as a buffalo.

Like the smith's dog, that sleeps at the sound of the hammer, and wakes at the crashing of the teeth.

He eats till he sweats, and works till he freezes.

1071. తిండికి వచ్చినావా తీర్థానకు వచ్చినావా.

Have you come to eat or to visit the shrine?

1072. తిట్టి చచ్చినవాడూ లేడు, దీవించి బ్రతికినవాడూ లేడు.

No man has ever died from cursing, or lived from blessing.

No one dies of threats. (Dutch.)*

---

* Van dreigen sterft man neit.

1073. తిట్టితే గాలికి పోతవి, తింటే లోగా పోతవి.

The abuse which is heaped on me goes to the winds, but the food which I eat goes within.

(See No. 397.)

A mean sycophant.

1074. తిట్టుగాదురా తొత్తు కొడకా.

I am not abusing you, my good son of a slut.

1075. తిన మరిగిన ప్రాణము అల్లాడి చచ్చినది.

The body accustomed to sumptuous living was distressed for want of food.

Applied to a man whose malpractices have been put a stop to, but who is eagerly seeking an opportunity of renewing them.

1076. తిన్న కుక్క తిని పోతే, కన్న కుక్కను పట్టి కాళ్లు విరగకొట్టినట్టు.

When the dog which had eaten [the food] ran off, he caught hold of another dog and broke its leg.

Making the innocent suffer for the guilty.

1077. తిన్నయింటి వాసాలు మెంచుతావేమిరా అంటే, పొరిగింటికి పోతే పూర్కుంటారా అన్నాడట.

When a man was asked why he was counting the rafters of the house in which he had been well treated, he replied, "Would they allow me to do it in the next house?"

(See Nos. 397, 636, 665, 1078, 1079, 1860.)

Gross ingratitude.

I taught you to swim, and now you'd drown me.

1078. తిన్నయింటి వాసాలు యెన్నేవాడు.

A man that counts the rafters of his benefactor's house.

A story is told of a man who counted the rafters, &c., of a house in order that he might take possession of it and found his claim to it on this knowledge. Hence the term is applied to a person basely attempting to swindle another, who had befriended him, out of his property.

(See Nos. 267, 636, 665, 1077, 1079, 1850.)

All's lost that's put into a riven dish.

1079. తిన్నయిల్లు గుద్దలించేవేమిరా అంటే, తినని యిల్లు నేనేమి యెరుగుదును అన్నాడట.

When asked, "Why are you digging [for treasure] in the house where you have eaten?" he replied, "What do I know of a house where I have not eaten?"

(See Nos. 267, 636, 665, 1077, 1078, 1850.)

Do good to a knave and pray God he requite thee not. (Danish.)*

1080. తిన్నవాడే మన్నవాడు, మన్నవాడే మహారాజు.

He that ate prospered, and he that prospered became a Mahârâja.

1081. తిమ్మన్న బంతికి తియ్యచారు అన్నము.

To a set of monkey-like scamps tasteless broth and plain rice [should be served].

1082. తిమ్మిని బ్రహ్మినీ, బ్రహ్మిని తిమ్మినీ చేస్తాడు.

He makes Timmi into Brâhmî and Brâhmi into Timmi.

(See No. 1215.)

Timmi is a familiar name for a she-monkey; Brâhmî (in the Proverb incorrectly *Brahmi*) is a name of Saraswatî, wife of Brahmâ.

He calls evil good, and good evil.

* Giör vel imod en Skalk, og bed til Gud han lönner dig ikke.

1083. తియ్యగా తియ్యగా రాగము, మూలగగా మూలగగా రోగము.

The more you practise the better you will sing; the more you groan the more will your illness increase.

1084. తియ్యని రోగములూ, కమ్మని మందులూ వున్నవా.

Are there sweet diseases, and delicious medicines?

1085. తిరగ మరిగిన కాలూ తిట్ల మరిగిన నోరూ వూరకుండవు.

The feet which are wont to wander, and the mouth which is accustomed to abuse, will never be quiet.

1086. తిరపతికి పోగానే తురక దాసరి అవునా.

Will a Mussulman become a Dâsari by going to Tirapati?

(See No. 609.—For *Dâsari* see No. 111.)

Tirapati (prop. *Tirupati*) is a sacred hill about 80 miles from Madras.

1087. తిరపతి మంగలవాడివత్తు.

Like the Tirapati barber.

(See No. 639.)

Has it all his own way. Pilgrims visiting the place have to get their heads shaved, and as one man has the entire monopoly he keeps them waiting for hours, taking payment in advance and shaving a little bit of one man's head and then a little bit of another, to prevent them from going away.

Applied to a person selfishly taking work out of others' hands which he is unable to complete himself.

1088. తిరిపెపు మజ్జిగకు వచ్చి పాడి బఱ్రెను బేరము చేసినట్టు.

Like coming to beg buttermilk, and bargaining for the milch buffalo.

Pretended wealth.

1089. తిలాః పాపహరా నిత్యం, తలా పిడికెడు పిడికెడు.

Sesamum seed always takes away sin, [give them] a handful a head.

Tila is the Sesamum Indicum.

A jocose proverb, half Sanscrit, half Telugu.

1090. తీగకు కాయ బరువా.

Is the gourd too heavy for the creeper?

Applied to having a large family to support.

1091. తీగ పట్టుకొంటే, పొద అంతా కదిలినట్టు.

When the creeper was pulled the whole bush shook.

Injury to the head of the house reaches to all the members.

1092. తీట పట్టినవాడు గోకుకొంటాడు.

The man with itch scratches himself.

(See No. 327.)

Let him that itches scratch himself. (French.)*

1093. తుంటిమీద కొట్టితే పండ్లు రాలినవట.

When the man received a blow on his back, he cried out that he had lost his teeth.

(See No. 1796.)

Applied to inappropriate actions or words.

1094. తుడుం తుడుం అంటే, దురాయి దురాయి అన్నట్టు.

When the drum sounded "tuḍum, tuḍum" a man called out "durâyi, durâyi."

Tuḍum is the (onomatopoetic) name of a kind of drum (Tom-tom). *Durâyi* is a form of adjuration in the name of Government.

(See No. 40.)

---

* Qui se sent galeux, se gratte.

1095. తుప్పర్ల పసేగాని, మంత్రాల పస లేదు.

The beauty of his slobberings, not of his mantras.

1096. తుమ్మితే పొయ్యేముక్కు యెన్నాళ్లు వుండును.

If your nose won't stand sneezing how long will it last?

(See No. 1138.)

1097. తుమ్ము తమ్ముడై చెప్పును.

A sneeze warns you as a younger brother.

On the commencement of an undertaking, if any one sneezes it is considered a bad omen.

1098. తురక దాసరికి యీత మజ్జిగ.

The butter-milk of a Mussulman mendicant is Toddy.

Applied to pretended sanctity.

1099. తురకలు గొట్టగా చుక్కకెదురా.

When a Mussulman raid is expected is one [afraid of] facing Venus?

Are omens observed in times of danger?

Necessity has no law. (Latin.)*

1100. తురకలు లేని వూళ్లో దూదేకులవాడు సయ్యదుమియ్యా.

In a village where there are no Mussulmans, the cotton cleaner is Saiyid Miyân.

(See Nos. 830, 1412, 1413.)

He is made much of.—The *Saiyids* are the high-born descendants of Husain, grandson of Muhammad. *Miyân* is a title. The cotton cleaners are 'mongrel Mussulmans.' (Brown).

---

* Necessitas non habet legem.

1101. తులసి కోటలో వుమ్మేశినావేమిరా అంటే, యజ్ఞవేదిక అనుకొన్నాను అన్నాడట.

When a man was asked why he spat on the Tulasi-Kôṭa, he replied that he thought it was an altar.

The irreverent answer of a sacrilegious sceptic, an altar being still more sacred.—*Tulasî* is the holy basil (Ocimum Sacrum). *Tulasi-Kôṭa* is the Telugu name for the altar-like bed in which it is grown, in the inner yard of a Hindu house.

1102. తులసి వనములో గంజాయి మొక్క మొలిచినట్టు.

Like a hemp plant growing in a Tulasî garden.

(For *Ganjâyi* see No. 1034.)

A black sheep in the family.

1103. తుళ్లే యెద్దే గోనె మోశేది.

A frisky bullock carries a good load.

A spirited man works well.

1104. తూమెడు వడ్లు తూర్పారపెట్టేటప్పటికి యేదుము వడ్లు యెలుకలు తిని పోయినవి.

While he was winnowing one Tûm of rice, the rats devoured five Tûms.

(See Nos. 619, 1794.)

***Tûm* is the Indian bushel.**

1105. తృణము మేరువ, మేరువ తృణము.

A straw as Mount Mêru, Mount Mêru as a straw.

The slightest favour done to a good man is gratefully acknowledged, but a bad man forgets the greatest benefits.

1106. తెగించి దానము చేస్తాను తేరా పిడికెడు ఆళ్లు అన్నట్టు.

I have determined on being liberal, bring a handful of grain.

(For *Âḻḻu* see No. 82.)

1107. తెగించిన వానికి తెడ్డే లింగము.

The man who is determined [to worship] uses his ladle as a lingam.

Where there's a will, there's a way.

The will is everything. (Italian.)*

The will is the soul of the work. (German.)†

1108. తెగించి వెనకకు పోయినంత తెలివి తక్కువ లేదు.

There is no greater folly than turning back after having once ventured to run the risk.

(See No. 1890.)

Turning back after putting one's hand to the plough.

Fortune lost, nothing lost; courage lost, much lost; honour lost, more lost; soul lost, all lost. (Dutch.)‡

1109. తెగువ దేవేంద్ర పదవి.

Liberality leads to Indra's heaven.

1110. తెచ్చుకొంటే భోంచెయి జగన్నాయకా, లేకుంటే వూరకుండు జగన్నాయకా.

If you get any thing eat it O Jagannâyaka! if you don't get any thing do without it O Jagannâyaka!

Jagannâyaka is the idol at Jagannâtha, in Orissa.

---

* La volontà è tutto. † Der Wille ist des Werkes Seele.

‡ Goed verloren, niet verloren; moed verloren, veel verloren; eer verloren, meer verloren; ziel verloren, al verloren.

1111. తెడ్డు నాకి వుపవాసములు మాన్పినట్టు.

Like licking the ladle when you're hungry.

1112. తెడ్డు యేది అంటే, కొయ్య యేది అన్నట్టు.

One said "Where's the ladle ?" the other said "Where's the stick ?"

Two lazy fellows.

1113. తెడ్డు వుండగా చెయ్యి కాల్చుకొన్నట్టు.

Burning his hand when he had a ladle.

To stir the rice with.

1114. తెలకుల వాడి ముడ్డికింది రాయివలెనే.

Like the oilmonger's stone seat.

Of permanent utility.

1115. తెలివి తక్కువ, ఆకలి యెక్కువ.

Little sense, great appetite.

Eating one's senses away.

1116. తెలిశి తెలిశి బొందను పడ్డట్టు.

Although he knew the pit well, he fell into it.

1117. తెలిశే వరకు బ్రహ్మవిద్య, తెలిస్తే కూసువిద్య.

Before you know it, it's hard ; when you know it, it's easy.

(See No. 94.)

Every thing is easy when you know it.

All things are difficult before they are easy.

All beginnings are hard, said the thief, and began by stealing an anvil. (Dutch.)*

---

* Alle beginselen zijn zwaar, zei de dief, en voor de eerste maal stal hij een aanbeeld.

1118. తేమానం తెగబారెడు.

Your sluggishness is equal to a full fathom.

The word *Bâra* properly signifies the length of the arms extended as when a man stretches himself.

1119. తేరగాడికి యేమిరా తెల్ల జొన్ననూగు.

What is the roughness of the ear to the man who gets grain for nothing?

(See No. 1482.)

1120. తేర గుర్రము, తంగేడు బరికె.

A horse for nothing, a Tangêḍu switch.

Tangêḍu is the Cassia Auriculata.—" When you ride gratis you use your cudgel well." (Brown's Tel. Dicty.)

1121. తేర సొమ్ము బీర పీచు.

Property got for nothing is Bîra peel.

Bîra Kâya is the Luffa Foetida.

1122. తేలుకు పుట్టి చలిపురుగు అయినట్టు.

Born to a scorpion and becoming a black ant.

An unworthy scion of a noble stock.

1123. తేలుకు పెత్తనమిస్తే, తెల్లవార్లూ అంటపొడిచినదట.

When the scorpion was given power, it continued stinging until the morning.

(See No. 1540.)

Applied to the abuse of authority by evil persons.

1124. తేలుకు యెవరు అపకారము చేశినారు.

Who did evil to the scorpion?

Thoroughly bad by nature injuring others without provocation.

1125. తేళ్లలో కొండి, పాములలో పడగ.

The sting among the scorpions, the hood among the snakes.

The worst among the bad.

1126. తొంగున్న సుంకరి తలమూట దింపు అన్నట్టు.

Like a man waking up the sleeping custom house officer to help him to put down his load.

A "green trick."

1127. తొండకు వెలుగు సాక్షి.

The bear is witness for the bloodsucker *or*
The hedge is witness for the bloodsucker.

(For *Tonḍa* see No. 1128.)

According to the first interpretation, a band of Mahomedan freebooters, when seeking on one occasion to discover treasure which had been buried by the inhabitants of a plundered village, having perceived first a chameleon nodding on certain spots and afterwards a bear sniffing in the same places, spent much labour in digging up the earth, but all in vain.—The application is that natural habits are not to be taken notice of.

According to others, the hedge where the chameleon lives should be questioned as to the latter's veracity and character,—the application being that the evidence of one man should be corroborated by that of another.

Ask my chum if I am a thief. (Italian.)*

1128. తొండ ముదిరి వూసరవిల్లి అయినట్టు.

The Tonḍa grew old, and became an Ûsaravilli.

Tonḍa is a bloodsucker (chameleon) which when old is called *Ûsaravilli.*

Vice growing with age.

1129. తొంభై తొమ్మండ్రుగురు పోగయి తోలు చిరగ పొడిచినారు.

Ninety-nine persons joined together [attacked a man, but only] succeeded in scratching his skin.

A cowardly mob.

---

* Domanda al mio caro se sono ladro.

1130. తొక్కలేనమ్మ తొక్కులో నీళ్లు పోసినదట.

The woman who couldn't pound, put water into the condiments.

She was too lazy to pound the condiments and therefore purposely spoilt them.

1131. తొత్తుకు శివము యెత్తితే మొక్కక తీరునా.

If a slut be inspired by the Deity, can one escape saluting her?

Respect must be paid to those in power, however low their origin.

1132. తోక దొక్కిన పాములాగున లేచినాడు.

He sprang up like a serpent when its tail is trodden on.

Applied to a sudden burst of anger in any one on his evil ways being exposed.

1133. తోచీ తోచనమ్మ తోడికోడలి చెల్లెలి పెండ్లికి పోయినదట.

A stupid woman going to the marriage of her husband's brother's wife's sister.

Doing useless things.

1134. తోట కూరకు కడిగి పెట్టిన యెసరే చాలును.

The water which remains in greens after they have been washed is sufficient to boil them in.

ద.

1135. దండమయ్యా బాపనయ్యా అంటే, మీ తండ్రి నాటి పాత బాకీ యిచ్చి పొమ్మన్నాడట.

When the Śûdra saluted the Brahman, the latter in return asked him to pay an old debt due by his father.

Rudeness in return for civility.

1136. దండుగకు రూపాయీలూ, తద్దినానకు కూరలూ పోగు కాకుండా పోవు.

Rupees to meet the exorbitant demands of Government, and vegetables for the annual ceremony of a deceased relative are never wanting.

Foolishly giving aid in matters which bring no personal profit.

1137. దండులోకి పోతే, రెంట్లో వకటి.

If you go to the wars, it will be one out of two.

Either victory or defeat.

1138. దగ్గితే నిలవని ముక్కు తుమ్మితే నిలుచునా.

Will the nose that can't stand a cough bear a sneeze?

(See Nos. 458, 1096, 1324.)

1139. దగ్గిరికి పిలిచి దాసరీ నీ కన్ను లొట్ట అన్నట్టు.

Beckoning to a religious mendicant and then telling him that one of his eyes is hollow.

Leading a person to suppose you wish to confer a benefit on him, and then insulting him.

1140. దత్త పుత్ర శోకము.

Grief for an adopted son.

Slight grief.

1141. దయగల మొగుడు దండుకు పోతూ, రోలు తీశి రొమ్మున వేల వేశి పోయినాడట.

When the kind husband went to the wars, he hung the mortar round his wife's neck.

(See No. 368.)

Rôlu is a large heavy mortar used for pounding rice in.

Said ironically of a bad husband cruel to the last.

1142. దయ దర్రుమంటే, నెత్తి చుర్రుమంటుంది.

When your favor answers my call with a Darr-rr my head will ache with a Çurr-rr.

Darr is a whirring sound; *Çurr* is applied to acute or burning pain.

Said by a man to another in whose friendship he puts no faith.

1143. దయ్యపు కంటికి పేల గింజ వేంగెము.

In the eye of a devil, parched grain is evil.

1144. దయ్యము కొట్టనూ బిడ్డ బ్రతకనా.

When the devil attacks will the child live?

Said of a meddling fool.

1145. దయ్యముల ముందర బిడ్డ బ్రతుకునా.

Could a child live in front of devils?

1146. దరిద్రుడు తల కడగపోతే, వడిగండ్ల వాన వెంబడే వచ్చినది.

When the poor man was about to anoint his head, it began to hail.

Difficulties always attend an unfortunate person.

He who is born to misfortune stumbles as he goes, and though he fall on his back will fracture his nose. (German.)*

1147. దర్యామే కష్కష్.

A Poppy seed in the ocean.

(Corrupted from the Hindustani).

A drop in the ocean.

---

* Wer Unglück soll haben, der stolpert im Grase, fällt auf den Rücken und bricht seine Nase.

1148. దశ దానాలకూ తోటకూర కట్ట.

For the ten gifts, [I give you] a bundle of greens.

(See No. 1321.)

The *Daśa Dânâlu* (ten gifts to Brahmans) are as follows :—

గోభూతిలహిరణ్యాజ్యవాసోధాన్యగుడానిచ।
రౌప్యంలవణమిత్యేతేదశదానాఃప్రకీర్తితాః॥

A cow; land; sesamum seed; gold; ghee; cloth; grain; molasses; silver; and salt.

Cheating the Brahmans.

1149. దాఁగ పోయిన చోట దయ్యాలు పట్టుకొన్నట్టు.

The devils caught him in the place he went to hide in.

One ill calls another. (Italian.)*

1150. దానము అయితే యివ్వలేను, దండగ అయితే పెట్టగలను.

As for charity, I can't give; as for fines, I can pay.

Said by a quarrelsome ruffian.

1151. దారిని పొయ్యే వ్యాజ్యము కొని తెచ్చుకొన్నట్టు.

Buying and bringing a suit which was going along the road.

Buying the right to carry on a heavy law suit from a stranger.

(See No. 974.)

1152. దాసరి తప్పు దండముతో సరి.

The crime of a Dâsari is excused with an apology.

(For *Dâsari* see No. 111.)

1153. దాసరి పాటకు ముష్టి ముజరా.

For the song of a Dâsari an alms is the payment.

All that his singing is worth.

Small payment for bad work.

---

* Un mal chiama l'otro.

1154. దాసరి పాట్లు పెరుమాళ్లకు యెరుక.

The troubles of a Dâsari are known only to Perumâḷ.

(For *Perumâḷ* see No. 761.)

1155. దాసరివా జంగమవా అంటే, ముందరి వూరికొద్దీ అన్నాడట.

When a mendicant was asked whether he was a Dâsari or a Jangam (i. e. a follower of Vishṇu or Śiva) he replied "Oh that depends on the next village!"

A time server.

1156. దాసీ కొడుకయినా కాసు గలవాడు రాజు.

A man with money is a king though he be the son of a slave girl.

1157. దాస్తిని వేరుండు మొగుడా.

I have saved [money] live separate with me, husband.

Said by a wife to her husband to induce him to quit his father's house. After he had yielded to her importunity and left his father's house, he enquired the amount of her savings when she replied "I have saved myself for you."

1158. దిక్కులేని దివాణముగా వున్నది.

A government which affords no protection.

1159. దిక్కులేని యింట్లో దయ్యాలు కాపురము చేస్తవి.

In a neglected house, devils take up their abode.

1160. దిక్కులేని వారికి దేవుడే దిక్కు.

God is the help of the helpless.

God is where He was.

1161. దిగులు పడితే, వెతలు తీరునా.

If you fear, will the pain be less?

1162. దినగండము వెయ్యేండ్లు ఆయుస్సు.

Daily danger of death, but duration of life a thousand years.

Snakes are believed to live 1000 years if they do not meet with a violent death.

Applied to a man always in danger of losing his situation.

1163. దినము మంచిదని తెల్లవార్లూ దొంగిలినట్టు.

Trusting to the "lucky day" the thief let the dawn overtake him.

Taking advantage of liberty.

1164. దివిటీ కింది దీపము.

A lamp under a torch.

One insignificant before the other.

1165. దివ్వె తీశిన గూడు వలె వున్నది.

Like a niche with the lamp taken out of it.

The reality wanting.

1166. దిసమొలవాడా కాళ్లకట్టు వానికి కప్పుమన్నట్టు.

Like saying "O naked man! cover him lying at your feet."

1167. దిసమొలవాడి దగ్గిరికి దిగంబరుడు వచ్చి బట్ట అడిగినట్టు.

Like one naked man asking another naked man for a cloth.

1168. దీపము ముడ్డి కింద చీకటి.

It is always dark underneath a lamp.

Roguery hides under the judgment seat.

1169. దీపము వుండగానే చక్కపెట్టుకో వలసినది.

Put all things in order while the lamp is yet burning.

(See Nos. 77, 507, 508.)

Make good use of your opportunities.

1170. దుక్కిటెద్దు దేశాంతరము వెళ్లినట్టు.

Like the ox being away when wanted for the plough.

Absent when most wanted.

1171. దున్నక చల్లితే, కొయ్యక పండినది.

When the field was sown without being ploughed it yielded without being reaped.

i. e. it yielded nothing.

If you neglect the use of the right means you must expect poor results.

1172. దున్నపోతు యీనినదంటే, దూడను కట్టి వేయుమన్నట్టు.

When one said "The male buffalo has calved" the other replied "Then tie up the calf."

(See No. 390.)

1173. దున్నబోతే దూడలలోనూ, మేయబోతే ఆవులలోనూ.

When [wanted for] ploughing it goes among the calves; when grazing it goes with the cows.

(See Nos. 73, 518, 1070, 1331, 1886.)

The best at eating, the worst at working.

1174. దున్నేవాండ్లకు లేళ్ల చూపించినట్టు.

Like pointing out antelope to ploughers.

Diverting the attention of people from their work.

1175. దుబ్బు కౌగెడు, వెన్ను మూరెడు, దూసితే దోశెడు, వూదితే యేమీ లేదు.

The stock of the millet is as large as you can embrace; the ear is a cubit in length; when you pluck the corn out it is a double handful; when you blow all goes.

Great show but no reality.

1176. దుష్టునికి దూరముగా వుండ వలశినది.

Shun a wicked man.

1177. దూడ కుడిచినట్టా దుత్తలో పడ్డట్టా.

Is it that the calf has sucked, or that [the milk] has fallen into the pail?

In either way beneficial.

1178. దూడ కుడిస్తేగాని, ఆవు చేపదు.

Unless the calf sucks, the cow will not let milk into her udder.

1179. దూడలేని పాడి దుఃఖపు పాడి.

Where there is no calf, the milk is got with pain.

1180. దూడా బఱ్ఱే వుండగా గుంజ అరిచినదన్నట్టు.

Like blaming the post when the calf or the she buffalo bellowed.

1181. దూరపు కొండలు నునుపు, దగ్గిరికి పోతే రాళ్లూ గుండ్లూ.

Mountains are smooth at a distance, but rugged when near.

'Tis distance lends enchantment to the view,
And robes the mountain in its azure hue. Campbell.

1182. దెబ్బకు దయ్యము సహా అడలుతుంది.

A devil even takes fright at a blow.

Strong measures will set things to right.

1183. దేవుడిచ్చునేగాని తినిపించునా.

God will give, but will He put the food in your mouth ?

God helps those who help themselves.

1184. దేవుడితోడు నా మీద దయ వుంచ వలశినది.

I adjure you by God to show me favor.

Attempting to obtain a person's favor by force.

1185. దేవుడి పెండ్లికి అందరూ పెద్దలే.

At the marriage ceremony of a god all are rulers.

Where there is no head, every one does what he likes.

1186. దేవుడు వరమిచ్చినా పూజారి వరమివ్వడు.

Although God grant a boon, yet the priest will not grant it.

1187. దొంగకు చేను పచ్చి లేదు.

The thief does not care if the corn be not quite ripe.

(See No. 1199.)

A man is not particular about that which does not belong to him.

1188. దొంగకు తలుపు తీసి దొరను లేపేవాడు.

He opens the door for the robber and then awakes his master.

A double dealing rascal.

1189. దొంగకు దొరికినదే చాలును.

A thief is content with what he gets.

(See No. 1187.)

1190. దొంగ చిక్కెనోయి అంటే, కరిచేనోయి అన్నాడట.

When one cried out "I have got the thief" the other said "Take care! he'll bite."

A cowardly fellow.

1191. దొంగ చెయ్యి దాచిపెట్టితే, అమావాస్య వచ్చినప్పుడు అల్లల్లాడి నట్టు.

The thief's hand that was kept began to shake when the dark night of the new moon came.

The time it had been accustomed to steal.

1192. దొంగతో కూడా దయ్యము వెంబడే వచ్చును.

The devil follows close on the thief.

To urge him on.

1193. దొంగను తేలు కుట్టినట్టు.

Like a robber stung by a scorpion.

A man does not cry out when he suffers from his own folly.

1194. దొంగను పుట్టించిన వాడు మతిభ్రష్టును పుట్టించక మానడు.

He that created a knave will not fail to create a dupe.

A fool only is cheated.

1195. దొంగల తల్లికి యేడవ భయము.

A robber's mother fears to weep.

When her son is caught.

A person will suffer rather than criminate or bring shame upon himself.

1196. దొంగలు కొట్టిన ఆరు మాసములకు కుక్కలు మొరిగినవి.

The dogs barked six months after the robbery.

1197. దొంగలు తోలిన గొడ్లు యే రేవున దాటినా వకటే.

It matters not which ford was crossed by the stolen ox.

When one suffers a loss the cause matters little.

1198. దొంగ వాకిట మంచము వేసినట్టు.

Putting your bed in the yard of a thief's house.

To watch his doings.

Outwitting a crafty man.

1199. దొంగవాడి పెండ్లాము యెప్పుడూ ముండమోపే.

A thief's wife is always a widow.

She is always in danger of becoming one.

1200. దొంగా మనిషే.

A thief is but a man.

1201. దొంగిల బోతే మంగలం దొరికినది.

When he went to steal, he only got an earthen dish.

Disappointment in evil designs.

1202. దొడ్డెడు గొడ్లను దొంగలు తోలుకొని పోతే, గొడ్డు గేదె శ్రీ మహా లక్ష్మి అయినది.

After the whole of the cattle had been stolen from the shed, the barren buffalo became as valuable as Mahâ Lakshmî (the goddess of fortune).

1203. దొరలు యిచ్చిన పాలుకన్నా ధరణి యిచ్చిన పాలు మేలు.

The share given by the earth is better than that given by the government.

Free lands are better when fertile, than shares of grain allotted by government.

1204. దొరికిన సొమ్ముకు దొంగ అవుతాడా.

Does a man become a thief by finding property?

1205. దోవలో కూర్చుండి దొబ్బులు తిన్నట్టు.

Sitting in the middle of the road and being abused by every passer by.

1206. ద్వారపూడి పచ్చెపువాడి వత్తు.

Like a pickpocket of Dvârapûḍi.

Dvârapûḍi is a notorious village in the Godavery District.

ధ.

1207. ధనియాల జాతి.

The coriander-seed caste.

Said of Kômaṭis (No. 712) because treating a Kômaṭi roughly is the only way of dealing with him, as rubbing the coriander-seed before it is sown is the only way of making it sprout.

1208. ధర్మపురిలో దొంగిలించబోతూ ధార్వాడలోనుంచి వంగుకొని పోయినాడట.

[The thief] going to rob in Dharmapuri went crouching from Dhârwâḍa (Dharwar).

(See Nos. 461, 1696.)

1209. ధాష్టీకానికి ధర్మము లేదు, గుడ్డి కంటికి చూపు లేదు.

There is no justice in oppression, and no sight in a blind eye.

1210. ధీరుడయినా కావలె, దీనుడయినా కావలె.

You must get a hero or a beggar [for a husband].

1211. ధైర్యములేని రాజు, యోచనలేని మంత్రి.

A king without courage, a minister without judgment.

1212. ధ్వంస పారాయణము, దంటు మంట.

Useless reading, like the blazing of millet stalks.

న.

1213. నంగి వంగలు మేస్తే నారికేళాలు దూడమేశినది అన్నాడట.

" When the Nangi ate up the brinjals, the calf ate up the cocoanuts" said he.

(For *Vanga* see No. 97.)

A certain Śûdra named Vêṇu before going on a pilgrimage delivered over charge of his brinjal garden to a Komaṭi called Kustumbha. When he returned and applied for his garden his friend told him that the *Nangi* had eaten up all the brinjals. Vêṇu knew that no such animal existed, but remained quiet and waited his opportunity to pay off the Kômaṭi. Shortly afterwards Kustumbha required a man to watch his cocoanut garden and engaged Vêṇu for this work. The Śûdra sold all the cocoanuts and appropriated the proceeds. On being questioned by the Kômaṭi, Vêṇu told him that the calf had eaten all the cocoanuts. " How is that?" asked Kustumbha, " How could it reach them?" "Oh" replied Vêṇu " When the *Nangi* ate the brinjals could not the calf eat the cocoanuts?" The Kômaṭi, knowing his own dishonesty, could give no answer.

1214. నంగీ నమలక మింగవే అంటే, వుడికిన చేపలు కరుస్తవి అన్నదట.

"Swallow without chewing, Nangi."—"The boiled fish are biting me" she replied.

(See Nos. 150, 483, 1839, 2084.)

Nangi is a name given to a woman who is never at a loss for an excuse however paltry.

1215. నంది అంటే నంది, పంది అంటే పంది.

If he says it's Śiva's bull, it is Śiva's bull; if he says it's a pig, it is a pig.

(See No. 1082.)

Said of the power of a great and unjust man.

1216. నంబి పెట్టినదే ప్రసాదము.

What the priest gives is sacred.

1217. నంబీ, తంబళీ, నాగుబామూ, చెవుల పిల్లీ, యెదురైతే చేటువస్తుంది.

If you meet a Nambi, a Tambaḷi, a cobra da capello, or a hare, it will be worse for you.

(For *Nambi* see No. 274 and for *Tambaḷi* see No. 178.)

1218. నంబీ నంబీ నా పెండ్లికి యేమి సహాయము చేస్తావంటే, నీ పెండ్లికి నేను యెదురుగా రాకపోవడమే సహాయమన్నాడట.

"O Nambi! Nambi! what assistance will you render at my marriage?" said one. "I will help you by my absence," replied the priest.

Meeting a *Nambi* is an ill omen. (See No. 1217.)

Negative advantages.

1219. నక్క గూసి పిల్లలకు దోవ తెచ్చును.

The jackal howls and brings evil upon its whelps.

1220. నక్క జిత్తులన్నీ నావద్ద వుండగా నన్ను మోసము చేశెనే తాబేటి బుర్ర.

Although I was as cunning as a fox, I was deceived by a tortoise.

A man sat on the back of a tortoise not knowing what it was, and sank with it.

1221. నక్కను చూచిన వాడెల్లా వేటకాడే.

Every one who sees a jackal hunts it.

1222. నక్క పోయిన వెనక బొక్క కొట్టుకొన్నట్టు.

After the jackal had departed, the hole lamented and wept.

Great sorrow in a household.

1223. నక్క యెక్కడ, దేవలోకమెక్కడ.

Where is the jackal ? where is heaven ?

What prospect has the jackal of entering heaven ?

A hopeless idea.

1224. నక్క రేలకాయ సామ్యము.

Like the effect of the Cassia fruit on a jackal.

Rêla is the Cassia (Cathartocarpus) Fistula.

1225. నక్కలు యెరగని బొక్కలూ నాగులు యెరగని పుట్టలూ వున్నవా.

Are there holes unknown to jackals, or anthills to snakes ?

1226. నట్టేట పుట్టి మునిగినట్టు.

Like a basket boat sinking as it reached the middle of the river.

A break down half way, in any business.

1227. నడమంత్రపు దాసరి పొద్దుమానము యెరగడు.

A man who has become a Dâsari in middle age, is not punctual in his duties.

(For *Dâsari* see No. 114.)

Business habits must be learnt in youth.

1228. నడమంత్రపు శిరి, నరాలమీది కురుపు.

A fortune obtained in middle age is like a boil on the sinews.

It spoils a man.

1229. నడవలేని అమ్మకు నాలుగు పక్కలా సవారి.

A lady who can't walk must have carriages on all sides.

Said of a lazy woman.

1230. నడిచే కొద్దీ డొంక, పెట్టే కొద్దీ కుదురు.

As you walk you widen the path, as you put [earth] you raise the ledge.

Donka is a path between two fields. *Kuduru* is a ledge made with earth round a mortar in which grain is pounded.

1231. నత్తగుల్లలన్నీ వకరేవున, ముత్యపు చిప్పలన్నీ వకరేవున.

Common oysters are in one spot, and pearl oysters in another.

(See Nos. 736, 1668, 1686, 1346, 1969.)

1232. నన్ను నేనే యెరగను, నిన్ను నేనేమి యెరుగుదును అన్నాడట.

He said "I don't know myself, how can I know you?"

Said of a supercilious fellow.

1233. నమల కూడని నారికేళము.

A cocoanut which cannot be chewed.

(See Nos. 253, 737, 1729, 1757.)

A difficult business.

1234. నమాజు చెయ్యబోతే, మశీదు మెడను పడ్డది.

When he went to pray, the mosque fell on his neck.

The management of the mosque was forced upon him.

1235. నమ్మితి రామన్నా అంటే, నా అంతవాణ్ని చేస్తానన్నట్టు.

When a man expressed his trust in Râmanna, the latter promised to make him as great a man as himself.

Râmanna was really a beggar though pretending to be a great man.

1236. నమ్మి నానబోసితే, పులిసి బుర్రటలాడెను.

I trusted it and put it to soak, it became acid and began to ferment.

Misplaced confidence.

1237. నరము లేని నాలుక నాలుగు విధాలు.

The tongue without nerves goes all ways.

When the conscience is dead, moral restraint disappears.

1238. నరుని కంట నల్లరాయి పగులును.

By the look of a man's eye, granite will be broken.

The power of an evil eye.

1239. నలపాకము భీమపాకముగా వున్నది.

It is like the cooking of Nala and Bhîma.

Said ironically to a bad cook.

1240. నల్లిని గూర్చి మంచానికి పెట్లు.

Beating a bedstead on account of the bugs.

(See Nos. 266, 1940.)

1241. నల్లేరు మీద బండి పారినట్లు.

Like a cart running over Nallêru.

Nallêru is the Vitis (Cissus) Quadrangularis.

1242. నవాబు సాతుల్లా ఖాన్ అవ్వ నాటిది.

Of the days of Nawâb Sa'âdat-ullah Khân's grandmother.

As old as the hills.

1243. నవాయతీ పొట్టా తమలపాకుల కట్టా తడుపుతూ వుండవలెను.

You must keep a Nawâyati lad and a bundle of betel leaves wet.

Nawâyati is a sect of Muhammadans (See the "Qanoon-e-Islam" page 12 et seq.).—Water is thrown on betel leaves by the bazar-men to keep them fresh and to prevent their being blown away.

1244. నమిలేవానికన్నా మింగేవాడు ఘనుడు.

He who swallows is better off than he who chews.

He gets along at a greater pace.

(See No. 1885.)

Said of an energetic man.

1245. నవ్వ చెప్పేవాడు చెడ జెప్పును, యేడవ చెప్పేవాడు బ్రతక చెప్పును.

He who speaks to make you laugh, speaks to your ruin; he who speaks to make you weep, speaks to your profit.

A friend's frown is better than a fool's smile.

1246. నవ్విన నాపచేనే పండుతున్నది.

The field of young millet which is laughed at will be fruitful.

Hindu cultivators assemble round a field which is in want of rain and laugh at it, taunting it with its unfruitfulness. By this means they believe that rain is brought down.

1247. నవ్వుతూ తిట్టితివో నరకాన పడితివో.

Laughing, you reviled, and you have fallen into hell!

1248. నవ్వు నాలుగందాల నష్టకారి.

Silly laughter produces much harm.

Laughter is the hiccup of a fool.

1249. నవ్వే ఆడదాన్ని యేడ్చే మొగవాణ్ని నమ్మరాదు.

A laughing woman and a crying man should not be trusted.

1250. నాం బడా, దర్శన్ థోడా.

Great in name, but little to look at.

(See Nos. 230, 240, 278, 613, 1542, 1796.)

The words of this proverb are Hindustâni.

1251. నాకు ఆయుష్యమస్తు, నాకు ఆరోగ్యమస్తు.

Let me have long life! let me have health!

(See No. 1253.)

A selfish man blessing himself.

Priests bless themselves first. (German.)*

---

* Pfaffen segnen sich zuerst.

1252. నాకు పరీక్షా, నా రాగి చెంబుకు పరీక్షా.

Am I to be examined, or is my copper pot?

Said by an ignorant Vaidika who with great pretentions to learning knew nothing, and wished his pot to be examined instead of himself.

1253. నాకూ నా పిల్లలకూ నూరేండ్లు ఆయుస్సు, నా పెనిమిటికి లోకము తోటిపాటు.

As for me and my children, let our age be a hundred years; as for my husband, let him take his chance in the world.

(See Nos. 1251, 1818.)

The prayer of a wife who did not love her lord.

1254. నాకూ శిగ్గులేదు, రేపు వచ్చే అమావాస్యకూ శిగ్గులేదు.

I am not ashamed, the Amâvâsya which is coming to-morrow is not ashamed.

1255. నాకోడి కుంపటి లేకపోతే, యేలాగు తెల్లవారుతున్నది.

If it were not for my cock and chafing-dish, how would the world go round?

(See No. 750.)

A story is told of an old woman who fancied that the crowing of her cock woke the whole village, and that all the inhabitants were dependent on her for fire.

Daylight will come, though the cock do not crow. (Danish.)*

1256. నాగవల్లి తీరినట్టు.

The last day of the marriage over.

Or, according to some,

The great day of the marriage has come.

Nâgavalli is the concluding ceremony at a Hindu's marriage.

Dulness after gaity, *or* festivity at its height.

---

* Det bliver vel Dag om end Hanen ei galer.

1257. నాగవల్లి నిష్ఠురము.

Squabbling on the fourth day of the marriage.

(For *Nágavalli* see No. 1256.)

Any disputes with regard to the presents, &c., are brought forward on the fourth day ; until then no one can open his mouth.

Forgetting many past benefits on account of one slight fault.

1258. నా చెయ్యి నొస్తున్నది, నీ చేత్తో మొత్తుకో.

My hand is aching, beat with your hand upon your mouth.

Mourning by proxy.

1259. నా చేతి మాత్ర, వైకుంఠ యాత్ర.

The pill in my hand, [will take you on] a pilgrimage to Vaikuṇṭha (Vishṇu's heaven).

(See No. 478.)

Said jokingly to a quack.

Bleed him, and purge him ; if he dies, bury him. (Spanish.)*

1260. నాజూకు నక్కలు దేకితే, నరిశిన గడ్డము కుక్కలు పీకినవి.

When the jackals slid on his delicacy, the dogs pulled out his grey beard.

Said of a hoary old humbug.

1261. నాటకములు బూటకములు, బోటితనములు నీటులు.

Plays are unreal, your wit is your beauty.

1262. నాథుడు లేని రాజ్యము నానా దారులు అయినది.

A kingdom without a ruler becomes disorganized in all ways.

---

* Sangrarle y purgarle ; si se muriere, enterrarle.

1263. నానాటికి తీశిపెట్టు నాగంభొట్లు.

Pine away day by day, Nâgambhoṭlu.

Said to a hypocritical Brahman, who was neglected when his tricks became known.

1264. నానా రుచులు పారి నాలికమీద కొరివి పెట్టుకొన్నట్టే వున్నది.

All kinds of savours run over my tongue, [and taste] just as if a firebrand was put on it.

Said by a man to a wretched cook.

1265. నా పతివ్రతా ధర్మము నా మొదటి పెనిమిటికి తెలుసును.

My chastity is known to my first husband.

Said by a widow who had passed herself off as a maid, and married again.

1266. నా పప్పు కలిశినంతా నేనే తింటాను.

I will eat as much of the rice as my Dâl has been mixed with.

(For *Dâl* see No. 183.)

Said by the greater of two men who, when travelling together, had mixed their food, the big man having brought dâl and the other rice.

Applied to a grasping, selfish man.

1267. నా పాదమే గతి అన్నట్టు.

My foot is my safety.

The disciples of a Guru on commencing to cross a river said "May the holiness of our master's feet preserve us!" After they had crossed it in safety the self righteous Guru believing that his presence had preserved them, stepped into the water saying "My foot is my safety" and was carried away by the stream, and drowned.

1268. నా ముందర బానెడు గంజా.

What is a big pot of gruel to me ?

Said by a glutton.

1269. నా యింటికి నేనే పెద్దను, పిల్లికి పెట్టరా పంగనామము.

I am the head of my house, I order you to put a Panganâmam on the cat's face.

(For *Panganâmam* see No. 780.)

The folly of a mean man in power.

1270. నాలికా నాలికా వీపుకు దెబ్బలు తేక.

O Tongue! Tongue! don't bring strokes on my back.

The tongue talks at the head's cost.

Let not the tongue utter what the head must pay for. (Spanish.)*

1271. నాళ్లల్లోకెల్లా చిన్ననాడే మేలు.

Of all times, childhood is the best, *or*
Of all sects, the little sect is the best.

Nâḍu signifies a sect, it also means time. When Appâji the minister was asked by the king which sect was superior to the others, he cleverly evaded the question, by making a pun on the word.

1272. నా వేలు పుచ్చుకొని నా కన్నే పొడిచినావా.

Have you poked my eye with my own finger?

To confute a man's reasoning with his own arguments.

1273. నా శిరికన్నా అక్క శిరి ఘనము, అక్క శిరికన్నా నా శిరి ఘనము.

My sister's fortune is greater than mine, and my fortune is greater than my sister's.

One no better off than the other.

---

* No diga la lengua por do pague la cabeza.

1274. నిండు కుండ తొణకదు.

A full pot will not spill.

(See Nos. 454, 502.)

True learning is humble.

Empty vessels give the greatest sound.

Deep rivers move in silence, shallow brooks are noisy.

1275. నిజమాడితే నిష్ఠురము.

If you tell the truth [it causes] annoyance.

(See Nos. 320, 321.)

Truth is bitter food. (Danish.)*

1276. నిజము నిలకడమీద తెలుసును.

Truth will be known in time.

Truth is the daughter of time.

1277. నిత్యము చచ్చేవారికి యేడ్చేవారు యెవరు.

Who are the mourners over people that die every day?

Those who always say their death is near.

Said of a man continually requiring to be corrected in his work.

1278. నిద్రపొయ్యేవాణ్ని లేపవచ్చునుగాని, మేలుకొన్నవాణ్ని లేపకూడదు.

You can wake a person who is asleep, but not one who is awake.

None so deaf as those who won't hear.

None so blind as those who won't see.

---

* Sandhed er en suur Kost.

1279. నిద్రపోయిన వాడి కాళ్లకు మొక్కినట్టు.

Like falling at the feet of a sleeping man.

Useless endeavours at a wrong time.

1280. నిన్న కుప్ప నేడు ఆళ్లు.

Yesterday there was a heap [of cut corn], to-day there is Âḷḷu [thrashed].

(For *Âḷḷu* see No. 82.)

Sudden advancement, speedy progress.

Yesterday a cowherd, to-day a cavalier. (Spanish.)*

1281. నిప్పుకు చెదలంటునా.

Will white ants attack fire?

1282. నిప్పుకూ నీళ్లకూ వుండే స్నేహము.

The friendship existing between fire and water.

They agree like cats and dogs.

1283. నిప్పు కొట్టితే రెండు అవునుగాని, నీళ్లు కొట్టితే రెండు అవునా.

If you cut fire it will be divided, but if you cut water will it divide?

(See Nos. 469, 1949.)

Inseparable friendship.

They are finger and thumb.

1284. నిప్పు ముట్టనిదీ చెయ్యి కాలదు.

Don't touch fire, and your hand won't be burnt.

(See Nos. 148, 836.)

Don't play with the bear if you don't want to be bit. (Italian.)†

---

* Ayer vaquero, hoy caballero.
† Non ischerzar coll'orso, se non vuoi esser morso.

1285. నిప్పుల బుర్రకు నీళ్ల బుర్ర.

A bowl of water to a bowl of fire.

An answer to a threat.

1286. నిప్పులు వళ్లో కట్టుకొని వున్నాడు.

He has fire in his skirt.

1287. నిమ్మకు నీరెత్తినట్టు.

Like watering a lime tree.

1288. నిర్భాగ్యునికి నిద్ర, అభాగ్యునికి ఆకలి.

Sleep to an unfortunate man, hunger to a poor man.

Over sleeping is considered by Hindus to be a sign of misfortune, and hunger a sign of poverty.

1289. నిలవ నీడా పట్ట కొమ్మా లేదు.

No shade to stand under, or branch to clutch.

Helpless and forlorn.

1290. నిలుచుండడానకు జాగా దొరికితే, కూర్చుండడానకు అప్పుడే దొరుకుతున్నది.

If you get a place to stand in, you will soon be able to get room to sit in.

Give me a seat, and I will make myself room to lie down. (Spanish.)*

1291. నివురు కప్పిన నిప్పు సామిత.

Fire covered with embers.

Said of a very learned and humble man.

---

* Dame donde me asiente, que yo me haré donde me acueste.

1292. నిశ్చితార్థము నాడే నీలగ వలశినది, నాగవల్లి దాకా వుండడము నా అదృష్టమే గదా.

He ought to have died on the day of betrothal, it is my good fortune that he has lived until the fourth day of the marriage.

Said ironically by a girl who had been married to an old man who died before the completion of the ceremonies.

1293. నిష్ఠ నీళ్ల పాలు, మంత్రము మాలల పాలు.

His religious rites go to the water, and his Mantras to the Pariahs.

Said of a great formalist.

Most of the religious rites of the Brahmans are performed with water. The sacred formulas (Mantras) ought according to the Śástras to be pronounced in a low voice, inaudible to the people.

1294. నీ అరచేతికి పండ్లు వస్తే చూతాము.

When teeth grow in the palm of your hand, I'll listen to you.

1295. నీకు రానిదీ నాకు విన సహించనిదీ పాడుమన్నట్టు.

Sing something that you don't know and that I cannot bear to hear.

Asking something which is impossible.

1296. నీకు రానిదీ, నేను విననిదీ, భూలోకములో లేనిదీ చెప్పుమన్నట్టు.

Tell me something that you never knew, that I never heard, and that never existed in the world.

1297. నీకు వక దండము, నీ బువ్వకు వక దండము.

A bow to you, a bow to your food.

Said when offered bad food.

1298. నీకూ నాకూ కాదు, రోకలెత్తి తలబ్రాలు పోయుమన్నట్టు.

You and I don't like each other; let us throw the mortar over each other's heads instead of rice.

(For *Rólu* see No. 1141.)

Said by one of an ill matched pair at their marriage.—*Talabrâlu* is the rice poured over the head of the bride and bridegroom.

1299. నీతి కాని మాట రాతి వేటు.

An unjust word is the throwing of a stone.

1300. నీతిలేని వాడు కోతికన్న బీడు.

An unjust man is worse than a monkey.

1301. నీ నొసటనే ప్రొద్దు పొడిచినదా.

Did the sun rise on *your* forehead only?

Are you the greatest in the world?

1302. నీ పత్తుపణం పాడుగానూ, నా వొరుపణం కుప్పలు కుప్పలు పెట్టు.

Ruin take your ten fanams, put my one fanam in heaps.

The words *Pattu paṇam* and *Oru paṇam* are Tamil.

Said by a Telugu man, ignorant of Tamil, who was owed one fanam, and owed ten.

1303. నీ పెండ్లి పాడుగా వున్నది గాని నా పెండ్లి తాంబూలానికి రమ్మన్నాడట.

Your marriage is rubbish, come to my marriage and betel.

1304. నీ పేరంటమే అక్కరలేదంటే, కరకంచు చీరకట్టుకొని వస్తానన్నదట.

If you refuse to admit me to the entertainment given in your house for the poor, I will come to dinner in a rich dress.

(See Nos. 1060, 1962.)

Said by a poor woman to a rich man.—At many Brahminical ceremonies gifts and food are distributed to the wives of the Vaidikas while a superior entertainment is provided for those of the Laukikas of the Niyyôgi class.

Forcing oneself upon another.

1305. నీ ముష్టి లేకపోతే మానెగాని, నీ కుక్కను కట్టివెయ్యి.

If there are no alms for me, never mind, but tie up your dog.

(See No. 311.)

Said by a beggar.

1306. నీ యెడమ చెయ్యి తియ్యి, నా పుర్ర చెయ్యి పెట్టుతాను.

Take away your left hand, I will use my sinister hand.

(See No. 295.)

As broad as long.

1307. నీరు నీరు వంకనే పారుతున్నది.

Water runs towards water.

Men haste to help those of their own caste, &c.

1308. నీరు పల్లమెరుగును, నిజము దేవుడెరుగును.

Water finds the low ground, God knows the truth.

(See Nos. 1401, 1910.)

1309. నీలి నీళ్లకు పోతే, బావి లోతుకు పోయినది.

When the jade went to the well, the water was too low.

Said of a lazy person glad of any excuse to get off work.

1310. నీళ్లలో నిమ్మలు బ్రతికినవి, అడివిలో తుమ్మలు బ్రతికినవి.

Lime trees lived in the water, acacia trees lived in the jungle.

(For *Tumma* see No. 360.)

Very common.

1311. నీళ్లు మూటకట్టినట్టు.

Tying up water in a bundle.

He draws water with a sieve.

1312. నీవు కాకపోతే నీ అబ్బ మరివకడాయెను.

If you won't do it, your father will.

i. e. a better person.

1313. నీవు చచ్చిన రోజూ లేదు, నేను యేడ్చిన రోజూ లేదు.

The day of your death has not come, nor the day of my mourning.

(See No. 1263.)

Said by a wife who hated her husband.

1314. నీవు చస్తే లోకమెల్లా బొకెలా.

If you were to die, would the whole earth be bones?

(See No. 1337.)

1315. నీవు పెట్టకపోయినా పెట్టేయిల్లు చూపించుమన్నట్టు.

Though you don't give alms, point out a house where they do.

1316. నీవు వకందుకు పోస్తే, నేను వకందుకు తాగుతున్నాను.

If you pour for one thing, I drink for another.

A woman poured out stale rice-water to make a man eat less solid food afterwards. The drink however has the property of increasing the appetite.

Diamond cut diamond.

1317. నీ సాకు చట్టుబండలు కానూ, నాలుగు బేకులు బేకు అన్నాడట.

May your Sâkus become stones! Give me four Bêkus.

Said by a greedy Telugu man at an entertainment given by a Canarese gentleman. The servant handed round the dishes a second time with the usual enquiry "*Sâku?*" (enough?) Some of the guests would reply "*Bêku*" (wanted) and help themselves moderately. The Telugu man not understanding Canarese, cried out "None of your *Sâkus*, give me some of your *Bêkus*."

1318. నుయ్యి తియ్యబోతే, దయ్యము బయిలు వెళ్లినది.

When they began to dig a well, a devil came out.

Applied to a sudden and heavy misfortune.

1319. నువ్వుకు నూరు రోగాలు.

A hundred diseases to the Sesamum.

Nuvvu is the Sesamum Indicum. The Sesamum crops are peculiarly liable to attacks of sap worm, blight, &c.

1320. నువ్వులూ నూనే వకటి, గాండ్లవాడు వేరు.

Oil seed and oil are one, the oil-crusher is another.

(For *Nuvvu* see No. 1319.)

Joining to oppose a common enemy.

1321. నూటికి నూలిపోగు, కోటికి గోవృతోక.

Instead of a hundred [cloths] a bit of thread; instead of a crore [of cows] a cow's tail.

(See No. 1148.)

1322. నూతి కప్పకు సముద్రము చేరువా.

Is the sea near to a frog in a well?

Applied to a clumsy fellow.

1323. నూనె పోగొట్టుకొన్నవాడూ యేడ్చినాడు, బొండాపకాయల వాడూ పొర్లి పొర్లి యేడ్చినాడు.

The man who lost the oil cried, and the cocoanut man cried bitterly.

A bullock laden with pots of oil belonging to one man and unpeeled cocoanuts belonging to another rolled over. The pots broke, but the cocoanuts were none the worse. The first man cried quietly, but the second was loud in his lamentations.

Making a fuss about nothing.

1324. నూరి భరించ లేనమ్మ తాగేమి భరించును.

Can she drink [medicine] who could not bear to grind it?

(See Nos. 466, 1138.)

1325. నూరు కల్లలాడి అయినా, వక యిల్లు నిలప వలెను.

You should save another even by telling a hundred lies.

1326. నూరు కాకులలో వక కోవెల యేమి చెయ్యగలదు.

Among a hundred crows, what could a single cuckoo do?

What can one good man do among so many bad men?

1327. నూరు నోములూ వక రంకుతో సరి.

One act of adultery does away with a hundred meritorious deeds.

1328. నూరుమంది గుడ్డివాండ్లు పోగయి వక పాడు నూతిలో పడ్డట్టు.

Like a hundred blind men falling into a well.

An ignorant assemblage.

1329. నూరుమంది మొండిచేతులవాండ్లు పోగయి వక గొడ్డు గేదెను పాలు పితక లేక పోయినారు.

A hundred fingerless people together could not milk a barren buffalo.

A thing in every way impossible.

1330. నూరు మాటలు వక వ్రాతకు యీడు కావు.

A hundred words are not equal to one writing.

1331. నూలిపోగు అతుకు.

A thread joined in weaving.

No strength.

1332. నెత్తి మూటకు సుంకమడిగినట్టు.

Like demanding duty for a bundle carried on the head.

1333. నెమలి కంట నీరు కారితే వేటగానికి ముద్దా.

If the peacock shed tears, will the hunter's heart be moved?

(See No. 869.)

1334. నెలకు మూడామడ బిళ్ల పెట్టుగా నడిచేవాడు.

He walks thirty miles in a month, as fast as a round plate can be thrown.

1335. నెల తక్కువ అయినా రాజు యింట పుట్టుమన్నట్టు.

Never mind though you be a seven months' child, be born in a king's house.

1336. నెల బాలుడికి నూలిపోగు.

A thread to the new moon.

When Hindus see the new moon, they unravel a thread from one of their garments and offer it, asking for a new cloth.

1337. నేడు చస్తే రేపటికి రెండు.

If you die to-day, to-morrow will be two.

i. e. the second day, on which milk will be poured on his bones, according to custom, after his body has been burnt.

(See No. 1314.)

1338. నేతగాడికేలరా కోతిపిల్ల.

What does a weaver want with a young monkey?

(See Nos. 808, 732, 1360, 1363, 1498.)

The monkey would do much mischief.

Imprudent association with bad people.

1339. నేతికుండ నేలబెట్టి వట్టికుండ వుట్టిమీద పెట్టేవాడు.

A man that puts the pot of ghî on the floor, and the empty pot in the sling.

(For *Uṭṭi* see No. 304.)

The eye is blind if the mind is absent. (Italian.)*

1340. నేతిగూనచేత బూని నిచ్చెన యెక్కినట్టు.

Mounting a ladder with a jar of ghî in one's arms.

1341. నేతి బీరకాయ సామ్యము.

Like a tasteless cucumber.

(See Nos. 230, 240, 276, 613, 1250, 1542, 1798.)

Nêti bîrakâya is the ghî cucumber.

Grand in name but not worth anything.

---

* Cieco è l'occhio, se l'animo è distratto.

1342. నేను పుట్టకపోతే నీకు పెండ్లామే లేకపోను అంటే, నీవు పుట్టక పోతే నీ తల్లినే పెండ్లాడి వుందును అన్నాడట.

When a wife said "If I had not been born, you would not have had a wife," the husband replied "If you had not been born, I should have married your mother."

i. e. a better woman.

1343. నేల విడిచి సాము చేసినట్టు.

Rising off the ground and fencing in the air.

If you loose your footing you will loose your power. (Brown's Tel. Dict.)

1344. నొసట వ్రాసిన వ్రాలు తప్పవు.

The writing written on the forehead never fails.

Hindus believe that their fate is mysteriously written by the Creator's hand in the sutures of the skull.

1345. నోటికీ చేతికీ యెంగిలి లేదు.

No pollution is caused by the hand being put in the mouth.

Engili literally means saliva.

Said by a careless Brahman.

1346. నోటి ముత్యాలు రాలి పోతవా.

Would the pearls fall out of your mouth?

If you were to speak.

1347. నోటివట్టుం గంజి పెడమూట.

[By] a slip of the mouth, a bundle of food on the back.

In Ujjayini (Ougein) there lived a merchant called Dîptimanta. He went to Jângala to trade. There he met another merchant named Vivêkamanta who on one occasion said to him "Tell me a story that is not known in the world, that has not come to your ears, and that I have not heard." After being twitted often by Dîptimanta on account of his inability to comply with this unreasonable request, Vivêkamanta undertook to perform the task, provided Dîptimanta should not pronounce his story to be false, and in the event of his doing so, should pay him 100 pagodas. Dîptimanta having agreed, Vivêkamanta said "On one occasion my great grand-father Vaṇikpati when going to trade in another country met your great grand-father Pṛithikpati and they entered into partnership. Shortly afterwards they reached a spot where grew a large and beautiful Banyan tree near which was a tank. Liking the place, they agreed that Vaṇikpati should remain there and sell the goods which Pṛithikpati would send him from another country. This was carried on for some time and afterwards when they met and compared their accounts, it was found that Pṛithikpati was in Vaṇikpati's debt 100 pagodas. For long I have sought you," added Vivêkamanta, "and now I beg you will pay me the balance due." Dîptimanta being unable to deny the truth of the story lest he should incur the forfeit, was compelled to pay the 100 pagodas, and beg his way to his own country, carrying what food was given to him in a bundle on his back. Some people who met him enquired what bundle he was carrying, to which he replied "By a slip of the mouth, have I been reduced to carry a bundle of food on my back."

The evil consequences of an idle word.

1348. నోట్లో ఆవగింజ దాగదు.

Even a mustard seed cannot be hidden in his mouth.

A gossipping fellow who repeats all he hears.

1349. నోరు అంబాళపు పండు, చెయ్యి బలుసు ముల్లు.

Your mouth is like a sweet plum and your hand is like a thorn-bush.

(See Nos. 658, 1711, 1696.)

Ambâḷam is the Spondias Mangifera; *Balusu* is the Canthium Parviflorum.

You speak sweetly with your mouth, but you give nothing with your hand.

Fair words don't fill the pocket. (German.)*

---

* Schöne Worte füllen den Sack nicht.

1350. నోరు కలిగితే బ్రతుకుతాడు.

If he has a mouth he will live.

The son of the minister of a king of Ayodhya (Oudh) was caught stealing the king's flowers.—As he was being taken to the palace, his father called out "It is of no consequence, if he has a mouth he will live" The son took the hint, ate up the flowers, denied the offence, and was believed by the king, who punished his accusers. (See Telugu Selections, 36th story.)

1351. నోరు కొవ్వి నీళ్లు కారడము.

When the mouth gets fat, it is made to salivate.

A man suffers for his arrogance.

1352. నోరు మంచిదయితే వూరు మంచిది.

If your words are good, the world will be good to you.

1353. నోరు మాట్లాడుతూ వుంటే, నొసలు వెక్కిరిస్తూ వుంటున్నది.

Speaking with the mouth but mocking with the forehead.

Insincerity.

1354. నోరు మూస్తే మూగ, నోరు తెరిస్తే రాగ.

If you shut up her mouth she remains like a dumb woman, if you let her open her mouth she's a vixen.

1355. న్యాయము తప్పని వానికి ఆచార్య కటాక్షమెందుకు.

What does a just man care for the favor of the priest?

ప.

1356. పంచపాండవులు మంచం కోళ్లవలె ముగ్గురు అంటారేగాని, యిద్దరే అని వక వేలు చూపినాడట.

"The five Pâṇḍavas they say are *three* like the legs of a bed, but there are only two," said he, showing *one* finger.

Said of a stupid accountant.

1357. పంచశుభం పంచాశుభం.

Five good things, five bad things.

Differently interpreted to mean five good and five bad qualities; the five senses applied to good and to bad uses, &c.

1358. పంచాంగములు పోతే నక్షత్రములు పోనా.

If the almanacks are lost, do the stars go also?

Can the original source not be applied to, when that derived from it has been lost?

1359. పంచాగ్ని మధ్యమందు వున్నట్టు.

Standing in the middle of five fires.

An act of penance.

Said of a person being unable to extricate himself from a difficult position in which he is surrounded by his enemies.

1360. పంజెకేలరా పత్తి ధర.

What has a beggar to do with the price of cotton?

1361. పండగ తొల్నాడు గుడ్డల కరువు, పండగనాడు అన్నము కరువు, పండగ మర్నాడు మజ్జిగ కరువు.

The day before the festival, there is a scarcity of cloth; on the festival day, a scarcity of food; and on the day after the festival, a scarcity of buttermilk.

1362. పండు జారి పాలల్లో పడ్డట్టు.

The fruit slipped, and fell into the milk.

(See Nos. 185, 1425, 1430, 1886.)

Happy go lucky.

1363. పందికి యేలరా పన్నీరు గిండి.

What can a pig do with a rose water bottle ?

Gindi is a narrow mouthed vessel used for rose water.

1364. పందిని నందినీ, నందిని పందినీ చేశేవాడు.

He can make a common pig into Śiva's bull, and Śiva's bull into a common pig.

(See Nos. 1082, 1215.)

Ability in argumentation.

1365. పందిలి పడి చచ్చిన వారూ యిల్లు పడి బ్రతికిన వారూ లేరు.

No men die from the falling of a Pandili ; no men live after the falling of a house.

(For *Pandili* see No. 61.)

1366. పందుం తిన్నా పరకడుపే, యేదుం తిన్నా యేకాదశే.

Though he eat ten Tûms of food he will say he is starving ; and though he eat five Tûms, he will say it is a fast.

(For *Tûms* see No. 619.)

1367. పక్కపుండు పెంచుతావేమి.

Why do you increase the sore in my side ?

1368. పక్కలో కత్తి.

A sword by the side [on a bed].

(See Nos. 999, 1002.)

1369. పగటి మాటలు పనికి చేటు, రాత్రి మాటలు నిద్రకు చేటు.

Talking in the day time spoils one's business ; talking in the night time spoils one's sleep.

1370. పగలు చస్తే వాతికి లేదు, రాత్రి చస్తే దీపముకు లేదు.

If he dies in the day, there is no rice to put in his mouth; if he dies in the night, there is no oil for a lamp.

Rice is put into the mouth of the dead at the funeral ceremony.

Said of a miserably poor person.

1371. పగలెల్లా బారెడు నేశినాను, దివ్వెతేవే దిగ నేస్తాను.

Like a weaver saying in the evening to his wife "woman during the day I have woven two yards, if you bring a lamp now I'll undo it all again."

Said of an idle fellow.

1372. పగవానింట పది బిచ్చాలు పోయినా పోయినవేను.

If alms are given ten times in an enemy's house, so much the better.

1373. పచ్చి గడ్డి వేస్తే భగ్గుమని మండుతున్నది.

Put green grass [between two rivals], and it will blaze up.

1374. పచ్చి వెలగకాయ గొంతున పడ్డట్టు.

Like an unripe wood apple sticking in one's throat.

Distress caused by continual worrying.

1375. పట్టపగలు కన్నము వేస్తావేమిరా అంటే, నా కక్కురితి నీకు యేమి తెలుసును అన్నాడట.

A burglar being asked why he was house-breaking in the day time, replied "What do you know of my necessities?"

Distress tempts to crime.

1376. పట్టపగలు చుక్కలు పొడిపిస్తాడు.

In the full light of day, he makes the stars appear.

Professing to do wonders. Applied to a great cheat.

1377. పట్టినది చింత కొమ్మ గాని ములగ కొమ్మ కాదు.

What I am clinging to is a Tamarind bough, not a Mulaga.

The tamarind wood is pliable, but the *Mulaga* (Hyperanthera Moringa) is brittle.

Said by a parasite of his staunch protector.

1378. పడమట కొరడు వేస్తే, పాడుగుంటలన్నీ నిండును.

If there be a rainbow in the west, all the dry tanks will be filled.

1379. పడిశెము పది రోగాల పెట్టు.

One cold in the head is as bad as ten diseases.

1380. పడుచుల కాపరం, చితుకుల మంట.

A house full of young girls, and a fire of little twigs.

Difficult to manage.

1381. పత్తిగింజలు తింటావా బసవన్నా అంటే ఆహా అన్నాడట, గంత కట్టనా బసవన్నా అంటే వూహూ అన్నాడట.

When Basavanna was asked if he would eat cotton seed, he said "Âhâ"; when Basavanna was asked whether he would have on the pack saddle he said "Ùhû."

(See Nos. 73, 518, 1070, 1385.)

Basavanna is the name of a bull sacred to Śiva. Bullocks are often familiarly called by this name. *Âhâ* is an exclamation signifying consent. *Ûhû* signifies refusal.

1382. పదిమందితోటి చావు పెండ్లితో సమము.

With many people death is equal to marriage.

Applied to an honorable death in a good cause.

1383. పదిమందిలో పడ్డపాము చావదు.

A snake falling among a lot of people will not die.

A bad man often escapes through the difference of opinion among others as to his guilt, as a snake does through the Hindu's superstitious dread of killing it.

1384. పదిరాళ్లు వేస్తే వకరాయి అయినా తగలదా.

If you throw ten stones, will not one hit?

(See No. 107.)

1385. పని అంటే నా వొళ్లు భారగిస్తుంది, భోజనమంటే నా వొళ్లు పొంగి వస్తుంది.

If you talk of work, my body becomes heavy; if you talk of dinner, my body swells [with delight].

(See Nos. 73, 518, 1070, 1381.)

The trade of thick-headed Michael: eating, drinking, and idling. (Dutch.)*

1386. పని చెయ్యనివాడు యింటికి దొంగ, పన్ను యివ్వనివాడు దివాణానకు దొంగ.

A man who does not work robs the house, a man who pays no taxes robs the government.

(See No. 1069.)

* Dat is het ambacht van dikken Michiel: drinken, eten, en wandelen.

1387. పనిలేని పాపరాజు యేమి చేస్తున్నాడంటే, కుందేటి కొమ్ముకు రేఖలు తీరుస్తున్నాడు అన్నాడట.

When they asked what idle Pâpa Râzu was about, they were told that he was carving lines on a hare's horn.

(See Nos. 319, 1388, 1389.)

1388. పనిలేని మంగలి పిల్లి తల గొరిగినాడట.

The barber without work shaved the cat's head.

(See Nos. 319, 1387, 1389.)

A man pretending to be fully employed.

1389. పనిలేని మాచకమ్మ పిల్లిపాలు పితికినదట.

The jade who had nothing to do milked the cat.

(See Nos. 319, 1387, 1388.)

1390. పన్నెండు ఆమడ మధ్య బ్రాహ్మణుడు లేకపోతే యజ్ఞము చేయిస్తాను అన్నాడట.

If there is no Brahman within a hundred miles, I'll conduct the sacrifice.

An ignorant professor gets on well in the absence of the learned.

1391. పప్పన్నమంటే పది ఆమడ అయినా పరుగెత్త వలెను.

When we hear of Dâl and rice we should run for it, even though it be hundred miles off.

(For *Dâl* see No. 183.)

Said of a greedy Brahman.

1392. పప్పుతో పది కబళాలు తింటే, పులుసు యెందుకు బుగ్గిలోకా.

If one gets a few mouthfuls of rice with Dâl, why should one want vegetables dressed with acid? To throw among the ashes?

Said by an epicure.

1393. పప్పులేని పెండ్లి వుప్పులేని కూరా వున్నదా.

Is there a marriage without Dâl, or a vegetable dressed without salt?

(See No. 2075.)

Said to a great friend whose presence at an entertainment is indispensable.

1394. పయికము లేనివాడు పరస్త్రీ వర్జితుడు.

A man without money is chaste.

1395. పయిపడ్డ మాటా, మడి పడ్డ నీళ్లూ పోతవా.

Will an accusation [be forgotten], will water which falls in a banked field escape?

(See No. 1928.)

Throw much dirt, and some will stick.

An ill wound may be cured, but not an ill name.

1396. పరద్రవ్యాణి బెల్లవత్.

The property of others is as sweet as molasses.

(See Nos. 3, 910, 1560.)

Being liberal at others' expence.

To cut large shives of another man's loaf.

1397. పరుగెత్తుతూ పాలు తాగేకన్నా, నిలుచుండి నీళ్లు తాగడము మేలు.

It's better to stand and drink water, than to run and drink milk.

A comfortable berth with a moderate salary, is better than a bad situation with a larger income.

1398. పరుగెత్తేవాణ్ని చూస్తే తరిమే వాడికి లోకువ.

The man that runs away, is inferior to the man who follows him.

1399. పరువిచ్చి పరువు తెచ్చుకో.

Give honor, get honor.

1400. పలకని వాండ్లతో పది వూళ్లవాండ్లూ గెలవ లేరు.

The people of ten villages cannot overcome men who won't open their mouths.

1401. పల్లము వుండే చోట నీళ్లు నిలుస్తవి.

Water lies in the low ground.

(See No. 1308.)

Truth will out at last.

1402. పసుపు కొమ్ము యివ్వని కోమటి పసారమంతా కొల్ల యిచ్చినాడు.

As impossible as that a Kômaṭi who would not give away a bit of turmeric should allow his whole store to be plundered.

1403. పసుపూ బొట్టూ పెట్టి పెండ్లికి పిలిస్తే వెళ్లక పెంకు పట్టుకొని పులుసుకు వెళ్లినట్టు.

When turmeric was rubbed on her feet and a mark put on her forehead and she was invited to the marriage feast she would not go, but afterwards she went with a broken pot to beg for broth.

Suffering by pride.

1404. పక్షిమీద గురి పెట్టి మృగమును వేసినట్టు.

He aimed at the bird and shot the deer.

He fired at the pigeon and he killed the crow.

1405. పాండవుల వారి సంపాద్యము దుర్యోధనుల వారి పిండాకూళ్లకు సరి.

The wealth gained by the Pâṇḍavas was only sufficient for the funerals of the Duryôdhanas (Kauravas).

(See No. 146.)

Ill use of well gotten gains.

1406. పాకలపాటి వారి రణకొమ్ము.

The war horn of the Pâkalapâṭi family.

Said of a loquacious person.

1407. పాగావంటి బంధువుడూ లేడు, అంగరకావంటి హరాంఖోరూ లేడు.

There is no relation like your turband, there is no scamp equal to your jacket.

A turband can be tied so as to hide all holes, which is not the case with the jacket; the turband is therefore likened to a trustworthy friend, and the jacket to an unfaithful fellow.

1408. పాటిమీది గంగానమ్మకు కూటిమీదనే లోకము.

The goddess Gangânamma who presides over the burial ground, thinks of nothing but eating [the corpses].

Entirely given to the selfish pursuit of one object.

1409. పాటు కలిగితే కూటికి కొదవా.

If you get work, will food be wanting?

1410. పాటు పడితే భాగ్యము కలుగును.

If you are industrious, you will become rich.

1411. పాడిందే పాడరా పాచిపండ్ల దాసరి.

Sing again what you have sung, O Dâsari with dirty teeth.

Said to an ignorant imposter.

Give the piper a penny, and two pence to leave off.

1412. పాడు వూరికి నక్క తలారి.

A jackal is the watchman of a ruined village.

(See Nos. 830, 1413.)

Applied to a person who gets on well with his work when there is no one to question him.

1413. పాడు వూరికి మంచపు కోడు పోతరాజు.

In a ruined village, the leg of a bed is Pôta Râzu.

(See Nos. 830, 1412.)

Pôta Râzu is a rustic deity.

1414. పాడు వూళ్లో పొగిడేవారు లేరు, నాకు నేనే పొగుడుకొంటానన్నాడట.

He said " in this ruined village there is no one to praise me, so I praise myself."

Your trumpeter's dead, and so you trumpet yourself.

1415. పాతముండలందరూ పోగయి క్రొత్తముండ తాడు తెంపినట్టు.

Like the old widows assembling to break the marriage cord of a new widow.

A gang of rascals conspiring to ruin a new comer, who they fear will be in their way.

1416. పానకములోని పుల్ల.

A bit of straw in sherbet.

1417. పాపటకాయ కొరకనెంత యాక పెట్టనెంత.

A bramble is neither large enough to bite nor to place on a dish.

(See No. 339.)

Pâpaṭa is the Pavetta Indica.

A quantity quite inadequate to one's wants.

1418. పాపి సొమ్ము పరులపాలు, ద్రోహి సొమ్ము దొంగలపాలు.

The riches of a sinner go to strangers ; the riches of a traitor go to thieves.

1419. పాముకాళ్లు పామునకెరుక.

The snake only knows where it's feet are.

(See No. 802.)

The Hindus believe that a snake has feet, though they are invisible.

A man knows his own business best.

1420. పాముకు పాలుపోశినట్లు.

Feeding a snake with milk.

(See Nos. 636, 665, 1432.)

Showing kindness to an ungrateful person.

1421. పాము చుట్టము పడిగ పగ.

The snake is your relation, and it's hood your enemy.

Being on friendly terms with members of a family though on bad terms with the head of the house.

1422. పాముతో చెలిమి, కత్తితో సాము.

Friendship with a snake, fencing with a sword.

1423. పామునూ చావనివ్వడు, బడితే విరగనివ్వడు.

He won't allow the snake to die, and he won't allow the stick to be broken.

(See No. 43.)

Applied to a trimmer.

1424. పాములలో మెలగ వచ్చునుగాని, స్వాములలో మెలగ కూడదు.

You may walk among snakes, but keep clear of Vaishṇava priests.

1425. పాయసములో నెయ్యి ఒలికినట్టు.

Like the ghî falling into the milk pudding.

(See Nos. 195, 1362, 1430, 1886.)

When a pot of ghî slipped from a woman's hand, it fortunately fell into a pudding.

He is like a cat, he always falls on his fest.

1426. పారవేసుకొన్న చోటనే వెతుక్కో వలసినది.

You must look for a thing in the place where you lost it.

Seek redress from the person who has injured you.

1427. పారే చీమ చప్పుడు వినేవాడు.

A man who hears the noise of a creeping ant.

As wary as a blind horse.

He is so wary that he sleeps like a hare with his eyes open.

1428. పాలకు వచ్చి ముంత దాచినట్టు.

Begging for milk and hiding his cup.

(See Nos. 20, 856, 1608, 1792.)

Poverty and pride.

1429. పాలబుట్టితే మాత్రము మేలు గుణము కలుగునా.

Does every thing that comes from milk possess good qualities?

Good qualities are not always possessed by people of high birth.

1430. పాలల్లో పంచదార వ్రులికినట్టు.

Like sugar dropped into milk.

(See Nos. 195, 1362, 1425, 1886.)

1431. పాలును చూడనా భాండాన్ని చూడనా.

Are we to look at milk or at the pot?

The pot is only valued for the milk in it.

The jewel is not to be valued for the cabinet.

1432. పాలుపోశి పెంచినా పాము కరవక మానదు.

Although you feed a snake with milk, it will not refrain from biting you.

(See Nos. 967, 636, 1077, 1078, 1079, 1420, 1850.)

1433. పాలే కుడిచి రొమ్మే గుద్దినాడు.

He sucked the milk, and struck the breast.

(See Nos. 1077, 1078, 1079.)

1434. పాశిన కూడు పదునుకు వస్తున్నదా.

Can rotten food ever be made sweet?

Past reformation.

1435. పిండి బొమ్మను చేశి పీటమీాద కూర్చుండ బెట్టితే, ఆడబిడ్డతనాన అదిరదిరి పడ్డదట.

When they made an image of an Âḍa Biḍḍa of flour and put it on a seat, it shook itself about [in threatening postures] and gave itself great airs.

Âḍa Biḍḍa (literally "a female child") is the familiar name for a husband's sister, who manages her brother's household in the absence of her mother.

1436. పిండి యెంతో నిప్పటి అంతే.

The cake will be as much as the flour.

Payment in proportion to work. Results according to labor.

1437. పిండీ ప్రోలూ లేనిదీ పెండ్లి అవునా.

Can there be a marriage without flour and a procession?

(See Nos. 1398, 2075.)

Indispensable accompaniments.

1438. పిందెలో పండిన పండు.

A fruit ripened after being plucked.

Said of a precocious youth.

1439. పిచ్చికమీద బ్రహ్మాస్త్రమా.

Attacking a sparrow with a Brahmâstra.

(For *Brahmâstra* see No. 1658.—See Nos. 615, 820, 880.)

He takes a spear to kill a fly.

1440. పిచ్చుగుంటలవాని పెండ్లి యెంత వైభవమెంత.

How long does a gypsy's marriage take? how long does an entertainment last?

Applied to the grandeur of arrogant people.

1441. పిట్ట కొంచెము కూత ఘనము.

A little bird with a great cry.

A little man sometimes casts a long shadow. (French.)*

A little dog, a cow without horns, and a short man are generally proud. (Danish.)†

---

* Un petit homme projette parfois une grande ombre.
† Stakket Hund, kuldet Ko, og liden Mand ere gierne hov modige.

1442. పిట్టా పిట్టా పోరు పిల్లి తీర్చినట్టు.

Like the cat settling the dispute between two birds.

By eating them both up (See Telugu Panchatantra, page 94.)

1443. పిఠాపురము వెళ్లి పిడతెడు నీళ్లు తెచ్చినట్టు.

He went to Piṭhâpuram, and brought a little potful of water.

(See No. 1667.)

1444. పిడుగుకూ బియ్యానకూ ఒకటే మంత్రము.

[He has] one Mantra for the thunderbolt and for the rice.

Hindus believe that repetition of the ten names of Arjuna

అర్జునః ఫల్గునః పార్థః కిరీటీ శ్వేతవాహనః।
బీభత్సో విజయః కృష్ణః సవ్యసాచీ ధనంజయః॥

drives away thunderbolts. An ignorant Brahman is said to have repeated this Ślôka when receiving a dish of raw rice.

Applied to impostors.

1445. పితికే బర్రెను యిచ్చి పొడిచే దున్నను తెచ్చినట్టు.

He bartered a milch she buffalo for a goring he buffalo.

1446. పినతండ్రి పెండ్లాము పినతల్లి కాదు, మేనమామ పెండ్లాము మేనత్త కాదు.

Your paternal uncle's wife is not your maternal aunt; your maternal uncle's wife is not your paternal aunt.

1447. పిరికి బంటుకు తుమ్మాస్థ.

A cowardly soldier is stopped by a sneeze.

A sneeze is considered a bad omen among the Hindus.

Ready for any excuse.

1448. పిలవని పేరంటము చెప్పని వక్క పొద్దు.

Attending a feast to which you are not invited, a fast you are not asked to observe.

(For *Pêranṭam* see No. 68.)

Fidders' dogs an' flees come to a feast unca'd. (Scotch.)

1449. పిలిస్తే బిగిస్తే సరిగాని వస్తే వాడి అబ్బ తరమా.

If I invite him and he is too proud to come, it will be all right; but if he does come, how shall I manage it?

Said by a poor man who was obliged to show hospitality which he could ill afford.

1450. పిల్లకాకి యేమి యెరుగును వుండేలు దెబ్బ.

What does a young crow know about the blow of a pellet?

Inexperience.

1451. పిల్లకాయలకూ పీటకోళ్లకూ చలిలేదు.

Children and the legs of a stool do not feel the cold.

To a child all weather is cold.

1452. పిల్లగలవాడు పిల్లకు యేడిస్తే, కాటివాడు కాసుకు యేడ్చినాడు.

When the father cried for his child, the sexton cried for his money.

(See Nos. 809, 930.)

Crows bewail the dead sheep and then eat them.

1453. పిల్లముడ్డి గిల్లి వుయ్యాల వూచే వాడు.

Pinching the child while swinging the cradle.

Done by a lazy fellow who wanted to make it appear that the child did not like him.

1454. పిల్లలేని యింట్లో తాత తడువులాడినట్టు.

Like a grandfather groping for the children in a house where there are none.

1455. పిల్లి కండ్లు పోగోరును, కుక్క పిల్లలు కలగకోరును.

The cat wishes to see your eyes out, and the dog wishes to see you have children.

Both will then be well fed.

1456. పిల్లి కండ్లు మూసుకొని పాలు తాగుతున్న యెవరూ యెరుగరని యెంచుకొన్నట్టు.

Like a cat shutting her eyes, and fancying that no one could see her drinking the milk.

A man fancying that he is unseen when committing some crime.

The forest has ears, the field has eyes. (German.)*

1457. పిల్లికి చెలగాటము యెలికకు ప్రాణసంకటము.

Sport to the cat, death to the rat.

What is sport to the cat is death to the mouse. (German.)†

What is play to the strong is death to the weak. (Danish.)‡

1458. పిల్లికి రొయ్యల మొలతాడు కట్టితే, అవుంటా బోయి నోట్లో వేసుకొన్నదట.

When they tied a waist cord of prawns round the cat's loins it went a little way and then ate up the whole.

Want of appreciation of honors conferred.

---

* Der Wald hat Ohren, das Feld hat Augen.
† Der Katzen Scherz, der Mäuse Tod.
‡ Staerke Mands Spil er kranke Mands Død.

1459. పిల్లిని చంకబెట్టుకొని పెండ్లికి వెళ్లినట్టు.

Going to a marriage with a cat under your arm.

(See Nos. 310, 806.)

The cat is a bad omen.

Transgressing the rules of society.

1460. పిల్లిని చంపిన పాపము నీది, బెల్లము తిన్న పాపము నాది.

You take the sin of killing the cat, I'll take the sin of eating your molasses.

Said by a stingy Kômaṭi to a Brahman priest to whom he had presented tha cheapest possible offering that would expiate the sin he had committed by killing a cat, viz., a little image of a cat made of molasses, which he afterwards was greedy enough to take back again and swallow.

1461. పిల్లి బ్రహ్మహంత.

Kill a cat, kill a Brahman.

Doing harm to a cat is considered as sinful as injuring a Brahman.

1462. పిల్లి బ్రాహ్మణుడు, పీట ముత్తైదువ.

A cat [is as sacred as] a Brahman, and the stool (used for prayers, &c.) is as sacred as his wife.

1463. పీటకూ పిర్రకూ వయిరము.

Enmity between the posteriors and the seat.

1464. పీతాంబరము మెరువిచ్చినమ్మ పీట వెంబడి పట్టుకొని తిరగవలశినది.

The lady who lent a woman a silk cloth, must walk after her with a stool.

If you lend any thing good to a careless person you must take measures to prevent his spoiling it, as the silk cloth would have been spoiled had the woman sat upon the ground.

1465. పీనుగకు చేసిన జాతర.

Carrying a corpse in procession.

(See No. 2052.)

A vain ceremony.

1466. పుంగనూరు సంస్థానము.

Like the Punganûru state.

Punganûru is in the North Arcot District.

No government.

1467. పుచ్చకాయ దొంగ అంటే, భుజము తడిమి చూచుకొన్నాడట.

When the robber of the water melon was spoken of, he felt his shoulders.

(See No. 786.)

Guilty conscience.

1468. పుచ్చిన మిరియాలయినా, జొన్నలకు సరి తూగక పోవు.

Though the pepper be worm eaten, it will weigh as much as the millet.

A brave spirit under adverse circumstances.

1469. పుట్టడము చావడము కొరకే.

To be born is but for death.

1470. పుట్టని బిడ్డకు పూసలు కట్టినట్టు.

Tying beads round an unborn child.

(See Nos. 204, 528, 936, 1471.)

Don't reckon your eggs before they are laid. (Italian.)*

1471. పుట్టని బిడ్డకు పేరు పెట్టుతాడు.

He gives a name to an unborn child.

(See Nos. 204, 528, 936, 1470.)

To celebrate the triumph before the victory. (Latin.)†

---

* Far conta dell' uovo non ancor nato.
† Ante victoriam canere triumphum.

1472. పుట్ట మీద తేలు కుట్టినా, నాగుమయ్య మహిమేనా.

If one is stung by a scorpion on an ant hill has it the venom of the snake-god?

Puṭṭa is a white ant hill, where snakes are found.

Applied to a person supposing himself to have been injured through the malice of an enemy.

1473. పుట్టించినవాడు పూరి మేపుతాడా.

Would your Maker feed you with grass?

(See No. 904.)

The Creator provides suitable food for all his creatures; the benefactors of others need not therefore be proud.

1474. పుట్టిన నాటనుంచి పుల్లిగాడే మొగుడా.

Has Pulligâḍu been my husband ever since I was born?

Applied to ungrateful servants or dependants.

1475. పుట్టిననాటి బుద్ధి పుడకలతో గాని పోదు.

The faggots of the funeral pile alone remove the [evil] qualities with which a man is born.

(See Nos. 259, 371, 515, 571, 578, 632, 924, 1494.)

What belongs to nature lasts to the grave. (Italian.)*

1476. పుట్టిన పిల్లలు బువ్వకు యేడిస్తే, అవ్వ మొగుడికి యేడ్చినది.

When the children cried for food, the grandmother cried for a husband.

Wishing for something quite unsuitable to one's age.

---

* Chi l'ha per natura, fin alla fossa dura.

1477. పుట్టిన యిన్నాళ్లకు పురుషుడు యజ్ఞము చేశెను.

After living for so many years the man performed a sacrifice.

Good luck comes at last.

Fortune knocks once at least at every man's gate.

Fortune is like the market, where if you bide your time, the price will fall.

1478. పుట్టిన వానికి తమ్ముడు, పుట్టే వానికి అన్న.

The younger brother of him who is born, the elder brother of him who is about to be born.

Said jokingly of a dwarf.

1479. పుట్టుచాయేగాని పెట్టుచాయ వచ్చునా.

The natural colour will remain, but will the artificial colour stand ?

False pretensions.

1480. పుట్టెడాముదము పట్టించుకొని పొర్లాడినా అంటేదే అంటును గాని అంటనిది అంటదు.

Although a man besmear himself with a Puṭṭi of castor oil and roll [among the grain] only what sticks, will stick to him, what does not, won't.

(See No. 1790.)

A *Puṭṭi* is 500 lbs.

A man can only obtain that which his destiny has prepared for him.

Every man hath his lot.

No butter will stick to his bread.

1481. పుణ్యము పుట్టెడు, పురుగులు తట్టెడు.

A bushelful of good works, and a dishful of worms.

A great show of piety, but the prospect of future punishment for evil deeds.

1482. పుణ్యానికి పుట్టెడిస్తే, పిచ్చుకుంచమని పోట్లాడినట్టు.

When a man was given a Puṭṭi of corn he complained of short measure.

(For *Puṭṭi* see No. 1480—see No. 1119.)

Look not a gift horse in the mouth. (Latin.)*

1483. పుణ్యానికి పెట్టే అమ్మా నీ మొగుడితో సమముగా పెట్టుమన్నట్టు.

Like a beggar who said "O charitable lady, give me food like that which you give to your husband."

An absurd request.

1484. పుత్రుడనై వేధింతునా, శత్రుడనై వేధింతునా, పేరులేని దయ్యమునై వేధింతునా, పెనిమిటినై వేధింతునా.

Shall I torment you as a son? shall I torment you as an enemy? shall I torment you as a nameless devil? or shall I torment you as a husband?

1485. పునుగు చట్టము పిండినట్టు.

Like squeezing an empty civet bag.

You cannot get blood out of a stone.

---

* Noli equi dentes inspicere donati.

1486. పుబ్బ రేగినా బూతు రేగినా నిలవదు.

If Pubba bursts forth (in rain) or if obscenity breaks out, they won't stop.

Pubba is the eleventh lunar mansion.

If the first of July it be rainy weather,
'Twill rain more or less for four weeks together.

1487. పురిట్లోనే సందు కొట్టినది.

The child was demon-struck before it was ten days old.

A Hindu infant is not taken out of the house during the mother's *Puruḍu* or ten days of ceremonial uncleanness after its birth. During this time the child is thought to be perfectly safe from the evil spirits, to attacks from which it is afterwards liable.

1488. పుర్రు కారుతూ వుంటే, పోతరాజు శివమాడినట్టు.

When a man was dying from diarrhœa, some one played pranks as if possessed by Pôta Râzu.

(For *Pôta Râzu* see No. 1413.)

1489. పులగము మీదికి తెడ్డెడు పప్పు.

A ladleful of Dâl on Pulagam.

For *Dâl* see No. 183—*Pulagam* is rice mixed with pulse (called in Hindustani *Khichṛi.*)—To add more dâl is considered barbarous.

1490. పులిగాడికి గిలిగాడు.

A ruffian even has his bugbear.

1491. పులి నాకి విడిచినట్టు.

The tiger licked him and left him.

A marvellous escape.

1492. పులిని జూచి నక్క వాత పెట్టుకొన్నట్టు.

The jackal branded himself with spots like a tiger.

Vulgar display.

Apeing one's superiors.

1493. పులి పక్కను జోరీగ వున్నట్టు.

Like a gadfly on a tiger's side.

A safe refuge.

1494. పులిపిల్ల పులిపిల్లే, మేకపిల్ల మేకపిల్లే.

A tiger-cub is a tiger-cub, a kid is a kid.

(See Nos. 259, 371, 515, 571, 573, 832, 924, 1475.)

Cat after kind.

1495. పులి మీసములు పట్టుకొని వుయ్యాల వూగినట్టు.

Taking hold of a tiger's mustaches and swinging one's self.

A rash enterprise.

1496. పువ్వు పుయ్యగానే తెలుసును పరిమళము.

As soon as a flower is full blown, it's fragrance is perceived.

A man's worth is known when he is grown up.

1497. పూజ కొద్దీ పురుషుడు, పుణ్యము కొద్దీ పుత్రుడు.

A husband according to the worship [of the wife], a son according to the good works [of the father].

1498. పూటకూళ్లకు వచ్చిన వారికి పుట్ల ధర యెందుకు.

What have people buying cooked food, to do with the price of Puṭṭis [of grain] ?

(For *Puṭṭi* see No. 1480.)

1499. పూటకూళ్లమ్మ పుణ్యమెరగదు.

The cateress has no conscience.

Said of the women who provide meals to travellers, and give them wretched food.

1500. పూతకు ముందే పురుగు పట్టినది.

Worm eaten before blossoming.

(See No. 1487.)

Premature. Precocious.

1501. పూరా మునిగిన వానికి చలియేమి గాలి యేమి.

When a man plunges into the water does he care for cold or wind ?

Overwhelmed with grief.

1502. పూలచేరెత్తినట్టు.

Like lifting up a string of flowers.

A very easy business.

1503. పూస కూర్చిన చందము.

Like stringing beads.

All in harmony.

1504. పూస పోగు వుంటే, బుజమెక్క వలెనా.

Although a man has necklace and earrings is he to sit on [another man's] shoulder ?

Should a rich man be puffed up with pride ?

1505. పెండ్లికి వెళ్లుదామంటే, వెళ్లిపోదామంటాడు.

One man said " Let us go to the marriage," the other replied " Let us leave the country."

(See Nos. 111, 232, 435.)

A spirit of contradiction.

1506. పెండ్లినాటి సౌఖ్యము లంఖణమునాడు తలుచుకొన్నట్టు.

Thinking of the good fare at the marriage when suffering from the effects of it afterwards.

1507. పెండ్లి మర్నాడు పెండ్లి కొడుకు ముఖాన పెద్దమ్మ వేలాడుతున్నది.

The day after the marriage the goddess of misfortune appeared in the face of the bridegroom.

The bridegroom looked a poor creature when stripped of all his finery.

1508. పెండ్లివారు వచ్చి పెరట్లో దిగినారా.

Are the people coming to the marriage waiting in the back-yard?

i. e. "Why such haste?"

1509. పెట్టగల బచ్చలిపాదు కొనగల గేదె మేశిపోయినది.

The buffalo you intended to buy has eaten up the vegetables I intended to plant.

(For *Bachchali* see No. 510.)

Taunting a man who is always talking but never acts.

1510. పెట్టనమ్మ పెట్టనే పెట్టదుగాని, పెట్టేముండకు యేమి వచ్చినది రోగము.

A woman who does not give [alms] will never give; what evil has happened to the jade who does give?

(See Nos. 243, 264.)

Said by a beggar of one from whom he generally received alms.

1511. పెట్టితే తింటారుగాని, తిట్టితే పడేవారు లేరు.

If you feed, [people] will eat; but if you abuse none will bear it.

1512. పెట్టితే పెండ్లి, పెట్టక పోతే శ్రాద్ధము.

If you feast me [I shall consider it] a marriage and if not, a funeral.

(See Nos. 243, 284.)

Fair and foul words.

1513. పెట్టినమ్మకు ప్రాణహాని చెప్పినమ్మకు జన్మహాని.

She that gives will lose her life, she that advised will lose [the advantage of] her birth.

The story runs thus: In the city of Matipuram, dwelt a king named Nayaśâli. He had three wives named Sumêdâḥ, Suvarchalâ, and Nîtimati. Sumêdâḥ was blessed with a son; her rival wives, being barren, were less loved by the king. This caused them to be jealous of Sumêdâḥ, and Nîtimati counselled Suvarchalâ to poison the son, saying that afterwards they would share the king's favor equally with their more fortunate rival. Suvarchalâ consulted in the matter with her intimate friend Vichitravati, the minister's daughter: Vichitravati after some deliberation replied " She that gives will lose her life, she that advised will lose her birth" (i. e. will be banished from the king's presence.) Suvarchalâ profiting by her friend's advice and perceiving the fatal consequences which would follow the commission of the intended crime, desisted from her wicked purpose.

1514. పెట్టిన వానికి తెలుసును నిక్షేపము.

The treasure is known to the man who buried it.

1515. పెట్టిన వారికి పుట్టినదే సాక్షి, పెట్టని వారికి పుట్టనిదే నిజము.

The alms received witness to those who gave; those who gave not, truly do not receive.

If the charitable become poor, they will not ask for help in vain; but the uncharitable will obtain nothing.

1516. పెట్టి పొయ్యనమ్మ కొట్టి పొమ్మన్నదట.

She that gave neither food nor drink, beat [me] and said "be off."

Said by a beggar.

1517. పెట్టు చుట్టము, పొగుడు భాగ్యము.

Entertainments [bring] relations, flattery [brings] fortune.

(See Nos. 1534, 1857.)

While the pot boils friendship blooms. (German.)*

1518. పెట్టు పోతలు శాశ్వతములా.

Will the meat and drink last for ever?

Can one expect to live always on the bounty of others ?

1519. పెద బావగారు ఆడంగులతో సమము.

The elder brother-in-law is like a woman.

Said of a stupid clumsy person.

1520. పెదిమకు మించిన పల్లు, ప్రమితకు మించిన వత్తి.

A tooth projecting beyond the lip, a wick too big for the oil dish.

Said of an insolent fellow.

He is on the high ropes.

1521. పెదిమ దాటితే, పెన్న దాటుతున్నది.

If it passes your lips it will go over the Penna river.

(For *Penna* see No. 1528—See Nos. 47, 525, 685.)

A secret revealed spreads quickly abroad.

Three may keep counsel if two be away.

Two eyes, two ears, only one mouth. (German.)†

---

* Siedet der Topf, so blühet die Freundschaft.
† Zwei Augen, zwei Ohren, nur ein Mund.

1522. పెద్ద కొడుకు పెండ్లి, అసుర భోజనము.

The eldest son's marriage, and the giant's dinner.

(See Nos. 99, 711.)

A giant had to be supplied with a man daily by the villagers in turn. (See Vikramârka Tales in Telugu Selections Page 41.)

A happy event and a great misfortune coming together.

1523. పెద్ద తల లేకపోతే, గొర్రె తల తెచ్చుకొమ్మన్నారు.

If you can't get a head for the family get a sheep's head.

(See Nos. 312, 314, 1906.)

Better than nothing.

When you can't get bread, oat cakes are not amiss. (Spanish.)*

1524. పెద్ద పులి తరుముక వచ్చినా, హజారము ముందరికి పోరాదు.

Though you be pursued by a tiger, you should not pass in front of the royal court.

(See No. 1525.)

Applied to a tyrannical Government.

1525. పెద్ద పులి యెదటనయినా పడ వచ్చునుగాని, నగరి వారి యెదట పడరాదు.

You may face a royal tiger but you should not face a government official.

(See No. 1524.)

1526. పెద్దలతోఁ వాదు, పెతరులతోఁ పొందు.

Disputing with the aged [is as wrong as] keeping company with ghosts.

1527. పెద్దల వుసురు పెనుబామై తాకును.

The sorrow [you have caused] to the pious will come upon you again like a great serpent.

"*His mischief shall return upon his own head.*" Psalm vii. 16.

---

* A mengua de pan, buenas son tortas.

1528. పెన్న దాటితే, పెరుమాళ్ల సేవ.

When we have crossed the Penna we can visit Perumâḷ.

The meaning is "Let us get over the river first and talk of visiting Perumâḷ (Vishṇu) afterwards.—The Penna (Pennar) falls into the sea near Nellore. It is rapid and deep during the monsoon, though its bed is nearly dry for 5 or 6 months of the year.

1529. పెన్నలో మాన్యము చెప్పినట్టు.

Like allotting glebe land in the Penna.

A doubtful benefit.

1530. పెరటి చెట్టు మందుకు రాదు.

The tree in the back yard won't do for medicine.

That which is near is not valued.

Far fetch'd and dear bought is good for ladies.

A cow from afar gives plenty of milk. (French.)*

1531. పెరుగుట విరుగుట కొరకే.

To grow is but to be broken.

Ruin follows speedy exaltation.

Fortune and glass soon break, alas! (Dutch.)†

1532. పెరుగు పెత్తనము చెరుచును.

Your curds take away the respect due to age.

Because they cause eructation.

1533. పెరుగూ వడ్లూ కలిపినట్టు.

Like mixing rice in the husk with curds.

1534. పేగు చుట్టమా, పెట్టు చుట్టమా.

Is he a blood relation, or a dinner relation?

(See Nos. 1517, 1557.)

A table friend is changeable. (French.)‡

---

* Vache de loin a lait assez.
† Geluk en glas breekt even ras.
‡ Ami de table est variable.

1535. పేడ కుప్పకు దృష్టి మంత్రమా.

Must the effects of an evil eye be removed from a dunghill ?

A cringing speech. "Should such a worm as I be honored ?"

1536. పేడలో పొదిగిన వుల్లిగడ్డ.

Like an onion set in cow-dung.

A bad man in like company.

1537. పేదల బిగువు.

Poor men's superciliousness.

1538. పేదవాని కోపము పెదవికి చేటు.

When a poor man is angry, he only bursts his own lips.

Anger without power is folly. (German.)*

Anger makes a rich man hated, and a poor man scorned.

1539. పేను కుక్కినా కుక్కుతాడు, చెవ్వి కరిచినా కరుస్తాడు.

[The monkey] may either kill the louse, or bite off the ear.

(See No. 2009.)

1540. పేనుకు పెత్తనమిస్తే, తలంతా తెగకొరికినది.

When power was given to a louse, it bit all over the head.

(See No. 1123.)

Abuse of authority.

1541. పేరంటానికి వచ్చి పెండ్లి కొడుకు వరస యేమి అన్నట్టు.

When she came to the marriage feast she began to enquire how the bridegroom was related to her.

i. e. she was enamoured with him.

Very unseemly behaviour.

---

* Zorn ohne Macht wird verlacht.

1542. పేరు గంగానమ్మ, తాగబోతే నీళ్లు లేవు.

Your name is mother Gangâ, but when I want a drink I find you have no water.

(See Nos. 230, 240, 276, 613, 1209, 1798.)

Where you think there are flitches of bacon there are not even hooks to hang them on. (Spanish.)*

1543. పేరు పల్లకీ మీద, కాలు నేల మీద.

His name is in the palankin, and his legs on the ground.

i. e. he once rode, but now walks.

(See No. 1546.)

1544. పేరు పెద్ద, వూరు దిబ్బ.

A great name but the village a heap [of ruins].

1545. పేరు పెనిమిటిది, అనుభవము మామగారిది.

The name is my husband's, the suffering is my father-in-law's.

Said by Sîtâ to the Ṛishis' wives when they condoled with her on her husband's sufferings. She knew that Râma's misfortune was not to be compared with that of her father-in-law Daśaratha who died of grief, cursed by the old hermit whose son he had accidentally killed.

(See No. 7.)

The name with one, the reality with another.

1546. పేరు పెన్న మోసింది, వొళ్లు నేల మోసింది.

His name is borne by the Penna, and his body by the ground.

(For *Penna* see No. 1528—See No. 1543.)

Said of a wretched fellow with a great name.

Fame is a magnifying glass.

---

* Adó pensas que hay tocinos, no hay estacas.

1547. పైన పారే పక్షికింద పారే చీమ.

Like the ant that crawls below a bird flying above.

It has no chance.

1548. పొంగేదంతా పొయి పాలు.

All that boils over goes to the fire-place.

Said of a silly man puffed up with conceit, whose vanity ruins him.

1549. పొక్కటి రాళ్లకు పోట్లాడినట్టు.

Fighting for the fire-dogs.

(See No. 741.)

Pokkaṭi Râḷḷu are three clods of earth, or round stones used as a temporary fire place.

Quarrelling for something of no value.

1550. పొట్టకరుకులు తిన్న వారికి వూచ బియ్యాలు లేవు.

There is no young corn for those who eat the ears.

1551. పొట్టకు పుట్టెడు తిని అట్లకు ఆదివారము.

Having eaten a bushel of food, [he begs] for cakes as it's Sunday.

Sunday is a fast day among some sects.

Great greediness.

1552. పొట్టి గట్టి, పొడుగు లోడుగు.

Short and strong, tall and weak.

A short man needs no stool to give a great lubber a box on the ear.

1553. పొట్టి పోతరాజు కొలువు.

The service of Poṭṭi Pôta Râzu.

(See No. 1[illegible].)

A worrying fellow, of whom it is said that when his followers were behind him, he abused them for treating him as their (Pariah) guide; when they went before him, he accused them of acting as if they were his superiors; and when they travelled at each side of his palankin, he reprimanded them for daring to place themselves on an equality with himself.

1554. పొట్టి వాడికి పుట్టెడు బుద్ధులు.

A short man has a Puṭṭi of wisdom.

(For *Puṭṭi* see No. 1480.)

1555. పొత్తుల మగడు పుచ్చి చచ్చెను.

The joint-husband was neglected and died.

(See No. 331.)

The ass that is common property is always the worst saddled. (French.)*

1556. పొదుగు కోసి పాలు తాగినట్టు.

Like cutting the udder, and drinking the milk.

Ruining one's self by ambition.

1557. పొయ్యి అరిస్తే బంధువులు, కుక్కలు కూస్తే కరువు.

If the fire place cries out (i. e. if the wood sings) relations [are coming], if the dogs bark a famine [may be expected].

(See Nos. 1517, 1534.)

Let us have florins and we shall find cousins. (Italian.)†

1558. పొయ్యిలో పిల్లి యింకా నిద్రపోతూ వున్నది.

The cat in the fireplace is still sleeping.

No preparations for cooking, little prospect therefore of dinner.

---

* L'âne du commun est toujours le plus mal bâté.

† Abbiamo pur florini che troveremo cugini.

1559. పొయ్యి వూదుమంటే, కుండ బద్దలు కొట్టినాడు.

When asked to blow the fire, he broke the pot which was on it.

To do much harm when asked to do a little favor.

1560. పొరిగింట చూడరా నా పెద్ద చెయ్యి.

Look in my neighbour's house, and see how openhanded I am!

When I distribute his alms.

(See Nos. 3, 910, 1336.)

It is easy to be generous out of another man's purse. (Danish.)*

Broad thongs are cut from other men's leather. (Latin.)†

1561. పొరిగింటి కలహము విన వేడుక.

Quarrelling in one's neighbour's house is pleasant to listen to.

1562. పొరుగు పచ్చగా వుంటే, పొయిలో నీళ్లు పోసుకొన్నట్టు.

When his neighbour prospered he poured water on his own hearth.

(See Nos. 53, 396.)

An envious act.

To lose one eye that you may deprive another of two. (Spanish.)‡

1563. పొల్లు దంచి బియ్యము చేశినట్టు.

Like trying to get rice by pounding empty husk.

(See No. 1485.)

1564. పోకలకుండ చట్రాతి మీద పగలకొట్టినట్టు.

Like breaking a pot full of areca nuts on a stone slab.

A noisy brawl.

---

* Det er godt at være kostfri af en andens Pung.

† Ex alieno tergore lata secantur lora.

‡ Quebrarse un ojo para sacar á otro los dos.

1565. పోడుబాము సామిత.

Like the Boa Constrictor.

(See No. 1615.)

Applied to indolent persons; or to those who, from religious motives, separate themselves from the world and strive to quench all natural emotions.

1566. పోతేపల్లివారికి పప్పే సంభావన.

To the men of Pôtêpalli, Dâl is the money present.

(For *Dâl* see No. 183.)

Said of very poor Brahmans ready to rush to feasts for the sake only of the food, although they know that they will not receive a present in money.

Pôtêpalli literally means "Going-village."

1567. పోయిన కంటికి మందు వేస్తే, వున్నకన్నూ వూడ్చుకొని పోయినది.

When he applied medicine to his bad eye, the sight of the other eye was lost.

(See Nos. 489, 681, 846.)

1568. పోయినది వర, వుండేది కత్తి.

That which is gone is the scabbard, that which remains is the sword.

(See No. 301.)

"He who is dead is nothing to his successor." (Brown.)

1569. పోరాని చుట్టము వచ్చినాడు, తమలపాకులు బొడ్డు వంచి కోయు మన్నట్టు.

"A near relation has come," said he "stoop and pluck the betel leaves."

The owner of the garden unwillingly complied with his relation's demand to be supplied with betel leaf gratis, and instructed his gardener with the ambiguous phrase "stoop and pluck," which the relation understood to mean that the order was to be obeyed with alacrity, the object really being that the worst leaves, which are always nearest the ground, should be given. The word translated "near" signifies literally "one who goes not."

Applied to that which is done because politeness requires it, but unwillingly.

1570. పోరాని చోట్లకు పోతే, రారాని నిందలు రాక మానవు.

If you go where you ought not, you will not escape scandal.

(See Nos. 148, 336.)

1571. పోరిన పొరుగూ రాచిన కుండలూ మనవు.

[In] a quarrelsome neighbourhood there is no thriving, pots rubbing together will not last.

1572. పోరు నష్టి, పొత్తు లాభము.

Strife is loss, friendship is gain.

(See No. 401.)

Where there are friends there is wealth. (Latin.)*

1573. పోలిగాడి చెయ్యి బొక్కలో పడ్డది.

Pôligâḍu's hand fell on the hole.

Where the money was kept.

A lucky chance.

1574. పోలీ పోలీ నీ భోగము యెన్నాళ్లే అంటే, మా అత్త మాలవాడ నుంచి వచ్చే వరకూ అన్నట్టు.

One said to a wife "O Pôli, Pôli, how long will you enjoy yourself?" "Till my mother-in-law comes back from the Pariah quarter" she replied.

When the cat's away the mice play.

1575. పోల్నాటిలో పోకకు పుట్టెడు అమ్మితే, ఆ పోకా దొరకక పొర్లి పొర్లి యేడ్చినదట.

When a Puṭṭi of grain was sold in Pôlnâḍu for an areca nut, she rolled herself on the ground and cried, for she could not even get that.

(For *Puṭṭi* see No. 1480.)

Very unfortunate.

---

* Ubi amici, ibi opes.

1576. ప్రతిష్ఠకు పెద్దినాయుడు చస్తే, యీడవ లేక యింటివాండ్లు చచ్చి నారు.

When Peddinâyuḍu died for fame, the members of his household suffered greatly in dragging away his body.

Peddinâyuḍu here means a Nâyuḍu, (a title borne by certain castes) great both in social position and bodily frame.

1577. ప్రయాణము అబద్ధము, ప్రసాపాటు నిబద్ధి.

The journey was a sham, but eating (the provisions prepared) was a reality.

(See No. 448.)

1578. ప్రసూతి వైరాగ్యము, పురాణ వైరాగ్యము, శ్మశాన వైరాగ్యము.

Three causes of transient repentance, viz., the pains of travail, the effects of preaching, and the sight of death.

(See No. 182.)

The chamber of sickness is the chapel of devotion.

Vows made in storms are forgotten in calms.

1579. ప్రాణము తీపా, బెల్లము తీపా.

Is life sweeter than molasses?

Said of a peculiarly timid nervous man.

1580. ప్రాణము పోయినా, మానము దక్కించుకోవలెను.

Though you lose your life, you must preserve your honor.

(See No. 1716.)

1581. ప్రీతితో పెట్టినది పిడికెడే చాలును.

If given with love, a handful is sufficient.

(See No. 76.)

1582. ప్రీతిలేని కూడు పిండాకూటితో సమము.

Food given without affection, is as food offered to the dead.

బ.

1583. బంగారపు కత్తి.

A golden knife.

Said of something of intrinsic value but of no utility.

1584. బంగారపు పిచ్చుక.

A golden sparrow.

The Telugu term for the grossbeak (Loxia Philippina).

Pretty to look at but of no use.

1585. బంగారు పొల్లు వున్నదిగాని మనిషి పొల్లు లేదు.

There is dross in gold, but there is no defect in man.

1586. బండి దొంగరికము.

Stealing a cart.

Open robbery.

1587. బందేడు పచ్చి కోడలి క్రొత్తా లేదు.

There is no greenness in Bandêḍu, nor newness in a daughter-in-law.

(See No. 588.)

Bandêḍu is the Dodonaea Burmanniana, a light wood that ignites like touch-wood.

1588. బగబగమను వాని పంచనుండ వచ్చునుగాని, నాలిముచ్చు నట్టింట నుండరాదు.

You may live in the verandah of a hot-tempered man's house but you should not dwell in the middle of the house of a man who conceals his resentment.

1589. బట్ట తలలకూ మోకాళ్లకూ ముడివేసినట్టు.

Like tying bald heads and knees in a knot.

Said of a very cunning person.

1590. బట్టప్పు పొట్టప్పు నిలవదు.

Debts for food and clothing do not remain long unpaid.

1591. బడాయి బారెడు, పొగచుట్ట మూరెడు.

His arrogance is two yards long and his cheroot a cubit long.

1592. బడాయి బావగారా అంటే, యేమే గుడ్డికంటి మరదలా అన్నాడట.

When a woman said "O conceited brother-in-law," he answered "Well, one eyed sister-in-law."

1593. బడే సాయబు జ్యోశ్యులూ తొలి యేకాదశి యెన్నడు.

Like asking Baṛê Sâḥib the astronomer on what day the feast of Toli Yêkâdaśî would fall.

Asking a man something which he cannot possibly answer.

1594. బఱ్ఱె కొమ్ము అంటే, యిఱ్ఱి కొమ్ము అంటాడు.

When one says it is a she-buffalo's horn, the other says it is a doe's.

Foolish argumentation.

1595. బఱ్ఱె చస్తే పాడి బయిట పడుతుంది.

When the buffalo dies, it comes out how much milk she gave.

1596. బఱ్ఱె దూడ వద్దా పాత అప్పుల వాడి వద్దా వుండరాదు.

You should not stay near a young buffalo, or an old creditor.

1597. బలవంత మాఘ స్నానము.

Forced bathing in Mâgha.

The mornings of the month Mâgha (January—February) are cold.

A disagreeable duty.

1598. బలవంతుని సొమ్ముగాని బాపడి సొమ్ము కాదు.

Property is the strong man's not the poor Brahman's.

Might overcomes right.

1599. బలిజె పుట్టుక పుట్టవలె, బతాయి బుడ్డి కొట్టవలె.

You must be born a Balije to toss off Batavia arrack.

Balije is a caste.

1600. బాపనవాని కొలువూ తెల్ల గుఱ్ఱపు కొలువూ కొలువ కూడదు.

You should not serve a Brahman or a white horse.

There is no end to your labor.

1601. బారకాడివలె పడ్డావు, నీవెవరవురా మా యింటి దేవుడికి మొక్కను.

You have fallen like a log, who are you to worship our household god?

Bârakâḍi is a long yoke used for training bullocks.

Said to a stranger who, under pretence of worshiping the god, came for food.

1602. బావ మరిది బ్రతకకోరును, దాయాది చావ కోరును.

Your wife's brother will wish you to live, your paternal relatives will wish you to die.

When a Hindu dies his widow is supported by her relatives, and his portion of the family property goes to his relations on the father's side.

1603. బావా నీ భార్య ముండమోశినదోయి అంటే, మొర్రో అని యేడ్చినాడట.

When his brother-in-law said to him "O brother-in-law! your wife has become a widow," he cried bitterly.

Said of a blockhead.

1604. బావిలోతు చూడ వచ్చునుగాని, మనస్సులోతు చూడ కూడదు.

You can see the depth of a well, but not the depth of the mind.

No one can see into another further than his teeth. (Danish.)*

1605. బాస తప్పినవాడూ బడిం తిరిగినవాడూ వకటి.

A man that breaks his word and a vagrant are alike.

1606. బిచ్చపు కూటికి శనేశ్వరమడ్డగించినట్టు.

Saturn prevented the [eating of] food got by begging.

1607. బిచ్చపు వాణ్ని చూస్తే బీద వానికి కోపము.

The sight of a beggar rouses a poor man's anger.

(See No. 75.)

Said impertinently by a beggar when he gets nothing.

1608. బిచ్చానకు పోయినా బిగువు తప్పలేదు, దుప్పటి పోయినా వల్లె వాటు తప్పలేదు.

Although he goes to beg his pride is not diminished, although his cloth has gone the scarf is not removed from his neck.

(See Nos. 90, 856, 1792.)

There's nothing agrees worse, than a proud mind and a beggar's purse.

---

* Man kan ikke see en Anden længer end til Tænderne.

1609. బిడ్డ చక్కిలము వలె యెండిపోయినాడంటే, చక్కిలాలు యిమ్మని యేడ్చినాడట.

When one said "the child has shrunk up like a Çakkilam" the child cried out "give me Çakkilams."

Çakkilamu is "a biscuit made of twisted rings of paste without sugar" (Brown.)

1610. బిడ్డను వేశి లోతు చూచినట్టు.

Like throwing a child into a well to find out the depth.

(See Nos. 1, 412.)

1611. బిడ్డ యెదిగితే కుండ యెదుగును.

As the child grows, the pot grows.

i. e. It eats more.

A growing youth has a wolf in his belly.

1612. బిడ్డ లేని ముద్దు, వాన లేని వరద.

Fondling without a child, a flood without rain.

1613. బీద వాడు బిచ్చపు వాడికి లోకువ.

A poor man is even lower than a beggar.

1614. బురద గుంటలో పంది సామిత.

Like a pig in the mire.

1615. బురదబుక్కడము వంటివాడు.

A man like an eel.

(See No. 1565.)

Sloth. Apathy.

1616. బుర్రకు వక గుణము, జిహ్వాకు వక రుచి.

Every head has its idiosyncrasy, and every tongue its taste.

All tastes are tastes. (Italian.*)

There is no disputing of tastes, appetites, and fancies.

---

* Tutti i gusti son gusti.

1617. బూడిద గుంటలో కుక్క సామెత.

Like a dog lying in the warm ashes.

Keeping quiet for a while, but soon returning to mischief.

1618. బూడిదలో చేసిన హోమము.

Like pouring out an offering on ashes.

(See Nos. 89, 1619.)

A useless or unprofitable work.

1619. బూడిదలో పోసిన పన్నీరు.

Like sprinkling rose water on ashes.

(See Nos. 89, 1618.)

Wanton waste.

1620. బెదిరించి బెదిరించి బెల్లపు కుండకు తూటు పొడిచినదట.

All her threats ended in making a hole in the molasses pot.

1621. బెల్లపు పిళ్లారికి ముడ్డి గిల్లి నైవేద్యం.

Offering the Molasses Gaṇêśa a bit nipped off his own person.

Said of a stingy man.

1622. బొంకరా బొంకరా పోలిగా అంటే, టంగుటూరి మిరియాలు తాటి కాయలంతేసి అన్నాడట.

"Go on with your lies Pôliga," said one, "The Ṭanguṭúru pepper is as big as Palmyra fruit," he replied.

(See Nos. 423, 584, 841.)

He may lie boldly who comes from afar. (French.)*

---

* A beau mentir qui vient de loin.

1623. బొంత కుట్టుకొన్నవాడు కప్పుకో లేడా.

Can he who has sewn himself a quilt, not cover himself with it?

1624. బొగ్గులలో రామచిలుక.

A beautiful parrot (Râmachiluka) among coals.

A good thing found in a bad place.

1625. బొచ్చు కాల్చితే బొగ్గులవునా.

If you burn hair will it become charcoal?

Vain economy.

1626. బొట్నవేలు సున్నమయితే బోర్ల పడుతాడు.

When he has chunam on his thumb, he is upset with conceit.

(See No. 1737.)

Having "chunam on the thumb" means ability to afford to eat a little betel nut. Chunam is rubbed on the leaf with the thumb.

1627. బోగం వలపూ బొగ్గు తెలుపూ లేదు.

There is no love in harlots or whiteness in coals.

1628. బోడి తలకు బొడ్డు మల్లెలు ముడిచినట్టు.

Like decorating a bald man with a jasmine garland.

Boddu Malle is the Jasminum Sambac.

Something being thrown away upon a person.

1629. బోడి నెత్తిన టెంకాయ కొట్టినట్టు.

Like beating a shaven head with a cocoanut.

As used to be done to a *Sannyâsî* (religious mendicant) by his disciples when he was about to die.

1630. బోడెద్దుకు పోటు మప్పడము.

Training a hornless bullock to gore.

Leading the innocent to vice.

1631. బ్రతకని బిడ్డ తెగబారెడు.

The dead infant is always a fine child.

(See Nos. 840, 841.)

Thought more of when dead than when living.

Far folks fare well, and fair children die.

1632. బ్రతికి వుంటే, బలుసుకూర తిని వుండ వచ్చును.

If I live, I can exist on Balusukûra.

Balusukûra is the Canthium Parviflorum.

Preferring hardship to oppression. " Submission to any necessity however grievous." (Elliot.)

What can't be cured must be endured.

1633. బ్రతికి వుండగా పాలు లేదు గాని, చచ్చిన వెనక గంగి గోవును దానము చేస్తానన్నట్టు.

While he lived no milk was given to him, but he was promised that a sacred cow would be presented [on his account] to a Brahman, after his death.

1634. బ్రతికే బిడ్డ అయితే, పాశిన వాసన యెందుకు వస్తున్నది.

If the child is to live, why should there be such an offensive smell ?

Said of a sure sign.

1635. బ్రహ్మకూ పుట్టుతున్నది రిమ్మ తెగులు.

Brahmâ himself becomes enamoured.

1636. బ్రహ్మ తలిస్తే ఆయుస్సుకు తక్కువా, మొగుడు తలిస్తే దెబ్బలకు తక్కువా.

If Brahmâ wishes, will there be any lack in the length of your days ? If the husband wishes, will there be any lack of blows ?

1637. బ్రహ్మ వ్రాసిన వ్రాలు తిరుగునా.

Will the writing written by Brahmâ fail?

(See No. 1344.)

1638. బ్రహ్మాస్త్రానికి తిరుగు లేదు.

There is no turning to a Brahmâstra.

Brahmâstra is the fabulous weapon of Brahmâ.

Said of anything which is irresistible.

1639. బ్రాహ్మణుని చెయ్యీ యేనుగ తొండమూ వూరకుండవు.

A Brahman's hand and an elephant's trunk are never quiet.

1640. బ్రాహ్మణుని మీది సంధ్యా కోమటి మీది అప్పూ నిలవదు.

The prayers due by a Brahman will not remain [unsaid], and the debt due by a Kômaṭi will not remain [unpaid].

1641. బ్రాహ్మణులలో చిన్న, బెస్తలలో పెద్ద.

The youngest among Brahmans, the eldest among fishermen.

Are made drudges.

1642. బ్రాహ్మణులలో నల్లవాణ్ణి మాలలలో యెర్రవాణ్ణి నమ్మరాదు.

You should not trust a black man among Brahmans, or a fair man among Pariahs.

భ.

1643. భక్తిలేని పూజ పత్రి చేటు.

Worship without faith is a mere waste of flowers.

Flowers are used in offerings.

1644. భరతుడి పట్నము, రాముడి రాజ్యము.

The city of Bharata, the kingdom of Râma.

(See Nos. 168, 278, 1887.)

Said of any thing neglected, as Râma's kingdom was neglected during his absence by his half brother Bharata.

1645. భల్లూకపు పట్టు.

A bear's hug.

Obstinacy.

1646. భాగ్యము వుంటే, బంగారు తింటారా.

If you are rich, will you eat your gold ?

A man, however rich, can only live by food, like other men.

1647. భారీముద్ర భారీముద్రే, కరుకు కరుకే.

A bad coin is a bad coin, a good coin is a good coin.

Bad is ever bad, good is ever good.

1648. భూమికి రాజు న్యాయము తప్పితే, గ్రామము వారందరు యేమి చెయ్య గలరు.

If the king of the earth fails in justice, what can all the people of the village do?

1649. భూమికి వాన మేలా అంటే, మేలే అన్నట్టు.

When one asked "Is rain good for the earth?" another replied "It is good."

1650. భోజనము చేశిన వానికి అన్నము పెట్ట వేడుక, బోడి తల వాడికి తలంట వేడుక.

The fun of setting food before a man who has had his dinner, or of anointing a shaven head.

1651. భోజనానికి ముందు, స్నానానికి వెనక.

First to dinner, last to bathe.

The first at dinner gets the best of the fare, the last to bathe gets the best supply of warm water.

1652. భోజునివంటి రాజు కలిగితే, కాళిదాసువంటి కవి అప్పుడే వుంటాడు.

When a king like Bhôja Râzu comes, a poet like Kâlidâsa will follow.

Bhôja Râzu was a king famous for his liberality and for his bountiful patronage of learning and poetry.

మ.

1653. మంగలవాడి పెంట తవ్వగిస్తే, బొచ్చు బైలు వెళ్లుతున్నది.

If you dig into the dunghill of a barber you will only find hair.

Unprofitable labour.

1654. మంగలిని చూచి యెద్దు కాలు కుంటినది.

The bullock began to limp when it saw the barber.

Who would take out a thorn, &c.

Malingering.

1655. మంగలి పాత, చాకలి కొత్త.

An old barber and a new washerman.

An old physician, a young lawyer.

A barber learns to shave by shaving fools.

1656. మంచి ప్రాణానికి మండలము వరకు భయము లేదు.

There is no fear for a good life for forty days.

A strong man can exist without food for that period.

1657. మంచి వానికి మరణమే సాక్షి.

Death is witness to a good man.

A good man's character is borne testimony to, after his death.

Good men must die, but death cannot kill their names.

"*The memory of the just is blessed.*" Proverbs x. 7.

1658. మంచి వానికి మాట్లాడనిదే మందు.

To a good man silence is reproof.

1659. మంచి వానికే వచ్చెనా మరణ కాకితము.

Alas! has a death warrant come to a good man?

Regretting the loss of some good man.

1660. మంచి వారికి మాటే మందు.

A word is medicine to the wise.

A word to the wise is sufficient. **(Latin.)***

1661. మంచి వారికి వక మాట, మంచి గొడ్డుకు వక దెబ్బ.

One word to a good man, one stroke to a good bullock.

A nod for a wise man, and a rod for a fool.

1662. మంత్రము చెప్ప మల్లుభొట్లు, తినడముకు యెల్లుభొట్లు.

Mallubhoṭlu to read the prayers, and Ellubhoṭlu to eat.

It was Ellubhoṭlu's part to read the prayers, but as he was an ignorant man Mallubhoṭlu officiated for him, while he attended to the eating part of the ceremony.

1663. మంత్రము లేని సంధ్యకు మరి చెంబెడు నీళ్లు.

For the Sandhyâ without Mantras another pot of water.

A man who pretends to perform the *Sandhyâ* without really repeating the sacred formula, uses twice as much water as is necessary.

---

* Verbum sat sapienti.

1664. మంత్రసాని ముందర మర్మము దాచినట్టు.

Like covering the body before the midwife.

Hide nothing from thy minister, physician, and lawyer.

1665. మంత్రాలకు మామిడి కాయలు రాలుతున్నవా.

Can unripe mangoes be made to drop by magic?

(See Nos. 421, 2032, 2077.)

Said of excessive leniency or ineffective measures.

1666. మంది యెక్కువయితే మజ్జిగ పలచన.

If there are more people, the buttermilk will be thinner.

i. e. more water will be added.

1667. మక్కాకు పోయి కుక్క మలము తెచ్చినట్టు.

Going to Mekka and bringing back dog's dirt.

(See Nos. 610, 612.)

1668. మక్ఖీకి మక్ఖీ.

A fly to a fly. (Hind.)

(See Nos. 735, 1231, 1666, 1646, 1969.)

1669. మఖ పుబ్బలు వరపయితే, మహత్తయిన క్షామము.

When there's a drought in Makha or Pubba, a great famine will follow.

Makha and *Pubba* are the 10th and 11th lunar mansions.

1670. మఖలో పుట్టి పుబ్బలో పోయినాడు.

Born in Makha, he died in Pubba.

(For *Makha* and *Pubba* see No. 1669.)

1671. మఖ వురిమితే, మదురు మీది కర్ర అయినా పండును.

If Makha thunders, even the millet stalks on the coping of the walls will yield.

i. e. there will be such fine rain.

(For *Makha* see No. 1669.)

1672. మగడు వల్లనమ్మను మారీ వల్లదు.

Even the goddess of pestilence passes over the woman unloved by her husband.

Because her misery cannot be augmented; death would only release her from her sufferings. *Mâri* or *Mâriyamma* (Sans. *Mârî*) is the fury supposed to preside over the small-pox and other epidemical diseases.

You cannot damage a wrecked ship. (Italian.)*

1673. మగ్గానకు వక రాయి మరవకుండా పట్టండి.

Don't forget to pick up a stone for each loom.

Said by one of a party of weavers;—until thus betrayed, their sticks had been mistaken by robbers for matchlocks, and they had been permitted to proceed with impunity.

1674. మట్టి గుర్రమును నమ్మి యేట్లో దిగినట్టు.

Going into a river upon a mud horse.

(See No. 631.)

Relying upon a man who pretends to have influence.

1675. మట్టి తిన్న పామువలె వున్నాడు.

He is like a snake which has eaten earth.

In a stupid state.

The Hindus say that snakes sometimes eat earth, when in want of food.

1676. మట్టి యెద్దయినా, మా యెద్దే గెలవ వలెను.

Although it is an earthen one, yet my ox will beat [the real ox].

(See No. 1048.)

Excessive obstinacy.

1677. మట్టు మీరిన మాటకు మారు లేదు.

A person gets no answer when he transgresses the bounds of politeness.

A rude speech gets no reply.

---

* Non puoi mal fare a nave rotta.

1678. మణులు చెక్కిన సంకెళ్లు.

Fetters set with gems.

Fetters still.

1679. మతి లేని మాట, శ్రుతి లేని పాట.

A senseless speech, a tuneless song.

1680. మదురు మీది పిల్లి వలె వున్నాడు.

He is like the cat on the coping.

i. e. lying steadily in wait.

Said of a cool, calculating, selfish man.

1681. మనమడు నేర్చుకొన్నట్టు, అవ్వకు దురద తీరినట్టు.

The grandson learnt his lesson, and the grandmother's itching was taken away.

The grandmother made her grandson write the alphabet on her back.

To kill two birds with one stone.

To bring down two apples with one stick. (Dutch.)*

1682. మనమెరగని చెవులకు మద్ది కాయలా.

[Are we to put] ear ornaments on ears that we have never heard of?

Said of persons whose pretensions to learning are not acknowledged.

1683. మనసు మహామ్మేరు దాటుతున్నది, కాలు కడప దాట లేదు.

The mind travels over Mahammeru, but the foot does not pass over the threshold.

(See No. 1708.)

Meru or *Mahammeru* is the fabulous mountain on which Brahmâ is said to reside attended by Rishis, &c. It appears really to be the high land of Tartary immediately north of the Himâlayas. (Wilson).

---

* Twee appelen met éénen stok afwerpen.

1684. మనసు లేని మనుము.

An unhappy match.

1685. మనిషి కాటుకు మందు లేదు.

There is no medicine for the bite of a man.

The bite of an enraged man is said to be fatally poisonous.

1686. మనిషికి రాక మ్రాకుకు వస్తున్నదా.

Will [calamity] come to a tree and not to a man?

Human beings are more liable to injury than inanimate objects.

1687. మనిషికి వున్నది పుష్టి, పసలానకు తిన్నది పుష్టి.

A man gets fat by doing nothing, a beast gets fat by eating.

1688. మనిషి పేద అయినా, మాట పేద కాదు.

Although the man be poor, his word is not poor.

(See No. 1706.)

Great words with an empty purse.

1689. మనిషి పోచికోలు కాదు.

No man is useless.

1690. మనో వ్యాధికి మందు లేదు.

There is no medicine for mental affliction.

Gold is no balm to a wounded spirit.

1691. మన్మథుడే పురుషుడయినా, మాయలాడి తన మంకు బుద్ధి మానదు.

Although Cupid himself were the husband of a bad woman, she would not give up her evil practices.

1692. మరిచి పోయి మారుబొట్టులో మజ్జిగ పోశినది.

By mistake she poured buttermilk into buttermilk.

Absence of mind, but no harm done.

1693. మర్యాద రామన్న మాట తప్పినా, నా వేటు తప్పదు.

Though the word of Maryâda Râmanna fail, my blow will not fail.

Maryâda Râmanna ('the respected Râmanna') was a famous minister, renowned for his judgment and the wisdom of his decisions.

1694. మలప సన్న్యాసికీ మాచకమ్మకూ జత.

The helpless Sannyâsî and the jade are a match.

1695. మల్లె పట్టిన చేనివలె.

Like a field attacked by worms.

Sudden and overwhelming ruin.

1696. మళయాలములో చెవులు కుట్టుతారని, మాయవరములోనుంచి చెవులు మూసుకొని పోయినట్టు.

[Having heard that] they bore in Maḷayâlam, she covered up her ears all the way from Mâyavaram.

(See Nos. 461, 1906.)

Mâyavaram is near Combaconum.

1697. మశి పూశి నేరేడు కాయ చేసినట్టు.

Like smearing anything with lamp black and making it like a rose apple.

Nêrêḍu is the Eugenia (Syzygium) Jambolana.

Deceit.

1698. మసి ముఖము వాడూ, చమురుకాళ్ల వాడూ పోగయినట్టు.

Like a black faced villain joining an oily legged sinner.

(See Nos. 735, 1231, 1668, 1846, 1969.)

Burglars disguise their faces, and lepers oil their sores.

Birds of a feather flock together.

1699. మహా మహా వారు మదుళ్లకింద వుంటే, గోడ చాటు వారికి శరణు శరణు.

When great men are under the coping, "Śaraṇu! Śaraṇu!" [is said] to those who live under the wall.

Śaraṇu Śaraṇu here means "you may go, you may go."

When a superior is in want, an inferior must expect to be neglected.

1700. మహా లక్ష్మి పరదేశము పోయినట్టు.

Like the goddess of fortune emigrating.

Said of an avaricious person going to seek for some small gains.

1701. మాంసము తింటామని బోకెలు గుచ్చి మెడను వేసుకోనా.

May we hang a string of bones round the neck, saying "we eat meat?"

1702. మాంసము మాంసమును పెంచును.

Flesh increases flesh.

1703. మాటకు మాట తెగులు, నీళ్లకు నాచు తెగులు.

Word upon word spoils speech as weeds spoil water.

1704. మాట ఘనము, మానిక పిచ్చు.

Great words, but small measure.

(See Nos. 661, 1708.)

A *Mânika* is a dry measure.

The greatest talkers are always the least doers.

1705. మాట తప్పిన వాడు మాల వాడు.

He that breaks his word is a Pariah.

1706. మాటలకు పేదరికము లేదు.

He is not wanting in words.

(See No. 1688.)

He ruins himself in promises, and clears himself by giving nothing. (French.)*

1707. మాటలకు మల్లి, పనికి యెల్లి.

He talks like Malli and works like Yelli.

Malli and *Yelli* are women's names. The former means 'again' the latter 'tomorrow.'

Applied to a man who is great in words, but slow in action.

Say well, and do well end with one letter ;
Say well is good, but do well is better.

1708. మాటలు కోటలు దాటుతవి, కాలు కడప దాట లేదు.

His words leap over forts, his foot does not cross the threshold.

(See Nos. 661, 1683, 1704.)

Great vaunters, little doers. (French.)†

---

* Il se ruine à promettre, et s'acquitte à ne rien donner.
† Grand vanteurs, petits faiseurs.

1709. మాటలు తేటలు మా యింటను, మాపటి భోజనము మీా యింటను.

Let us have a talk in my house, and dinner in your's.

A regular screw.

He is no friend that eats his own by himself and mine with me. (Portuguese.)*

'Tis good feasting in other men's houses. (Italian.)†

1710. మాటలు నేర్చిన కుక్కను వేటకు బంపితే, వుస్కో అంటే వుస్కో అన్నట్టు.

When "Hiss!" was said to the dog that had been taught to speak, "Hiss!" the dog replied.

The consequence of too much petting or spoiling.

1711. మాటలు మా తల్లి మాటలు, పెట్టు మా మారు తల్లి పెట్టు.

She talks like a mother, but she feeds me like a step mother.

(See Nos. 858, 1349, 1986.)

Said of a step mother.

1712. మాటాడితే మల్లెలు, కాటాడితే కందిరీగలు పైలుకుతవి.

When he talks his words are jasmine, but when he wrangles they are hornets.

1713. మాదిగ మంచానకు కాళ్లవైపూ తలవైపూ వక్కటే.

The head and the foot of a cobbler's bed are alike.

Said of an unprincipled sensualist.

---

* Naõ me pago do amigo, que come o seu só, e o meu comigo.
† Le feste sono belle a casa d'altri.

1714. మాదిగ మళ్లి, కంసాలి రెల్లి.

Cobblers say "Again," goldsmiths say "Tomorrow."

Dilatory in work.

1715. మాధవభొట్లకు పడిశెము యేటా రెండు మార్లు రావడము, వచ్చి నప్పుడెల్లా ఆరేశి మాసములు వుండడము.

Mâdhavabhoṭlu gets a cold twice a year, and on each occasion it lasts six months.

Said of a man always in hot water.

1716. మానము పోయిన వెనక ప్రాణమెందుకు.

When honor has gone, why life?

(See No. 1580.)

Take away my good name, and take away my life.

Either live or die wi' honour.

1717. మానిన రోగానికి మందు వద్దు, యీనిన కుక్క యింట వున్నది వైద్యుడా అన్నా డట.

"Holloa Doctor! we don't want medicine for a cured disease, there's a bitch with pups in the house."

Doing the Doctor, when he called for his fees.

1718. మాని పోయిన పుండు మళ్లీ రేపినట్టు.

Like irritating a healed sore.

Bringing up old quarrels.

To rip up old sores.

1719. మానును చూచేవా, మానును పట్టిన భూతాన్ని చూచేవా.

Will you look to the tree or the devil which has possessed the tree?

You must pay respect even to a low fellow in power, because of his influence with those in authority.

1720. మాను పండ్లు మాను కిందనే రాలుతవి.

The tree's fruits fall below the tree.

(See No. 1480.)

What is in your lot, that you will have.

Every man hath his own planet.

1721. మానుపిల్లి అయినా, మట్టి పిల్లి అయినా, యెలుకను పట్టినదే పిల్లి.

A cat which kills a rat is a cat, whether it be of wood or mud.

If the work be well done, never mind the instrument.

1722. మాను పేరు చెప్పి పండ్లు అమ్ముకో వచ్చును.

Having named the tree, you may sell fruit.

As having been plucked from it.

1723. మానెడు పిండవచ్చును గాని, చిట్టెడు యెక్కించ కూడదు.

You can milk down a Mânika, but you cannot put up a Chiṭṭi.

Mânika and *Chiṭṭi* are measures. One of the former equals 16 of the latter.

1724. మాల కూటికి లోబడ్డా, పప్పు బద్ద దొరకదు.

Although you may be driven to eat in a Pariah's house, you won't get any Dâl there.

(For *Dâl* see No. 183.)

Undergoing much and yet suffering disappointment.

1725. మాల పల్లెలో మంగళాష్టకాలు.

The "Eight prayers" said in a Pariah hamlet.

1726. మాలలకు మంచాలు, బ్రాహ్మణులకు పీటలు.

Cots for Pariahs, stools for Brahmans.

Caste customs.

1727. మాలాయ గారికి కోలాయ గారు గురువు.

Mâlâya's priest is Kôlâya.

Mâlâya means a Pariah ; *Kôlâya* is an imaginary name.

Said contemptuously of a Pariah.

1728. మింగ మెతుకు లేదు, మీసాల మీదికి సంపెంగనూనె.

Not a grain to eat, but scented oil for his mustaches.

(See Nos. 539, 1033.)

Love of outward show disproportionate to one's means.

1729. మింగరాని కడి.

A lump that cannot be swallowed.

(See Nos. 259, 737, 1283, 1787.)

A powerful oppressor who cannot be overcome.

1730. మింటికన్నా పొడుగు, నగరి కన్నా ధాష్టీకము లేదు.

There is no greater height than the sky, there is no greater oppression than that of the palace.

1731. మిండడి యీవి యెంతో లంజ మక్కువ అంతే.

The harlot's affection is in proportion to the gifts of her paramour.

1732. మిండలను మరిగిన అమ్మా, మీగడలు తిన్న అమ్మా వూరకుండరు.

She who has used paramours, and she who has eaten the skim of boiled milk will never cease to do so.

Once an use, and ever a custom.

1733. మిడతంభొట్ల జ్యోస్యము.

The prophecy of Miḍatambhoṭlu.

A man is said to have been given that name by a king for guessing that a grasshopper (*Miḍata*) was in the king's hand when the diviners were all at a loss.

Making one's fortune by a lucky chance.

1734. మిద్దె మీది పరుగు.

Running on the terrace of a house.

A hasty beginning.

1735. మిన్ను విరిగి మీద పడ్డట్టు.

As if the sky had broken and fallen upon him.

Said of any one sustaining a great shock by suddenly receiving bad news.

Thunder-struck.

1736. మీకు మాట, నాకు మూట.

A word to you, a bag to me.

An influential person can by a word do great things for others.

1737. మీగాలి మీద మెతుకు పడితే మిట్టి మిట్టి పడ్డాడు.

When a grain of rice fell on his foot, he started with conceit.

It is only when a man has plenty to eat that he lets a grain fall.

1738. మీగాళ్లు వాచినమ్మా మీ యింట్లో పెండ్లి యెప్పుడంటే, మోకాళ్లు వాచినమ్మా మొన్ననే పోయినదన్నట్టు.

"When will the marriage be in your house, swollen-insteps?" said [one woman,] "It was all over the day before yesterday, swollen-knees" retorted the other.

1739. మీ గొడ్డుకు యింత తవుడు అంటే, మీ బిడ్డకు యిన్ని పాలు అన్నాడట.

One said "Here is bran for your cow," the other replied "Here is milk for your child."

(See No. 863.)

Interchange of kindly acts.

One good turn deserves another.

1740. మీ యింటికి వస్తాను నాకేమి యిస్తావు, మా యింటికి వస్తే నాకేమి తెస్తావు.

When I come to your house what will you give me? and when you come to my house what will you bring?

1741. ముంజేతి కంకణానకు అద్దము కావలెనా.

Do you require a looking glass to see the bracelet on your wrist?

(See Nos. 119, 285.)

A thing obvious and plain, requiring no demonstration.

As plain as the nose on a man's face.

As clear as the sun.

1742. ముండ కొడుకే కొడుకు, రాజు కొడుకే కొడుకు.

A widow's son is a son, a king's son is a son.

A king's son and a widow's son are both greatly indulged.

1743. ముండ పెంచిన బిడ్డ ముగదాడు లేని యెద్దుతో సమానము.

A child brought up by a widow is like a bullock without a nose-rope.

1744. ముండ ముప్పావుకు చెడ్డది, నరకడు పావుకు చెడ్డాడు.

The widow lost three quarters of a pagoda, the man lost a quarter of a pagoda.

(See No. 281.)

When a man asked a widow to lend him a pagoda, she said she would only do so on his paying her twenty-five per cent. discount. He complied, but never repaid the principal.

1745. ముండ మొయ్య వచ్చును, నింద మొయ్య రాదు.

You may become a widow but you should not bring on yourself dishonor.

1746. ముండా కాదు, ముత్తయిదా కాదు.

Neither a widow, nor a married woman.

Said by a man kept in suspense, neither granted nor refused a request, and not knowing whether he was to be as fortunate as a married woman or as unfortunate as a widow.

1747. ముంతెడు నీళ్లకే జడిస్తే, బానెడు నీళ్లు యెవరు పోసుకొంటారు.

If you take fright at a cupful of water, who will bathe with a boilerful?

1748. ముంతెడు పాలకు, ముత్యమంత చేమిరి.

A drop of buttermilk, the size of a pearl, to a whole pailful of milk.

(See No. 335.)

A little leaven leavens a great mass. (French.)*

"*A little leaven leaveneth the whole lump.*" I Corinthians v. 6.

1749. ముందర పల్లము, వెనక మిట్ట.

In front a ditch, behind a mound.

(See No. 1751.)

A precipice ahead, wolves behind. (Latin.)†

To be between the horns of a dilemma.

1750. ముందర వున్నది ముసళ్ల పండగ.

The old men's feast is still to come.

i. e. burial.

Said of greater troubles still to be borne.

* Peu de levain aigrit grand'pâte.

† A fronte praecipitium, a tergo lupi.

1751. ముందరికి వస్తే గొయ్యి, వెనక్కు పోతే నుయ్యి.

If you come on, there's a pit; if you go back, there's a well.

(See No. 1749.)

Go forward, and fall; go backward, and mar all.

1752. ముందు పొయ్యే ముతరాచవాణ్ని, వెనక వచ్చే బోయవాణ్ని, పక్కను వచ్చే పట్రాతివాణ్ని నమ్మరాదు.

You should not trust a Mutarâça man going in front of you, a Bôya man going behind you, or a Paṭrâti man going along side of you.

The *Mutarâças* are "a tribe of Hindus, descendants from feudal tenants who were holders in black mail." (Brown.) The *Bôyas* are a tribe of hill men. The *Paṭrâtis* or *Paṭras* are a wandering tribe.

Dangerous companions.

1753. ముందు వచ్చిన చెవులకన్నా, వెనక వచ్చిన కొమ్ములు వాడి.

The horns which came last are sharper than the ears which came first.

Said of a new comer wishing to usurp authority over his seniors.

1754. ముందు వచ్చినది ముత్తైద, వెనక వచ్చినది వెధవ.

The first one was a wife, the last one was a widow.

i. e. the first died while her husband was alive, the last was degraded to the position of a widow.

Old things are thought much of, new ones are not valued.

1755. ముక్కిడికి తోడు పడిశెము.

A noseless man with a running.

(See Nos. 801, 1690.)

Worse and worse.

1756. ముక్కు చొచ్చి కంట్లో ప్రవేశించే వాడు.

Having entered the nose, he gets into the eye.

A skilful rogue.

1757. ముక్కు పట్టని ముత్యము.

A pearl that does not suit the nose.

(See Nos. 253, 737, 1233, 1729.)

1758. ముక్కులో యే వేలు పెట్టినా వాటేను.

Every finger fits the nose.

1759. ముక్కు వుండేవరకు పడిశెము వుంటున్నది.

As long as you have a nose, you will have a running from it.

Continual liability.

1760. ముఖము చూస్తే కనపడదా మీాగాళ్ల వాపు.

If you look at the face, will not the dropsy in the feet be seen?

(See No. 932.)

The face also shows the swelling.

Said of a man whose stupidity is shown in his face.

In the forehead and the eye, the lecture of the mind doth lie.

The countenance is the index of the mind. (Latin.)*

1761. ముఖము మాడుపు దీపము యింటికి కొరగాదు, రంకుబోతు పెండ్లాము మొగుడికి కొరగాదు, యేడ్పుగొట్టు బిడ్డ చంకకు కొరగాదు.

A flickering lamp is unpropitious in a house; a faithless wife is a shame to her husband; a crying child is not fit for the hip.

Hindu women carry children astride on the hip. The word *Çanka* literally signifies "armpit."

---

* Vultus est index animi.

1762. ముగ్గురిని కూర్చెరా మూల దేవుడు.

Alas! God has collected three of us.

Said by one of a number of helpless people.

1763. ముగ్గురి మధ్య ముంత దాగినది.

The large pot disappeared in the midst of three.

i. e. it could not possibly be carried off from the midst of a number of people without some one perceiving it.

1764. ముడి మూరెడు సాగదు.

A knot cannot be lengthened a cubit.

1765. ముడ్డి కిందికి నీళ్లు వస్తే లేవక మానరు.

They won't fail to rise up when the water reaches their posteriors.

(See No. 970.)

Alluding to a flood. Said of apathetic persons who won't move to get out of danger until they are actually obliged.

1766. ముడ్డిమీద కొట్టితే, నోటి పండ్లు రాలెను.

When hit in the back his teeth fell out.

1767. ముడ్డీ ముఖము లేని బిడ్డ, మొదలు లేని పాట.

A child without face or posteriors, a song without beginning.

1768. ముదిమాను చేవ.

An old tree has a firm core.

A brave heart in a weak body.

1769. ముదిమి తప్పితే మూడు వర్ణాలు.

When extreme old age is reached there are three castes.

The distinctive rules of the three castes are no longer observed.

Dotage.

1770. ముదిముప్పున అంగిటముల్లు.

The quinsy in extreme old age.

1771. ముద్దు ముఖము గరుడసేవా.

Is your sweet face like Garuḍasêva?

Garuḍasêva is the name of a feast held at Conjeveram in honor of Varadarâzulu (Vishṇu) whose vehicle is the man bird (Garuḍa).

Said ironically to an ugly fellow.

1772. ముద్దులు గులకరా ముదిపెండ్లి కొడకా అంటే, పెండ్లికి వచ్చిన పేరంటాండ్లు అందరూ నా పెద్ద పెండ్లాలు అన్నట్టు.

When an elderly bridegroom was jokingly asked to say something funny, he replied "All the married ladies who have come to the marriage are my old wives."

A person making himself ridiculous.

1773. మున్నూటి కులానకు ముప్పూ లేదు, మొండి కాలికి చెప్పూ లేదు.

The pedigree of a family numbering three hundred branches cannot be traced nor can a shoe be made to fit a maimed foot.

A hopeless task.

1774. మున్నూరు శిఖలయినా కూడ వచ్చునుగాని, మూడు కొప్పులు కూడ రాదు.

Three hundred Śikhas (i. e. men) may come together, but three Koppus (i. e. women) should not get together.

Śikha is the top-lock worn by men and *Koppu* is a woman's chignon.

1775. ముప్పయి తట్టల పేడ మోసే పోలికి, మూడు పుంజాల దండ బరువా.

Would a necklace of three skeins of thread be heavy for Pôli who carries thirty baskets of cowdung ?

1776. ముప్పయి యేండ్ల ఆడదీ, మూడేండ్ల మొగవాడూ వకటి.

A woman thirty years old and a man three years old are one [in strength].

1777. మురదన్న సందేహాము నిస్సందేహాము.

Muradanna's doubt is cleared.

Said of a man who while wavering and doubting about some undertaking is forestalled by another.

1778. మురిపెముకు మూడు నల్ల పూసలు, కొలిక్కి వక తిరగట్రాయి.

Three black beads for affection, and a mill stone for a clasp.

When a man was told that out of affection three black beads had been tied round a boy's neck, he said " Then use a mill stone for a clasp."

(See No. 93.)

1779. మురిపెము తిరిపెము చేటు, ముసలి మొగుడు ప్రాణముకు చేటు.

Encouraging beggars causes a great expenditure, an old husband is the plague of one's life.

1780. ములకకాయకు తగిన ముండ్లు యెప్పుడు వున్నవో, కాకరకాయకు తగిన గరుకులు అప్పుడే వున్నవి.

As there are thorns on the nightshade so is there roughness on the Kâkara.

(For *Kâkara* see No. 555.)

Mulaka is the Solanum Trilobatum.

One man foolish in one way and one man in another.

1781. ముల్లాలు తిండికి లేక మొత్తుకొంటూ వుంటే, పీర్లకు పంచదార.

While their priests are starving, [the Mussalmans] give sugar [in honor of] their standards.

Pirs or *'Alams* are representations of the standards of 'Alî and Husain set up during the Muḥarram festival.

(See Nos. 227, 799, 989, 1798.)

Caring for the dead and neglecting the living.

1782. ముల్లు దీసి కొర్రడచినట్లు.

Like filling up a hole in a drill-plough with a thorn.

1783. ముల్లు ముంట తీస్తే పొయ్యేదానికి దబ్బనాన తీశినట్లు.

Like taking out with a packing needle, a thorn which could have been extracted with a thorn.

(See No. 820.)

1784. ముష్టికి మూడు సంచులా.

Does a beggar want three bags ?

Applied to an ostentatious display unsuited to a man's position.

1785. ముసలమ్మ సుద్దులు.

An old woman's tales.

(See Nos. 157, 1066.)

1786. ముసలమ్మా బుర్ర వణికిస్తావేమి అంటే, వూరుకుండి నేనేమి చేస్తాను అన్నదట.

When an aged lady was asked "Why do you shake your head?" she replied "Because I have nothing better to do."

A foolish question, and a smart answer.

1787. ముసుకులో గుద్దులాట.

Fisticuffs under a veil.

Two men wishing to converse privately put a veil over their heads; having fallen out they took to pommelling each other.

1788. మూగవాని ముందర ముక్కు గోకుకొన్నట్టు.

Like scratching your nose in front of a dumb man.

This enrages him.

Deriding the defects of another.

1789. మూటికీ ముడివేస్తే, యేమీ లేదు.

If you join the three, there's nothing.

Various interpretations are given.—One is that a man devoid of pride, modesty, and shame, cares for nothing.

1790. మూడు నాళ్ల ముత్తయిదువతనానికి ఆరు జోళ్ల లక్క ఆకులా.

Are three pairs of leaf-earrings [wanted] for three days of wedlock?

Earrings of palm leaves, coloured with *lac* are worn by brides.

Said of an unfortunate young widow.

1791. మూడు నెలలు సాముచేశి, మూలనున్న ముసలిదాన్ని పొడిచినాడు.

After practising fencing for three months he thrust through the old woman in the corner.

Learning to no advantage.

1792. మూడు బోనాలూ సిద్ధమయినవి, దివ్వెకట్ట ముడికి వచ్చినది, దొర గారూ సువారానకు రావచ్చును.

Sir, three kinds of food have been prepared and the lamps are lighted, come to the dining room.

(See Nos. 20, 856, 1608.)

This was a clever speech of the maid servant of a proud but poor Velama to conceal the poverty of her master before visitors; the three kinds of food being the three divisions of the palmyra fruit, and the phrase used regarding the lamps being also susceptible of the meaning " The straw torch has burnt to the knot" i. e. to the end.

You can't fare well, but you must cry roast-meat.

1793. మూడు మూరా వక చుట్టు, ముప్ఫయి మూరా వక చుట్టు.

Three cubits once round, thirty cubits once round [the body].

A woman on being given cloths of different lengths, complained in each case that the cloth would go only once round her body.

Not to be satisfied.

1794. మూరెడు పోనేల, బారెడు కుంగనేల.

Why advance a cubit, and sink a fathom ?

(See Nos. 619, 1104.)

1795. మూరెడు యింట్లో బారెడు కర్ర.

A stick two yards long in a room one cubit square.

A defiant speech in answer to a threat.

1796. మూర్తి కొంచెమయినా కీర్తి విస్తారము.

Small in body, great in fame.

(See Nos. 230, 276, 613, 1250, 1542.)

1797. మూలము అంటే, నిర్మూలము అంటాడు.

When one said "root" the other said "rot."

One attempted to explain, the other pooh poohed him.

1798. మూలవిగ్రహాలు ముష్టి యెత్తుకొంటూ వుంటే, వుత్సవవిగ్రహాలకు దధ్యోదనము.

When the great idols were begging for alms, the little idols asked for rice and curds.

(See Nos. 227, 799, 969, 1781.)

Mûlavigrahas are the large idols made of stone which always remain in the temple; the *Utsavavigrahas* are, as the name denotes, the smaller images that are carried in procession.

Forwardness. Impertinent demands.

1799. మూల వున్నదాన్ని ముంగిట్లోకి తెచ్చినట్టు.

Bringing into the yard that which was in the corner.

Treacherously revealing the secrets of another.

1800. మూలిగే నక్క మీద తాటికాయ పడ్డట్టు.

Like a palmyra fruit falling on a groaning jackal.

A misfortune caused by a strange coincidence.

1801. మూలుగులు ముందటివలెనే, తిండి యెప్పటి వలెనే.

Groanings as before, but glutting as usual.

(See under No. 1173.)

A skulk.

1802. మూశిపెట్టితే, పాశిపోయినది.

When covered, [the food] became bad.

The evil consequences of a crime are aggravated by its concealment.

1803. మెచ్చి మేకతోలూ కోరి గొర్రెతోలూ కప్పుతారు.

If they approve of you they will cover you with a goat-skin; and if they choose you, with a sheepskin.

1804. మెట్టను మాత, పల్లాన భార్య.

The mother on the edge of the precipice and the wife on the brink of the pool.

The two having quarrelled each threatens to destroy herself unless the man takes her part.

A difficult dilemma.

1805. మెట్టనువున్నా యేనుగే, పల్లానవున్నా యేనుగే.

The elephant is an elephant whether on high ground or low.

(See No. 444.)

True greatness is not affected by a change of circumstances.

1806. మెడ తడవడము పూసల కొరకే.

Feeling the neck for beads.

Said of a wheedling scoundrel.

1807. మెరుగు వెయ్యకగాని మృదువుకాదన్నము.

Rice is not soft unless you put ghî.

1808. మేక మెడ చన్ను.

The wattle on a goat's neck.

(See Nos. 731, 1063.)

A useless appendage.

1809. మేకవన్నె పులి.

A goat-coloured tiger.

A wolf in sheep's clothing.

1810. మేడికాయ పై మిసిమి.

The lustre of a green fig.

It often has worms in it.

(See Nos. 1809, 1911.)

Outwardly fine, but inwardly bad.

1811. మేత కరణము.

A Karaṇam to graze.

i. e. up to any amount of bribery and corruption.

(See Nos. 669, 2042.)

1812. మేలు మేలంటే, మెడ విరగపడ్డట్టు.

When they cried "Bravo! Bravo!" he jumped down and broke his neck.

Said of a vain man, who makes a fool of himself to please others.

1813. మొండికి శిగ్గూ లేదు, మొరడుకు గాలీ లేదు.

A pig-headed fellow [feels] no shame, the trunk of a tree [feels] no wind.

1814. మొండికీ బండకూ నూరేండ్లు ఆయుస్సు.

Pig-headed people live for a hundred years.

1815. మొండికెక్కినదాన్ని మొగుడేమి చేసును, రచ్చకెక్కినదాన్ని రాజేమి చేసును.

What can a husband do to a refractory wife? What can a king do to a woman who enters the hall of audience?

1816. మొండిచేతితోటి మొత్తుకొన్నట్టు.

Like beating one's mouth (lamentation) with a maimed hand.

Doing any thing clumsily.

1817. మొండిచేతివానికి నువ్వులు తిన నేర్పినట్టు.

Like teaching a man without hands to eat Sesamum seed.

Attempting impossibilities.

1818. మొండిముక్కున ముక్కెర వున్నట్టు.

A nose jewel in a torn nose.

1819. మొండివాడు రాజుకన్నా బలవంతుడు.

An obstinate person is stronger than a king.

The power of importunity.

1820. మొక్కపోయిన దేవుడు యెదురుగా వచ్చినట్టు.

The god he went to worship met him in the way.

(See No. 174.)

1821. మొక్కుబడే లేదంటే, వక్క దాసరికయినా పెట్టుమన్నట్టు.

As you say you have made no vow, feed at least one Dâsari.

(For *Dâsari* see No. 111.)

Importunity.

1822. మొక్కేవారికి వెరవనా, మొట్టేవారికి వెరవనా.

Shall I fear those who salute me? or those who rap me with their knuckles?

(See No. 103.)

Yielding to force and not to entreaties.

1823. మొగుడి తలమీద మిరియాలు నూరినట్టు

Like grinding pepper on the husband's head.

Said of a hen pecked husband.

The wife wears the breeches.

The grey mare is the better horse.

1824. మొగుడు కొట్టినందుకు కాదుగాని, తోడికోడలు దెప్పుతున్నదని విచారము.

I am not grieved because my husband beat me, but because his brother's wife will taunt me.

Ridicule is feared more than pain.

1825. మొగుడు కొట్టినా కొట్టెను, ముక్కు చీమిడి పోయెను.

My husband has done well in beating me, for [crying] has cleared my nose.

Assumed indifference.

1826. మొగుణ్ని కొట్టి, మొగసాల యెక్కినది.

Beating her husband and then lodging a complaint against him.

1827. మొత్తుకోళ్లోయి ముత్తమశెట్టి.

Senseless howlings O Muttama Śeṭṭi!

Said of people wrangling without reason.

1828. మొదటికి మోసము, లాభానికి గుద్దులాట.

Fighting for the profits after losing the capital.

Neglecting great things for small.

1829. మొదలు దుర్బలం, అందులో గర్భిణి.

Weak to begin with and pregnant besides.

(See Nos. 150, 483, 1214, 2834.)

Sick of the idle crick, and the belly-wark in the heel.

1830. మొదలే మన్ను, కరువు వస్తే గడ్డలు.

Nothing but earth to begin with, and by want of rain, clods.

(See Nos. 801, 1755.)

Worse and worse.

1831. మొప్పులేని వాడే మొదటి సుజ్ఞాని.

The man without evil is the best of wise men.

1832. మొప్పెకు మూరెడు నోరు.

A fool has a mouth a cubit broad.

1833. మొయిలును నమ్మి చెరువు తెగకొట్టినట్టు.

Trusting to the cloud, he cut open the tank.

Prematurely giving up what you have, in the hopes of getting more.

1834. మొయిలు విడిచిన యెండా, మొగుడు విడిచిన ముండా, పట్టి విడిచిన మండా, మెత్తి విడిచిన కుండా తీక్ష్ణము.

The heat of the sun emerging from the clouds—the passion of a meretricious woman separated from her husband—the violence of a bough bent and let go—the force of a pot lifted up and dropped—are great.

"Give the water no passage; neither a wicked woman liberty to gad abroad." *Ecclesiasticus* xxv. 25.

A man under no restraint is a bear without a ring.

1835. మొర్రో మొర్రో వద్దనగా లింగము కట్టేరుగాని, మొక్క చేతులు తేగలరా.

They may tie a Lingam round a man's neck however much he resist it, but can they make him worship it?

A man may lead a horse to the water, but he cannot make him drink unless he will.

Ane may lead a horse to the water, but four an' twenty canna gar him drink. (Scotch.)

1836. మొలమట్టు దుఃఖములో మోకాలుమట్టు సంతోషము.

Up the waist in grief, up to the knees in joy.

1837. మొసలిబావా కడింవేరాయెగాని, కాలయినా యింతేగదా.

O my friend alligator! If this root had been my leg you would have treated it in the same way, would you not?

An alligator enticed a man into the water with fair promises. But afterwards caught him by the leg. The man in turn deceived the alligator by a ruse and escaped.

1838. మోచెయ్యి ఆడితే, ముంజెయ్యి ఆడుతుంది.

If the elbow moves, the wrist moves with it.

1839. మోటకు మొదటి చోట కంపు, వన్నెగాడికి వళ్లంతా కంపు.

A fastidious person suffers more than one who is less particular.

(See Roebuck's *Persian and Hindustani Proverbs*, No. 776, Part II. Sect. I.)

1840. మోటు గాలికి వెరవడు.

A rough man does not fear the wind.

1841. మోశేవానికి తెలుసును కావడి బరువు.

The weight of a load is known to him who carries it.

No one knows the weight of another's burden.

1842. మోక్షానకు పోతే, మొసలి యెత్తుకొని పోయినది.

When he went for salvation, an alligator carried him off.

He was bathing in holy water for the attainment of eternal beatitude.

య.

1843. యజ్ఞానికి యేమి యత్నమంటే, కత్తులూ కటార్లూ.

When asked what preparations had been made for the offering, he said "Here are swords and daggers."

A religious Brahman is not permitted even to touch a lethal weapon.

An impertinent, unbecoming reply.

ర.

1844. రంకాడనేర్చినమ్మ బొంకాడనేరదా.

Will the woman who has learnt to play the harlot, not learn to lie?

1845. రంభ చెక్కిలి కొట్టి రాట్నము తెచ్చినట్టు.

She slapped Rambhâ's cheeks, and then brought a spinning-wheel.

A woman thought she excelled Rambhâ (No. 1066) in beauty, but really was an ugly creature, only fit to sit at the spinning-wheel.

1846. రత్నాలన్నీ వక చోట, నత్తగుల్లలన్నీ వక చోట.

All the gems in one place, all the snails in another.

(See Nos. 735, 1231, 1668, 1696, 1909.)

Like will to like.

1847. రత్నాలు తినే పక్షికి రత్నాలు, రాళ్లు తినే పక్షికి రాళ్లు.

To the bird that lives on gems, gems; to the bird that lives on stones, stones.

(See No. 1473.)

God provides all his creatures with that which they need.

1848. రవుతు కొద్దీ గుర్రము.

As rider, so horse.

The horse goes according to the skill of the rider.

1849. రవుతు మెత్తనయితే, గుర్రము మూడు కాళ్లతో నడుస్తున్నది.

If the rider be bad, the horse will go on three legs.

If the headman be soft, the subordinates will be careless.

1850. రక్షించినవాణ్ని భక్షించనా.

Are you to devour the man who has protected you?

(See Nos. 967, 636, 665, 1077, 1078, 1079.)

Save a thief from the gallows, and he will be the first to cut your throat.

1851. రాగల శని రామేశ్వరము పోయినా తప్పదు.

Even if you perform a pilgrimage to Râmêśvaram, the predestinated evil will not fail to overtake you.

(See No. 1371.)

1852. రాగానకు నేను, అందానకు మా అక్క.

I for singing, my eldest sister for beauty.

Said by an ass of itself and the camel by way of praise.

Applied to a braggart.

Did you ever before hear an ass play upon a lute?

1853. రాఘవా స్వస్తి, రావణా స్వస్తి.

Blessings on Râghava, blessings on Râvaṇa.

The deities were compelled outwardly to bless the tyrant Râvaṇa, but they inwardly blessed Râghava (Râma,) whom they wished to be victorious.

1854. రాచ పీనుగ తోడు లేకుండా చావదు.

A king will not die alone.

The Hindus believe that when a royal personage dies, some other person dies at the same time to keep him company.

When a great man suffers he drags others with him into trouble.

1855. రాజు చేశిన కార్యాలకూ రాముడు చేశిన కార్యాలకూ మెన్నిక లేదు.

There is no questioning the actions of a king or of Râma.

1856. రాజును చూచిన కంట మొగుణ్ని చూస్తే మొట్టబుద్ధి అయినది.

When she looked at her husband with the eye which had beheld the king, she had a mind to thump him.

1857. రాజు భార్య మేడ యెక్కితే, కుమ్మరవాడి కోడలు గుడిశె యెక్కినది.

When the king's wife went on the top of the palace, the potter's daughter-in-law went on the top of the hut.

(See No. 22.)

1858. రాజు మెచ్చినది మాట, మొగుడు మెచ్చినది రంభ.

That's the word, which pleases the king; she is Rambhâ, who is loved by her husband.

1859. రాజు యెంతో ధర్మమంతే.

As is the king, so will the virtue [of the people] be.

(For *Rambhâ* see No. 1066.)

1860. రాజులేని వూళ్లు, పూజలేని గుళ్లు.

Villages without a king, temples without worship.

1861. రాజ్యాలు చెడ్డా లక్షణాలు చెడ లేదు.

Though the kingdom be lost, the air of royalty still remains.

(See No. 221.)

Applied to a man who bears the appearance of having seen better days.

1862. రాట్నము వస్తున్నది, బండి తియ్య వలశినది.

The spinning wheel is come, out the way with your cart.

I ask your pardon, coach; I thought you were a wheelbarrow when I stumbled over you. (Irish.)

1863. రాత నార తీశినట్టు.

Like taking the bark off a stone.

(See No. 59.)

To milk a he goat. (Latin.)*

1864. రాతి కుండకు యినప తెడ్డు.

An iron ladle for a stone pot.

Severe measures for stubborn people

To a hard kust a hard wedge. (Spanish.)†

1865. రాత్రి పడ్డ గోతిలో పగలు కూడా పడనా.

Shall we fall in the day time into the pit into which we fell at night?

Shall we not benefit by experience?

Bought wit is best.

Experience teaches. (Latin.)‡

---

* Mulgere hircum.
† A mal ñudo mal cuño.
‡ Experientia docet.

1866. రానివాడి మీద రాయి.

A stone on him who won't come!

An imprecation used with reference to a man who refuses an invitation.

1867. రామరాజ్యముగా వున్నది.

Like Râma's kingdom.

(See Nos. 166, 278, 1644.)

Neglected.

1868. రామాయణము రంకు, భారతము బండు, భాగవతము బొంకు.

The Râmâyaṇa is [a tale of] adultery; the Bhârata is obscene; the Bhâgavata is a lie.

1869. రామాయణములో పిడకల వేట్లాట.

Like pelting one another with cowdung cakes, during the reading of the Râmâyaṇa.

Inattention and disrespect.

1870. రామాయణమంతా విని రాముడికి సీత యేమి కావలెను అని అడిగినట్టు.

Like asking what relation Sitâ was to Râma after listening to the whole Râmâyaṇa.

A dunderhead.

1871. రామేశ్వరము పోతే, శనేశ్వరము కూడా వచ్చినది.

When he went to Râmeśvaram, Śaneśvaram followed him.

(See No. 1851.)

His bad luck followed him.—Śaneśvaram is an incorrect name given to the planet Saturn; it appears to be a corruption of Śanaischara.

1872. రాయడి తలది, చాకలి మొలది.

Round the lord's head, round the washerman's waist.

i. e. the lord's head cloth is used by the washerman for a lower garment.

1873. రాయి గుద్దనేల, చెయ్యి నొవ్వనేల.

Why thump a stone? Why should your hand be pained?

Why bring trouble on your own head?

1874. రాళ్లచేనికి గుంటక తోలినట్టు.

Like harrowing a field of stones.

A foolish exploit.

1875. రాష్ట్రం దాగినా, రంకు దాగదు.

Although the country be hid, adultery cannot be concealed.

i. e. it were easier to conceal the whole realm.

1876. రూక లేని వాడు పోక చెయ్య లేదు.

A man without money is not worth an areca nut.

A man without money is a bow without an arrow.

Who has not, is not. (Italian.)*

1877. రెక్కలు విరిగిన పక్షివలె వున్నాడు.

Like a bird with broken wings.

Utterly helpless.

---

* Chi non ha, non è.

1878. రెడ్డి వచ్చినాడు, మొదటినుంచి పాడుమన్నట్టు.

The Reḍḍi has come, begin your song again.

A person being continually asked to recommence his song or story on the arrival of every person of consequence.

1879. రేగుచెట్టు కింది ముసలామె సామిత.

Like the old woman under the Rêgu tree.

(For *Rêgu* see No. 119.)

To knock off the fruit, boys were throwing stones into the tree, and they fell on the old woman who was too infirm to move away.

An unfortunate position.

1880. రేపల్లె వాడ చందము.

Like a row of houses in Rêpalle.

Rêpalle (or Vrêpalle) is the Telugu name of Nandavraja, the scene of the youthful exploits of Kṛishṇa.

It was famous for its prosperity according to some—according to others, for the unchastity of its women.

1881. రేపు అనే రోజు వున్నదా.

Is there a day called tomorrow?

Tomorrow comes never.

No one has seen tomorrow. (Portuguese.)*

1882. రేల పూచినట్టు.

As the Cassia blossoms.

Rêla cheṭṭu is the Cassia (Cathartocarpus) Fistula.

(See No. 969.)

---

* O dia de amanhã ninguem o vio,

1883. రొట్టెకు రేవు లేదు.

There is no fixed spot to a wheaten cake.

i. e. there is no rule for breaking it.

1884. రొట్టె తగవు కోతి తీర్చినది.

The monkey settled the bread dispute [between two birds,] by eating it up.

(See No. 1442.)

Swindling others under pretence of arbitration.

1885. రొట్టెలవానికంటే, తునకలవాడు ఘనుడు.

The beggar of crumbs gets more than the beggar of loaves.

1886. రొట్టె విరిగి నేత పడ్డట్టు.

The bread broke and fell into the ghî.

(See Nos. 195, 1362, 1425, 1430.)

His bread fell into the honey. (Spanish.)*

1887. రోకటికి చిగురు పట్టినట్టు.

Like a rice pounder budding.

Said of a hopelessly ignorant fellow.

1888. రోకలి మూడు మాడలు.

Three half-pagodas for a rice pounder.

Said of any thing purchased at an exorbitant price.

1889. రోగిన్ని పాలే కోరినాడు, వైద్యుడున్ను పాలే చెప్పినాడు.

The patient longed for milk, and the doctor too prescribed it.

A fortunate coincidence.

---

* Cayósele el pan en la miel.

1890. రోట్లో బుర్ర పెట్టి, రోకటి దెబ్బకు జడిశినట్టు.

Putting one's head in the mortar, and then fearing the blow of the pestle.

(See No. 1108.)

Undertaking a business and then holding back through fear.

The gladiator, having entered the lists, is taking advice. (Latin.)*

1891. రోలు కరువు యెరగదు.

The rice mortar feels not the famine.

(See No. 354.)

Some grain or other is always pounded in it.

Said of a person who is exempted by his position from the loss which falls upon others, or of one who escapes a general misfortune.

1892. రోలు వెళ్లి మద్దెలతోటి చెప్పుకొన్నది.

The mortar complaining to the drum.

The mortar is beaten on *one* side (by the pestle)—the drum is beaten on *both* sides.

1893. రోషములేని బంటుకు మోసము లేదు.

A mean-spirited servant is in no danger [of losing his life.]

1894. రోషానకు రోలు మెడను కట్టుకొన్నట్టు.

Like tying the rice-mortar to his neck out of rivalry.

Two men were dancing.—One had a drum round his neck ; the other, not to be out-done, hung the mortar round his neck.

ల.

1895. లంకలో పుట్టినవారెల్లా రాక్షసులే.

Every man that is born in Lankâ is a Râkshasa.

Coming from a bad stock.

---

* Gladiator in arenâ consilium capit.

1896. లంజకు పిల్ల తగలాటము.

A child is a hindrance to a harlot.

1897. లంజ చెడి యిల్లాలు అయినది.

The changed harlot became an honest woman.

Ironical.

Chastity gone once, gone for ever.

1898. లంజ బిడ్డకు తండ్రి యెవరు.

Who is the father of a harlot's child?

1899. లడాయి వచ్చినప్పుడా కత్తులు చేసుకోవడము.

To make swords when the war comes.

(See No. 2069.)

1900. లక్షణాలు గల బావగారికి రాగి మీసాలు, అవలక్షణాలు గల బావగారికి అవీ లేవు.

The good looking brother-in-law has red mustaches, the ugly brother-in-law has none at all.

1901. లాభము గూబలలోకి వచ్చినది.

The profit has come into the drums of the ears.

A dealer in *ghî* suffering from the ear-ache put a little of it into his ears. This was all his profit.

Applied to any unprofitable transaction.

1902. లాభము లేనిదీ శెట్టి యేటపడడు.

Unless there is something to be gained by it, the Śeṭṭi will not venture into the river.

(See No. 181.)

The *Śeṭṭis* and *Kômaṭis* are very greedy and very cowardly.

People do not risk their lives unless they have some great object to gain by it.

1903. లేక లేక లోకాయ పుట్టితే, లోకాయ కన్ను లొట్ట పోయినది.

When after being long childless, Lôkâya was born to them, Lôkâya's eye was sunken.

1904. లేకుండా చూచి పోకుండా పట్టు అన్నాడట.

If you see he's not there, catch him and don't let him go.

Said by a cowardly man to another with reference to a thief.

1905. లేడికి లేచినదే ప్రయాణము.

The antelope has only to rise to be ready for a journey.

Said of a man ready to go any where.

1906. లేనిబావకంటే గుడ్డిబావ అయినా మేలు.

A blind brother-in-law is better than none at all.

(See Nos. 312, 314, 776.)

Better a bare foot than no foot at all.

Better a blind horse than an empty halter. (Dutch.)*

1907. లేని వుదారికంటే కలిగిన మొండి మేలు.

A rich stingy man is better than a poor liberal man.

1908. లేవలేని అత్తకు వ్రాపలేని కోడలు.

A bed-ridden mother-in-law and a lazy daughter-in-law.

A useless couple.

1909. లేస్తే కొరగాను భాయీ.

If I get up, I'll give it you, my boy!

The story is that a certain custom house official had no legs, but he used to threaten travellers who attempted to evade payment of duty, until the secret was found out.

Applied to powerless threats.

If you cannot bite, don't show your teeth.

---

* Beter een blind paard, dan een leege halter.

1910. లోగుట్టు పెరుమాళ్లకు యెరుక.

The secrets of the heart are known to Perumâḷ (Vishṇu).

'[*God*] *knoweth the very secrets of the heart.*' Psalm xliv. 21. (Psalter.)

1911. లోన వికారము, బయిట శృంగారము.

Inwardly bad, outwardly fair.

(See Nos. 1809, 1810.)

All saint without, all devil within.

1912. లోభికి నాలుగందాలా నష్టము.

A miser suffers loss on all sides.

False economy.

A stingy man is always poor. (French.)*

1913. లోభిని చంపవలెనంటే, డబ్బు అడిగితే చాలును.

If you wish to kill a miser, to ask him for a Ḍabb is sufficient.

A *Ḍabbu* is one-third of an Aṇâ (anna), and is equivalent to a half-penny.

1914. లోభి సొమ్ము దొంగవాడి పాలు.

A miser's property falls to the lot of the thief.

1915. లోవి ముయ్యగలరుగాని, లోకము ముయ్యగలరా.

You may cover the mouth of a pot but can you cover up the world ?

You may shut one man's mouth, but you cannot shut the mouth of the world.

---

* Homme chiche jamais riche.

1916. వంకర టింకర కాయలు యేమిటివి అంటే, చిన్ననాడు అమ్మిన చింత కాయలు అన్నాడట.

When she asked "What are those crooked pods?" they replied "The unripe tamarinds you sold in your youth."

The story goes that the daughter of very poor parents who in her youth had to go about selling the unripe tamarinds she was able to gather from under the trees, afterwards became the wife of a rich man. Passing through the streets one day in her grand palankin, she superciliously enquired what a tamarind girl was selling, when her bearers replied as above, "These are the tamarinds Madam, which you sold in your youth."

To take one a peg lower.

You used to be a baker though now you wear gloves. (Spanish.)*

1917. వంకాయ రుచి తోటవాడు యెరుగును, అరటికాయ రుచి రాజు యెరుగును.

The gardener knows the taste of the brinjal; the king knows the taste of the plantain.

(For *Brinjal* see No. 97.)

Brinjals should be cooked and eaten fresh from the garden. Plantains when used in an unripe state as a vegetable, should be kept a few days. Before the brinjals are set before a king they have lost some of their flavour, and as the gardener cannot afford to keep the plantains he plucks, he cooks them before they are ready for the pot.

1918. వంగతోటవానికి కని గుడ్డు, ఆకుతోటవానికి విని చెవుడు.

The brinjal gardener is blind, though he sees; the betel gardener is deaf, though he hears.

(For *Brinjal* see No. 97.—See No. 1278.)

In the first case, the gardener on being asked to give brinjals pretends he cannot find any; in the second case, the gardener when called to by some one outside the garden for betel pretends he cannot hear.—(Brahmans and some high caste Śûdras are forbidden by their Śâstras to enter a betel garden).

None so deaf as he that won't hear. (French.)†

---

* Panadera erades antes, aunque ahora traels guantes.
† Il n'est pire sourd que celui qui ne veut pas entendre.

1919. వంట అంతా అయినదిగాని, వడ్లు వక పొలుపు యెండ వలశి వున్నది.

The dinner is quite ready, the paddy merely requires another drying.

Paddy is an Anglo Indian term for rice in the husk.

A hasty and ridiculous answer.

1920. వండలేని అమ్మకు వొప్పులు మెండు, తేలేని అయ్యకు తిండి మెండు.

The lady who cannot cook seeks for much praise; the gentleman who cannot earn his livelihood is a great eater.

He earns a farthing and has a penn'orth of thirst. (Dutch.)*

1921. వండిన కుండలో వక మెతుకే పట్టి చూడడము.

Taking one grain out of the pot and feeling [whether it is soft or not].

One action tells what a man is worth.

From one circumstance judge of all. (Latin.)†

You may judge of Herles from his foot. (Latin.)‡

1922. వండుతూ వుండగా వాంతి వస్తున్నది అంటే, వుండి భోజనము చేశి పొమ్మన్నదట.

When he said "[The sight of] your cooking makes me sick," she replied "Please stay and eat your dinner before you go."

1923. వగచినట్టూ వుండవలె, వాత పెట్టినట్టూ వుండవలె.

Pretend to condole when you cauterize.

1924. వగలమారి వంకాయ శెగలేకనే సగమయినది.

The feigning brinjal shrunk into half its size, when there was no heat.

Simulating fear.

---

* Hij verdient een' stuiver en heeft wel voor een' braspenning dorst.
† Ex uno specta omnia.
‡ Ex pede Herculem.

1925. వగ్గు కోతికి సివము వచ్చినట్టు.

Like the fury of a weak monkey.

(See No. 1536.)

Impotent rage.

1926. వచ్చిన కర్మము వద్దంటే పోతున్నదా.

Will the result of your deeds go away at your bidding ?

(See No. 287.)

1927. వచ్చిన దోవనే పోతున్నది.

It will go the way it came.

So got, so gone.

Lightly come, lightly go.

I llgot, ill spent.

1928. వచ్చిన వాదు చచ్చినా పోదు.

Calumny is not removed even by death.

(See No. 1395.)

Slander leaves a slur.

Give a dog an ill name, and you may as well hang him.

1929. వచ్చిన వారికి వరమిస్తాను, రాని వారికి రాయి వేస్తాను.

I will grant a boon to those who come, and cast a stone on those who do not come.

Supposed to have been said by a deity.

Used threateningly by a great personage.

1930. వచ్చీ రాని మాటలు రుచి, వూరీ వూరని వూరుగాయ రుచి.

The half articulated words [of children] are pleasant [to the ear] and half pickled vegetables to the taste.

1931. వచ్చే కాలము కన్నా, వచ్చిన కాలము మేలు.

The past is better than the future.

"The good old times."

1932. వచ్చేదెల్లా రాని, పొయ్యేదెల్లా పోని.

Let what is to come come, and what is past be past.

Let bygones be bygones.

1933. వట్టింటికి పోచిళ్లు చల్లినట్లు.

Like sprinkling grains of rice over an empty house.

Pôchiḷḷu is a superstitious rite in which a man having thrown grains of rice on a neighbour's house, listens for any words he can overhear, and elicits a meaning from them.

A profitless proceeding.

1934. వట్టి గొడ్డుకు అరుపులు మెండు, వరపుఏటికి మెరుపులు మెండు.

The barren cow bellows much, and in the year of drought there is much thunder.

Much smoke and little roast. (Italian.)*

All talk and no go.

1935. వట్టి నిందలు చెప్పితే, గట్టి నిందలు వచ్చును.

If you accuse others falsely, you will be accused truly in turn.

1936. వట్టి మాటలవల్ల పొట్టలు పూడుతవా.

Will empty words fill bellies?

(See Nos. 858, 1349, 1711.)

We must assist in deeds not in words. (Latin.)†

Words don't fill the belly. (Portuguese.)‡

---

* Molto fumo, e poco arrosto.
† Re opitulandum non verbis.
‡ Palavras naõ enchem barriga.

1937. వడ్డించేవాడు తనవాడు అయితే, కడబంతిని కూర్చున్నా వక్కటే.

If the person who serves the food is your friend, your sitting at the end won't matter.

A friend in court makes the process short.

1938. వడ్డి ఆశ మొదలు చెరుచును, గుడ్డిది ఆలయితే కుండలు చెరుచును.

By seeking usury, the principal suffers; if the wife be blind, the pots suffer.

1939. వడ్ల గాదెలో పందికొక్కును పెట్టినట్టు.

Like putting a bandicoot in a corn bin.

1940. వడ్లతోకూడా దాగర యెండ వలశి వచ్చినది.

The basket must bake in the sun with the paddy.

(See Nos. 256, 1240.)

Sharing the sufferings of others.

1941. వడ్ల రాశి వరదబోయినా వానతో శేగి లేదు.

Though the heap of rice be carried away by the flood, there will be no damage from the rain.

Though one suffer many will be benefited.

1942. వన్నెచీర కట్టుకొన్న సంభ్రమమేగాని, వెర్రికుక్క కరిచినది యెరగదు.

She was thinking so much of the coloured cloth she had put on, that she did not know that she had been bitten by a mad dog.

Engrossed in pleasure, and blind to danger.

1943. వయసు తప్పినా వయూరము తప్పలేదు.

Though he is old he is still a fop.

1944. వరహాకన్నా వడ్డీ ముద్దు, కొమారునికన్నా మనముడు ముద్దు.

Interest is sweeter than the principal; a grandson is dearer than a son.

1945. వరికి వకవానా, వూదకు వకవానా.

Is one rain for paddy and another for Úda?

(For Úda see No. 303.)

'[*God*] *sendeth rain on the just and on the unjust.*' Matthew v. 45.

Impartiality.

1946. వరికి వాక, దొరకు మూక.

A stream for a rice-field, a troop for a chief.

1947. వలశివస్తే మేనమామకూతురు వావి కాదన్నట్టు.

When his uncle's daughter wanted to marry him, he excused himself on the plea that she was not of the right affinity.

Proudly refusing, because it was voluntarily offered, a good thing which at another time would have been thankfully accepted.

Note. Among Hindus (especially Kômaṭis) it is obligatory for a man to marry his maternal uncle's daughter if there be one.

1948. వసిష్ఠుని వాక్కున విశ్వామిత్రుడు బ్రహ్మర్షి అనిపించుకో వలెను.

Viśvâmitra must have himself called a Brahmarshi from the mouth of Vaśishṭha.

Vasishṭha was a celebrated priestly sage (Brahmarshi). Viśvâmitra, once a king, had by penance become a royal Ṛishi (Râjarshi) but persisted in austerities until Vaśishṭha was compelled to acknowledge him as a Brahmarshi. (See *Bâlakâṇḍa* of the *Râmâyaṇa*.*—Also Muir's *Sanscrit Texts* Part. I.)

---

* ब्रह्मवेदविदां श्रेष्ठो ब्रह्मवेदविदामपि।
ब्रह्मपुत्रो वशिष्ठो मामेवं वदतु देवताः॥

1949. వాండ్లు పొక్కటి రాళ్ల రీతిగా వున్నారు.

They are like fire dogs.

(See Nos. 460, 1283.—For *Pokkaṭirāḷḷu* see No. 1549.)

Bosom friends.

1950. వాకిలి దాటి వారణాశి యెంత దూరమన్నట్టు.

Like a man asking when he had just got outside his door, how far off Benares was.

Talking about the completion of a great undertaking before you have well commenced it.

1951. వాచినమ్మకు పాశినకూడు పెట్టితే, మా అత్త పరమాన్నము పెట్టినది అని యిరుగింట పొరుగింట చెప్పినదట.

When an ill-treated daughter-in-law at last got some bad food from her mother-in-law, she told the neighbours she had been sumptuously fed.

Real want is not dainty.

1952. వాడ పగిలిన కళాసుల సామిత.

Like the crew of a wrecked ship.

In a miserable plight.

Said of something sudden and alarming.

1953. వాడమీాద వుండేవరకు వాడమల్లప్ప, దిగగానే బోడిమల్లప్ప.

As long as he was on board his ship, he was "Ship Mallappa" as soon as he landed he was "Bald-headed Mallappa."

1954. వాడలో నా పోకచెక్క సగం వున్నది భాయీ.

My half areca nut is in the ship, brother!

A merchant was returning to his country in a ship which he had laden with areca-nuts. A friend on board cunningly dropped half of a nut which he was eating into the hold, exclaiming "My half nut is in the ship, brother!" The merchant laughing replied that he would restore it, on which the other, pretending to carry on the joke, made him give a bond to the effect that his half areca-nut was in the ship. The phrase also could be construed as meaning that half the areca-nuts in the ship were his. On arriving at their destination the merchant was prosecuted by the swindler and cheated out of half his cargo.

Said of a clever cheat.

1955. వాడవదినెకేల వావి వర్తనములు.

What has a harlot to do with degrees of relationship, and good manners?

Vâvi signifies those degrees of relationship within which cohabitation is incest.

1956. వాడి పని గూట్లోకి వచ్చినది.

His business has come into the niche.

(See No. 1957.)

He is on his last legs.

1957. వాడి పని తెల్లవారినది.

His business has dawned.

(See No. 1956.)

He's blown up.

He has shut up his shop windows.

1958. వాడి మాట పిండికీ అవుతుంది, పిడుక్కూ అవుతుంది.

His speech will answer for flour or for a thunderbolt.

Said of an ambiguous speech.

1959. వాడు ఆడినది ఆట, పాడినది పాట.

What he dances is a dance, what he sings is a song.

(See Nos. 1960, 1990.)

1960. వాడు చెప్పినది వసిష్ఠ వాక్యము.

What he says is Vaśishṭha's dictum.

(For *Vaśishṭha* see No. 1948—See Nos. 1959, 1990.)

1961. వాడు వెక్కిరిస్తే నీకు యెక్కడ మొర్రిపోయినది.

When he mocked you where were you maimed?

Words break no bones.

1962. వానతో సేగి మొగుడితో పేదరికము లేదు.

There is no loss by rain, or poverty with a husband.

1963. వానరాకడ, ప్రాణము పోకడ, యెవరికి తెలియదు.

The coming of rain, and the going of life, are known to none.

Sorrow an' ill weather come unsent for. (Scotch.)

Death keeps no calendar.

1964. వానలు కురిస్తే వాతలు మానునా, బిడ్డలు కంటే రంకులు మానునా.

If it rains, will brands disappear? If children be born, will adultery be discontinued?

1965. వానలు కురుస్తుంటవి, కప్పలు అరుస్తుంటవి.

Rain will fall, frogs will croak.

Said of any thing which must be expected as a matter of course.

1966. వానలేని వట్టిపిడుగు.

A thunderbolt without rain.

A useless thing.

1967. వానిపని యేకాధ్వర్యమాధవకరముగా వున్నది.

His business is flourishing greatly, even to the extent of begging alms.

A sarcastic speech used with reference to the downfall of a bad man.

1968. వాని యింట్లో యిలిభిక్షము బలిభిక్షము పుట్టదు.

In his house neither Ili nor Bali is offered.

(See Nos. 286, 964, 2027.)

Ili is applied to the grains of raw rice religiously offered to ants, &c. *Bali* is the food given in the same manner to crows before commencing a meal.

He'll flay a flint.

Dogs run away with whole shoulders.

1969. వాసానికి తగ్గ కూసము.

A peg for the rafter.

(See Nos. 735, 1231, 1663, 1696, 1846.)

A well matched pair.

1970. వింటే భారతము వినవలె, తింటే గారెలు తినవలె.

If you listen, listen to the Bhârata; if you eat, eat cakes.

1971. వింతలేని ఆవలింత పుట్టదు.

There is no yawn without a wonder.

Pratáparudrudu king of Ôrugallu, (Wurrangal) had a very sagacious minister, by name Yugandharudu, who was summoned by the Sultan to be employed in his court. The king refusing to send him, was taken prisoner and confined in the capital. His faithful minister having declared that he would rescue him and bring him back openly, went disguised to the capital and there feigning madness, ran daily through the streets calling out "Ho! I am going to take away Ôruganti Pratáparudrudu." The Sultan, suspecting that his madness was assumed, caused him to be watched. The spies discovered that he cooked under a tree at midnight, and a man was concealed in the tree to watch him when he thought himself alone. According to his custom the minister came at midnight to cook his food, and while doing so, *yawned*. He immediately thought to himself that there must be some cause for this, and glancing furtively up the tree perceived the spy. He then said in a loud voice 'There is no yawn without a wonder,' and commenced breaking his pots and acting the mad man. The minister was then reported as really mad and his ravings were unheeded. Shortly afterwards a ship laden with valuables, was sent by the minister's contrivance to the port. The Sultan hearing this, was anxious to inspect the cargo, and being informed that the imprisoned king was a connoisseur in gems ordered him to be brought with him on board the vessel. The minister also managed to get on board and while the Sultan was engaged in examining the precious stones, caused the anchor to be weighed. The Sultan then learnt the trick that had been played upon him and commending the sagacity of the minister, pardoned both him and the king, who returned rejoicing to Ôrugallu.*

---

* A somewhat different version of the story is given in the *Madras Church Missionary Record* for October 1865 by the Rev. F. W. N. Alexander:—

"I could get very little information from my informant about this ancient king, one thing only is certain that in his days the Mohammedans invaded this part of India and besieged Wurrangal, but the Fort was not taken in his days. The story told to me by several people is very contradictory and unlikely in many respects. The most credible version seems to be, that Wurrangal was besieged by the Padasha of Delhi in person, and for 7 years the assailants were baffled by the thickness of the walls and by the supplies raised within the Fort itself from the large space enclosed by the walls. Failing in this way, they at last took the king by stratagem. The Mohammedans feigned a desire for peace and decoyed Pratáparudrudu outside the gates on pretence of making peace, and then seized him in a chariot and carried him off to Delhi and kept him there many days. Meanwhile things went on badly in Wurrangal. In the absence of their king the people refused to obey the minister, and anarchy reigned in the city. The minister resolved to deliver his lord from confinement, and restore him to his subjects. He went to Delhi and began to tell in the most public manner that he was come to release Pratáparudrudu, the imprisoned king. For this he was imprisoned and beaten. After a time he was released, and as before proclaimed everywhere that he was going to release the king. He was imprisoned and beaten again and again, till at last he was regarded as a mad man and no heed was taken of his sayings or doings. Roaming through the city, he at last found out where his lord was, and brought to him two legs of the carved ebony cot on which the king used to sleep in Wurrangal, and offered them for sale. They were recognized at once; and the pretended seller was asked where he got them and where the remaining pair was to be found. The king was told that the missing pair would be found on board a ship in the river, and he was asked to come and see them. To this the king assented, and somehow brought with him the Padasha of Delhi. They both went on board the ship indicated, and at the helm was seen the pretended mad man who was in truth the minister of the king. In an instant the ship was loose, and the sails spread, keeping in mid-stream they escaped down the river before they could be apprehended, and entering the Godaveri the king and the Padasha made their way to Wurrangal. The latter it is said was subsequently released by ransom, and Pratáparudrudu died peaceably in his own city."

1972. విందు మర్నాడు మందు.

The day after a feast a dose.

(See No. 1506.)

After a feast a man scratches his head. (French.)*

1973. విందులేని కూడు మందు.

Food without a feast is medicine.

To dine alone is disagreeable.

1974. విఘ్నేశ్వరుడి పెండ్లికి విఘ్నాలు వెయ్యి.

There are thousand obstacles in the way of Vighneśvara's marriage.

Vighneśvara (Gaṇeśa) is the god of obstacles, the deity 'supposed capable of either causing or removing difficulties or impediments.' (Wilson.)

Applied to an unlucky man.

1975. విడిబడితే గుర్రము గాడిదెతో సమానము.

If a horse gets loose it is like an ass.

i. e. it snorts and kicks.

Applied to wickedness unrestrained.

1976. విడువుమంటే పాముకు కోపము, పట్టుమంటే కప్పకు కోపము.

If you say "let it go" the snake will be angry, if you say "hold it" the frog will be angry.

A difficulty in pleasing both parties in the settlement of a dispute.

It is hard to please a' parties. (Scotch.)

1977. విత్తనము వకటి వేస్తే, మొక్క వకటి మొలుచునా.

Will the plant differ from the seed?

(See Nos. 175, 185, 1019.)

A chip of the old block.

He that was born of a hen loves to be scratching. (French.)†

---

* Après la fête on gratte la tête.

† Qui naît de geline il aime à grater.

1978. విత్తనాలకు పోయిన రెడ్డి ప్రాదెలెత్తగా వచ్చినాడు.

The farmer who went for seed, returned after the harvest.

(See No. 28.)

Applied to a slow coach.

1979. విదియనాడు రాని చంద్రుడు తదియనాడు తానే వస్తాడు.

The moon which does not come (i. e. cannot be seen) on the second [of the month] will come himself on the third.

Applied to the necessity of having patience.

1980. విధివస్తే పొదలడ్డమా.

When fate meets you can bushes stop it?

(See No. 1984.)

Nothing can interfere with one's destiny.

That which must be, will be. (Danish.)*

1981. వినాయకుడి మీంది భక్తా ఉండ్రాళ్ల మీంది భక్తా.

Is it devotedness to Vinâyaka or to the cakes?

Vinâyaka is one of the names of Gaṇeśa (No. 1974.)

Cupboard love.

1982. విని రమ్మంటే, తిని వచ్చినట్టు.

When he was sent to find out, he ate and returned.

(See No. 537.)

1983. విన్నమ్మ వీపు కాలినది, కన్నమ్మ కడుపు కాలినది.

Vinnamma's back burned, Kannamma's belly burned.

The first mourned the loss of a son-in-law, the second that of a son.— *Kannamma* signifies 'she who bore;' *Vinnamma* signifies 'she who heard' [of the death.]

---

* Det kommer vel der skee skall.

1984. విల్లూరి మఱ్ఱికింద విధి వున్నది.

Your fate is under the Banyan tree at Villûru.

(See No. 1980.)

A certain king consulting on one occasion an astrologer was told that he would in two years be hanged as a thief on the western bough of the Banyan tree at Villûru. The king laughed at this but the astrologer only replied "Your fate is under the Banyan tree at Villûru." The king afterwards believing his predictions, went far away to the Himâlayas and there having caused himself to be maimed so that he could not walk, practised penance. At the expiration of the two years, Yama the god of death suddenly came and mounted the unfortunate king on a horse which flew with him through the air, and threw him under the Banyan tree at Villûru. The same night a band of robbers having plundered a Râja's palace brought their booty and divided it under the Banyan tree. The doomed king enquired from them where he was, and having learnt to his dismay that he was at Villûru, and on the *western* side of the tree, he crawled round with difficulty to the eastern side. There he was found by the Raja's men, and beside him a jewel which the robbers had accidently left behind them. In vain he pleaded innocence. The Raja was informed that one of the robbers had been found, the jewel was identified, and the unfortunate king was hanged on the eastern bough. Immediately this was done the tree turned round and the astrologer's prediction was fulfilled.

This story is told as a wonderful instance of the power of fate.

He that is born to be hanged shall never be drowned.

What will be, will be. (Italian.)*

1985. విశిరినమ్మకు బొక్కినదే కూలి.

The grinding woman's hire is what she gobbles up.

1986. విషపాల విత్తు, నేపాలపుగింజ.

A Vishapâla seed, a Nêpâla seed.

Vishapâla is the Hoya Pendula.—*Nêpâla* is the Physic-nut (Jatropha Curcas) ; in large doses the seeds are an energetic poison (Eng. Cyclop.)

Said of a person of a vicious disposition.

---

* Che sarà, sarà.

1987. విషపుంజము.

A mass of poison.

Wickedness.

1988. విస్తరి కొదవా సంసారపు కొదవా తీర్చేవారు లేరు.

There are none who can remedy the defect in a platter or in a family.

It is difficult to entertain people to their satisfaction, or to remove all dissensions in a family.

1989. విస్తళ్లు యెత్తమంటే, భోజనము చేశినవారు యెందరు అన్నట్టు.

When told to remove the leaves, he asked how many people had dined.

An impertinent question.

1990. విస్సన్న చెప్పినది వేదము.

What Vissanna says is the Veda.

(See Nos. 1959, 1960.)

All that he says is law.

1991. వీపుమీద కొట్టవచ్చును గాని, కడుపుమీద కొట్టరాదు.

You may beat on the back but not on the belly.

i. e. Punish me but don't touch my pay.

1992. వీసముగల రెడ్డికి విడవా ముడవా సరి.

The time of a rich Reḍḍi is taken up in untying and tying [his purse].

1993. వెంటరావద్దంటే, యెత్తుకొమ్మని యేడ్చినాడట.

When [a child] was told not to follow, it asked to be carried.

(See No. 1060.)

Asking much when denied a little.

1994. వెంట్రుకలు వుంటే, యే కొప్పు అయినా పెట్టవచ్చును.

If there is hair, it may be dressed in any fashion.

(See No. 824.)

If you have means, you can do any thing you like.

1995. వెట్టికి పుట్టిన బిడ్డ నెత్తికి లేక యేడ్చినదట.

A child born where there was no love [between the parents] suffered for want [of oil] for its head.

1996. వెట్టిగదరా పోలా అంటే, యెడవక తీరదే అయ్యా అన్నాడట.

When one said "O Pôla! is it not work without pay?" he replied "Alas! Sir, there is no way to get out of it."

Said of any disagreeable duty, which must be performed without remuneration.

To have nothing but one's labour for one's pains.

Like the tailor who sewed for nothing and found thread himself.

Better sit idle than work for nought.

1997. వెధవకు దణ్ణము పెట్టితే, తన్ను బోలి బ్రతుకుమన్నది.

When the widow was saluted, she replied with "May you live like me."

A doubtful blessing.

Depending upon the helpless.

1998. వెధవముండా వేరుండుమన్నట్టు.

Live separately, you wretched creature.

Said when turning out any member of the household.

1999. వెనకకు వెళ్లితే తన్ను, ముందుకు వస్తే పోటు.

If you go behind you are kicked, if you go in front you are gored.

(See No. 1553.)

Not to be pleased in any way.

2000. వెనక చింతించుట వెర్రితనము.

Thinking over the past is folly.

Vain regrets.

2001. వెనకా ముందూ చూచి మాట్లాడండి అన్నట్టు.

Having looked before and behind, speak, Sir.

A story is told of a corrupt judge behind whose seat one of the parties in a suit placed a bag of money and when he perceived that the case was going against him, called out "Look before and behind you Sir, and decide." The judge, perceiving the bribe, adroitly turned his judgment against the opposite party.

2002. వెన్న దగ్గిర వుంచుకొని నేతికి తడుముకొన్నట్టు.

Looking for ghî when you have got butter.

(See No. 118.)

Asking others to help you when you have all in your own power.

2003. వెన్న పుచ్చుకొని వేశినవారిని రాయి పుచ్చుకొని వేతురా.

Will you throw stones on those that threw butter?

Returning evil for good.

2004. వెన్నలో వెంట్రుక తీశినట్టు.

Like taking a hair out of butter.

(See No. 130.)

Said of a very easy business.

How easily a hair gets into butter! (German.)*

2005. వెయ్యికాళ్ల జెర్రి.

A scolopendra with a thousand legs.

Said of a very restless man.

2006. వెయ్యి రూపాయీలు కావలెనా, వెధవ తోడబుట్టినది కావలెనా.

Do you want the thousand Rupees, or the widow sister?

Among the Vaishṇava Brahmans the widows make themselves very useful and earn something for their livelihood. The proverb refers to a partition of the property.

---

* Wie leicht kommt nicht ein Haar in die Butter!

2007. వెఱ్ఱిముండ వేడుక చూడబోతే, వెతకనిద్దరు యేడవనిద్దరు.

When the daft creature went to see the show, two had to search, and two to cry [for her.]

2008. వెఱ్ఱిమొద్దుకేల వేదశాస్త్రములు.

What has a dunderhead to do with the Vedas and the Śâstras ?

2009. వెఱ్ఱివాడి చేతి రాయి.

A stone in a madman's hand.

(See No. 1539.)

A dangerous experiment.

Put not a naked sword in a madman's hand.

2010. వెఱ్ఱివాడి పెండ్లాము వాడవదినె.

A madman's wife is common property.

The helpless are mocked and ill-treated.

2011. వెఱ్ఱి వెయ్యివిధాలు, పైత్యము పదివేల విధాలు.

Idiocy [takes] a thousand forms, and madness ten thousand.

2012. వెలమవారి పెండ్లికొడుకు మారడగనేరడు, వున్నదంతా వూడ్చి పెట్టు మన్నట్టు.

The Velama bridegroom cannot ask, sweep it all on to his platter.

(See Nos. 36, 241.)

Men of the Velama caste are said to be reserved and modest.

2013. వెల సులభము, ఫల మధికము.

Small in price, but great in value.

2014. వెలుగు నీడ, గ్రామము తోడు.

The hedge is [my] shade, and the village [my] help.

Utterly helpless.

2015. వెల్లకిత్తలా వేశిపాడిస్తే, వక దెబ్బకే చస్తున్నదని సన్న్యాసులమయిన మేము యెందుకు చెప్పవలెను.

Why should we, Sannyâsîs, tell you that the tortoise can be killed by one blow if you turn it over?

Hypocrisy. Feigned friendship.

2016. వెల్లటూరిలో యెద్దునూ పరుచూరిలో పడుచునూ యివ్వకూడదు.

Never dispose of a bullock in Vellaṭûru, or of a girl in Paruçûru.

The former village is bad for bullocks on account of the miry soil, the latter is bad for women as the wells are distant.

Don't bring on yourself another's curse.

2017. వెళ్లిపొమ్మంటే చూరుపట్టుకొని వేలాడినట్టు.

When told to go away, he swung on the eaves.

(See Nos. 340, 605.)

Said of a parasite who could not be shaken off.

2018. వేటుకు వేటు, మాటకు మాట వుండవలె.

There must be a blow for a blow, and a word for a word.

One word brings on another. (Italian.)*

2019. వేడుకకు వెలలేదు.

There is no price [fixed] for a show.

i. e. you may remunerate performers as you please.

2020. వేణ్ణీళ్లకు చన్నీళ్లు, చన్నీళ్లకు వేణ్ణీళ్లు.

Cold water to hot water, hot water to cold water.

The beneficial union of different dispositions.

2021. వేణ్ణీళ్లకు వొర్వనమ్మ సాగుమానము చేస్తానన్నదట.

The woman who could not bear warm water said she would become Satî.

(See Nos. 204, 496.)

---

* Una parola tira l'altra.

2022. వేణ్ణీళ్లకూ వేసంగికీ యెంత చలవో, నీకూ నాకూ అంత చలవ.

There is as much coolness between you and me as there is in hot water and hot weather.

Coolness is here a term for friendship.

Said ironically.

2023. వేణ్ణీళ్లు పోస్తే యిల్లు కాలునా.

Can your house be burnt down with hot water?

(See Nos. 421, 1865, 2077.)

Applied to lenient or ineffective measures.

2024. వేలం వెఱ్ఱి.

Auction madness.

Said of foolish extravagance.

2025. వేలిమీద గోరు మొలిచినది, వేరుపోదాము రారా వెఱ్ఱిమొగుడా అన్నట్టు.

A nail has grown on my finger, let us go and live separately—come, come, silly husband.

Said by a cunning wife to her daft husband to persuade him to leave her father-in-law's house.

2026. వేలుకు వేలు యెడము.

There is space between each finger.

Said by a distant connexion envying the favor conferred on a near relative.

2027. వేలు కోసుకొన్నా, సున్నము పెట్టడు.

Even if one cuts his finger, he will not give a bit of chunam.

To stop the bleeding.

(See Nos. 286, 364, 1968.)

A heartless man.

2028. వేలు చూపి వుత్తది అనిపించుకొన్నట్టు.

Pointing the finger and coming off worst.

(See No. 919.)

Said of a man who accuses another without being able to substantiate his allegations.

2029. వేలు వంగబెట్టనిదీ, వెన్న అయినా రాదు.

(See No. 1009.)

Without bending the finger, even butter cannot be got.

Without obsequiousness, nothing is to be had.

2030. వేశినట్టే వేస్తే, వెర్రివాడు అయినా గెలుచును.

With continued attempts, even a fool may win.

A fool's bolt may sometimes hit the mark.

2031. వేశినదే వక గంతు, విరిగినదే వక కాలు.

One leap leapt, one leg broken.

Loss in the first venture.

2032. వేశిన వెదుళ్లల్లారా కాలిన యిండ్లకు పొండి.

O heap of bamboos, go to the houses which are burnt down.

Making use of an idle person on an emergency.

2033. వేశ్యా మోహము.

A harlot's love.

2034. వేషాలమారికి వేవిళ్లువస్తే, వున్నచోటు విడవను అన్నదట.

When the feigning woman became pregnant, she declared that she would not move from the place where she was.

(See Nos. 150, 483, 1214, 1829.)

2035. వేసాలెల్లా గ్రాసాలకే.

Every garb (i. e. occupation) is for food.

(See No. 706.)

2036. వేస్తివిరా కన్నము అంటే, చేస్తివే కాపరము అన్నట్టు.

"So you've broken into the house, have you?" [said a wretched woman to a burglar] "So you live in great style, do you?" [replied the thief].

Disappointed expectations.

2037. వైదికుని చేతి విడెము.

Betel nut in the hand of a clerical Brahman.

2038. వైద్యము నేరనివాడూ, వానకు తడియనివాడూ లేడు.

There is not a man who knows not medicine, nor one who has not been wet by rain.

Every man is a fool or a physician at forty.

2039. వైరికిగాని వడ్లు మెదగవు.

The rice will not be pounded except by the enemy.

i. e. the rice-pounder.

Severe measures are required for the stubborn.

2040. వ్యాసప్రోక్తమా, పరాశరప్రోక్తమా.

Is it the dictum of Vyâsa or Parâśara?

Parâśara was the father of the celebrated saint Vyâsa.

Said by one disputing the authority of another.

2041. వ్రతము చెడ్డా, సుఖము దక్కవలెను.

If the vow be broken, some enjoyment must be obtained.

There must be some inducement to transgress the bounds of virtue.

2042. వ్రాతకరణము.

A Karaṇam to write.

(For *Karaṇam* see No. 154.– See Nos. 660, 1811.)

A mere scribe.

2043. వ్రాతగడే కూతురా అంటే, కోతిమొగుడే అమ్మా అన్నట్టు.

"It is your fate, my daughter" [said a mother] "My husband is a monkey" [replied the daughter.]"

The allusion is to a bad match.

Finding things even worse than anticipated.

2044. వ్రాయగా వ్రాయగా కరణము, దగ్గగా దగ్గగా మరణము.

Writing, writing, a Karaṇam; coughing, coughing, death.

(For *Karaṇam* see No. 154.)

By working we become workmen, (Latin.)*

Constant dropping wears the stone.

2045. వ్రాశేవాణ్ణి కోశేవాణ్ణి గీశేవాణ్ణి నమ్మరాదు.

You should not trust a man who writes, cuts, or pares.

i. e. a village accountant, a butcher, or a toddy-drawer.

(See Nos. 354, 579.)

Put a miller, a weaver, and a tailor in a bag and shake them, the first that comes out will be a thief.

2046. వ్రైదికపు ప్రిల్లీ వ్రృత్తిప్రలకవే అంటే, మ్రావు మ్రావు అన్నదట.

"O clerical cat! you must pronounce with an accent"— "Mrâu, Mrâu" answered the cat.

A joke against the clerical Brahmans who are fond of pedantic language. The words were used by a secular Brahman (*Laukika*) to the cat of a clerical Brahman (*Vaidika*) and are all ridiculously spelt with the pedantic r (which is admissible in certain words only). The cat replied in the same style mewing *mrâu, mrâu,* instead of *mâu, mâu.*

---

* Fabricando fabri fimus.

2047. శంఖములో పోస్తేగాని, తీర్థము కాదు.

The water is not holy, unless it be poured into the shell.

2048. శత డబ్బు, సహస్ర డబ్బు.

[One who can tell] a hundred lies, [one who can tell] a thousand lies.

Ten times as bad.

2049. శని విరగడ, పని వొబ్బిడి.

When ill fortune departs, the business will be completed.

2050. శరణార్థిని లింగప్పా అంటే, కందులు మూడు మాడలు అన్నాడట, చిన్నా పెద్దా బాగున్నారా అంటే, పప్పు లక్క వలెనే వుడుకుతున్నది అన్నాడట.

"Lingappa I salute you" [said one deaf Jangam to a deaf friend,] "I have got three half pagodas' worth of Kandi" [replied the second;] "Are you all well at home"? [asked the first,] "The Dâl will boil as soft as sealing wax" [said his friend in reply.]

(For *Kandi* and *Dâl* see Nos. 32, 183.—See Nos. 927, 928, 929.)

Said jokingly when a person is inattentive.

2051. శల్య సారథ్యము.

Like the driving of Śalya.

Śalya, king of Madra having undertaken to drive the chariot of Karṇa continually endeavoured to dishearten him. (See *Karṇa Parva* of the *Mahâbhârata*).

A faithless ally.

2052. శవానకు చేశిన అలంకారము.

The decoration of a corpse.

(See No. 1465.)

A foolish undertaking.

He paints the dead.

2053. శాస్త్రులవారింట జన్మించి, సోమయాజులవారింట చొచ్చి, లవణమంటే దూడరేణమని యెరగనా.

Having been born in the house of a Śâstrî, and having married into the house of a Somayâjî, don't I know that Lavaṇam means calf-dung ?

Somayâjî is a sacrificing priest; *Lavaṇam* is salt.—Said by a stupid woman proud of her education, and acquaintance with pedantic terms.

Display of ignorance.

2054. శింగన్నా శింగన్నా అద్దంకి పోయి వచ్చినావా అంటే, పోనూ పోయి నాను రానూ వచ్చినానన్నాడట.

"Śinganna, Śinganna, have you been to Addanki ?" they asked. "I have been and come back" he replied.

Śinganna was a simpleton who having heard that he was to be sent on an errand to Addanki, went off in the night without having received his message.

2055. శింగినాదం జీలకర్ర.

Trumpet and cummin seed.

Similar to the English slang expression "Bosh."

2056. శింగి బిడ్డకంటే శింగడు కారము తిన్నట్టు.

When Śingi brought forth a child, Śingaḍu ate of the medicine.

Śingaḍu and Śingi are cant names for men and women of the wandering tribes (*Erukalas* and *Ênâdis* or *Yânâdis*). The men are polygamists and their wives out of jealousy often attempt to poison each other. The husband therefore tastes the medicine first.

2057. శిగ్గు అనగా తోటకూరవంటిది.

Modesty is like garden greens.

They sprout again after being cut.

Tōṭakūra is specially applied to the Amaranthus Tristis.

2058. శిగ్గుచెడ్డా బొజ్జపెట్టితే చాలును.

Although I be disgraced, if I grow fat (i. e. rich) it is enough.

2059. శిగ్గులచేటు పెద్దలపెండ్లి.

Old men's marriages are shameful.

2060. శిగ్గులేని ముఖానకు నవ్వే అలంకారము.

A laugh is the ornament of the face without shame.

Hiding a blush with a simper.

2061. శిరికొద్దీ చిన్నెలు, మగనికొద్దీ వన్నెలు.

The style of living is according to one's means; a wife's decorations depend upon the husband.

i. e. upon her love for him, and the amount of attention he pays her.

2062. శిరి పోయినా చిన్నెలు పో లేదు.

Although the wealth has gone, the finery has not gone.

Hiding one's losses and keeping up the former style.

2063. శిలాభోగం, స్థలభోగం, నరభోగం, కానరావు.

The fortune of a stone, a place, and a man cannot be foreseen.

The first may be formed into an idol and be worshipped; the second may be cultivated and made fruitful, or adorned with a beautiful edifice; and the third may become wealthy and be raised to a position of influence.

2064. శిలా శాసనం, ఫలా పాదకం.

An inscription on stone is profitable.

Said of an honest man's word.

2065. శివుని ఆజ్ఞలేక చీమ అయినా కుట్టదు.

Without the permission of Siva, even an ant will not bite you.

2066. శిష్యా శిష్యా నా కాళ్లను చెప్పులున్నవా అంటే, నక్షత్రమండలం యీ మధ్య కనపడలేదు అన్నాడట.

When [the Guru] said "O disciple! disciple! are there shoes on my feet? [the pupil] replied "I don't see them between this and the stars."

The Guru and his pupil were both gluttons, but the disciple excelled his master. On one occasion when the Guru—who had eaten so much that he could not see his toes which were numb—asked his pupil to inform him whether his shoes were on, the latter—who was filled up to his neck and was obliged to keep his face towards the sky—replied as above.

To have a belly up to one's mouth. (Spanish)*

2067. శుభము పలకరా పెండ్లికొడకా అంటే, యెవడి ఆలి తాడు తెగితే నాకు యేమి, నాకు వేశే పిండాకూడు నాకు వేస్తే అవి రేణికుండలకాడ చచ్చినట్టే తొంగుంటాను అన్నాడట.

When the bridegroom was asked to use auspicious words, he said "What is to me whose wife becomes a widow? If you feed me with the rice ball offered to the dead, I will lie down and sleep like a corpse near the painted pots."

Annoying others with unsuitable speeches.

---

*Tener la barriga á la boca.

2068. శుష్కప్రియములు, శూన్యహస్తములు.

Sweet words, empty hands.

(See Nos. 658, 1349, 1711, 1936.)

Speaking kindly, but rendering no assistance.

Deeds are love, and not fine phrases. (Spanish.)*

Words are female, deeds are male. (Italian.)†

2069. శెట్టి శృంగారించేలోగా పట్నమంతా కొల్లపోయినది.

By the time the Śeṭṭi had equipped himself, the whole town was plundered.

(See No. 680.)

He brings his machines after the war is over.

2070. శెట్టి శేరు, లింగం అరవీశెడు.

The Śeṭṭi [weighs] a seer and his lingam two and a half.

(See Nos. 117, 2074.)

2071. శెనగలు తింటూ వులవలని చెప్పి, పత్తివిత్తులు చేత్లో పెట్టేవాడు.

When eating Bengal gram he says it's horse gram, and when he gives it, it's cotton seed.

Śenagalu is the Cicer Arietinum; *Ulavalu* is the Dolichos Uniflorus.

A man of crooked ways.

2072. శెనగలు తిని, చెయ్యి కడుగుకొన్నట్టు.

Like washing one's hands after eating Bengal gram.

This gram is so clean, that the washing of the hands is a superfluous act.

Separating one's self wholly from anything.

---

*Obres son amores, que no buenas razones.

† Le parole son femmine, e i fatti son maschi.

2073. శేరుకు సవాశేరు.

For one seer a seer and a quarter.

A greater ruffian than another.

To a rogue a rogue and a half. (French.)*

2074. శేరు దొరకు, మణుగు బంటు.

The master is a seer, the servant is a maund.

(See Nos. 117, 2070.)

The servant is the master.

2075. శొంఠి లేని కషాయము లేదు.

No decoction without ginger.

(See Nos. 1368, 1437.)

An indispensable accompaniment.

No flying without wings.

ష.

2076. షండునికి యేలరా పత్నీధారణ.

What has a eunuch to do with taking a wife?

స.

2077. సంగీతమునకు చింతకాయలు రాలునా.

Will singing make the tamarinds drop?

(See Nos. 421, 1666, 2623.)

2078. సంజయ రాయభారము.

The embassy of Sanjaya.

Sanjaya was employed as an ambassador by the Kurus and showed no zeal for his party. (See the *Mahâbhârata.*)

Applied to a person who takes no real interest in the performance of his duty.

---

* A fripon fripon et demi.

2079. సంతపాక తొత్తు సన్న్యాసిని యెరుగునా.

Does the wretched harlot know [the virtues of] the Sannyâsî?

2080. సంతమెరుగు, సానిమెరుగు.

The decorations of a fair and of a loose woman.

Ornament which soon disappears and exposes the real wretchedness.

2081. సంతోషం సగం బలము.

Happiness is half [a man's] strength.

2082. సంపన్న గృహస్తు వస్తున్నాడు, తప్పేలాలు ముంతలు తీశి యింట్లో వేయుమన్నట్టు.

The honourable man is coming, put away the pots and pans.

Said of a plausible swindler.

2083. సంబరపు చలిగాలికి యెదురు వాకిలి.

A door opposite to the deliciously cool wind.

Said ironically of a bitterly cold wind.

2084. సంసారము గుట్టు, వ్యాధి రట్టు.

Family affairs [should be kept] secret, disease should be divulged.

2085. సకలగుణాభిరాముడు.

Endowed with every grace.

Said ironically.

2086. సత్తెరాజువారింటికి నీవెక్కడి తొత్తవే.

Whence have you come from to be a slave in the house of Satte Râzu ?

The *Satte Râzu* family are said to have been noted for their uprightness; they would never keep slaves.

Said of an improbable story.

2087. సత్యములు పొత్తుగుడుచునా, బాసలు కలిశివచ్చునా.

Will oaths bring harmony ? Will adjurations bring profit ?

2088. సత్యహరిశ్చంద్రుడయ్యా.

As truthful as Hariśchandra.

(See Nos. 2131, 2132.)

Used ironically.

2089. సన్న నూలు వడుకుతున్నాడు.

He is spinning fine thread.

Wasting away.

2090. సన్న్యాసి పెండ్లికి జుట్టుకాడినుంచి యెరువు.

At a Sannyâsî's wedding every thing is on loan from his top-lock downwards.

2091. సబా అంటే, ఆరు నెలలు.

When he says 'Tomorrow' [it means] six months.

(See No. 62.)

From tomorrow till tomorrow time goes a long journey. (French.)*

One to-day is better than ten tomorrows. (German.)†

---

* De demain à demain le temps s'en va bien loin.
† Ein Heute ist besser als zehn Morgen.

2092. సమయానకులేని బాకా చచ్చినవెనకటికా.

Can the horn not [blown] in time, [be sounded] after death?

Said by a beggar, who blew his horn when he was being carried away by a tiger, thus scaring the animal and saving his life.

2093. సముఖానకు వచ్చి రాయభారమా.

When you have come to the presence, why send a message?

Things done unnecessarily in an indirect manner.

2094. సముద్రము యీదవచ్చునుగాని, సంసారము యీదరాదు.

You may swim over the sea, but not over family [annoyances].

2095. సముద్రానకు చెల్లెలికట్ట హద్దు.

The shore is the limit of the sea.

The word Chellelikaṭṭa signifies 'sister bank.' The idea is that the shore is as inviolate as a sister.

Used in cautioning others not to transgress due bounds.

2096. సముద్రానకు యేతము వేశినట్లు.

Like fixing a pump to the sea.

For full description of the *Êtam*, *Êtâm* or *Yâtâm* (the Indian swape called by the English *Picota*) see Buchanan's Mysore.

He is building a bridge over the sea.

2097. సరసము విరసముకే.

Joking causes a breach [of friendship].

Better lose a jest than a friend.

A joke never gains an enemy, but often loses a friend.

Familiarity breeds contempt.

2098. సర్వాంకషప్రజ్ఞ కళవాడు.

One who knows everything.

Jack of all trades and master of none.

2099. సవరణ సంతకు పోతే, యేకులబుట్ట యెదురుగా పోయినది.

When Mr. Grand-style went to the fair, the spinning basket met him in the way.

Said of a man being brought to his bearings.

2100. సాగితే యిడవలె, జారితే పడవలె.

If you can, you must give ; if you slip, you must fall.

2101. సాతాని పీకులాట.

A Sâtâni dispute.

The Sâtânis (Râmânujas) admit as members of their body all classes amongst the worshippers of Vishṇu, who consequently dispute each other's rank in assemblies.

2102. సామజము చెరుకు మేస్తే, దోమలు యెన్ని అయినా తోలగలవా.

When an elephant feeds on the sugar-cane, can any number of mosquitos drive him away ?

2103. సాయబుకు యెంత దవులతు వచ్చినా, బీబీలకు కుట్టుపోగులే.

However rich the Ṣâḥib may become, the Bîbîs will wear boring-wires in their ears.

It is customary for the Mussalman women to wear little rings *(Danḍiyâṅ)* along the border of the ear, which resemble the wires used by Hindu women for keeping open the aperture, when not wearing their ornaments.

2104. సాహెబూ చిక్కిపోయినావేమంటే, యింకా చిక్కుతాం, మరీ చిక్కుతాం, మనసూ వస్తే చచ్చిపోతాం, నీకేమి అన్నాడట.

When the Ṣâḥib was asked how it was he had grown so thin, he said "We will grow thinner, and still thinner, and if we like we will even die, what's that to you?"

Said of a supercilious fool.

2105. సాలెకూ జంగానికీ సంధి కుదురుతుందా.

Can the weaver and the tailor be reconciled?

This is a joke :—the tailors cut up the weavers' cloth.

2106. సాలెజాండ్ర సభామధ్యే సాతానిః పండితాయతే।
వుల్లీవనసమూహేషు జోరీగః కోకిలాయతే॥

A Sâtâni is a Panḍit among the weavers; the gad-fly is a cuckoo in the onion gardens.*

(See No. 2107.)

To the unskilled the voice of the sparrow is music. (Latin.)†

2107. సాలె సభకు సాతాని పెద్ద, వుల్లివనానకు జోరీగ కోకిల.

In a council of weavers a Sâtâni presides; in an onion garden the gad-fly is a cuckoo.

(See No. 2106.)

2108. సింహాము యేనుగను చంపునేగాని, చచ్చిన కుక్కను తినునా.

A lion will kill an elephant, but will it eat a dead dog?

A noble-minded man is above mean actions.

2109. సిద్దన్నా కవులూరన్నట్టు.

Like saying to Siddanna "Here is Kavulûru."

---

* In this proverb Telugu is mixed with Sanscrit and the Telugu words are used in an absurd manner with Sanscrit case-endings. It reads as ridiculously as
Alum si sit stalum non est malum;
Beerum si sit cleerum est synocerum.

† Inter indoctos etiam corydus sonat.

2110. సిలార్, పిల్లలూ నేనూ తయార్.

"Silâr!" [cried the Chief,] "Ready with my children" [he replied].

When a chieftain called his Mussalman retainer to go and fight the enemy, that worthy replied that he was ready with his family for the flight!

A sham warrior.

2111. సీతకు వ్రాశినది శీమకు వ్రాయవలెనా.

Is the fate of Sítâ to be common to all?

Sítâ the wife of Râma suffered much during the greater part of her life.

2112. సుఖము కష్టముకే.

Happiness [is followed by] trouble.

Grief borders on the extremes of gladness. (Latin.)*

If you laugh to-day you may cry to-morrow.

2113. సుత్తె ముందా కారు ముందా.

Was the hammer first, or were the tongs?

(See No. 905.)

2114. సున్నము పుట్టని వూళ్లో అన్నము పుట్టునా.

Can food be expected in a village where chunam is refused?

A small quantity of fine *chunam* (lime) is eaten with betel leaf.

2115. సున్నములో వున్నది సూక్ష్మము, సూక్ష్మములో వున్నది మోక్షము.

In the chunam is the trick; in the Supreme Soul is salvation.

Chunam is an indispensable accompaniment to betel leaf—The word *Sûkshma* signifies "ingenuity," "craft" and also "The Supreme Soul, the subtle and invisible spirit that pervades all existence," (Wilson) to know which is salvation.

---

* Extrema gaudii luctus occupat.

2116. సువ్వీ అంటే, రోకటిపాట.

. As for "Suvvi," 'tis the rice pounder's song.

The word *Suvvî* is used as a chorus in songs sung by women when beating rice.

Said in disparagement of anything very common.

2117. సూది గొంతు, బాన కడుపు.

His throat is like the eye of a needle, and his belly is like a large jar.

A slow eating glutton.

The eye is bigger than the belly. (German.)*

2118. సూదివలె వచ్చి దబ్బనమువలె తేలినట్టు.

Coming like a needle and turning out a packing needle.

The reverse of No. 688 q. v.

2119. సూరన్న సుఖవాశి, పేరన్న పెద్దవాడు, అయ్యకెత్తరా కోళ్లగంప.

Sûranna is a delicately brought up man, Pêranna is an elderly man, so put the basket of fowls on the head of the priest.

Want of respect for those to whom it is due.

2120. సైంధవుడు అడ్డపడ్డట్టు.

Like the hindrance of Saindhava.

2121. సొగసు సోమవారముపోతే, మొగుడు యాయవారము పోయినాడట.

Her beauty went on Monday, and her husband went to beg.

The jingle of the original is lost in the translation i. e. Monday—*Sômavâram*, begging—*Yâyavâram*.

2122. సొమ్మూ పోయి దిమ్మూ పట్టినది.

Money went and madness came.

---

* Die Augen sind weiter dann der Bauch.

2123. స్తన శల్య పరీక్ష చేస్తాడు.

He searches for bones in a woman's breast.

(See No. 835.)

Applied to a very minute enquiry.

2124. స్థానబలిమిగాని తనబలిమి కాదు.

It is the strength of his position, not his own strength.

2125. స్థూలము కనుగుడ్డు, సూక్ష్మము కనుపాప.

The eye-ball is large, but the pupil is small.

2126. స్వతంత్రము స్వర్గలోకము, పరతంత్రము ప్రాణసంకటము.

Independence is heaven, dependence is harassing to the life.

2127. స్వర్గానకు జెత్తెడు.

There is only a span between you and heaven.

Said ironically to a hypocrite.

2128. స్వర్గానకు వెళ్లినా, వడేకులు తప్పవు.

Even if you go to heaven, you will not escape spinning.

Said reproachfully to a very poor person.

2129. స్వాతికొంగలమీదికి సాళువ పోయినట్టు.

Like a hawk attacking a flock of cranes.

Svâtikonga is a kind of crane which emigrates in *Svâti*, the 15th lunar mansion. *Sâḷuva* is a hawk used in hunting.

2130. స్వాతి వానకు ముత్యపుచిప్పలెదురుచూచినట్టు.

Like oysters looking out for the rain in Svâti.

(For *Svâti* see No. 2129.)

The oyster-shells are said to rise to the surface of the water and lie open until the rain falls in *Svâti*, closing and sinking to the bottom immediately after receiving the drops, which turn into pearls.

Anxious expectation.

హా.

2131. హరిశ్చంద్రుడి నోట అబద్ధమూ రాదు, నా నోట నిజమూ రాదు.

A lie never came out of the mouth of Hariśchandra, truth never comes out of my mouth.

(See No. 2066.)

Said of an audacious liar.

2132. హరిశ్చంద్రుణ్ని లంపకాయ కొట్టి పుట్టినాడు.

He slapped (i. e. overcame) Hariśchandra and was born.

Said jokingly of a great liar.

2133. హాస్యగాణ్ని తేలు కుట్టినట్లు.

Like a scorpion stinging a jester.

No one believes it.

One may cry " Wolf !" too often.

క్ష.

2134. క్షేత్రమెరిగి విత్తనము, పాత్రమెరిగి దానము.

Knowing the soil, [sow] seed; knowing the worthiness [give] gifts.

సంస్కృతలోకోక్తులు.

SANSCRIT PROVERBS.

अ.

1. अंगारश्शतधौतेन मलिनत्वं न मुंचति ॥
అంగారశ్శతధౌతేన మలినత్వం న ముంచతి॥

The blackness cannot be removed from charcoal by a hundred washings.

स्वभावो यादृशो यस्य न जहाति कदाचन।
अंगारश्शतधौतेन मलिनत्वं न मुंचति ॥ इतिचाणक्यधृतं ॥
స్వభావో యాదృశో యస్య న జహాతి కదాచన।
అంగారశ్శతధౌతేన మలినత్వం న ముంచతి॥ ఇతిచాణక్యధృతం॥

Whatever one's nature be, it never changes ; the blackness is not removed from charcoal by a hundred washings. (Kavitâratnâkara 161).

" Can the Ethiopian change his skin or the leopard his spots ?"
Jeremiah xiii. 23.

2. अंततोश्मापि जीर्यति ॥
అంతతోశ్మాపి జీర్యతి॥

The stone is worn away at last.

3. अंतस्तापो बहिश्शीतं ॥
అంతస్తాపో బహిశ్శీతం॥

Inward heat, outward coolness.

(See TELUGU No. 4, &c.—also No. 2022.)

Outward friendship, inward hate.

4. अंधस्य दीपो बधिरस्य गीतं मूर्खस्य शास्त्रं किमु सानुरागं ॥
అంధస్య దీపో బధిరస్య గీతం మూర్ఖస్య శాస్త్రం కిము సానురాగం॥

Is a lamp pleasing to the blind, a song to the deaf, or science to the fool ?

5. अग्निनाग्निस्समिध्यते ॥
అగ్నినాగ్నిస్సమిధ్యతే॥

With fire, fire is kindled.

Like produces like.

अग्निनाग्निः समिध्यते कविर्गृहपतिर्युवा। हव्यवाड् जुह्वास्यः ॥
అగ్నినాగ్నిః సమిధ్యతే కవిర్గృహపతిర్యువా। హవ్యవాడ్జుహ్వాస్యః॥

"Agni, the ever young and wise, the guardian of the dwelling (of the sacrificer), the bearer of offerings, whose mouth is (the vehicle) of oblations is kindled by Agni." (Ṛig-veda-saṁhitâ 12, 6.—Wilson's trans.)*

6. अग्निर्वैद्यमतःपरं ॥
అగ్నిర్వైద్యమతఃపరం॥

Hereafter treatment by fire.

An ambiguous phrase used by a physician : it may either refer to cauterization of the affected part, or to cremation of the whole body.

7. अजायुद्धे ऋषिश्राद्धे प्रभाते मेघडंबरे।
दंपत्योः कलहे चैव बह्वारंभो लघुक्रिया ॥
అజాయుద్ధే ఋషిశ్రాద్ధే ప్రభాతే మేఘడంబరే।
దంపత్యోః కలహే చైవ బహ్వారంభో లఘుక్రియా॥

In the fighting of she-goats, in a Ṛishi's obsequial rites, in the gathering of clouds at the dawn, in the squabbles of husband and wife, the beginning is great, and the doings are small.

---

* "That is, the *Âhavanîya* fire, into which the oblation is poured, is lighted by the application of other fire whether taken from the household fire or produced by attrition." (Wilson's note.)

8. अति सर्वत्र वर्जयेत् ॥
అతి సర్వత్ర వర్జయేత్॥

Excess is to be avoided in all things.

अतिदानाद्धतः कर्णस्त्वतिलोभात्सुयोधनः ।
अतिकामाद्दशग्रीवस्त्वति सर्वत्र वर्जयेत् ॥
అతిదానాద్ధతః కర్ణస్త్వతిలోభాత్సుయోధనః।
అతికామాద్దశగ్రీవస్త్వతి సర్వత్ర వర్జయేత్॥

Karṇa was ruined by excessive liberality, Suyodhana by excessive avarice, Daśagrîva by excessive lust—Excess is to be avoided in all things.

9. अति सर्वत्र गर्ह्यते ॥
అతి సర్వత్ర గర్హ్యతే॥

Excess is blamed in all things.

10. अतिस्नेहः पापशंकी ॥
అతిస్నేహః పాపాశంకీ॥

Excessive friendship [causes] doubt of sin.

11. अत्युच्छ्रायः पतनहेतुः ॥
అత్యుచ్ఛ్రాయః పతనహేతుః॥

Too great exaltation is the cause of a downfall.

(See TELUGU No. 1531.)

12. अदानदोषेण भवेद्दरिद्रो दारिद्र्यदोषेण करोति पापं ।
पापादवश्यं नरकं प्रयाति पुनर्दरिद्रः पुनरेव पापी ॥
అదానదోషేణ భవేద్దరిద్రో దారిద్ర్యదోషేణ కరోతి పాపం।
పాపాదవశ్యం నరకం ప్రయాతి పునర్దరిద్రః పునరేవ పాపీ॥

By the crime of not giving alms, [a man] becomes poor; by the defect of poverty, he commits sin; by sin he certainly goes to hell; again [he becomes] poor, again [he becomes] a sinner.

13. अदृष्टपादपे देशे एरंडोपि द्रुमायते ॥
అదృష్టపాదపే దేశే ఏరండోపి ద్రుమాయతే॥

In the country where no tree is seen, even the castor oil plant is called a tree.

यत्र विद्वज्जनो नास्ति श्लाघ्यस्तत्राल्पधीरपि।
निरस्तपादपे देशे एरंडोपि द्रुमायते ॥
యత్ర విద్వజ్జనో నాస్తి శ్లాఘ్యస్తత్రాల్పధీరపి।
నిరస్తపాదపే దేశే ఏరండోపి ద్రుమాయతే॥

Where there is no learned man, there even one of little intellect is to be praised; in a place without trees, even the castor-oil plant is considered a tree.—Hitopadeśa, Book I.

14. अद्य भक्ष्यो धनुर्गुणः ॥
అద్య భక్ష్యో ధనుర్గుణః॥

To-day the bow string is to be eaten.

Referring to the story of the parsimonious jackal in the Hitopadeśa, Book I.

15. अद्य युद्धं त्वया मया ॥
అద్య యుద్ధం త్వయా మయా॥

Now a combat between thee and me!

सप्तसिंहा जिताः पूर्वं पंचव्याघ्रास्त्रयोगजाः।
पश्यंतु देवतास्सर्वा अद्य युद्धं त्वया मया ॥ इतीतिहासः ॥
సప్తసింహాః జితాః పూర్వం పంచవ్యాఘ్రాస్త్రయోగజాః।
పశ్యంతు దేవతాస్సర్వా అద్య యుద్ధం త్వయా మయా॥ ఇతీతిహాసః॥

Seven lions, five tigers, and three elephants have ere this been conquered by me; to-day a combat between thee and me, let all the gods behold it! (Kavitāratnākara 17.)

16. अधमा सेवकावृत्तिः ॥
అధమా సేవకావృత్తిః॥

Servitude is the lowest occupation.

17. अधिकस्याधिकं फलं ॥

అధికస్యాధికం ఫలం॥

More is the fruit of much.

18. अनभ्यासे विषं शास्त्रमजीर्णे भोजनं विषं ॥

అనభ్యాసే విషం శాస్త్రమజీర్ణే భోజనం విషం॥

Want of practice [makes] science poison, indigestion [makes] food poison.

(cf. Böhtlingk's *Indische Sprüche*, 1. 87).

A little knowledge is a dangerous thing.

Practise not your art, and 'twill soon depart. (German.)*

19. अनाथप्रेतसंस्कारात्कोटियज्ञफलं लभेत् ॥

అనాథప్రేతసంస్కారాత్కోటియజ్ఞఫలం లభేత్॥

By performing the obsequies of an unclaimed corpse, the reward of ten million sacrifices will be obtained.

20. अनाथो देवरक्षकः ॥

అనాథో దేవరక్షకః॥

The destitute has God for his protector.

(See TELUGU No. 1160.)

" Thou art a God of the afflicted, an helper of the oppressed, an upholder of the weak, a protector of the forlorn, a Saviour of them that are without hope." Judith ix. 11.

21. अनामिका सार्थवती बभूव ॥

అనామికా సార్థవతీ బభూవ॥

The nameless has become possessed of a meaning.

Anâmikâ (" having no name") is the ring finger.

---

* Wer die kunst nicht übt, verlernt sie bald.

पुरा कवीनां गणनाप्रसंगे कनिष्ठिकाधिष्ठितकालिदासा ।
अद्यापि तत्तुल्यकवेरभावादनामिका सार्थवती बभूव ॥
పురా కవీనాం గణనాప్రసంగే కనిష్ఠికాధిష్ఠితకాలిదాసా।
అద్యాపి తత్తుల్యకవేరభావాదనామికా సార్థవతీ బభూవ॥

Formerly on an occasion of numbering the poets, Kâlidâsa having been placed on the little finger (i. e. first) and no poet equal to him having up to this time existed, the nameless (ring finger) has become possessed of a meaning.

(cf. Böhtlingk's *Indische Sprüche*, 2. 1798).

22. अनायका विनश्यंति नश्यंति शिशुनायकाः ।
स्त्रीनायका विनश्यंति नश्यंति बहुनायकाः ॥
అనాయకా వినశ్యంతి నశ్యంతి శిశునాయకాః।
స్త్రీనాయకా వినశ్యంతి నశ్యంతి బహునాయకాః॥

Those without a leader perish ; those with a youthful leader perish ; those with a female leader perish ; those with many leaders perish.

23. अनाश्वासितदुःखिते मनसि सर्वमसह्यं ॥
అనాశ్వాసితదుఃఖితే మనసి సర్వమసహ్యం॥

When the mind is grieved and unconsoled, all is disgust.

24. अनित्यानि शरीराणि विभवोनैव शाश्वतः ।
नित्यं सन्निहितो मृत्युः कर्तव्यो धर्मसंग्रहः ॥
అనిత్యాని శరీరాణి విభవోనైవ శాశ్వతః।
నిత్యం సన్నిహితో మృత్యుః కర్తవ్యో ధర్మసంగ్రహః॥

Bodies are transitory ; riches are not lasting ; death is always at hand ; [therefore] virtue should be practised.

25. **अन्नदातस्सुखी भव ॥**

అన్నదాతస్సుఖీ భవ॥

O giver of food! be happy.

A phrase used in returning thanks.

26. **अन्नमूलं बलं पुंसां ॥**

అన్నమూలం బలం పుంసాం॥

The strength of men is rooted in food.

अन्नमूलं बलंपुंसां बलमूलंहि जीवनं ।
तस्माद्यत्नेन संरक्षेत्बलंच कुशलो भिषक् ॥

అన్నమూలం బలంపుంసాం బలమూలంహి జీవనం।
తస్మాద్యత్నేన సంరక్షేత్ బలంచ కుశలో భిషక్॥

The strength of man is rooted in food, the life is rooted in strength; therefore the skilful physician should carefully preserve the strength. (Kavitâratnâkara 201.)

27. **अन्नस्य क्षुधितं पात्रं ॥**

అన్నస్య క్షుధితం పాత్రం॥

The hungered is worthy of food.

28. **अन्नानुरूपास्तनुरूपबुद्धयः ॥**

అన్నానురూపాస్తనురూపబుద్ధయః॥

The body, form, and sense depend upon the food.

29. **अन्यथा चिंतितं कार्यं दैवमन्यत्र चिंतयेत् ॥**

అన్యథా చింతితం కార్యం దైవమన్యత్ర చింతయేత్॥

A plan considered [by man] in one way is considered by God in another.

(See TELUGU No. 1056.)

Human counsels are directed from heaven. (Latin.)*

---

* Humana consilia divinitus gubernantur.

30. अपृष्टोपि शुभं ब्रूयात् ॥
అపృష్టోపి శుభం బ్రూయాత్॥

Although unasked, you should speak auspiciously.

31. अबद्धंवा सुबद्धंवा कुंतीपुत्रो विनायकः ॥
అబద్ధంవా సుబద్ధంవా కుంతీపుత్రో వినాయకః॥

Be it truth, or be it falsehood, Vinâyaka was the son of Kuntî.

32. अभावे विरक्तिः ॥
అభావే విరక్తిః॥

In not having is disgust.

Disgust is simulated with regard to that which is unattainable.

अभावे विरक्तिरसंभावितानां मंत्रावृत्तिर्दरिद्रस्य देवताभक्तिः ॥
అభావే విరక్తిరసంభావితానాం మంత్రావృత్తిర్దరిద్రస్య దేవతాభక్తిః॥

In the non-existence is disgust; there is repetition of Mantras by those who are unhonored; there is trust in God by the poor.

33. अभ्यासानुसरी विद्या बुद्धिः कर्मानुसारिणी ।
उद्योगानुसरी लक्ष्मीः फलं भाग्यानुसारि च ॥
అభ్యాసానుసరీ విద్యా బుద్ధిః కర్మానుసారిణీ।
ఉద్యోగానుసరీ లక్ష్మీః ఫలం భాగ్యానుసారిచ॥

Learning depends on practice, intellect on former deeds; wealth follows exertion, and success, good fortune.

34. अयं पटाटोपः कौपीनसंरक्षणार्थः ॥
అయం పటాటోపః కౌపీనసంరక్షణార్థః॥

This pomp is for the protection of the clout.

Said by a Sannyâsî when asked why his style of living was inconsistent with his profession. To protect his rags from the rats he got a cat, to get milk for the cat he bought a cow, to tend the cow he hired a servant, and for his servant he procured a wife.

35. अरसिकजनसंभाषणतोरसिकजनेन वरं वाक्कलहः ॥

అరసికజనసంభాషణతోరసికజనేన వరం వాక్కలహః॥

To quarrel with a man of good speech is better than to converse with a man of rude address.

36. अर्थस्य पुरुषो दासः ॥

అర్థస్య పురుషో దాసః॥

Man is the slave of money.

अर्थस्य पुरुषो दासो दासस्त्वर्थो न कस्यचित् ।
इति सत्यं महाराज बद्धस्त्वार्थेच कौरवैः ॥

అర్థస్య పురుషో దాసో దాసస్త్వర్థో న కస్యచిత్।
ఇతి సత్యం మహారాజ బద్ధశ్చార్థేచ కౌరవైః॥

Man is the slave of money, money is the slave of no one ; this is true O Mahârâja! By money I have been made subject to the Kauravas.

(cf. Böhtlingk's *Indische Sprüche* 1. 214).

37. अर्था गृहे निवर्तंते श्मशाने मित्रबांधवाः ।
सुकृतं दुष्कृतंचैव गच्छंतमनुगच्छति ॥

అర్థా గృహే నివర్తంతే శ్మశానే మిత్రబాంధవాః।
సుకృతం దుష్కృతంచైవ గచ్ఛంతమనుగచ్ఛతి॥

Wealth stops at the house, friends and relatives at the grave ; good deeds and evil deeds follow the dying man.

38. अर्थातुराणां न गुरुर्न बंधुः कामातुराणां न भयं न लज्जा ।
विद्यातुराणां न सुखं न निद्रा क्षुधातुराणां न रुचिर्न पक्वं ॥

అర్థాతురాణాం న గురుర్న బంధుః కామాతురాణాం న భయం న లజ్జా।
విద్యాతురాణాం న సుఖం న నిద్రా క్షుధాతురాణాం న రుచిర్న పక్వం॥

Those eager to amass wealth regard neither priests nor relations; those eager to indulge lust feel neither fear nor shame; those eager in the pursuit of knowledge care not for comfort or sleep; those eager to satisfy hunger regard neither the flavour nor the cookery.

(cf. Böhtlingk's *Indische Sprüche* 3. 3597.)

39. अर्थानामार्जने दुःखमार्जितानां च रक्षणे ।
नाशे दुःखं व्यये दुःखं किमर्थं दुःखभाजनं ॥

అర్థానామార్జనే దుఃఖమార్జితానాంచ రక్షణే।
నాశే దుఃఖం వ్యయే దుఃఖం కిమర్థం దుఃఖభాజనం॥

There is pain in acquiring wealth, pain in preserving what has been acquired, pain in its loss, and pain in its expenditure—why have such a receptacle of sorrow?

40. अर्थेन सर्वे वशाः ॥

అర్థేన సర్వే వశాః॥

All are made subject by money.

माता निंदति नाभिनंदति पिता भ्राता न संभाषते ।
भृत्यः कुप्यति नानुगच्छति सुतः कांता च नालिंगते ।
अर्थप्रार्थनशंकया न कुरुतेप्यालापमात्रं सुहृत् ।
तस्मादर्थमुपार्जयश्रृणुसखे चार्थेन सर्वे वशाः ॥

మాతా నిందతి నాభి నందతి పితా భ్రాతా న సంభాషతే।
భృత్యః కుప్యతి నానుగచ్ఛతి సుతః కాంతాచ నాలింగతే।
అర్థప్రార్థన శంకయానకురుతే ప్యాలాపమాత్రం సుహృత్।
తస్మాదర్థముపార్జయశృణుసఖే చార్థేన సర్వే వశాః॥

The mother rails, the father is displeased, the brother speaks not, the servant sulks, the son accompanies not, the wife embraces not, and for fear of being asked for money even the friend addresses not—listen therefore O friend! Acquire wealth, for all are made subject by money. (Kavitâratnâkara 20.)

41. अल्पविद्यो महागर्वः ॥

అల్పవిద్యో మహాగర్వః॥

Little learning, much pride.

(See TELUGU No. 454, &c.)

42. **अल्पारंभः क्षेमकरः ॥**

అల్పారంభః క్షేమకరః॥

A small beginning is good.

To attempt too much at first is unwise.

Every beginning is feeble. (Latin.)*

43. **अवश्यं पितुराचारः ॥**

అవశ్యం పితురాచారః॥

A father's rule is binding [on the son.]

Âchâra is "an established rule of conduct." (Wilson.)

44. **अवश्यमेव भोक्तव्यं कृतं कर्म शुभाशुभं ॥**

అవశ్యమేవ భోక్తవ్యం కృతం కర్మ శుభాశుభం॥

[The reward of] deeds done, be they good or evil, will assuredly be received.

मा भुक्तं क्षीयते कर्म कल्पकोटिशतैरपि ।
अवश्यमेव भोक्तव्यं कृतं कर्म शुभाशुभं ॥

మా భుక్తం క్షీయతే కర్మ కల్పకోటిశతైరపి।
అవశ్యమేవ భోక్తవ్యం కృతం కర్మ శుభాశుభం॥

The result of [evil] deeds, unsuffered, decays not even by hundreds of crores of Kalpas.

45. **अवस्था पूज्यते राजन्नशरीरं शरीरिणां ॥**

అవస్థా పూజ్యతే రాజన్నశరీరం శరీరిణాం॥

O king! the position, not the body of corporeal beings is worshipped.

अवस्था पूज्यते राजन्नशरीरं शरीरिणां ।
तदा वनचरो राम इदानीं नृपतां गतः ॥

అవస్థా పూజ్యతే రాజన్నశరీరం శరీరిణాం।
తదా వనచరో రామ ఇదానీం నృపతాం గతః॥

O King! the position—not the body—of corporeal beings is worshipped; Râma who once was a wanderer in the forests has now obtained kinghood. (Kavitâratnâkara 140.)

* Omne principium est debile.

46. अविचारपुरीमध्ये यः पलायति जीवति ॥
అవిచారపురీమధ్యే యః పలాయతి జీవతి॥

He who flees from an ill-governed town will live.

47. अव्यवस्थितचित्तस्य प्रसादोपि भयंकरः ॥
అవ్యవస్థితచిత్తస్య ప్రసాదోపి భయంకరః॥

Even the favor of a man of ill-regulated mind is to be dreaded.

क्वचिद्रुष्टः क्वचित्तुष्टो रुष्टस्तुष्टः क्षणेक्षणे ।
अव्यवस्थितचित्तस्य प्रसादोपि भयंकरः ॥
క్వచిద్రుష్టః క్వచిత్తుష్టో రుష్టస్తుష్టః క్షణేక్షణే।
అవ్యవస్థితచిత్తస్య ప్రసాదోపి భయంకరః॥

Sometimes angry, sometimes pleased, angry one moment and pleased another: even the favor of a man of ill-regulated mind is to be dreaded.

48. असंतुष्टो द्विजो नष्टस्संतुष्ट इव पार्थिवः ॥
అసంతుష్టో ద్విజో నష్టస్సంతుష్ట ఇవ పార్థివః॥

A discontented Brahman is lost [to the world] like a contented king.

49. असतां धर्मबुद्धिश्चेत्सतां संतापकारणं ॥
అసతాం ధర్మబుద్ధిశ్చేత్సతాం సంతాపకారణం॥

If bad men become charitable, it will be a cause of grief to the good.

50. असह्यं ज्ञातिदुर्वाक्यं ॥
అసహ్యం జ్ఞాతిదుర్వాక్యం॥

An evil word from a cousin is insufferable.

वरं रामशरस्सह्यो न च वैभीषणं वचः ।
असह्यं ज्ञातिदुर्वाक्यं मेघांतरितरौद्रवत् ॥
వరం రామశరస్సహ్యో న చ వైభీషణం వచః।
అసహ్యం జ్ఞాతిదుర్వాక్యం మేఘాంతరితరౌద్రవత్॥

Râma's dart is easier to bear than Vibhîshaṇa's word; an evil word from a cousin is insufferable, like the fury in the clouds.

51. असारे खलु संसारे सारं श्वशुरमंदिरं ॥

అసారే ఖలు సంసారే సారం శ్వశురమందిరం॥

Worldly pursuits are surely unprofitable, but there is something to be had in the father-in-law's house.

असारे खलु संसारे सारं श्वशुरमंदिरं ।
हिमालये हरश्शेते हरिश्शेते महोदधौ ॥

అసారే ఖలు సంసారే సారం శ్వశురమందిరం।
హిమాలయే హరశ్శేతే హరిశ్శేతే మహోదధౌ॥

There is truly nothing profitable in the world, the father-in-law's house is best; Śiva sleeps on the Himâlayas (father of Durgâ) and Vishṇu sleeps on the great ocean (father of Lakshmî). (cf. Böhtlingk 1. 290.)

52. अहिंसा परमो धर्मः ॥

అహింసా పరమో ధర్మః॥

Non-injury is the highest duty.

(cf. Hitopadeśa Book I. and Böhtlingk's *Indische Sprüche* 1. 301.)

आ.

53. आकारो ह्रस्वः गुणास्तु विपुलाः ॥

ఆకారో హ్రస్వః గుణాస్తు విపులాః॥

The form is small, the qualities are great.

A little body often harbours a great soul.

54. आचारः प्रथमो धर्मः ॥

ఆచారః ప్రథమో ధర్మః॥

The observance of ordinances is the first duty.

55. आजगाम यदा लक्ष्मीर्नारिकेलफलांबुवत् ।
निर्जगाम यदा लक्ष्मीर्गजभुक्तकपित्थवत् ॥ इतिनीतिशास्त्रं ॥

ఆజగామ యదా లక్ష్మీర్నారికేలఫలాంబువత్।
నిర్జగామ యదా లక్ష్మీర్గజభుక్తకపిత్థవత్॥

When the goddess of wealth came, it was like the water in a cocoanut; when she departed it was like the wood-apple eaten by an elephant.

(See TELUGU No. 445.)

56. आतुरे नियमो नास्ति ॥

ఆతురే నియమో నాస్తి॥

For the sick man, there is no rule.

He is exempted from the observance of the ceremonial law.

57. आत्मच्छिद्रं न जानंति परच्छिद्रानुसारिणः ॥

ఆత్మచ్ఛిద్రం న జానంతి పరచ్ఛిద్రానుసారిణః॥

They know not their own defects who search for the defects of others.

58. स्त्रीबुद्धिः प्रलयंकरी ॥

స్త్రీబుద్ధిః ప్రలయంకరీ॥

Woman's counsel is destructive.

आत्मबुद्धिस्सुखंचैव गुरुबुद्धिर्विशेषतः ।
परबुद्धिर्विनाशाय स्त्रीबुद्धिः प्रलयंकरी ॥

ఆత్మబుద్ధిస్సుఖంచైవ గురుబుద్ధిర్విశేషతః।
పరబుద్ధిర్వినాశాయ స్త్రీ బుద్ధిః ప్రలయంకరీ॥

One's own resolve is happy, the priest's advice is better; another's advice is for one's ruin, woman's counsel is destructive.

59. आत्मवत्सर्वभूतानि यः पश्यति स पश्यति ॥
ఆత్మవత్సర్వభూతాని యః పశ్యతి స పశ్యతి॥

He who looks upon all living beings as upon himself, sees.

मातृवत्परदारांश्च परद्रव्याणि लोष्टवत् ।
आत्मवत्सर्वभूतानि यः पश्यति स पश्यति॥
మాతృవత్పరదారాంశ్చ పరద్రవ్యాణి లోష్టవత్।
ఆత్మవత్సర్వభూతాని యః పశ్యతి స పశ్యతి॥

He who looks upon other men's wives as his mother, and other men's money as clods of earth, he who considers all creatures as himself—he sees [with spiritual wisdom].

(cf. Böhtlingk's *Indische Sprüche*, 2. 2173).

Do as you would be done by.

60. आत्मवन्मन्यते जगत् ॥
ఆత్మవన్మన్యతే జగత్॥

[Every man] thinks the world like himself.

61. आत्मशक्तिसमं कोपं यो जानाति स पंडितः ॥
ఆత్మశక్తిసమం కోపం యో జానాతి స పండితః॥

He is wise whose wrath is limited by his power.

If you cannot bite, never shew your teeth.

62. आत्मानं सततं रक्षेत् ॥
ఆత్మానం సతతం రక్షేత్॥

You should always save yourself.

आपदर्थं धनं रक्षेद्दारान्रक्षेद्धनैरपि ।
आत्मानं सततं रक्षेद्दारैरपि धनैरपि ॥
ఆపదర్థం ధనం రక్షేద్దారాన్రక్షేద్ధనైరపి।
ఆత్మానం సతతం రక్షేద్దారైరపి ధనైరపి॥

You should save money for [a time of] distress, you should save your wife even with [the expenditure of] money; you should always save yourself even with [the sacrifice of] wife and money.

Self is the first object of charity. **(Latin.)***

*** Prima sibi charitas.**

63. **आपदर्थे धनं रक्षेत् ॥**

ఆపదర్థే ధనం రక్షేత్॥

Money should be saved for a time of need.

आपदर्थे धनं रक्षेत् श्रीमतामापदः कुतः ।
सा चेदपगता लक्ष्मीस्संचितार्थो विनश्यति ॥

ఆపదర్థే ధనం రక్షేత్ శ్రీమతామాపదః కుతః।
సా చేదపగతా లక్ష్మీస్సంచితార్థో వినశ్యతి॥

Money should be saved for a time of need, how can distress reach the rich? If fortune depart, the wealth acquired will be lost.

64. **आयुरन्नं प्रयच्छति ॥**

ఆయురన్నం ప్రయచ్ఛతి॥

Duration of life gives food.

i. e. So long as a man is destined to live, food will not be wanting.

65. **आयुर्मर्माणि रक्षति ॥**

ఆయుర్మర్మాణి రక్షతి॥

Duration of life preserves the vital parts.

निमग्नस्य पयोराशौ पर्वतात्पतितस्य च ।
तक्षकेणापि दष्टस्य आयुर्मर्माणि रक्षति ॥

నిమగ్నస్య పయోరాశౌ పర్వతాత్పతితస్యచ।
తక్షకేణాపి దష్టస్య ఆయుర్మర్మాణి రక్షతి॥

Life preserves the vital parts of one sunk in the water, of one fallen from a mountain, even of one bitten by [the serpent] Takshaka. (Hitopadeśa, Book 2.)

66. **आयुर्याति दिनेदिने ॥**

ఆయుర్యాతి దినేదినే॥

Life goes day by day.

लोकः पृच्छति सद्वार्तां शरीरे कुशलं तव ।
कुतः कुशलमस्माकमायुर्याति दिनेदिने ॥

లోకః పృచ్ఛతి సద్వార్తాం శరీరే కుశలం తవ।
కుతః కుశలమస్మాకమాయుర్యాతి దినేదినే॥

People ask by way of compliment 'Are you in good health?' How can we be well when our life is waning day by day? (Kavitāratnākara 152.)

67. आलस्यादमृतं विषं ॥

ఆలస్యాదమృతం విషం॥

By delay [in using it] nectar [becomes] poison.

68. आशया बध्यते लोकः कर्मणा बहुचिंतया ॥

ఆశయా బధ్యతే లోకః కర్మణా బహుచింతయా॥

The world is bound by desire, fate, and much thinking.

69. आशावधिं को गतः ॥

ఆశావధిం కో గతః॥

Who has reached the limit of his desire ?

70. आशाशा परमं दुःखं निराशा परमं सुखं ॥

ఆశాశా పరమం దుఃఖం నిరాశా పరమం సుఖం॥

Desire upon desire [causes] the greatest sorrow; contentment, the greatest happiness.

71. आहारे व्यवहारेच त्यक्तलज्जस्सुखी भवेत् ॥

ఆహారే వ్యవహారేచ త్యక్తలజ్జస్సుఖీ భవేత్॥

In eating and in business he who discards modesty will be best off.

(cf. Morton's *Bengali and Sanscrit Proverbs* 805.)

72. आहारोपि मनुष्याणां जन्मना सह जायते ॥

ఆహారోపి మనుష్యాణాం జన్మనా సహ జాయతే॥

Food is provided with the birth of men.

धर्मंच चिंतयेत्प्राज्ञः स्वाहारं नैव चिंतयेत् ।
आहारोपि मनुष्याणां जन्मना सह जायते ॥

ధర్మంచ చింతయేత్ప్రాజ్ఞః స్వాహారం నైవ చింతయేత్।
ఆహారోపి మనుష్యాణాం జన్మనా సహ జాయతే॥

The wise should think of virtue and not of food: food also is created with the birth of men. (Kavitâratnâkara 101.)

इ.

73. इच्छामात्रा प्रभोस्सृष्टिः ॥
ఇచ్ఛామాత్రా ప్రభోస్సృష్టిః॥

The Lord's creation is His mere will.

"He commanded, and they were created." Psalm cxlviii. 5.

उ.

74. उत्तमं स्वार्जितं वित्तं मध्यमं पितुरार्जितं ।
अधमं भ्रातृवित्तंच स्त्रीवित्तमधमाधमं ॥
ఉత్తమం స్వార్జితం విత్తం మధ్యమం పితురార్జితం।
అధమం భ్రాతృవిత్తంచ స్త్రీ విత్తమధమాధమం॥

[To live upon] self-acquired property is good, [to live upon] that acquired by a father is middling, [to live upon] a brother's property is low, [to live upon] a woman's property is the lowest of the low.

75. उत्तमा कुलविद्या स्यात् ॥
ఉత్తమా కులవిద్యా స్యాత్॥

The caste-craft is the best.

Every man to his trade.

76. उत्तमा मानमिच्छंति धनमानौहि मध्यमाः ।
अधमा धनमिच्छंति मानोहि महतां धनं ॥
ఉత్తమా మానమిచ్ఛంతి ధనమానౌహి మధ్యమాః।
అధమా ధనమిచ్ఛంతి మానోహి మహతాం ధనం॥

Good men seek honor; middling men seek wealth and honor; base men seek wealth: honor itself is wealth to great men.

77. उत्तमेच क्षणं कोपो मध्यमे घटिकाद्वयं।
अधमे स्यादहोरात्रं पापिष्ठे मरणांततः॥
ఉత్తమేచ క్షణం కోపో మధ్యమే ఘటికాద్వయం।
అధమే స్యాదహోరాత్రం పాపిష్ఠే మరణాంతతః॥

In a good man, wrath [lasts] for a moment; in a middling man, for two hours; in a base man, for a day and night; in a great sinner, until death.

78. उत्तीर्णेच जलेपारे नौकया किं प्रयोजनं॥
ఉత్తీర్ణేచ జలేపారే నౌకయా కిం ప్రయోజనం॥

After the stream has been crossed what is the use of the boat on the other side?

79. उत्पथं प्रतिपन्नस्य परित्यागो विधीयते॥
ఉత్పథం ప్రతిపన్నస్య పరిత్యాగో విధీయతే॥

The forsaking of one who has gone out of the right way is enjoined.

80. उत्पद्यंते प्रलीयंते दरिद्राणां मनोरथाः॥
ఉత్పద్యంతే ప్రలీయంతే దరిద్రాణాం మనోరథాః॥

The desires of the poor spring up and perish.

81. उत्साहस्साहसं धैर्यं बुद्धिश्शक्तिः पराक्रमः।
षडेते यत्र तिष्ठंति तत्र देवोपि तिष्ठति॥
ఉత్సాహస్సాహసం ధైర్యం బుద్ధిశ్శక్తిః పరాక్రమః।
షడేతే యత్ర తిష్ఠంతి తత్ర దేవోపి తిష్ఠతి॥

Perseverance, daring, courage, wisdom, strength and valour—where these six are, there is God.

82. उदरनिमित्तो बहुकृतवेषः ॥
ఉదరనిమిత్తో బహుకృతవేషః॥

For the belly's sake many disguises are assumed.

जटिलो मुंडी लुंचितकेशः काषायांबर बहुकृतवेषः ।
पश्यन्नपिच न पश्यति मूढोह्युदरनिमित्तो बहुकृतवेषः ॥
జటిలో ముండీ లుంచితకేశః కాషాయాంబర బహుకృతవేషః।
పశ్యన్నపిచ న పశ్యతి మూఢోహ్యుదరనిమిత్తో బహుకృతవేషః॥

With matted hair, with shaven head, with cropped hair, or in the honored garb of red-dyed clothes, the fool, [though apparently] seeing, sees not [Brahma] :— for the belly's sake many disguises are assumed. (Chaturdasamanjarikāstotra.)

83. उद्योगः पुरुषलक्षणं ॥
ఉద్యోగః పురుషలక్షణం॥

Endeavour makes the man.

84. उद्योगिनं पुरुषसिंहमुपैति लक्ष्मीः ॥
ఉద్యోగినం పురుషసింహముపైతి లక్ష్మీః॥

Fortune favors the persevering and stout-hearted.

उद्योगिनं पुरुषसिंहमुपैति लक्ष्मीः
दैवेन देयमिति कापुरुषा वदंति ।
दैवं निहत्य कुरु पौरुष मात्मशक्त्या
यत्नेकृते यदि न सिध्यति कोऽत्र दोषः ॥
ఉద్యోగినం పురుషసింహముపైతి లక్ష్మీః
దైవేన దేయమితి కాపురుషా వదంతి।
దైవం నిహత్య కురు పౌరుష మాత్మశక్త్యా
యత్నేకృతే యది న సిధ్యతి కోఽత్ర దోషః॥

Fortune favors the persevering and stout-hearted man. Wretched creatures say "Destiny must give us." Regard not destiny but exercise all your powers; if your endeavours fail, what fault will there be?

85. उपकारेण नीचानामपकारोऽहि जायते ।
पयः पानं भुजंगानां केवलं विषवर्धनं ॥
ఉపకారేణ నీచానామపకారోహి జాయతే।
పయః పానం భుజంగానాం కేవలం విషవర్ధనం॥

By doing good to base men, evil results; the drinking of milk is to snakes only an increasing of poison.

86. उपायेनहि यच्छक्यं नतच्छक्यं पराक्रमैः ॥
ఉపాయేనహి యచ్ఛక్యం నతచ్ఛక్యం పరాక్రమైః॥

That which is possible by stratagem is not possible by valour.

(See Hitopadeśa Book II and Böhtlingk's *Indische Sprüche* 1. 498).

87. उपोदकी समायाति तिंत्रिणीमंत्रिणा सह ।
पलायध्वं पलायध्वं रेरे शाकविडंबकाः ॥
ఉపోదకీ సమాయాతి తింత్రిణీమంత్రిణా సహ।
పలాయధ్వం పలాయధ్వం రేరే శాకవిడంబకాః॥

Upodakî comes with his minister Tintriṇî—flee, flee, ye pretended vegetables.

Said of the excellence of the *Upodakî* (Basella Cordifolia) when accompanied by *Tintriṇî* (Tamarindus Indica).

88. उपोषितस्य व्याघ्रस्य पारणा पशुमारणं ॥
ఉపోషితస్య వ్యాఘ్రస్య పారణా పశుమారణం॥

The breaking fast of the fasting tiger is the killing of a cow.

89. उषः प्रशस्यते गार्ग्यश्शकुनंतु बृहस्पतिः ।
मनोजयंतु मांडव्यो विप्रवाक्यं जनार्दनः ॥
ఉషః ప్రశస్యతే గార్గ్యశ్శకునంతు బృహస్పతిః।
మనోజయంతు మాండవ్యో విప్రవాక్యం జనార్దనః॥

Gârgya [says] the dawn is best; Bṛihaspati, the omen; Mâṇḍavya, the victory of the mind; Janârdana, the voice of the Brahman.

Said with reference to fixing a time for setting out on a journey.

90. उष्णकाले भवेच्छीतं शीतकाले बहूष्णता ॥

ఉష్ణకాలే భవేచ్ఛీతం శీతకాలే బహూష్ణతా॥

In hot weather, [people say] 'Let there be cold'; in cold weather, 'Let there be great heat.'

91. उष्णमुष्णेन शीतलं ॥

ఉష్ణముష్ణేన శీతలం॥

Heat with heat [produces] cold.

Like cures like. (Latin.)*

ऋ.

92. ऋणं कृत्वा घृतं पिबेत् ॥

ఋణం కృత్వా ఘృతం పిబేత్॥

Having incurred debt you should eat ghî.

93. ऋणव्रणकलंकानां काले लोपो भविष्यति ॥

ఋణవ్రణకలంకానాం కాలే లోపో భవిష్యతి॥

Debt, a sore, and a stain will be effaced in time.

94. ऋणानुबंधरूपेण पशुपत्नी सुतालयाः ।
ऋणक्षये क्षयं यांति का तत्र परिवेदना ॥

ఋణానుబంధరూపేణ పశుపత్నీ సుతాలయాః।
ఋణక్షయే క్షయం యాంతి కా తత్ర పరివేదనా॥

Cattle, a wife, children, and a house are the cause of debt; if the debt is cleared, they go to ruin—what sorrow is there in that?

---

* Similia similibus curantur.

ए.

95. एकः पापानि कुरुते फलं भुंक्ते महाजनः ॥

ఏకః పాపాని కురుతే ఫలం భుంక్తే మహాజనః॥

One commits sin, many persons suffer the consequences.

96. एका भार्या सुंदरीवा दरीवा ॥

ఏకా భార్యా సుందరీవా దరీవా॥

One wife; a beautiful woman or a cave.

एको देवः केशवोवा शिवोवा एको वासः पत्तनेवा वनेवा ।
एकं मित्रं भूपतिर्वा यतिर्वा एकाभार्या सुंदरीवा दरीवा ॥
ఏకో దేవః కేశవోవా శివోవా ఏకో వాసః పత్తనేవా వనేవా।
ఏకం మిత్రం భూపతిర్వా యతిర్వా ఏకాభార్యా సుందరీవా దరీవా॥

One god, either Kêśava or Śiva; one place of abode, either in a town or a forest; one friend, either a king or a hermit; one wife, either a beautiful woman or a cave.

(cf. Böhtlingk's *Indische Sprüche* 1. 557.)

97. एकेनैवतु चक्रेण न रथस्य गतिर्भवेत् ॥

ఏకేనైవతు చక్రేణ న రథస్య గతిర్భవేత్॥

A chariot will not go on one wheel.

98. एति जीवंतमानंदो नरं वर्षशतादपि ॥

ఏతి జీవంతమానందో నరం వర్షశతాదపి॥

Happiness attends a living man even after a hundred years.

99. **एष्टव्या बहवः पुत्राः ॥**
ఏష్టవ్యా బహవః పుత్రాః॥

Many sons are to be desired.

एष्टव्या बहवः पुत्राः यद्येकोपि गयां व्रजेत् ।
गौरींवा वरयेत्कन्यां नीलंवा वृषमुत्सृजेत् ॥
ఏష్టవ్యా బహవః పుత్రాః యద్యేకోపి గయాం వ్రజేత్।
గౌరీంవా వరయేత్కన్యాం నీలంవా వృషముత్సృజేత్॥

Many sons are to be desired; for one at last may go to Gayâ, or may give away a pure virgin, or free a black bull.

औ.

100. **औदुंबराणि पुष्पाणि श्वेतवर्णंच वायसं ।**
मत्स्यपादं जले पश्येन्ननारीहृदयस्थितं ॥
ఔదుంబరాణి పుష్పాణి శ్వేతవర్ణంచ వాయసం।
మత్స్యపాదం జలే పశ్యేన్ననారీహృదయస్థితం॥

The flowers of the fig tree, a white-coloured crow, a fish's foot in the water, one may see—but not what is in a woman's mind.

Udumbara is the Ficus Glomerata—(See Telugu No. 59.)

क.

101. **कं न वशीकुरुते भुवि रामा ॥**
కం న వశీకురుతే భువి రామా॥

Whom on earth will a handsome woman not subdue ?

कुंकुमपंककलंकितदेहा गौरपयोधरकंपितहारा ।
नूपुरहंसरणत्पदपद्मा कन्न वशीकुरुते भुवि रामा ॥
కుంకుమపంకకలంకితదేహా గౌరపయోధరకంపితహారా।
నూపురహంసరణత్పదపద్మా కన్న వశీకురుతే భువి రామా॥

Whom on earth will a handsome woman—her body besmeared with saffron paste, a necklace dangling on her fair bosom, bells tinkling on her ankles—not subdue ? (Bhartṛihari.)

102. कः पापिष्ठो ममाधिकः ॥

కః పాపిష్ఠో మమాధికః॥

What great sinner is greater than I?

103. कथयति संवृतिरेव कामितानि ॥

కథయతి సంవృతిరేవ కామితాని॥

Concealment itself reveals the wishes.

104. कदलीवंध्या काकीवंध्या ॥

కదలీవంధ్యా, కాకీవంధ్యా॥

Barren as a plantain, barren as a crow.

A woman who has one child and then dies is like the plantain which produces one bunch and then perishes; a woman who brings forth once and is afterwards barren is like the crow which lays eggs but once.

105. करतलामलकं ॥

కరతలామలకం॥

Emblic Myrobalan in the palm of the hand.

To have a thing at one's fingers' ends.

106. कर्तव्यो नातिसंचयः ॥

కర్తవ్యో నాతిసంచయః॥

Great accumulations should not be made.

कर्तव्यस्संचयो नित्यं कर्तव्यो नातिसंचयः ।
अतिसंचयदोषेण धनुषा जंबुको हतः ॥

కర్తవ్యస్సంచయో నిత్యం కర్తవ్యో నాతిసంచయః।
అతిసంచయదోషేణ ధనుషా జంబుకో హతః॥

We should always lay up [for the future], but great accumulations should not be made; by the folly of excessive hoarding the fox was killed by the bow. (See Hitopadeśa Book I.)

107. कर्ता भोक्ता जनार्दनः ॥

కర్తా భోక్తా జనార్దనః॥

Janârdana is the doer and the enjoyer?

The merit of offering a sacrifice, as well as the favor of receiving it, is to be ascribed to Janârdana (Vishṇu.)

108. कर्मणा बाध्यते बुद्धिर्नबुध्या कर्म बाध्यते ॥

కర్మణా బాధ్యతే బుద్ధిర్నబుధ్యా కర్మ బాధ్యతే॥

The mind is ruled by fate, not fate by the mind.

कर्मणा बाध्यते बुद्धिर्न बुद्ध्या कर्म बाध्यते ।
सुबुद्धिरपि यद्रामो हैमं हरिणमन्वगात् ॥
కర్మణా బాధ్యతే బుద్ధిర్న బుద్ధ్యా కర్మ బాధ్యతే।
సుబుద్ధిరపి యద్రామో హైమం హరిణమన్వగాత్॥

Fate rules the mind; not mind the fate ;—with all his wisdom, Râma pursued the golden deer!

109. कष्टे फले ॥

కష్టే ఫలే॥

From labour, fruit.

The gods sell us everything for our labours. (Latin.)*

110. कांचनात्कर्ममोचनं ॥

కాంచనాత్కర్మమోచనం॥

By gold is [obtained] freedom from [the consequences of evil] deeds.

Through the priests.

111. काकः काकः पिकः पिकः ॥

కాకః కాకః పికః పికః॥

The crow is a crow; the cuckoo is a cuckoo.

काकः कृष्णः पिकः कृष्णस्त्वभेदः पिककाकयोः ।
आयाता मधुयामिन्यः काकः काकः पिकः पिकः ॥
కాకః కృష్ణః పికః కృష్ణస్త్వభేదః పికకాకయోః।
ఆయాతా మధుయామిన్యః కాకః కాకః పికః పికః॥

The crow is black, the cuckoo is black; there is no difference between the cuckoo and the crow: but as the spring nights appear, the crow is a crow, the cuckoo is a cuckoo. (i. e. the distinction between them becomes clear when the notes of the cuckoo are heard.)

When men are tried, their relative worth is known.

---

* Di nobis laboribus omnia vendant.

112. काकतालफलन्याय: ॥
కాకతాలఫలన్యాయః॥

The crow and the palm fruit.

As a crow happened to perch on a ripe fruit, it fell.
Said of a coincidence.

113. काकमांसं शुनोच्छिष्टं स्वल्पं तदपि दुर्लभं ॥
కాకమాంసం శునోచ్ఛిష్టం స్వల్పం తదపి దుర్లభం॥

The leavings of crow-flesh by a dog are small; that even is not obtainable.

A churl, when asked to give away a little of his food, first said it was crow-flesh; then, on being pressed, said it was the leavings of a dog; and at last swallowed the whole of it and said he had none left.

114. का कस्य परिवेदना ॥
కా కస్య పరివేదనా॥

Who feels pain?

एकवृक्षसमारूढा नानादेशविहंगमा: ।
प्रभातेतु दिशो यांति का कस्य परिवेदना ॥
ఏకవృక్షసమారూఢా నానాదేశవిహంగమాః।
ప్రభాతేతు దిశో యాంతి కా కస్య పరివేదనా॥

Birds of various countries alight upon one tree; but at the dawn, they each go their way—which of them feels pain?

दुर्दूरांतपथश्रांताश्छायां यांति च शीतलां ।
शीतलाश्च पुनर्यांति का कस्य परिवेदना ॥
దుర్దూరాంతపథశ్రాంతాశ్ఛాయాం యాంతి చ శీతలాం।
శీతలాశ్చ పునర్యాంతి కా కస్య పరివేదనా॥

Wayworn travellers come under the cool shade [of a tree;] but as soon as they are refreshed, they start again—which of them feels pain? Kavitáratnákara 88.)

115. काचः काचो मणिर्मणिः ॥

కాచః కాచో మణిర్మణిః॥

Glass is glass; a gem is a gem.

मणिर्लुठति पादेन काचश्शिरसि धार्यते ।
यथैवास्तु तथैवास्तु काचः काचो मणिर्मणिः ॥
మణిర్లుఠతి పాదేన కాచశ్శిరసి ధార్యతే।
యథైవాస్తు తథైవాస్తు కాచః కాచో మణిర్మణిః॥

A diamond is trodden under foot and glass is worn on the head; let them be even in that state, glass is glass and a gem a gem.

116. का चिंता मरणे रणे ॥

కా చింతా మరణే రణే॥

What fear is there in death or the battle-field?

यदि कृष्ण पदे चिंता भक्तिस्ते पदपंकजे ।
विषमे दुर्गमे वापि का चिंता मरणे रणे ॥
యది కృష్ణ పదే చింతా భక్తిస్తే పదపంకజే।
విషమే దుర్గమే వాపి కా చింతా మరణే రణే॥

If we O Krishṇa! contemplate, if we have faith in your lotus-like feet, what fear [need we feel] in trouble or difficulty—in death or the battle field?

117. कार्येषु दासी करणेषु मंत्री रूपे च रंभा क्षमया धरित्री ।
भोज्येषु माता शयने तु वेश्या षट्कर्मयुक्ता खलु धर्मपत्नी ॥
కార్యేషు దాసీ కరణేషు మంత్రీ రూపే చ రంభా క్షమయా ధరిత్రీ।
భోజ్యేషు మాతా శయనే తు వేశ్యా షట్కర్మయుక్తా ఖలు ధర్మపత్నీ॥

In work, a slave; in business, a minister; in form a Rambhâ; in patience, [like] the earth; in [providing] food, a mother; in conjugal enjoyments, a courtesan:— is not she who possesses these six qualities, a dutiful wife?

118. कालः क्रीडति गच्छत्यायुः ॥

కాలః క్రీడతి గచ్ఛత్యాయుః॥

Time sports; life goes.

दिनमपि रजनी सायं प्रातश्शिशिरवसंतौ पुनरायातः ।
कालः क्रीडति गच्छत्यायुस्तदपि न मुंचत्याशापाशः ॥
దినమపి రజనీ సాయం ప్రాతశ్శిశిరవసంతౌ పునరాయాతః।
కాలః క్రీడతి గచ్ఛత్యాయుస్తదపి న ముంచత్యాశాపాశః॥

Day and night, evening and morning, winter and spring, come again and again; time sports, life goes, but nevertheless the chain of desire loosens not.

(cf. Böhtlingk's *Indische Sprüche* 3. 4181.)

119. कालस्य कुटिला गतिः ॥

కాలస్య కుటిలా గతిః॥

The ways of time are capricious.

अप्सु प्लवंति पाषाणा मानुषा घ्नंति राक्षसान् ।
कपयः कर्म कुर्वंति कालस्य कुटिला गतिः ॥
అప్సు ప్లవంతి పాషాణా మానుషా ఘ్నంతి రాక్షసాన్।
కపయః కర్మ కుర్వంతి కాలస్య కుటిలా గతిః॥

Stones float on water; men kill giants; monkeys perform works; the ways of time are capricious.

120. कालो हि बलवत्तरः ॥

కాలో హి బలవత్తరః॥

Time is stronger [than all things else.]

Death awaits all.

(Morton's *Bengali and Sanscrit Proverbs* 871.)

121. कीर्तिर्यस्य सजीवति ॥
కీర్తిర్యస్య సజీవతి॥

He lives, who has acquired fame.

चलच्चित्तं चलद्वित्तं चलज्जीवन यौवनं ।
चलाचलमिदं सर्वं कीर्तिर्यस्य सजीवति ॥
చలచ్చిత్తం చలద్విత్తం చలజ్జీవన యౌవనం।
చలాచలమిదం సర్వం కీర్తిర్యస్య సజీవతి॥

Mind is transitory; wealth is transitory; life is transitory; youth is transitory; all this is fleeting: he [only] lives who has acquired fame.

122. कुपुत्रेण कुलं यथा ॥
కుపుత్రేణ కులం యథా॥

As a family [is ruined] by a bad son.

एकेनापि कुवृक्षेण कोटरस्थेन वह्निना ।
दह्यते तद्वनं सर्वं कुपुत्रेण कुलं यथा ॥
ఏకేనాపి కువృక్షేణ కోటరస్థేన వహ్నినా।
దహ్యతే తద్వనం సర్వం కుపుత్రేణ కులం యథా॥

By the fire generated in its hollow, a single small tree burns a whole forest, even as a single wicked son brings ruin on his whole family.

123. कुसुमे कुसुमोत्पत्तिश्श्रूयते न च दृश्यते ॥
కుసుమే కుసుమోత్పత్తి శ్శ్రూయతే న చ దృశ్యతే॥

The production of a flower in a flower, has never been heard of, nor seen.

A riddle propounded by King Bhoja, through his mistress, to Kâlidâsa. The poet, addressing her, replied—completing the couplet—

बाले तव मुखांभोजे दृष्टमिंदीवरद्वयं ॥
బాలే తవ ముఖాంభోజే దృష్టమిందీవరద్వయం॥

O girl! two blue lotuses (eyes) are seen in the lotus of your face.

124. कृतस्य करणं नास्ति मृतस्य मरणं यथा।
गतस्य शोचना नास्ति एतद्वेदविदां मतं॥
కృతస్య కరణం నాస్తి మృతస్య మరణం యథా।
గతస్య శోచనా నాస్తి ఏతద్వేదవిదాం మతం॥

There is no doing of a thing done; there is no death for a dead man; there is no [advantage in] grief for that which is passed—this is the opinion of the learned in the Vedas.

125. कृपणस्य धनं याति वह्नितस्करपार्थिवैः॥
కృపణస్య ధనం యాతి వహ్నితస్కరపార్థివైః॥

A miser's wealth goes by fire, robbers, and kings.

126. कोकिलानां स्वरो रूपं पातिव्रत्यं तु योषितां।
विद्या रूपं विरूपाणां क्षमा रूपं तपस्विनां॥
కోకిలానాం స్వరో రూపం పాతివ్రత్యం తు యోషితాం।
విద్యా రూపం విరూపాణాం క్షమా రూపం తపస్వినాం॥

The voice is the beauty of cuckoos; chastity is the beauty of women; learning is the beauty of the deformed; patience is the beauty of ascetics.

127. कोपः पापस्य कारणं॥
కోపః పాపస్య కారణం॥

Anger is a cause of sin.

128. कोरुक् हितमितभुक्॥
కోరుక్ హితమితభుక్॥

Who is without disease? He who eats what agrees with him moderately.

Kâlidâsa's interpretation of a bird's cry "*koruk, koruk.*"

129. कोशवान् पंडितः खलु॥
కోశవాన్ పండితః ఖలు॥

Is not the man possessed of books a Paṇḍit?

130. कौपीनवंतः खलु भाग्यवंतः ॥

కౌపీనవంతః ఖలు భాగ్యవంతః॥

Are not those who have a clout the fortunate ?

i. e. Anchorites.

Said jokingly of a stingy fellow.

131. क्रियासिद्धिस्सत्वे भवति महतां नोपकरणे: ॥

క్రియాసిద్ధిస్సత్వే భవతి మహతాం నోపకరణైః॥

Success in an undertaking rests in the strength of great men, not in the means.

132. क्रोडेमनोधावति ॥

క్రోడేమనోధావతి॥

The mind runs to the [mother's] breast.

" The love of native country prevails in all." (Morton).

वासः कांचनपंजरे नृपकरांभोजे स्तनूमार्जनं ।
भक्ष्यं स्वादुरसालदाडिमफलं पेयं सुधाभं पयः ॥
पाटस्संसदि रामनाम सततं धीरस्य कीरस्य मे ।
हाहा हंत तथापि जन्मविटपिक्रोडे मनो धावति ॥

వాసః కాంచనపంజరే నృపకరాంభోజై స్తనూమార్జనం।
భక్ష్యం స్వాదురసాలదాడిమఫలం పేయం సుధాభం పయః॥
పాఠస్సంసది రామనామ సతతం ధీరస్య కీరస్య మే।
హాహా హంత తథాపి జన్మవిటపిక్రోడే మనో ధావతి॥

My residence is a golden cage ; my body is stroked by the lotus-like hands of kings ; I am fed with the delicious mango and pomegranite ; milk, equal to nectar, forms my drink ; the repetition of the name of Râma is my constant task in the assembly ; I am a clever parrot ; yet still, alas ! my heart yearns for the hollow of my native tree.

ख.

133. खलः केन निवार्यते ॥

ఖలః కేన నివార్యతే॥

By what can a wicked man be checked?

सर्पः क्रूरः खलः क्रूरः सर्पात्क्रूरतरः खलः ।
मंत्रौषधवशस्सर्पः खलः केन निवार्यते ॥

సర్పః క్రూరః ఖలః క్రూరః సర్పాత్ క్రూరతరః ఖలః।
మంత్రౌషధవశస్సర్పః ఖలః కేన నివార్యతే॥

The serpent is cruel; a wicked man is cruel; a wicked man is more cruel:—a serpent yields to spells and medicines, but by what can a wicked man be checked?

134. खलानां दुर्जनानां च द्विविधैव प्रतिक्रिया ।
उपायान्मुखभंगो वा दूरतो वा विसर्जनं ॥

ఖలానాం దుర్జనానాం చ ద్వివిధైవ ప్రతిక్రియా।
ఉపాయాన్ముఖభంగో వా దూరతో వా విసర్జనం॥

For the wicked and the evil, the remedy is of two kinds;—either to disgrace them by strategy, or to leave them at a distance.

ग.

135. गंडूषजलमात्रेण शफरी फरफरायते ॥

గండూషజలమాత్రేణ శఫరీ ఫరఫరాయతే॥

The Śapharî splashes in even a mouthful of water.

Śapharî is a small fish (Cyprinus Sophore.)—"Said of a low person unduly elated with a small advancement, and so assuming a ridiculous importance," (Morton).

136. गणाद्गृहीता वर्धेत गणस्य तु न किंचन ।
गणप्रदाता हीयेत गणस्य तु न किंचन ॥

గణాద్గృహీతా వర్ధేత గణస్య తు న కించన।
గణప్రదాతా హీయేత గణస్య తు న కించన॥

He who takes from a number will gain—it is nothing to a number; he who gives to a number will lose—it is nothing to a number.

137. गतं न शोचामि कृतं स्मरामि ॥

గతం న శోచామి కృతం స్మరామి॥

I mourn not for the past, I remember [the benefits] done [to me.]

(cf. Morton's Bengali and Sanscrit Proverbs 836.)

Vain repining is unprofitable but gratitude is a duty.

138. गतजलसेतुबंधनं ॥

గతజలసేతుబంధనం॥

Repairing the tank-bund after the water had escaped.

(See TELUGU No. 77.)

To cover the well when the child is drowned. (German.)*

139. गतानुगतिको लोको न लोकः पारमार्थिकः ।
सेतौ सैकतलिंगेन नष्टं मे ताम्रभाजनं ॥

గతానుగతికో లోకో న లోకః పారమార్థికః।
సేతౌ సైకతలింగేన నష్టం మే తామ్రభాజనం॥

Following those gone before, people reason not; by making a sand lingam at the bridge, my copper pot is lost.

A man having buried his copper pot to go and bathe at Adam's bridge near Rāmeśvaram made a sand *lingam* over it to mark the place; crowds of people following, senselessly did the same, so that it was a hopeless task for the owner to look for his property.

Silly sheep, where one goes, all go. (Spanish.)†

* Den Brunnen decken, so das kind ertrunken ist.
† Ovejas bobas, por do va una, van todas.

140. गता बहुतरा कान्ते स्वल्पा तिष्ठति शर्वरी ।
इति चित्ते समाधाय कुरुष्व जनरंजनं ॥
గతా బహుతరా కాంతే స్వల్పా తిష్ఠతి శర్వరీ।
ఇతి చిత్తే సమాధాయ కురుష్వ జనరంజనం॥

O beautiful woman! The night has mostly passed, little remains, bear this in mind and please the people.

Said to an actress, who had danced long but received no present.

141. गतो बहुतरः कालस्स्वल्प एवावशिष्यते ॥
గతో బహుతరః కాలస్స్వల్ప ఏవావశిష్యతే॥

Time has mostly gone, little only remains.

Therefore prepare for another world.

142. गुणदोषौ बुधो गृह्णन्निंदुक्ष्वेलाविवेश्वरः ।
शिरसा श्लाघते पूर्वं परं कंठे नियच्छति ॥
గుణదోషౌ బుధో గృహ్ణన్నిందుక్ష్వేలావివేశ్వరః।
శిరసా శ్లాఘతే పూర్వం పరం కంఠే నియచ్ఛతి॥

The wise man deals with virtues and faults as Śiva [dealt with] the moon and the poison; he praises the former with his head and keeps the latter in his throat.

i. e. he does not expose the faults of others, though he praises their good qualities.

Alluding to the 'Churning of the ocean'.

143. गुणिनि गुणज्ञो रमते नागुणशीलस्य परितोषः ।
अलिरेति वनात्कमलं न दर्दुरस्त्वेकवासोपि ॥
గుణిని గుణజ్ఞో రమతే నాగుణశీలస్య పరితోషః।
అలిరేతి వనాత్కమలం న దర్దురస్త్వేకవాసోపి॥

An appreciator of good qualities is pleased with a good man, but no pleasure [is experienced] by the bad man; the bee goes from the forest to the lotus, but not so the frog, though he lives with it.

144. गुणी गुणं वेत्ति न वेत्ति निर्गुणः ॥
గుణీ గుణం వేత్తి న వేత్తి నిర్గుణః॥

A good man appreciates virtue; a bad man appreciates it not.

गुणी गुणं वेत्ति न वेत्ति निर्गुणो बली बलं वेत्ति न वेत्ति निर्बलः।
पिको वसंतस्य गुणं न वायसः करी च सिंहस्य बलं न मूषिकः ॥
గుణీ గుణం వేత్తి న వేత్తి నిర్గుణో బలీ బలం వేత్తి న వేత్తి నిర్బలః।
పికో వసంతస్య గుణం న వాయసః కరీ చ సింహస్య బలం న మూషికః॥

The virtuous man appreciates virtue, the bad man appreciates it not; the strong man, and not the feeble, understands strength; the cuckoo, and not the crow, feels the influence of the spring; the elephant, and not the mouse, justly values the strength of the lion.

145. गुरुनिंदा अधोगतिः ॥
గురునిందా అధోగతిః॥

Reproaching a Guru is the road to perdition.

146. गृहीत इव केशेषु मृत्युना धर्ममाचरेत् ॥
గృహీత ఇవ కేశేషు మృత్యునా ధర్మమాచరేత్॥

You should practise virtue as if death had seized you by the hair.

147. ग्रामैकरात्रं ॥
గ్రామైకరాత్రం॥

One night in a village.

A wandering life.

घ.

148. घृतस्य पात्रमाधारो वा पात्रस्य घृतमाधारो वा ॥
ఘృతస్య పాత్రమాధారో వా పాత్రస్య ఘృతమాధారో వా॥

Does the vessel hold the ghî, or the ghî hold the vessel?

Said by a would-be logician, as he turned the jar upside down, and so lost all the contents.

Applied to foolish argumentation.

च.

149. चंदनं न वने ॥
చందనం న వనే॥

There is no sandal in the forest.

"The sandal tree grows not in every wood—Eminent persons are rarely seen." (Morton.)

150. चटकस्य मांसं भागशतं ॥
చటకస్య మాంసం భాగశతం॥

A hundred shares of a sparrow's flesh.

To make two bites of a cherry.

He'll make nineteen bits of a bilberry.

151. चर्वितचर्वणं ॥
చర్వితచర్వణం॥

Chewing the chewed.

Said of a man repeating a foolish speech.

He harps ay on ae string.

152. चिंता ज्वरो मनुष्याणां ॥
చింతా జ్వరో మనుష్యాణాం॥

Sorrow is the fever of men.

(See Böhtlingk's *Indische Sprüche* 1. 913.)

छ.

153. छिन्ने कर्णे लूने पुच्छे श्वाश्वैव नाश्वो न गर्दभः ॥
ఛిన్నే కర్ణే లూనే పుచ్ఛే శ్వాశ్వైవ నాశ్వో న గర్దభః॥

By slitting the ears and cutting the tail, a dog is but a dog—not a horse, not an ass.

(See TELUGU No. 571, &c.)

ज.

154. जनवाक्यंतु कर्तव्यं ॥

జనవాక్యంతు కర్తవ్యం॥

One should act according to the people's voice.

The voice of the people, the voice of God. (Latin.)*

155. जनिताचोपनेता च येन विद्योपदिश्यते ।

अन्नदाता भयत्राता पंचैते पितरस्स्मृताः ॥

జనితాచోపనేతా చ యేన విద్యోపదిశ్యతే।

అన్నదాతా భయత్రాతా పంచైతే పితరస్స్మృతాః॥

He who brought you forth; he who invested you with the sacred thread; he from whom you received instruction; the giver of food; he who saved you from danger—these five are to be remembered as fathers.

156. जन्मप्रभृति दारिद्र्यं दशवर्षाणि बंधनं ।

समुद्रतीरे मरणं कश्चिद्भोगो भविष्यति ॥

జన్మప్రభృతి దారిద్ర్యం దశవర్షాణి బంధనం।

సముద్రతీరే మరణం కశ్చిద్భోగో భవిష్యతి॥

There will be poverty from birth, ten years' imprisonment, death on the sea shore, and [then] a little enjoyment.

The divine writing on a skull (See Telugu No. 1344) picked up by Bhoja Râja; the "enjoyment" was interpreted by Kâlidâsa to be a ride in Bhoja Râja's palankin.

157. जातस्य मरणं ध्रुवं ॥

జాతస్య మరణం ధ్రువం॥

To him who is born, death is certain.

158. जामाता दशमो ग्रहः ॥

జామాతా దశమో గ్రహః॥

A son-in-law is the tenth planet.

A troublesome fellow.

---

* Vox populi, vox Dei.

159. जामात्रर्थं अर्पितस्य सूपस्यातिथिभ्यः ।
प्रथम परिवेषणे न प्राधान्यं हीयते ॥
జామాత్రర్థం అర్పితస్య సూపస్యాతిథిభ్యః।
ప్రథమ పరివేషణే న ప్రాధాన్యం హీయతే॥

The pre-eminence of the son-in-law is not diminished by first serving the guests with the pulse cooked for him.

160. जिघांसंतं जिघांसीयात् ॥
జిఘాంసంతం జిఘాంసీయాత్॥

You may kill him who wishes to kill you.

आततायिनमायांतमपि वेदांतगं रणे ।
जिघांसंतं जिघांसीयान्नतेन ब्रह्महा भवेत् ॥
ఆతతాయినమాయాంతమపి వేదాంతగం రణే।
జిఘాంసంతం జిఘాంసీయాన్నతేన బ్రహ్మహా భవేత్॥

You may kill a man on the field of battle who attempts to kill you though he be learned in the Vedanta; you will not by that become a Brahman-slayer.

Self-preservation is the first law of nature.

161. जिह्वाग्रे वर्तते लक्ष्मीर्जिह्वाग्रे मित्रबांधवाः ।
जिह्वाग्रे बंधनप्राप्तिर्जिह्वाग्रे मरणं ध्रुवं ॥
జిహ్వాగ్రే వర్తతే లక్ష్మీర్జిహ్వాగ్రే మిత్రబాంధవాః।
జిహ్వాగ్రే బంధనప్రాప్తిర్జిహ్వాగ్రే మరణం ధ్రువం॥

Fortune rests on the tip of the tongue; friends and relatives rest on the tip of the tongue; suffering imprisonment rests on the tip of the tongue; death rests on the tip of the tongue.

162. जीर्णमन्नं प्रशंसीयाद्भार्यां च गतयौवनां ।
रणात्प्रत्यागतं शूरं सस्यं च गृहमागतं ॥
జీర్ణమన్నం ప్రశంసీయాద్భార్యాం చ గతయౌవనాం।
రణాత్ప్రత్యాగతం శూరం సస్యం చ గృహమాగతం॥

You should praise food digested, a wife whose youth has gone, a hero returned from the battle-field, and the grain which has come to the house.

163. श्रेष्ठत्वंतु न हि ज्येष्ठे श्रेष्ठत्वं गुण उच्यते ॥
శ్రేష్ఠత్వంతు న హి జ్యేష్ఠే శ్రేష్ఠత్వం గుణ ఉచ్యతే॥

Superiority is not in seniority; superiority is attributed to virtue.

164. ज्वरांतेतु विरेचनं ॥
జ్వరాంతేతు విరేచనం॥

After a fever, a purge.

ट.

165. टीका टूकामपेक्षते ॥
టీకా టూకామపేక్షతే॥

The commentary requires a commentary.

Obscurum facere per obscurius.

त.

166. तंतुदेशं न पश्यामि यत्र भ्राता सहोदरः ॥
తంతుదేశం న పశ్యామి యత్ర భ్రాతా సహోదరః॥

I see not the country where a brother is.

देशेदेशे कलत्राणि देशेदेशे च बांधवाः ।
तं तु देशं न पश्यामि यत्र भ्राता सहोदरः ॥
దేశేదేశే కలత్రాణి దేశేదేశే చ బాంధవాః।
తం తు దేశం న పశ్యామి యత్ర భ్రాతా సహోదరః॥

Wives can be procured in all countries, and relatives as well, but I see not a country where there is a brother born of the same womb.

167. तवाप्यर्धं ममाप्यर्धं ॥
తవాప్యర్ధం మమాప్యర్ధం॥

Half yours, half mine.

Said by a Brahman impostor who was caught repeating sham Mantras.

(See TELUGU No. [illegible]).

168. तस्करस्य वधो दंडो दासीदंडस्तु मुंडनं ।
भार्यादंडः पृथक्छय्या मित्रदंडस्त्वभाषणं ॥
తస్కరస్య వధో దండో దాసీదండస్తు ముండనం।
భార్యాదండః పృథక్ఛయ్యా మిత్రదండస్త్వభాషణం॥

Death is the punishment of a robber, the punishment of a harlot is shaving the head; separation *a toro* is the punishment of a wife, the punishment of a friend is not speaking to him.

169. तावच्च शोभते मूर्खो यावत्किंचिन्न भाषते ॥
తావచ్చ శోభతే మూర్ఖో యావత్కించిన్న భాషతే॥

A fool shines so long as he says nothing.

दूरतश्शोभते मूर्खो लंबशाटपटावृतः ।
तावच्च शोभते मूर्खो यावत्किंचिन्न भाषते ॥
దూరతశ్శోభతే మూర్ఖో లంబశాటపటావృతః।
తావచ్చ శోభతే మూర్ఖో యావత్కించిన్న భాషతే॥

A fool looks well at a distance with his flowing garments; a fool shines so long as he says nothing.

Every fool is wise when he holds his tongue. (Italian.)*

A fool, if he holds his tongue, passes for wise. (Spanish.)†

170. तिलतंडुलन्यायः ॥
తిలతండులన్యాయః॥

Sesamum seed and rice.

Though mixed, their difference will always be seen.

---

*Ogni pazzo è savio quando tace.
† El bobo, si es callado, por sesudo es reputado.

171. तृणजलूकान्यायः ॥
తృణజలూకాన్యాయః॥

Like the leaping leech.

Which jumps along holding on by its head and tail alternately, not letting go its hold at one end until fixed at the other.

A bird in the hand is worth two in the bush.

172. तृणाल्लघुतरस्तूलस्तूलादपि च याचकः ।
वायुना किं न नीतोऽसौ मामयं याचयेदिति ॥
తృణాల్లఘుతరస్తూలస్తూలాదపి చ యాచకః।
వాయునా కిం న నీతో஽సౌ మామయం యాచయేదితి॥

Cotton is lighter than grass and a beggar is lighter (more insignificant) than cotton—why is he not carried away by the wind? "Lest he should beg of me" [fears the wind.]

173. तृष्णावधिं को गतः ॥
తృష్ణావధిం కో గతః॥

Who has reached the limit of desire?

निःस्वो ह्येकशतं शती दशशतं लक्षं सहस्राधिपो
लक्षेशः क्षितिपालतां क्षितिपतिश्चक्रेशवत्संपदं ।
चक्रेशः पुनरिंद्रतां सुरपतिर्ब्रह्मास्पदं वांछति
ब्रह्मा विष्णुपदं हरिर्हरपदं तृष्णावधिं को गतः ॥
నిఃస్వో హ్యేకశతం శతీ దశశతం లక్షం సహస్రాధిపో
లక్షేశః క్షితిపాలతాం క్షితిపతిశ్చక్రేశవత్సంపదం।
చక్రేశః పునరింద్రతాం సురపతిర్బ్రహ్మాస్పదం వాంఛతి
బ్రహ్మా విష్ణుపదం హరిర్హరపదం తృష్ణావధిం కో గతః॥

He who has nothing wishes for a hundred; he who has a hundred wishes for ten hundred; the possessor of a thousand desires a lakh; the owner of a lakh desires a kingdom; the ruler of a kingdom longs for an empire; the emperor again wishes for Indra's possessions; Surapati desires to be in Brahmâ's place; Brahmâ to be in Vishṇu's; Hari covets Hara's dominion —who has reached the limit of desire?

174. त्यजेदेकं कुलस्यार्थे ग्रामस्यार्थे कुलं त्यजेत् ।
ग्रामं जनपदस्यार्थे आत्मार्थे पृथिवीं त्यजेत् ॥
త్యజేదేకం కులస్యార్థే గ్రామస్యార్థే కులం త్యజేత్।
గ్రామం జనపదస్యార్థే ఆత్మార్థే పృథివీం త్యజేత్॥

You should forsake a man for the sake of your family; you should forsake your family for the sake of your village; you should forsake your village for the sake of your country; you should forsake the earth for the sake of yourself.

175. त्रिशंकुस्वर्गारोहणं ॥
త్రిశంకుస్వర్గారోహణం॥

Triśanku's mounting to heaven.

King Triśanku, a descendant of Ikshwâku, having been exalted to heaven by the power of Viśvâmitra was hurled from thence headlong by Indra, and remained ever after, in mid-air, head down and heels upward! (See Muir's *Sanscrit Texts*, Part I, pp. 100-103.)

The result of ambition—Applied also to a matter kept in suspense, neither settled one way nor the other. (cf. Morton's *Bengali and Sanscrit Proverbs* 810.)

द.

176. दंडो दशगुणो भवेत् ॥
దండో దశగుణో భవేత్॥

A stick has ten uses.

177. दर्दुरा यत्र वक्तारस्तत्र मौनं हि शोभनं ॥
దర్దురా యత్ర వక్తారస్తత్ర మౌనం హి శోభనం॥

Where frogs are the croakers, there silence is becoming.

भद्रं कृतं कृतं मौनं कोकिलैर्जलदागमे।
दर्दुरा यत्र वक्तारस्तत्र मौनं हि शोभनं॥
భద్రం కృతం కృతం మౌనం కోకిలైర్జలదాగమే।
దర్దురా యత్ర వక్తారస్తత్ర మౌనం హి శోభనం॥

Cuckoos do well to keep silent in the winter; where frogs are the croakers, there silence is becoming.

178. **दशमाता हरीतकी॥**
దశమాతా హరీతకీ॥

Harîtakî is [equal to] ten mothers.

Harîtakî is the Terminalia Chebula; "the tender buds of this tree are formed into galls which are much prized as an astringent medicine and also as a mordant in dyeing." (W. Elliot's *Flora Ândhrika.*) The fruit is used as a purgative.

179. **दाता दरिद्रः कृपणो धनाढ्यः पापी चिरायुस्सुकृती गतायुः।**
राजाकुलीनस्सुकुलेन सेव्यः कलौ युगे षड्गुणमाश्रयंति॥
దాతా దరిద్రః కృపణో ధనాఢ్యః పాపీ చిరాయుస్సుకృతీ గతాయుః।
రాజాకులీనస్సుకులేన సేవ్యః కలౌ యుగే షడ్గుణమాశ్రయంతి॥

In the Kali Yuga men will suffer these six changes: the liberal man will be poor; the miser will be rich; the sinner will be longlived; the good man will be short-lived; the king will be of low birth; and he will be served by a man of high birth.

180. **दातृत्वं प्रियवक्तृत्वं धीरत्वमुचितज्ञता।**
अभ्यासेन न लभ्यंते चत्वारस्सहजागुणाः॥
దాతృత్వం ప్రియవక్తృత్వం ధీరత్వముచితజ్ఞతా।
అభ్యాసేన న లభ్యంతే చత్వారస్సహజాగుణాః॥

Liberality, sweetness of speech, courage, judgment: these four natural qualities are not attained by practice.

181. दानं दातृवशं ॥

దానం దాతృవశం॥

Giving is in the power of the giver.

Giving or not giving depends upon the will of him who has the means of giving.

182. दारिद्र्यदोषो गुणराशिनाशकः ॥

దారిద్ర్యదోషో గుణరాశినాశకః॥

The defect of poverty is the destroyer of a host of virtues.

अंकस्य दोषो गुणसन्निपाते निमज्जतींदोरिति यो बभाषे ।
नूनं न दृष्टं कविनापि तेन दारिद्र्यदोषो गुणराशिनाशकः॥
అంకస్య దోషో గుణసన్నిపాతే నిమజ్జతీందోరితి యో బభాషే।
నూనం న దృష్టం కవినాపి తేన దారిద్ర్యదోషో గుణరాశినాశకః॥

The poet, who has said that the blemish of a dark spot is lost in the many beauties of the moon, surely did not observe that the defect of poverty is the destroyer of a host of virtues.

Poverty is no vice, but it is a sort of leprosy. (French.)*

183. दाक्षिण्याद्धननाशनं ॥

దాక్షిణ్యాద్ధననాశనం॥

Complaisance empties the purse.

184. दिवा काकरुताद्भीता ॥

దివా కాకరుతాద్భీతా॥

In the daytime she was frightened by the cawing of a crow.

The feigned timidity of a loose woman. (See the *Bhojacharitra.*)

---

* Pauvreté n'est pas vice, mais c'est une espèce de ladrerie.

185. दीर्घश्रृंगमनड्वाहं निर्लज्जां विधवां स्त्रियं ।
शूद्रमक्षरसंयुक्तं दूरतः परिवर्जयेत् ॥
దీర్ఘశృంగమనడ్వాహం నిర్లజ్జాం విధవాం స్త్రియం।
శూద్రమక్షరసంయుక్తం దూరతః పరివర్జయేత్॥

Keep clear of a bull with long horns, a widow without shame, and an educated Śûdra.

186. दुर्जनं दूरतस्त्यजेत् ॥
దుర్జనం దూరతస్త్యజేత్॥

Keep clear of a bad man.

Keep yourself from the anger of a great man, from the tumult of a mob, from a man of ill fame, from a widow that has been thrice married, from a wind that comes in at a hole, and from a reconciled enemy.

187. दुर्जनः परिहर्तव्यो विद्ययालंकृतोपि सन् ।
मणिना भूषितस्सर्पः किमसौ न भयंकरः ॥
దుర్జనః పరిహర్తవ్యో విద్యయాలంకృతోపి సన్।
మణినా భూషితస్సర్పః కిమసౌ న భయంకరః॥

Though he be adorned with learning, a bad man is to be shunned; is a snake adorned with a gem not to be feared?

A jewel called *Sarpamaṇi* (snake-stone) is said to be found in the head of a snake.

188. दुर्जनः प्रथमं पूज्यस्सज्जनस्तदनंतरं ।
पदप्रक्षालनं पूर्वं मुखप्रक्षालनं परं ॥
దుర్జనః ప్రథమం పూజ్యస్సజ్జనస్తదనంతరం।
పదప్రక్షాలనం పూర్వం ముఖప్రక్షాలనం పరం॥

The bad man to be honored first and the good man afterwards; the feet to be washed first, and the mouth afterwards.

189. दुर्जनः प्रियवादी च नैतद्विश्वासकारणं ।
मधु तिष्ठति जिह्वाग्रे हृदये तु हलाहलं ॥

దుర్జనః ప్రియవాదీ చ నైతద్విశ్వాసకారణం।
మధు తిష్ఠతి జిహ్వాగ్రే హృదయే తు హాలాహలం॥

Though a bad man speak soft words, that is no ground for confidence in him; it is honey on the tip of the tongue and poison in the heart.

(See TELUGU, No. 4, &c.)

190. दुर्बलस्य बलं राजा बालानां रोदनं बलं ॥

దుర్బలస్య బలం రాజా బాలానాం రోదనం బలం॥

The king is the strength of the weak, crying is the strength of children.

Because they obtain what they want by it.

191. दुर्भिक्षमल्पं स्मरणं चिराय ॥

దుర్భిక్షమల్పం స్మరణం చిరాయ॥

Famine for a short time, the remembrance of it long.

(See Morton's *Bengali and Sanscrit Proverbs* 830).

192. दुष्टा भार्या शठं मित्रं भृत्योऽहंकारसंयुतः ।
ससर्पे च गृहे वासो मृत्युरेव न संशयः ॥

దుష్టా భార్యా శఠం మిత్రం భృత్యోఽహంకారసంయుతః।
ససర్పే చ గృహే వాసో మృత్యురేవ న సంశయః॥

A wicked wife, a false friend, a servant with pride, living in a house with a snake are [causes of] death, without doubt.

193. दूरस्थाः पर्वता रम्यास्समीपस्थास्तु बर्बराः ॥

దూరస్థాః పర్వతా రమ్యాస్సమీపస్థాస్తు బర్బరాః॥

Mountains are beautiful at a distance, rugged when near.

(See TELUGU, No. 1181.)

194. दूषकश्च क्रियाशून्यो निकृष्टो दीर्घकोपनः ।
चत्वारः कर्मचंडाला जातिचंडाल उत्तमः ॥

దూషకశ్చ క్రియాశూన్యో నికృష్టో దీర్ఘకోపనః।
చత్వారః కర్మచండాలా జాతిచండాల ఉత్తమః॥

A foul mouthed man, a man without employment, a low fellow, a revengeful man — these four are base from their evil deeds; the base-born are better.

195. दृष्टिपूतं न्यसेत्पादं वस्त्रपूतं जलं पिबेत् ।
सत्यपूतां वदेद्वाचं मनःपूतं समाचरेत् ॥

దృష్టిపూతం న్యసేత్పాదం వస్త్రపూతం జలం పిబేత్।
సత్యపూతాం వదేద్వాచం మనఃపూతం సమాచరేత్॥

The foot should be placed [on a spot] seen to be clean, water should be drunk after having been strained through a cloth; a word should be spoken with truth, [a business] should be done with consideration.

196. दैवं पुरुषरूपेण ॥

దైవం పురుషరూపేణ॥

God in the form of man.

God works through men, as His instruments.

197. दैवस्य चित्रागतिः ॥

దైవస్య చిత్రాగతిః॥

Various are the ways of fortune.

198. दैवाधीनं जगत्सर्वं मंत्राधीनं तु दैवतं ।
तन्मंत्रं ब्राह्मणाधीनं ब्राह्मणो मम देवता ॥
దైవాధీనం జగత్సర్వం మంత్రాధీనం తు దైవతం।
తన్మంత్రం బ్రాహ్మణాధీనం బ్రాహ్మణో మమ దేవతా॥

The whole world is subject to God, God is subject to a Mantra, that Mantra is subject to the Brahman, the Brahman is my god.

199. दैवे बले दुर्बले ॥
దైవే బలే దుర్బలే॥

When fortune fails, [nothing can be done.]

200. दोषा वाच्या गुरोरपि ॥.
దోషా వాచ్యా గురోరపి॥

The defects, even of a Guru, should be told.

शत्रोरपि गुणा वाच्या दोषा वाच्या गुरोरपि ।
सर्वदा सर्वयत्नेन पुत्रे शिष्ये हितं वदेत् ॥
శత్రోరపి గుణా వాచ్యా దోషా వాచ్యా గురోరపి।
సర్వదా సర్వయత్నేన పుత్రే శిష్యే హితం వదేత్॥

Virtues, even in an enemy, should be acknowledged; defects, even in a Guru, ought to be pointed out: always, and with all endeavour, should the son and the scholar be taught wisdom.

201. द्रव्यं मूल्येन शुध्यति ॥
ద్రవ్యం మూల్యేన శుధ్యతి॥

A thing is valued for its price.

फलं तु क्षालनाच्छुध्येत् गोमयेन गृहं तथा ।
क्षारयोगेन वस्त्रं च द्रव्यं मूल्येन शुध्यति ॥
ఫలం తు క్షాలనాచ్ఛుధ్యేత్ గోమయేన గృహం తథా।
క్షారయోగేన వస్త్రం చ ద్రవ్యం మూల్యేన శుధ్యతి॥

A fruit becomes purified by washing; so a house by cow-dung; and a cloth by the use of fuller's earth; a thing is valued for its price.

ध.

202. **धनमूलमिदं जगत् ॥**

ధనమూలమిదం జగత్॥

In this world, money is the means.

203. **धर्मं च चिंतयेत्प्राज्ञः ॥**

ధర్మం చ చింతయేత్ప్రాజ్ఞః॥

A wise man should think of virtue.

204. **धर्मस्य सूक्ष्मा गतिः ॥**

ధర్మస్య సూక్ష్మా గతిః॥

The way of justice is mysterious.

यातः क्ष्मामखिलां प्रदाय हरये पातालमूलं बलिः ।
सक्तुप्रस्थविसर्जनात्सच मुनिस्स्वर्गं समारोपितः ॥
आबाल्यादसती सती सुरपुरीं कुंती समारोहयत् ।
हा सीता पतिदेवतागमदधो धर्मस्य सूक्ष्मा गतिः ॥

యాతః క్ష్మామఖిలాం ప్రదాయ హరయే పాతాలమూలం బలిః।
సక్తుప్రస్థవిసర్జనాత్సచ మునిస్స్వర్గం సమారోపితః॥
ఆబాల్యాదసతీ సతీ సురపురీం కుంతీ సమారోహయత్।
హా సీతా పతిదేవతాగమదధో ధర్మస్య సూక్ష్మా గతిః॥

Making over all the earth to Hari, Bali went down to the bottom of Pâtâla; with the offering of a measure of flour of fried corn, the celebrated Ṛishi [Kuchela] procured his elevation to Heaven; in spite of her unchaste character from youth, Kunti rose to the region of angels; while, alas, Sîtâ, in spite of her devotion to her husband, went down [into the earth];—the way of justice is mysterious.

205. धर्मो वर्धति वर्धति ॥

ధర్మో వర్ధతి వర్ధతి॥

Virtue increases and increases.

206. धारां तु पश्यति न कश्चन योगसिद्धः ॥

ధారాం తు పశ్యతి న కశ్చన యోగసిద్ధః॥

No gifted Yogi can see the stream.

आनंदतांडवपुरे द्रविडस्य गेहे ।
चित्रं वसिष्ठवनितासममाज्यपात्रम् ॥
हा हंत हंत परिनर्तति तत्र दर्वी ।
धारां तु पश्यति न कश्चन योगसिद्धः ॥

ఆనందతాండవపురే ద్రవిడస్య గేహే।
చిత్రం వశిష్ఠవనితాసమమాజ్యపాత్రం॥
హా హంత హంత పరినర్తతి తత్ర దర్వీ।
ధారాం తు పశ్యతి న కశ్చన యోగసిద్ధః॥

In the city of Anandatāṇḍava, in the house of a Draviḍa, there is a wonder—the ghī pot is like Vaśishṭha's wife, the spoon dances in it; Aha! Aha! no gifted Yogi can see the stream.

(See TELUGU No. 2411.)

Vaśishṭha's wife, Arundhatī, is the personification of one of the Pleiades. The allusion here is to the smallness of the star.

207. धूर्तैर्जगद्वंच्यते ॥

ధూర్తైర్జగద్వంచ్యతే॥

The world is deceived by the wicked.

208. धैर्यं सर्वत्र साधकं ॥

ధైర్యం సర్వత్ర సాధకం॥

Courage is in all things a means [of success.]

न.

209. नंदो राजा भविष्यति ॥

నందో రాజా భవిష్యతి॥

Nanda will become a king.

210. न गृहं गृहमित्याहुर्गृहिणी गृहमुच्यते ॥

న గృహం గృహమిత్యాహుర్గృహిణీ గృహముచ్యతే॥

It is not a house they call the house, but the housewife.

न गृहं गृहमित्याहुर्गृहिणी गृहमुच्यते ।
तया हि सहितस्सर्वान् पुरुषार्थान् समश्नुते ॥
న గృహం గృహమిత్యాహుర్గృహిణీ గృహముచ్యతే।
తయా హి సహితస్సర్వాన్ పురుషార్థాన్ సమశ్నుతే॥

It is not a house they call the house but the housewife; one possessed of her enjoys all the pleasures man is capable of.

211. न च दैवात्परं बलं ॥

న చ దైవాత్పరం బలం॥

There is no power greater than that of fate.

न च विद्यासमो बंधुर्न च व्याधिसमो रिपुः ।
न चापत्यसमः स्नेहो न च दैवात्परं बलं ॥
న చ విద్యాసమో బంధుర్న చ వ్యాధిసమో రిపుః।
న చాపత్యసమః స్నేహో న చ దైవాత్పరం బలం॥

No relative is equal to learning; no enemy is equal to disease; no affection is equal to that for a child; there is no power greater than that of fate.

212. न च धनगर्वितबांधवशरणं ॥

న చ ధనగర్వితబాంధవశరణం॥

Be not dependent on a purse-proud relation.

वरमसिधारा तरुतलवासो वरमिह भिक्षा वरमुपवासः ।
वरमपि घोरे नरके पतनं न च धनगर्वितबांधवशरणं ॥
వరమసిధారా తరుతలవాసో వరమిహ భిక్షా వరముపవాసః।
వరమపి ఘోరే నరకే పతనం న చ ధనగర్వితబాంధవశరణం॥

Better is the edge of a sword, or to live under a tree—better is it to beg, to starve, or even to fall into the dreadful hell, than to depend on a purse-proud relation.

213. न चलति खलु वाक्यं सज्जनानां कदाचित् ॥

న చలతి ఖలు వాక్యం సజ్జనానాం కదాచిత్॥

The words of the good will surely never fail.

उदयति यदि भानुः पश्चिमे दिग्विभागे ।
विकसति यदि पद्मः पर्वतानां शिखाग्रे ॥
प्रचलति यदि मेरुः शीततां याति वह्निः ।
नचलति खलु वाक्यं सज्जनानां कदाचित् ॥
ఉదయతి యది భానుః పశ్చిమే దిగ్విభాగే।
వికసతి యది పద్మః పర్వతానాం శిఖాగ్రే॥
ప్రచలతి యది మేరుః శీతతాం యాతి వహ్నిః।
నచలతి ఖలు వాక్యం సజ్జనానాం కదాచిత్॥

Even if the sun should rise in the west, even if the lotus should bloom on the peaks of the mountains, even if Meru should shake, even if fire should feel cold,—the words of the good will surely never fail.

214. नदीनां सागरो गतिः ॥

నదీనాం సాగరో గతిః॥

The ocean is the course of rivers.

Death is the common lot of all. (Latin.)*

* Mors omnibus communis.

215. **न दुःखं पंचभिस्सह ॥**

న దుఃఖం పంచభిస్సహ॥

With five [others] there is no sorrow.

स्थातव्यं पंचभिःसार्थं गंतव्यं पंचभिस्सह ।
भोक्तव्यं पंचभिस्सार्थं न दुःखं पंचभिस्सह ॥
స్థాతవ్యం పంచభిస్సార్థం గంతవ్యం పంచభిస్సహ।
భోక్తవ్యం పంచభిస్సార్థం న దుఃఖం పంచభిస్సహ॥

You should stop along with five [others]; walk along with five [others]; eat along with five [others]; with five [others] there is no sorrow.

Company in distress makes trouble less. (French.)*

216. **न देवस्सृष्टिनाशकः ॥**

న దేవస్సృష్టినాశకః॥

God is not the destroyer of his creation.

न माता शपते पुत्रं न दोषं लभते मही ।
न हिंसां कुरुते साधुर्नदेवस्सृष्टिनाशकः ॥
న మాతా శపతే పుత్రం న దోషం లభతే మహీ।
న హింసాం కురుతే సాధుర్న దేవస్సృష్టినాశకః॥

A mother curses not her son; the earth suffers not harm; a good man does no injury; God is not the destroyer of His creation.

217. **न दोषं लभते मही ॥**

న దోషం లభతే మహీ॥

The Earth does not feel evil.

---

* Qui ne souffre pas seul, ne souffre pas tant.

218. न भूतो न भविष्यति ॥
న భూతో న భవిష్యతి॥

It has not been and it will not be.

अन्नदानात्परं दानं न भूतं न भविष्यति ।
अन्नेन धार्यते सर्वं जगदेतच्चराचरं ॥
అన్నదానాత్పరం దానం న భూతం న భవిష్యతి।
అన్నేన ధార్యతే సర్వం జగదేతచ్చరాచరం॥

A greater gift than that of food, has not been and will not be; by food this whole world, animate and inanimate, is sustained.

219. नमंति फलिनो वृक्षा नमंति गुणिनो जना: ॥
నమంతి ఫలినో వృక్షా నమంతి గుణినో జనాః॥

Fruitful trees bend down, men of wisdom stoop.

The truly great are humble.

नमंति फलिनो वृक्षा नमंति गुणिनो जना: ।
शुष्ककाष्ठं च मूर्खश्च भिद्यते न च नम्यते ॥
నమంతి ఫలినో వృక్షా నమంతి గుణినో జనాః।
శుష్కకాష్ఠం చ మూర్ఖశ్చ భిద్యతే న చ నమ్యతే॥

Fruitful trees bend down, men of wisdom stoop;—a dry stick and a fool can be broken but not bent.

220. नमंति संतस्त्रैलोक्यादपि लब्धुं समुन्नतिं ॥
నమంతి సంతస్త్రైలోక్యాదపి లబ్ధుం సమున్నతిం॥

Good men bend to obtain the highest elevation, even above the three worlds.

221. न माता शपते पुत्रं ॥
న మాతా శపతే పుత్రం॥

A mother curses not her son.

(See No. 216.)

222. नराणां नापितो धूर्तः ॥
నరాణాం నాపితో ధూర్తః॥

Among men a barber is the [greatest] knave.

223. नव नव वयं पंच ॥
నవ నవ వయం పంచ॥

Nine, Nine—we [know] five.

When on one occasion, a voice was heard crying "*Nava, Nava,*" Kâlidâsa replied "we [only know] five [grammars].

224. न विद्या कारणं पुंसां भाग्यमेव हि कारणं ।
पाषाणस्य कुतो विद्या देवत्वमुपतिष्ठते ॥
న విద్యా కారణం పుంసాం భాగ్యమేవ హి కారణం।
పాషాణస్య కుతో విద్యా దేవత్వముపతిష్ఠతే॥

The learning of men is not a cause [of greatness]; what learning has a stone? but it obtains divinity.

(See TELUGU No. 2068.)

225. नष्टस्य कान्या गतिः ॥
నష్టస్య కాన్యా గతిః॥

What other resource has a ruined man?

भिक्षो मांसनिषेवणं किमुचितं किं तेन मद्यं विना ।
मद्यं चापि तव प्रियं प्रियमहो वारांगनाभिस्सह ।
वेश्याप्यर्थरुचिः कुतस्तव धनं द्यूतेन चौर्येण वा ।
चौर्यद्यूतपरिश्रमोऽस्ति भवतो नष्टस्य कान्या गतिः ॥
భిక్షో మాంసనిషేవణం కిముచితం కిం తేన మద్యం వినా।
మద్యం చాపి తవ ప్రియం ప్రియమహో వారాంగనాభిస్సహ।
వేశ్యాప్యర్థరుచిః కుతస్తవ ధనం ద్యూతేన చౌర్యేణ వా।
చౌర్యద్యూతపరిశ్రమోస్తి భవతో నష్టస్య కాన్యా గతిః॥

"Is it right, Hermit, to eat flesh?" "What is the use of it without liquor?" "You like liquor, too?" "Aha! I like it in the company of harlots." "A harlot is fond of money and how can you get it?" "Either by gambling or by theft." "Are you accustomed to gamble and steal?" "What other resource has a ruined man?"

226. न स्त्री स्वातंत्र्यमर्हति ॥

న స్త్రీ స్వాతంత్ర్య మర్హతి॥

A woman is not fit for independence.

227. न हिंसां कुरुते साधुः ॥

న హింసాం కురుతే సాధుః॥

A good man does no injury.

228. न हि प्रमाणं जंतूनामुत्तरक्षणजीवने ॥

న హి ప్రమాణం జంతూనాముత్తరక్షణజీవనే॥

There is no law for living beings of life for the next moment.

(See TELUGU No. 1963.)

229. न हि सर्वस्सर्वं जानाति ॥

న హి సర్వస్సర్వం జానాతి॥

No one knows everything.

230. न हि सर्वे भवादृशाः ॥

న హి సర్వే భవాదృశాః॥

All are not like you.

231. न हि सुखं दुःखैर्विना लभ्यते ॥

న హి సుఖం దుఃఖైర్వినా లభ్యతే॥

No pleasure is obtained without pain.

No rose without a thorn.

232. नानृतं वदेत् ॥

నానృతం వదేత్॥

A lie should not be told.

233. नानृतात्पातकं परं ॥
నానృతాత్పాతకం పరం॥

There is no greater sin than a lie.

234. नारदः कलहप्रियः ॥
నారదః కలహప్రియః॥

Nârada was a lover of strife.

The Muni Nârada had a knack of sowing discord between others.

235. नारीणां भूषणं पतिः ॥
నారీణాం భూషణం పతిః॥

A husband is the ornament of women.

236. नाविष्णुः पृथिवीपतिः ॥
నావిష్ణుః పృథివీపతిః॥

There is no king who is not Vishṇu.

i. e. in whom divinity does not dwell.

(See No. 196.)

237. नास्ति ग्रामः कुतस्सीमा ॥
నాస్తి గ్రామః కుతస్సీమా॥

There is no village—how can there be a boundary?

नास्ति ग्रामः कुतस्सीमा नास्ति विद्या कुतो यशः ।
नास्ति ज्ञानं कुतो मुक्तिर्भक्तिर्नास्ति कुतस्तु धीः ॥
నాస్తి గ్రామః కుతస్సీమా నాస్తి విద్యా కుతో యశః।
నాస్తి జ్ఞానం కుతో ముక్తిర్భక్తిర్నాస్తి కుతస్తు ధీః॥

There is no village — how can there be a boundary?
There is no learning — how can there be fame?
There is no wisdom — how can there be salvation?
There is no faith — how can there be understanding?

238. नाहंकारात्परो रिपुः ॥

నాహంకారాత్పరో రిపుః॥

There is no greater enemy than self-conceit.

न चापत्यसमस्नेहो न च दैवात्परं बलं ।

न च विद्यासमो बंधुर्नाहंकारात्परो रिपुः ॥

న చాపత్యసమస్నేహో న చ దైవాత్పరం బలం।

న చ విద్యాసమో బంధుర్నాహంకారాత్పరో రిపుః॥

No love is equal to that of [a parent for] a child ; no power greater than that of fate ; no relation is equal to knowledge ; no enemy greater than self-conceit.

239. नित्यं सन्निहितो मृत्युः ॥

నిత్యం సన్నిహితో మృత్యుః॥

Death is always present.

Death does not blow a trumpet. (Danish.)*

240. नियतिः केन बाध्यते ॥

నియతిః కేన బాధ్యతే॥

Who can control fate ?

मातुलो यस्य गोविंदः पिता यस्य धनंजयः ।

सोभिमन्यूरणे शेते नियतिः केन बाध्यते ॥

మాతులో యస్య గోవిందః పితా యస్య ధనంజయః।

సోభిమన్యూరణే శేతే నియతిః కేన బాధ్యతే॥

On the battle field lies Abhimanyu, whose maternal uncle is Govinda, and whose father is Dhananjaya ! — Who can control fate ?

241. निर्धनपुरुषः पशुः ॥

నిర్ధనపురుషః పశుః॥

A man without money is a beast.

(See TELUGU Nos. 1876, &c.)

---

* Döden blæser ei Lyd for sig.

242. निर्धनपुरुषस्तूलसमानः ॥
నిర్ధనపురుషస్తూలసమానః॥

A man without money is like cotton.

i. e. as insignificant as cotton is light.

(See No. 172—also TELUGU Nos. 1876, 2168, 2169.)

243. निर्वाणदीपे किमुतैलदानं चोरे गते वा किमु सावधानं ॥
నిర్వాణదీపే కిముతైలదానం చోరే గతే వా కిము సావధానం॥

What is the use of oil to an extinguished lamp? What is the use of care after the thief has gone?

(See TELUGU No. 77.)

When the head is broken the helmet is put on. (Italian.)*

To stop the hole when the mischief is done. (Spanish.)†

Every ditch is full of after-wit. (Italian.)‡

244. नीचाः कलहमिच्छंति संधिमिच्छंति साधवः ॥
నీచాః కలహమిచ్ఛంతి సంధిమిచ్ఛంతి సాధవః॥

Base men love contention, good men love peace.

245. नीचाश्रयो न कर्तव्यः कर्तव्यो महदाश्रयः ।
ईशाश्रयो महानागः पप्रच्छ गरुडं सुखं ॥
నీచాశ్రయో న కర్తవ్యః కర్తవ్యో మహదాశ్రయః।
ఈశాశ్రయో మహానాగః పప్రచ్ఛ గరుడం సుఖం॥

The protection of the base should not be sought, the protection of the great should be obtained; the great serpent protected by Îśa (Śiva) enquired after Garuḍa's health.

(See TELUGU No. 751.)

246. नीचो वदति न कुरुते न वदति कुरुते सज्जनः ॥
నీచో వదతి న కురుతే న వదతి కురుతే సజ్జనః॥

A mean fellow promises and does not; a good man promises not, but does.

---

* Rotta la testa, se mette la celata.
† Recabido ya el daño, atapar el horado.
‡ Del senno di poi è piena ogni fossa.

247. नीरुजस्य किमौषधैः ॥

నీరుజస్య కిమౌషధైః॥

Why medicine for a healthy man?

दरिद्रान् भर कौंतेय मा प्रयच्छेश्वरे धनं ।
व्याधितस्यौषधं पथ्यं नीरुजस्य किमौषधैः ॥

దరిద్రాన్ భర కౌంతేయ మా ప్రయచ్ఛేశ్వరే ధనం।
వ్యాధితస్యౌషధం పథ్యం నీరుజస్య కిమౌషధైః॥

Support the needy, O son of Kunti! bestow not your riches on the wealthy. Medicine is proper for a patient; why medicine for a healthy man?

248. नैषधं विद्वदौषधं ॥

నైషధం విద్వదౌషధం॥

The Naishadham is medicine for the Doctors.

It tests the powers of the learned.

प.

249. पंडिता मूर्खजीविनः ॥

పండితా మూర్ఖజీవినః॥

Pandits live on fools.

250. पंथा वातेन शुद्ध्यति ॥

పంథా వాతేన శుద్ధ్యతి॥

The road is cleansed by the wind.

रजसा शुध्यते नारी काष्ठं शुध्यति तक्षणात् ।
ताम्रमम्लस्य योगेन पंथा वातेन शुध्यति ॥

రజసా శుధ్యతే నారీ కాష్ఠం శుధ్యతి తక్షణాత్।
తామ్రమమ్లస్య యోగేన పంథా వాతేన శుధ్యతి॥

• • • Wood is beautified by chiselling; copper is polished by tamarind; the road is cleansed by the wind.

251. पक्वानां हि वधे सूत वज्रायंते तृणान्यपि ॥
పక్వానాం హి వధే సూత వజ్రాయంతే తృణాన్యపి॥

O Sûta! in killing those ripe [for death], blades of grass even are equal to Indra's weapon.

252. पटाटोपो भयंकरः ॥
పటాటోపో భయంకరః॥

[His] pomp is dreadful.

253. पत्रं पुष्पं फलं तोयं ॥
పత్రం పుష్పం ఫలం తోయం॥

A leaf, a flower, a fruit, water.

Said apologetically by a poor host to a grand guest.

पत्रं पुष्पं फलं तोयं यो मे भक्त्या प्रयच्छति ।
तदहं भक्त्युपहृतमश्नामि प्रयतात्मनः ॥
పత్రం పుష్పం ఫలం తోయం యో మే భక్త్యా ప్రయచ్ఛతి।
తదహం భక్త్యుపహృతమశ్నామి ప్రయతాత్మనః॥

"I accept and enjoy the holy offerings of the humble soul, who in his worship presenteth leaves and flowers, and fruit and water unto me." (*Bhagavad-gîta*, 9. 26. Wilkins' trans.)

254. पतितः पर्वतो लघुः ॥
పతితః పర్వతో లఘుః॥

A fallen mountain is [thought] light [of].

"When a person once prosperous declines in circumstances, he ceases to be respected." (Morton 822.)

255. पयसा सिंचितो नित्यं न निंबो मधुरायते ॥
పయసా సించితో నిత్యం న నింబో మధురాయతే॥

The Margosa tree will not sweeten, though it be constantly watered with milk.

256. परप्रतारणे पांडित्यं ॥

పరప్రతారణే పాండిత్యం ॥

Skill in defrauding others.

257. पराान्नं प्राणसंकटं ॥

పరాన్నం ప్రాణసంకటం॥

Another's food is distressing to the life.

Dependence on another for one's livelihood is a miserable state of existence.

(See TELUGU No. 2126)

258. परमे ब्रह्मणि कोपि न सक्तः ॥

పరమే బ్రహ్మణి కోపి న సక్తః॥

No one is devoted to the supreme Brahma.

259. परोपकारः पुण्याय पापाय परपीडनं ॥

పరోపకారః పుణ్యాయ పాపాయ పరపీడనం॥

To do good to others is meritorious, to injure others is sinful.

260. परोपकाराय सतां विभूतयः ॥

పరోపకారాయ సతాం విభూతయః॥

The riches of the good are [employed] for the benefit of others.

पिबंति नद्यस्स्वयमेव नांभः खादंति न स्वादुफलानि वृक्षाः।
पयोधरास्सस्यमदंति नैव परोपकाराय सतां विभूतयः ॥

పిబంతి నద్యస్స్వయమేవ నాంభః ఖాదంతి న స్వాదుఫలాని వృక్షాః।
పయోధరాస్సస్యమదంతి నైవ పరోపకారాయ సతాం విభూతయః॥

The rivers themselves drink not [their] water, nor do the trees eat [their own] sweet fruit; the clouds eat not the crops—the riches of the good are [employed] for the benefit of others.

261. परोपकारार्थमिदं शरीरं ॥
పరోపకారార్థమిదం శరీరం॥

This body is for doing good to others.

Our bodies are given to us as the means whereby we may assist our fellow men.

262. परोपदेशे पांडित्यं ॥
పరోపదేశే పాండిత్యం॥

Proficiency in advising others.

परोपदेशे पांडित्यं सर्वेषां सुकरं नृणां ।
धर्मे स्वीयमनुष्ठानं कस्य चित्तु महात्मनः ॥
పరోపదేశే పాండిత్యం సర్వేషాం సుకరం నృణాం।
ధర్మే స్వీయమనుష్ఠానం కస్య చిత్తు మహాత్మనః॥

Proficiency in advising others is easy to all men; few are the great men who themselves practise virtue.

Every one thinks himself able to advise another.

Nothing is so freely given as advice. (French.)*

Of judgment every one has a stock for sale. (Italian.)†

263. परोपि हितवान् बंधुः ॥
పరోపి హితవాన్ బంధుః॥

Though not of your kin, a friend is your [truest] relation.

(See TELUGU No. 909.)

Many kinsfolk, few friends.

परोपि हितवान् बंधुर्बंधुरप्यहितः परः ।
अहितो देहजो व्याधिर्हितमारण्यमौषधं ॥
పరోపి హితవాన్ బంధుర్బంధురప్యహితః పరః।
అహితో దేహజో వ్యాధిర్హితమారణ్యమౌషధం॥

One interested in our welfare is a relative, though a stranger; one injurious is a stranger, though a relative; disease is hurtful, though born in our body; medicine is beneficial, though produced in a forest.

---

* Rien ne se donne aussi libéralement que les conseils.
† Del judizio ognun ne vende.

264. पक्षिवृक्षन्याय: ॥

పక్షివృక్షన్యాయః॥

Like a bird and a tree.

265. पापात्मनां पापशतेन किं वा ॥

పాపాత్మనాం పాపశతేన కిం వా॥

What of a hundred sins to sinners?

गोमूत्रमात्रेण पयो विनष्टं तक्रस्य गोमूत्रशतेन किं वा ।
अत्यल्पपापैर्विपदष्शुचीनां पापात्मनां पापशतेन किं वा ॥
గోమూత్రమాత్రేణ పయో వినష్టం తక్రస్య గోమూత్రశతేన కిం వా।
అత్యల్పపాపైర్విపదశ్శుచీనాం పాపాత్మనాం పాపశతేన కిం వా॥

Milk is spoiled even by a little of cow's urine, what harm does a quantity of it do to buttermilk? The pure are involved in trouble by the smallest sins, how will even a hundred sins affect those already sinners?

(cf. Morton's *Bengali and Sanscrit Proverbs* 811.)

266. पिता च ऋणवाञ्छत्रुर्माता शत्रुरशीलिनी ।
भार्या रूपवती शत्रु: पुत्रश्शत्रुरपंडित: ॥
పితా చ ఋణవాఞ్ఛత్రుర్మాతా శత్రురశీలినీ।
భార్యా రూపవతీ శత్రుః పుత్రశ్శత్రురపండితః॥

A father in debt is an enemy [to his son]; a mother of bad conduct is an enemy [to her son]; a beautiful wife is an enemy [to her husband]; an unlearned son is an enemy [to his parents].

267. पितृदु:खं तु षण्मासं मातृदु:खं तु वत्सर: ।
भार्यादु:खं पुनर्भार्या पुत्रदु:खं निरंतरं ॥
పితృదుఃఖం తు షణ్మాసం మాతృదుఃఖం తు వత్సరః।
భార్యాదుఃఖం పునర్భార్యా పుత్రదుఃఖం నిరంతరం॥

Sorrow for [the loss of] a father [lasts] six months; sorrow for a mother, a year; sorrow for a wife until a second wife [comes]; sorrow for a son, for ever.

268. पिशाचानां पिशाचभाषयैवोत्तरं देयं ॥

పిశాచానాం పిశాచభాషయైవోత్తరం దేయం॥

Devils should be answered in devils' language.

269. पुमान् दुष्कीर्तिसंयुक्तो जीवन्नपि मृतोपमः ॥

పుమాన్ దుష్కీర్తిసంయుక్తో జీవన్నపి మృతోపమః॥

A man of evil repute is, though living, as one dead.

270. पुरुषाणामभावेन सर्वा नार्यः पतिव्रताः ॥

పురుషాణామభావేన సర్వా నార్యః పతివ్రతాః॥

In the absence of men, all women are chaste.

271. पुस्तकं वनिता वित्तं परहस्तगतं गतं ।
अथवा पुनरायाति जीर्णं भ्रष्टा च खंडशः ॥

పుస్తకం వనితా విత్తం పరహస్తగతం గతం।
అథవా పునరాయాతి జీర్ణం భ్రష్టా చ ఖండశః॥

A book, a woman, or money, when gone into the hand of another, is gone [indeed]; or it returns worn out, corrupted, or by bits.

272. पुस्तकेषु च या विद्या परहस्ते च यद्धनं ।
समये तु परिप्राप्ते न सा विद्या न तद्धनं ॥

పుస్తకేషు చ యా విద్యా పరహస్తే చ యద్ధనం।
సమయే తు పరిప్రాప్తే న సా విద్యా న తద్ధనం॥

Learning, in the book, is not learning, and money in the hand of another is not money when the time [of need] arises.

273. पृष्ठताडनाद्दंतभंगः ॥

పృష్ఠతాడనాద్దంతభంగః॥

Falling out of the teeth by a stroke on the back.

(See TELUGU No. 1766.)

Applied to inconclusive reasoning.

274. प्रथमकवले मक्षिकापातः ॥

ప్రథమకబళే మక్షికాపాతః॥

Fall of a fly into the first morsel [of food].

Said of an obstruction at the very commencement of an undertaking.

275. प्रयोजनमनुद्दिश्य न मंदोपि प्रवर्तते ॥

ప్రయోజనమనుద్దిశ్య న మందోపి ప్రవర్తతే॥

Without an object in view, not even a fool undertakes [a business.]

276. प्रवृत्तित्वावच्छिन्नं प्रति कृतिसाध्यताज्ञानं कारणं ॥

ప్రవృత్తిత్వావచ్ఛిన్నం ప్రతి కృతిసాధ్యతాజ్ఞానం కారణం॥

Knowledge of the possibility of the act is an inseparable motive to perseverance.

277. प्रक्षालनाद्धि पंकस्य दूरादस्पर्शनं वरं ॥

ప్రక్షాళనాద్ధి పంకస్య దూరాదస్పర్శనం వరం॥

Keeping away from the mire is better than washing it off.

278. प्राणमेव परित्यज्य मानमेवाभिरक्षतु ।

अनित्यो भवति प्राणो मान आचंद्रतारकं ॥

ప్రాణమేవ పరిత్యజ్య మానమేవాభిరక్షతు।

అనిత్యో భవతి ప్రాణో మాన ఆచంద్రతారకం॥

Even at the cost of his life, one should preserve his honor; life is transient, honor is as lasting as the moon and stars.

279. प्राप्तकालो न जीवति ॥
ప్రాప్తకాలో న జీవతి॥

He whose time has come, lives not.

नाकाले म्रियते कश्चिद्विद्धश्शरशतैरपि ।
स्पृष्टः कुशाग्रमात्रेण प्राप्तकालो न जीवति ॥
నాకాలే మ్రియతే కశ్చిద్విద్ధశ్శరశతైరపి।
స్పృష్టః కుశాగ్రమాత్రేణ ప్రాప్తకాలో న జీవతి॥

No one dies before his time even though pierced by hundreds of arrows; touched merely by a blade of grass, he lives not, whose time has come.

280. प्रायो गच्छति यत्र दैवहतकस्तत्रैव यांत्यापदः ॥
ప్రాయో గచ్ఛతి యత్ర దైవహతకస్తత్రైవ యాంత్యాపదః॥

Wherever the fate-stricken goes, there calamities generally go also.

खल्वाटो दिवसेश्वरस्य किरणैस्संतापिते मस्तके ।
गच्छन् देशमनातपं द्रुतगतिस्तालस्य मूलं गतः ॥
तत्राप्येकमहाफलेन पतता भग्नं सशब्दं शिरः ।
प्रायो गच्छति यत्र दैवहतकस्तत्रैव याञ्त्यापदः ॥
ఖల్వాటో దివసేశ్వరస్య కిరణైస్సంతాపితే మస్తకే।
గచ్ఛన్ దేశమనాతపం ద్రుతగతిస్తాలస్య మూలం గతః॥
తత్రాప్యేకమహాఫలేన పతతా భగ్నం సశబ్దం శిరః।
ప్రాయో గచ్ఛతి యత్ర దైవహతకస్తత్రైవ యాన్త్యాపదః॥

When a bald headed man having had his head scorched by the rays of the sun, seeking a cool place, went quickly under a palmyra tree, there by the falling of a large fruit his head was broken with a noise! Wherever the fate-stricken goes, there calamities generally go also.

ब.

281. **बकः परमधार्मिकः**

బకః పరమధార్మికః॥

The crane is very virtuous!

Ironically "applied to one of outward decency and pretence of virtue, but inwardly aiming at injury to others." (Morton, 832.)

शनैः शनैः क्षिपेत्पादौ प्राणिनां वधशंकया ।
पश्य लक्ष्मण पंपायां बकः परमधार्मिकः ॥

శనైః శనైః క్షిపేత్పాదౌ ప్రాణినాం వధశంకయా।
పశ్య లక్ష్మణ పంపాయాం బకః పరమధార్మికః॥

Behold, Lakshmana! for fear of destroying life it places its feet softly in the Pampa lake, the crane is very virtuous!

282. **बकध्यानं ॥**

బకధ్యానం॥

A crane's meditation.

Cranes appear to be meditating when they are ready to pounce on the fish.

Hypocrisy.

283. **बद्धमूलस्य मूलं हि महद्वैरतरोः स्त्रियः ॥**

బద్ధమూలస్య మూలం హి మహద్వైరతరోః స్త్రియః॥

Women are the great root of the firmly-rooted tree of enmity.

Women and dogs set men together by the ears.

A woman's vengeance knows no bounds. (German.)*

---

* Weiberrache hat keine Grenzen.

284. बलवंतं चिकित्सयेत् ॥

బలవంతం చికిత్సయేత్ ॥

The strongest should be cured.

उपस्थिते बहुविधे रोगे पित्तादि दोषजे।
हीनाहितकरं त्यक्त्वा बलवंतं चिकित्सयेत् ॥
ఉపస్థితే బహువిధే రోగే పిత్తాది దోషజే।
హీనాహితకరం త్యక్త్వా బలవంతం చికిత్సయేత్ ॥

When there are divers diseases sprung from bile and the like, the strongest (most dangerous) should be cured, leaving alone those less injurious.

285. बिंदुस्सिंधुस्सिंधुरप्येकबिंदुः ॥

బిందుస్సింధుస్సింధురప్యేకబిందుః ॥

A drop is as the ocean [to the good]; the ocean is as a single drop [to the base].

Referring to recipients of charity.

286. बुद्धिर्यस्य बलं तस्य निर्बुद्धेस्तु कुतो बलं ॥

బుద్ధిర్యస్య బలం తస్య నిర్బుద్ధేస్తు కుతో బలం ॥

He who is wise, is strong; the foolish man has no strength.

बुद्धिर्यस्य बलं तस्य निर्बुद्धेस्तु कुतो बलं ॥
पश्य सिंहो मदोन्मत्तश्शशकेन निपातितः ॥
బుద్ధిర్యస్య బలం తస్య నిర్బుద్ధేస్తు కుతో బలం।
పశ్య సింహో మదోన్మత్తశ్శశకేన నిపాతితః ॥

He who has wisdom, has strength; how comes strength to him who has no wisdom? Consider how the lion Madonmatta was drowned by the hare.

287. ब्रह्मज्ञानेन ब्राह्मणः ॥

బ్రహ్మజ్ఞానేన బ్రాహ్మణః ॥

By the knowledge of Brahma, a Brahman.

Spiritual wisdom makes the Brahman.

भ.

288. भवेन्नदीनामुदकं प्रधानं ॥
భవేన్నదీనాముదకం ప్రధానం॥

For rivers, water is the chief thing.

289. भक्षितेपि लशुने न शांतो व्याधिः ॥
భక్షితేపి లశునే న శాంతో వ్యాధిః॥

Though an onion was eaten, the disease was not cured.

To eat onions is forbidden by the Hindu Law.

Said when an object has not been gained even though a considerable sacrifice was made to secure it.

290. भाग्यं फलति सर्वत्र न विद्या न च पौरुषं ॥
భాగ్యం ఫలతి సర్వత్ర న విద్యా న చ పౌరుషం॥

Fortune is fruitful everywhere, not learning nor human efforts.

समुद्रमंथने लेभे हरिर्लक्ष्मीं हरो विषं ।
भाग्यं फलति सर्वत्र न विद्या न च पौरुषं ॥
సముద్రమంథనే లేభే హరిర్లక్ష్మీం హరో విషం।
భాగ్యం ఫలతి సర్వత్ర న విద్యా న చ పౌరుషం॥

At the churning of the ocean, Hari obtained Lakshmi and Hara, poison; fortune is fruitful everywhere, not learning nor human efforts.

291. भाग्यानि पूर्वतपसा खलु संचितानि ।
काले फलंति पुरुषस्य यथैव वृक्षाः ॥
భాగ్యాని పూర్వతపసా ఖలు సంచితాని।
కాలే ఫలంతి పురుషస్య యథైవ వృక్షాః॥

Fortune, acquired by former penance, brings forth fruit to a man in [due] time, as do the trees.

292. भुक्त्वा राजवदासीत ॥

భుక్త్వా రాజవదాసీత॥

One should eat and sit like a king.

293. भुक्त्वा शतपदं गच्छेत् ॥

భుక్త్వా శతపదం గచ్ఛేత్॥

After eating, walk a hundred paces.

After eating, either stand, or walk a mile. (Latin.)*

After dinner sit a while, after supper walk a mile.

294. भुजंग एव जानीते भुजंगचरणं सखे ॥

భుజంగ ఏవ జానీతే భుజంగచరణం సఖే॥

O friend! the serpent only knows the serpent's feet.

(See TELUGU No. 1419.)

295. भूते पश्यंति बर्बराः ॥

భూతే పశ్యంతి బర్బరాః॥

Fools learn by the past.

राजा पश्यति कर्णाभ्यां धिया पश्यंति पंडिताः ।

पशुः पश्यति गंधेन भूते पश्यंति बर्बराः ॥

రాజా పశ్యతి కర్ణాభ్యాం ధియా పశ్యంతి పండితాః।

పశుః పశ్యతి గంధేన భూతే పశ్యంతి బర్బరాః॥

A king perceives by his ears, the learned by their intellect; a beast perceives by scent, and fools by the past.

Experience is the mistress of fools. (Latin.)†

Experience is a dear school, but fools learn in no other.

---

* Post epulas stabis vel passus mille meabis.

† Experientia stultorum magistra.

296. भृंगकीटन्यायः ॥
భృంగకీటన్యాయః॥

Like the bee and the worm.

The large black bee is said to hum round a worm until it makes it, like itself, a bee.—" The similitude is used to point out the entire change produced in the mind of a pupil." (Brown.)

297. भेको बकबकायते ॥
భేకో బకబకాయతే॥

A frog croaks.

दिव्यं चूतफलं प्राप्य न गर्वं याति कोकिलः ।
पीत्वा कर्दमपानीयं भेको बकबकायते ॥
దివ్యం చూతఫలం ప్రాప్య న గర్వం యాతి కోకిలః।
పీత్వా కర్దమపానీయం భేకో బకబకాయతే॥

The cuckoo feels no pride in the possession of a delicious mango; a frog is set a croaking by a gulp of muddy water.

298. भ्रमरकीटन्यायः ॥
భ్రమరకీటన్యాయః॥

Like the bee and the worm.

(See No. 296.)

म.

299. मत्तकुंजरसंघातं भिनत्त्येकोपि केसरी ॥
మత్తకుంజరసంఘాతం భినత్త్యేకోపి కేసరీ॥

Even a single lion tears to pieces a herd of mad elephants.

300. मध्ये तिष्ठति माधवः ॥
మధ్యే తిష్ఠతి మాధవః॥

Mâdhava stands in the middle.

When two persons salute each other, it is as pleasing to Vishṇu as if he were himself worshipped by them both.

301. मन एव मनुष्याणां कारणं बंधमोक्षयोः ॥
మన ఏవ మనుష్యాణాం కారణం బంధమోక్షయోః॥

The mind of men is the cause of bondage and release.

It depends upon man himself to obtain final beatitude and release from mundane existence.

302. मनस्येकं वचस्येकं कर्मण्येकं महात्मनां ।
मनस्यन्यद्वचस्यन्यत्कर्मण्यन्यद्दुरात्मनां ॥
మనస్యేకం వచస్యేకం కర్మణ్యేకం మహాత్మనాం।
మనస్యన్యద్వచస్యన్యత్కర్మణ్యన్యద్దురాత్మనాం॥

At heart, in word, and in deed the good are one; in the wicked, heart differs from word and word from deed.

303. मरणांतानि वैराणि ॥
మరణాంతాని వైరాణి॥

Enmities end with death.

304. मर्कटकिशोरन्यायः ॥
మర్కటకిశోరన్యాయః॥

The monkey and its cub.

As the cub clings to its mother, so man seeks divine aid, and clings to his God.—The doctrine of the *Vaḍagalais.*

(See No. 319.)

305. मर्दनाद्गुणवर्धनं ॥
మర్దనాద్గుణవర్ధనం॥

Pounding improves the disposition.

दुर्जनं कांचनं भेरीं दुष्टस्त्रीं दुष्टवाहनं ।
इक्षुखंडान् तिलान्शूद्रान् मर्दयेद्गुणवृद्धये ॥
దుర్జనం కాంచనం భేరీం దుష్టస్త్రీం దుష్టవాహనం।
ఇక్షుఖండాన్ తిలాన్శూద్రాన్ మర్దయేద్గుణవృద్ధయే॥

A bad man, gold, a drum, a bad woman, a bad horse, stalks of sugar cane, sesamum seed, and Śûdras should be beaten to improve their qualities.

A spaniel, a woman and a walnut tree,
The more they be beaten, the better they be.

306. महागजाः पलायंते मशकानां तु का गतिः ॥

మహాగజాః పలాయంతే మశకానాం తు కా గతిః॥

When huge elephants run away, what hope is there for mosquitos?

307. महाजनो येन गतस्स पंथाः ॥

మహాజనో యేన గతస్స పంథాః॥

That is the road which is trodden by the great.

वेदा विभिन्नाः स्मृतयो विभिन्ना तथा मुनीनां मतयो विभिन्नाः।
धर्मस्य तत्वं निहितं गुहायां महाजनो येन गतस्स पंथाः ॥

వేదా విభిన్నాః స్మృతయో విభిన్నా తథా మునీనాం మతయో విభిన్నాః।
ధర్మస్య తత్వం నిహితం గుహాయాం మహాజనో యేన గతస్స పంథాః॥

The Vedas are divided, the Smṛitis are divided, so are Munis' minds divided; the reality of virtue is placed in a cave—that is the road which is trodden by the great.

308. मक्षिका मारुतो वेश्या याचको मूषकस्तथा।
ग्रामणीर्गणकश्चैव सप्तैते परबाधकाः ॥

మక్షికా మారుతో వేశ్యా యాచకో మూషకస్తథా।
గ్రామణీర్గణకశ్చైవ సప్తైతే పరబాధకాః॥

A fly, the wind, a harlot, a beggar, a rat, the head of the village, and the village accountant—these seven are annoying to others.

309. मांसं मांसेन वर्धते ॥

మాంసం మాంసేన వర్ధతే॥

Flesh is increased by flesh.

i. e. by eating it.

310. मातापुत्रविरोधाय हिरण्याय नमो नमः ॥

మాతాపుత్రవిరోధాయ హిరణ్యాయ నమో నమః॥

Salutation, salutation to the gold [which caused] enmity between the mother and the son.

The story runs as follows: A man found, while ploughing, a pot of money. His mother perceiving this from a distance, determined to kill her son and mixed poison with his food; the son noticing that his mother had seen the treasure and fearing that he would be made to divide it with his brothers, killed her with a blow of the yoke and soon afterwards himself died of the poison. The goddess of money then invited a Brahman, who was in a neighbouring tree, plucking leaves for platters, and had seen all that had happened, to appropriate the treasure, but he declined to have anything to do with it.

311. मातृहीनशिशुजीवनं वृथा कान्तहीननवयौवनं तथा ।
शान्तिहीनतपसः फलं वृथा तिन्त्रिणीरसविहीनभोजनं ॥

మాతృహీనశిశుజీవనం వృథా కాంతహీననవయౌవనం తథా।
శాంతిహీనతపసః ఫలం వృథా తింత్రిణీరసవిహీనభోజనం॥

Vain is the life of a motherless child, so is the prime [of a woman] without a husband; penance without quietism is fruitless, so is food without tamarind juice.

(See No. 87—also TELUGU No. 1028.)

312. मानं धर्मो हतो हरेत् ॥

మానం ధర్మో హతో హరేత్॥

Virtue lost, takes away honor.

313. मार्जालकिशोरन्यायः ॥

మార్జాలకిశోరన్యాయః॥

Like the cat and her kitten.

The stronger carrying and protecting the weaker; used to illustrate the free grace of God.—The doctrine of the *Tengalais*.

(See No. 304.)

314. मार्जालाभ्यंजनं ॥

మార్జాలాభ్యంజనం॥

Anointing a cat.

If oil be put on a cat's head, it is said she will scratch herself to death in a week.

Injuring another by indirect means.

315. मुखं पद्मदलाकारं वचश्चंदनशीतलं ।
हृत्कर्तरीसमं चातिविनयो धूर्तलक्षणं ॥

ముఖం పద్మదలాకారం వచశ్చందనశీతలం।
హృత్కర్తరీసమం చాతివినయో ధూర్తలక్షణం॥

A face shaped like the petals of the lotus, a voice as cool [pleasing] as sandal, a heart like a pair of scissors, and excessive humility—these are the signs of a rogue.

316. मुखे मुखे सरस्वती ॥

ముఖే ముఖే సరస్వతీ॥

Sarasvatî is in every mouth.

i. e. all have the power of speech.

317. मुनीनां च मतिभ्रमः ॥

మునీనాం చ మతిభ్రమః॥

The minds of Munis are [sometimes] confused.

जिह्वा टलति धीरस्य पादस्खलति हस्तिनः ।
भीमस्यापि रणे भंगो मुनीनां च मतिभ्रमः ॥

జిహ్వా టలతి ధీరస్య పాదస్ఖలతి హస్తినః।
భీమస్యాపి రణే భంగో మునీనాం చ మతిభ్రమః॥

The tongue of the brave, [sometimes] falters; the foot of the elephant shakes; Bhîma even is discomfited; and the minds of Munis are confused.

318. मुरारेस्तृतीयः पंथाः ॥

మురారేస్తృతీయః పంథాః॥

Murâri's is the third way.

The poet Murâri's style differs both from that of Kalidâsa and that of Bhavabhûti.

319. **मुसलः किसलायते ॥**
ముసలః కిసలాయతే॥

The rice pounder sprouts.

(See TELUGU No. 1867.)

320. **मूर्खस्य पुत्रो विधवा च कन्या ॥**
మూర్ఖస్య పుత్రో విధవా చ కన్యా॥

A stubborn son, a widowed daughter.

कुग्रामवासः कुजनस्य सेवा कुभोजनं क्रोधमुखी च भार्या ।
मूर्खस्य पुत्रो विधवा च कन्या विनाग्निना संदहते शरीरं ॥
కుగ్రామవాసః కుజనస్య సేవా కుభోజనం క్రోధముఖీ చ భార్యా।
మూర్ఖస్య పుత్రో విధవా చ కన్యా వినాగ్నినా సందహతే శరీరం॥

Residence in a hamlet, service under a low fellow, coarse food, an ill-tempered wife, a stubborn son, and a widowed virgin [daughter] burn the body without fire.

321. **मूर्खस्य नास्त्यौषधं ॥**
మూర్ఖస్య నాస్త్యౌషధం॥

There is no cure for the headstrong.

शक्यो वारयितुं जलेन हुतभुक् छत्रेण वर्षातपौ ।
नागेंद्रो निशितांकुशेन समदो दंडेन गोगर्दभौ ॥
व्याधिर्भेषजसंग्रहैश्च विविधैर्मंत्रप्रयोगैर्विषं ।
सर्वस्यौषधमस्ति शास्त्रविहितं मूर्खस्य नास्त्यौषधं ॥
శక్యో వారయితుం జలేన హుతభుక్ ఛత్రేణ వర్షాతపౌ।
నాగేంద్రో నిశితాంకుశేన సమదో దండేన గోగర్దభౌ॥
వ్యాధిర్భేషజసంగ్రహైశ్చ వివిధైర్మంత్రప్రయోగైర్విషం।
సర్వస్యౌషధమస్తి శాస్త్రవిహితం మూర్ఖస్య నాస్త్యౌషధం॥

It is possible to stop fire with water, rain and heat with an umbrella, a *must* elephant with a sharp hook, a bull or ass with a stick, a disease with medicines, and venom by the use of various spells; for every thing there is a remedy provided in the Śástras—but there is no cure for the headstrong.

322. मूर्खस्य मूर्खो गतिः ॥

మూర్ఖస్య మూర్ఖో గతిః॥

A fool's refuge is a fool.

323. मूर्खेण किं भाषणं ॥

మూర్ఖేణ కిం భాషణం॥

What speech with a fool?

"Talk not much with a fool, and go not to him who hath no understanding." Ecclesiasticus, xxii. 13.

324. मृत्पिंड एको बहुभांडरूपस्सुवर्णमेकं बहुभूषणात्मा ।
गोक्षीरमेकं बहुधेनुजातमेकः परात्मा बहुदेहवर्ती ॥

మృత్పిండ ఏకో బహుభాండరూపస్సువర్ణమేకం బహుభూషణాత్మా।
గోక్షీరమేకం బహుధేనుజాతమేకః పరాత్మా బహుదేహవర్తీ॥

One lump of clay [is moulded] into vessels of many forms, one gold [is made] into ornaments of many shapes; [all] cow-milk is one though yielded by many cows; so the one Supreme soul resides in many bodies.

325. मृत्युर्वै प्राणिनां ध्रुवं ॥

మృత్యుర్వై ప్రాణినాం ధ్రువం॥

Death is certain to all living creatures.

(See Nos. 120, 214.)

Man is a bubble. (Greek.)*

326. मौनं सर्वार्थसाधकं ॥

మౌనం సర్వార్థసాధకం॥

Silence gains all objects.

Silence is wisdom, when speaking is folly.

Who speaks, sows; who keeps silence, reaps. (Italian.)†

---

* Πομφόλυξ ὁ ἄνθρωπος.

† Chi parla semina, chi tace raccoglie.

327. मौनमर्धांगीकारः ॥
మౌనమర్ధాంగీకారః॥

Silence is half consent.

Silence is consent.

Who keeps silence, consents. (Italian.)*

He who says nothing, consents. (French.)†

328. मौनेन कलहो नास्ति नास्ति जागरतो भयं ॥
మౌనేన కలహో నాస్తి నాస్తి జాగరతో భయం॥

By silence there is no quarrel, by vigilance there is no fear.

By silence all occasion of strife is avoided, and by vigilance is removed all cause of sudden fear.

Silence seldom doth harm.
Silence is wisdom, and gets friends.

य.

329. यतो धर्मस्ततो जयः ॥
యతో ధర్మస్తతో జయః॥

Where there is justice, there is victory.

जयोस्तु पांडुपुत्राणां येषां पक्षे जनार्दनः ।
यतः कृष्णस्ततो धर्मो यतो धर्मस्ततो जयः ॥
జయోస్తు పాండుపుత్రాణాం యేషాం పక్షే జనార్దనః।
యతః కృష్ణస్తతో ధర్మో యతో ధర్మస్తతో జయః।

Success be to sons of Pāṇḍu, on whose side is Janârdana; where Krishna is, there is justice; where justice is, there is victory.

330. यत्र तिष्ठति धर्मात्मा तत्र देवोपि तिष्ठति ॥
యత్ర తిష్ఠతి ధర్మాత్మా తత్ర దేవోపి తిష్ఠతి॥

Where there is a virtuous man, there also is God.

God helps the good.

---

* Chi tace, acconsente.
† Qui ne dit mot, consent.

331. यत्र धर्मो ह्यधर्मेण सत्यं यत्रानृतेन च ।
हन्यते प्रेक्षमाणास्तु हतास्तत्र सभासदः ॥

యత్ర ధర్మో హ్యధర్మేణ సత్యం యత్రానృతేన చ।
హన్యతే ప్రేక్షమాణాస్తు హతాస్తత్ర సభాసదః॥

Where virtue is destroyed by vice, and truth by falsehood, there the courtiers who witness it become themselves depraved.

332. यत्र धूमस्तत्र वह्निः ॥

యత్ర ధూమస్తత్ర వహ్నిః॥

Where smoke, there fire.

Where there's smoke, there's fire.

No smoke without some fire.

Where there is no fire, no smoke rises. (Portuguese.)*

333. यथा पिता तथा पुत्रः ॥

యథా పితా తథా పుత్రః॥

As the father, so the son.

(See TELUGU No. 176.)

334. यथा बीजं तथांकुरः ॥

యథా బీజం తథాంకురః॥

As the seed, so the sprout.

(See TELUGU No. 1977.)

Bad crow, bad egg. (Greek.)†

335. यथा राजा तथा प्रजाः ॥

యథా రాజా తథా ప్రజాః॥

As the king, so the people.

Like king, like people. (Latin.)‡

---

* Onde fogo naõ ha, fumo naõ se levanta.

† Κακοῦ κόρακος κακὸν ᾠόν.

‡ Qualis rex, talis grex.

336. यथार्थवादी लोकविरोधी ॥

యథార్థవాదీ లోకవిరోధీ॥

A speaker of truth is the world's enemy.

(See TELUGU No. 320, &c.)

337. यथेच्छं विहर वृषभराज ॥

యథేచ్ఛం విహార వృషభరాజ॥

O king of bulls, roam freely at your will.

(See No. 90.)

A phrase used when liberating a bull in obsequial ceremonies. "The sacrifice of a cow or calf formed part of the ancient Śrāddha. It then became typical, or a bull was turned loose, instead of being slaughtered." (Wilson's note on Vishṇu-purāṇa, Book 111, Chap. 15.)

338. यदि किंचिद्वरे दोषः किं धनेन कुलेन किं ॥

యది కించిద్వరే దోషః కిం ధనేన కులేన కిం॥

If there be a defect in the son-in-law, what is wealth and what is birth?

आदौ तातो वरं पश्येत् ततो वित्तं ततः कुलं ।
यदि किंचिद्वरे दोषः किं धनेन कुलेन किं ॥

ఆదౌ తాతో వరం పశ్యేత్ తతో విత్తం తతః కులం।
యది కించిద్వరే దోషః కిం ధనేన కులేన కిం॥

A father should first look to [the person of] his son-in-law, then to his wealth and then to his family; if there be any defect in the son-in-law, what is wealth and what is birth?

339. यदि हृदयमशुद्धं तस्य सर्वं विरुद्धं ॥

యది హృదయమశుద్ధం తస్య సర్వం విరుద్ధం॥

If the heart be impure, all [the actions] will be wrong.

This can also be rendered "If a man's heart be impure, all things will appear opposed to him."

340. यद्गतं तद्गतं गतं ॥

యద్గతం తద్గతం గతం॥

What is gone, is gone, gone.

(See TELUGU Nos. 2000, 2162.)

341. यद्दिनं तद्दिनं नास्ति तद्दिनं दुर्दिनं मम ॥

యద్దినం తద్దినం నాస్తి తద్దినం దుర్దినం మమ॥

What day is not a "That-day", that day is a bad day for me.

(For *Taddina* [lit. "that day"] see TELUGU No. 271.)

Said by a poor Brahman who lived by attending obsequial ceremonies (*Śrâddha.*)

342. यद्विधेर्मनसि स्थितं ॥

యద్విధేర్మనసి స్థితం॥

As Fate wills it.

करोतु नाम नीतिज्ञो व्यवसायमितस्ततः ।
फलं पुनस्तदेवास्य यद्विधेर्मनसि स्थितं ॥

కరోతు నామ నీతిజ్ఞో వ్యవసాయమితస్తతః।
ఫలం పునస్తదేవాస్య యద్విధేర్మనసి స్థితం॥

Let a politic man certainly attempt this and that, but the fruit shall be as Fate wills it.

" There's a divinity that shapes our ends,
Rough-hew them how we will." Shakespeare.

343. यमस्य करुणा नास्ति तस्माज्जाग्रत जाग्रत ॥

యమస్య కరుణా నాస్తి తస్మాజ్జాగ్రత జాగ్రత॥

Yama has no mercy, be careful therefore, be careful!

Yama is the god of death, " the deity of *Naraka* or hell : he corresponds with the Grecian god Pluto and the judge of hell Minos, and in Hindu mythology is often identified with Death and Time." (Wilson.)

344. यस्य नास्ति स्वयं प्रज्ञा शास्त्रं तस्य करोति किं ॥

యస్య నాస్తి స్వయం ప్రజ్ఞా శాస్త్రం తస్య కరోతి కిం॥

Who has no sense of his own, what will the Sâstra do for him?

यस्य नास्ति स्वयं प्रज्ञा शास्त्रं तस्य करोति किं ।
लोचनाभ्यां विहीनस्य दर्पणः किं करिष्यति ॥

యస్య నాస్తి స్వయం ప్రజ్ఞా శాస్త్రం తస్య కరోతి కిం ।
లోచనాభ్యాం విహీనస్య దర్పణః కిం కరిష్యతి॥

What will the Sâstra do for him who has no sense of his own? what will a mirror do for him who has lost his eyes?

What has a blind man to do with a mirror? (Greek.)*

345. यस्यास्ति वित्तं स नरः कुलीनस्स पंडितस्स श्रुतवान् विधिज्ञः ।
स एव वक्ता स च दर्शनीयः सर्वे गुणाः कांचनमाश्रयंति ॥

యస్యాస్తి విత్తం స నరః కులీనస్స పండితస్స శ్రుతవాన్ విధిజ్ఞః।
స ఏవ వక్తా స చ దర్శనీయః సర్వే గుణాః కాంచనమాశ్రయంతి॥

Who has wealth, that man is of high birth, he is learned, he is a hearer [of the Vedas], he has a knowledge of the precepts, he is eloquent, he is handsome—all qualities follow gold.

Ironical.

Money makes the man.

Money is the god of the world.

All things are obedient to money. (Latin.)†

346. यस्मिन् जीवति जीवंति बहवस्स तु जीवति ॥

యస్మిన్ జీవతి జీవంతి బహవస్స తు జీవతి॥

He [truly] lives by whom many live.

He lives a worthy life who supports many lives besides his own.

---

* Τὶ τυφλῷ καὶ κατόπτρῳ.

† Pecuniae obediunt omnia.

347. यस्मिन् देशे यदाचारः पारंपर्यो विधीयते ॥

యస్మిన్ దేశే యదాచారః పారంపర్యో విధీయతే॥

In every country, that custom prevails which has come down from generation to generation.

न दोषो मगधे मद्ये चान्नयोनौ कलिंगके ।
ओड्रे भ्रातृवधूभोगे गौडे मत्स्यस्य भोजने ॥
दुहितुर्मातुलस्यापि विवाहे द्राविडे तथा ।
यस्मिन् देशे यदाचारः पारंपर्यो विधीयते ॥

న దోషో మగధే మద్యే చాన్నయోనౌ కలింగకే।
ఓడ్రే భ్రాతృవధూభోగే గౌడే మత్స్యస్య భోజనే॥
దుహితుర్మాతులస్యాపి వివాహే ద్రావిడే తథా।
యస్మిన్ దేశే యదాచారః పారంపర్యో విధీయతే॥

In Magadha, there is no crime in [drinking] liquor; in Kalinga, in [drinking] arrack; in Orissa, in co-habitation with a brother's wife; in Gauḍa, in eating fish; in Drâviḍa, in marrying a maternal uncle's daughter:—that custom obtains in every country, which has been handed down from generation to generation.

Every country has its custom. **(Spanish.)***

So many countries, so many customs. **(French.)†**

Every land its own custom, every wheel its own spindle. **(Portuguese.)‡**

348. यादृशः पुरुषस्यात्मा तादृशं संप्रभाषते ॥

యాదృశః పురుషస్యాత్మా తాదృశం సంప్రభాషతే॥

As a man's heart is, so does he speak.

As the life is, so will be the language. **(Greek.)§**

*** En cada tierra su uso.**

† Tant de pays, tant de guises.

‡ Cada terra com seu uso, cada roca com seu fuso.

§ Οἷος ὁ βίος, τοῖος ὁ λόγος.

349. **यादृशी भावना यस्य सिद्धिर्भवति तादृशी ॥**

యాదృశీ భావనా యస్య సిద్ధిర్భవతి తాదృశీ॥

As is the perception, so is the fulfilment.

Success depends upon faith.

दैवे तीर्थे द्विजे मंत्रे दैवज्ञे भेषजे गुरौ ।
यादृशी भावना यस्य सिद्धिर्भवति तादृशी ॥

దైవే తీర్థే ద్విజే మంత్రే దైవజ్ఞే భేషజే గురౌ।
యాదృశీ భావనా యస్య సిద్ధిర్భవతి తాదృశీ॥

In God, in pilgrimage, in a Brahman, in medicine and in a Guru, as is the perception, so is the fulfilment.

350. **यादृशी माता तादृशी पुत्री ॥**

యాదృశీ మాతా తాదృశీ పుత్రీ॥

Like mother, like daughter.

(See TELUGU No. 1019.)

351. **यावज्जीवं होष्यामि ॥**

యావజ్జీవం హోష్యామి॥

I shall make offerings all my life.

352. **यावन्मुखगतं पिंडं तावन्मधुरभाषणं ॥**

యావన్ముఖగతం పిండం తావన్మధురభాషణం॥

As long as there is food in the mouth, so long will the words be sweet.

(See TELUGU No. 399.)

353. **युक्तियुक्तं वचो ग्राह्यं बालादपि शुकादपि ॥**

యుక్తియుక్తం వచో గ్రాహ్యం బాలాదపి శుకాదపి॥

A reasonable word should be received even from a child or a parrot.

354. **युष्माकं बदरीमूलमस्माकं बदरीतरुः ।**
बादरायणसंबंधो यूयं यूयं वयं वयं ॥

యుష్మాకం బదరీమూలమస్మాకం బదరీతరుః।
బాదరాయణసంబంధో యూయం యూయం వయం వయం॥

Yours is the jujube root, mine is the jujube tree; ours is a jujube relationship—You are you, I am I.

Said by one who had pretended to be a relation.—*Badari* is the Zizyphus Jujuba.

355. येन केन प्रकारेण प्रसिद्धः पुरुषो भव ॥

యేన కేన ప్రకారేణ ప్రసిద్ధః పురుషో భవ॥

In some way or other, become a famous man.

356. येषामन्या गतिर्नास्ति तेषां वाराणसी गतिः ॥

యేషామన్యా గతిర్నాస్తి తేషాం వారాణసీ గతిః॥

For those who have no other resource, Vârâṇasî (Benares) is a refuge.

(See TELUGU No. 2690.)

मातापितृपरित्यक्ता ये त्यक्ता निजबंधुभिः ।
येषामन्या गतिर्नास्ति तेषां वाराणसी गतिः ॥

మాతాపితృపరిత్యక్తా యే త్యక్తా నిజబంధుభిః।
యేషామన్యా గతిర్నాస్తి తేషాం వారాణసీ గతిః॥

For such as are forsaken by their parents and relatives, and have no other resource, Benares is a refuge.

357. योग्यं योग्येन युज्यते ॥

యోగ్యం యోగ్యేన యుజ్యతే॥

Like joins with like.

(See TELUGU No. 735, &c.)

भार्या मे नर्त्तकी चेयमहं च यवनाधमः ।
जामाता षड्ढकश्चैव योग्यं योग्येन युज्यते ॥

భార్యా మే నర్తకీ చేయమహం చ యవనాధమః।
జామాతా షడ్డకశ్చైవ యోగ్యం యోగ్యేన యుజ్యతే॥

This my wife is a dancing girl, and I am the lowest of Yavanas; [so are] my son-in-law and wife's brother-in-law : like joins with like.

Like loves like. (Greek.)*

---

* Ὅμοιον ὁμοίῳ φίλον.

358. यो यस्य हृद्यो न हि तस्य दूरः ॥

యో యస్య హృద్యో న హి తస్య దూరః॥

What is dear to one's heart is not far off.

(See TELUGU No. 186.)

गिरौ कलापी गगने पयोदो लक्षांतरेर्कश्च जलेषु पद्मं ।
इंदुर्द्विलक्षे कुमुदस्य बंधुर्योयस्य हृद्यो न हि तस्य दूरः ॥

గిరౌ కలాపీ గగనే పయోదో లక్షాంతరేర్కశ్చ జలేషు పద్మం।
ఇందుర్ద్విలక్షే కుముదస్య బంధుర్యోయస్య హృద్యో న హి తస్య దూరః॥

The peacock is in the mountain and the clouds in the sky; at the distance of a hundred thousand yojanas is the sun, and the lotus is in the water; two hundred thousand yojanas away is the moon from its friend, the lily—what is dear to one's heart is not far off.

Kumuda is the white esculent water lily (Nymphæa esculenta) which expands its petals during the night.

र.

359. राजवत्पंचवर्षाणि दशवर्षाणि दासवत् ।
प्राप्ते तु षोडशे वर्षे पुत्रं मित्रवदाचरेत् ॥

రాజవత్పంచవర్షాణి దశవర్షాణి దాసవత్।
ప్రాప్తే తు షోడశే వర్షే పుత్రం మిత్రవదాచరేత్॥

A son should be treated as a prince for five years, as a slave for ten years, and in his sixteenth year, as a friend.

360. राजा मत्तः शिशुश्चैव प्रमादी धनगर्वितः ।
अप्राप्यमपि वांछंति किं पुनर्लभ्यतेपि यत् ॥

రాజా మత్తః శిశుశ్చైవ ప్రమాదీ ధనగర్వితః।
అప్రాప్యమపి వాంఛంతి కిం పునర్లభ్యతేపి యత్॥

A king, a drunken man, a child, a madman, a purse proud man desire what is not obtainable—how much more that which can be had?

361. राजा राष्ट्रकृतं पापं राजपापं पुरोहितः ।
भर्ता च स्त्रीकृतं पापं शिष्यपापं गुरुर्व्रजेत् ॥

రాజా రాష్ట్రకృతం పాపం రాజపాపం పురోహితః।
భర్తా చ స్త్రీకృతం పాపం శిష్యపాపం గురుర్వ్రజేత్॥

The king must answer for his country's sin; the priest for the king's sin; the husband for the wife's sin, and the Guru for the disciple's sin.

362. राजन् कनकवर्षाणि त्वयि सर्वत्र वर्षति ।
अभाग्यछत्रसंपन्ने मयि नायांति बिंदवः ॥

రాజన్ కనకవర్షాణి త్వయి సర్వత్ర వర్షతి।
అభాగ్యచ్ఛత్రసంపన్నే మయి నాయాంతి బిందవః॥

O king! a rain of gold falls from thee in all places, but no drops reach me, covered with the umbrella of misfortune.

363. रामरावणयोर्युद्धं रामरावणयोरिव ॥

రామరావణయోర్యుద్ధం రామరావణయోరివ॥

The battle between Râma and Râvaṇa is like that between Râma and Râvaṇa.

i. e., like nothing else—nothing can be compared to it.

गगनं गगनाकारं सागरस्सागरोपमः ।
रामरावणयोर्युद्धं रामरावणयोरिव ॥

గగనం గగనాకారం సాగరస్సాగరోపమః।
రామరావణయోర్యుద్ధం రామరావణయోరివ॥

The sky is like the sky, the ocean is like the ocean; the battle between Râma and Râvaṇa is like that between Râma and Râvaṇa.

364. रामाय स्वस्ति रावणाय स्वस्ति ॥
రామాయ స్వస్తి రావణాయ స్వస్తి॥

Blessings on Râma! Blessings on Râvaṇa!

(See TELUGU No. 1853.)

Applied to keeping on good terms with both parties in a quarrel, and not espousing the cause of either.

365. रूपयौवनसंपन्ना विशुद्धकुलसंभवाः ।
विद्याहीना न शोभंते निर्गंधा इव किंशुकाः ॥
రూపయౌవనసంపన్నా విశుద్ధకులసంభవాః।
విద్యాహీనా న శోభంతే నిర్గంధా ఇవ కింశుకాః॥

Though possessed of beauty and youth and sprung from a pure stock, the unlearned shine not, as the inodorous kiṁśuka flowers [are valueless].

Kiṁśuka is the Butea frondosa.

ल.

366. लंघनं परमौषधं ॥
లంఘనం పరమౌషధం॥

Fasting is the best medicine.

Feed sparingly, and defy the physician.

367. लज्जा स्त्रीभूषणं ॥
లజ్జా స్త్రీభూషణం॥

Modesty is the ornament of women.

"I will therefore that • • women adorn themselves • • with shamefacedness." 1 Timothy, ii. 8, 9.

368. ललाटलिखिता रेखा परिमार्ष्टुं न शक्यते ॥
లలాటలిఖితా రేఖా పరిమార్ష్టుం న శక్యతే॥

The line written on the forehead cannot be effaced.

(See TELUGU Nos. 1344, 1687.)

369. **ललाटलेखा न पुनः प्रयाति ॥**

లలాటలేఖా న పునః ప్రయాతి॥

The writing on the forehead will never fail.

(See TELUGU Nos. 2431, 2450.)

लब्धव्यमर्थं लभते मनुष्यो देवोपि तं वारयितुं न शक्तः ।
अतो न शोचामि न विस्मयो मे ललाटलेखा न पुनः प्रयाति ॥

లబ్ధవ్యమర్థం లభతే మనుష్యో దేవోపి తం వారయితుం న శక్తః।
అతో న శోచామి న విస్మయో మే లలాటలేఖా న పునః ప్రయాతి॥

Man obtains what wealth he is to obtain, even God is not able to prevent it; hence I neither grieve nor am surprised—the writing on the forehead will never fail.

370. **लोको भिन्नरुचिः ॥**

లోకో భిన్నరుచిః॥

The world is divided in tastes.

(See TELUGU No. 1616.)

व.

371. **वचने को दरिद्रः ॥**

వచనే కో దరిద్రః॥

Who is poor in speech?

Good words cost nothing, but are worth much.

372. **वसंतयौवना वृक्षाः पुरुषा धनयौवनाः ।**
सौभाग्ययौवना नार्यो युवानो बुद्धियौवनाः ॥

వసంతయౌవనా వృక్షాః పురుషా ధనయౌవనాః।
సౌభాగ్యయౌవనా నార్యో యువానో బుద్ధియౌవనాః॥

The spring is the youth of trees, wealth is the youth of men, beauty is the youth of women, intelligence is the youth of the young.

373. वस्त्रेण वपुषा वाचा ॥

వస్త్రేణ వపుషా వాచా॥

By dress, by body, and by speech.

374. वाग्दोषेण हता वयं ॥

వాగ్దోషేణ హతా వయం॥

We are ruined by foolish speech.

(See TELUGU No. 1347.)

375. वाणिज्ये वसते लक्ष्मीः ॥

వాణిజ్యే వసతే లక్ష్మీః॥

Fortune dwells in trade.

वाणिज्ये वसते लक्ष्मीस्तदर्धं कृषिकर्मणि।
तदर्धं राजसेवायां भिक्षायां नैव नैव च ॥

వాణిజ్యే వసతే లక్ష్మీ స్తదర్ధం కృషికర్మణి।
తదర్ధం రాజసేవాయాం భిక్షాయాం నైవ నైవ చ॥

Fortune dwells in trade; she is half in agriculture, half of that in Government service, and not at all in begging.

376. वादभ्रष्टो वैद्यश्रेष्ठः ॥

వాదభ్రష్టో వైద్యశ్రేష్ఠః॥

A ruined alchymist [makes] a capital doctor.

377. विद्यया सह मर्तव्यं न चैनामूषरे वपेत् ॥

విద్యయా సహ మర్తవ్యం న చైనామూషరే వపేత్॥

One should die with his learning, not sow it in a barren soil.

Better that a man's learning should die with him than that it should be thrown away on the foolish.

378. विद्यानाशाय कल्याणं सर्वनाशाय शोभनं ॥

విద్యానాశాయ కల్యాణం సర్వనాశాయ శోభనం॥

Marriage is ruin to learning, and the consummation of marriage is ruin to everything.

379. विद्यारत्नं महाधनं ॥

విద్యారత్నం మహాధనం॥

The gem of learning is great wealth.

ज्ञातिभिर्वण्टनेनैव चौर्येणापि न नीयते ।
दानेनैव क्षयं याति विद्यारत्नं महाधनं ॥
జ్ఞాతిభిర్వంటనేనైవ చౌర్యేణాపి న నీయతే।
దానేనైవ క్షయం యాతి విద్యారత్నం మహాధనం॥

The gem of learning is great wealth; it cannot be shared by cousins, nor lost by robbery, nor exhausted by liberality.

380. विद्यावान् धनवान् भवेत् ॥

విద్యావాన్ ధనవాన్ భవేత్॥

The possessor of learning becomes the possessor of wealth.

"Get learning with a great sum of money and get much gold by her." Ecclesiasticus li. 28.

381. विद्याविहीनः पशुः ॥

విద్యావిహీనః పశుః॥

One void of learning is a beast.

विद्या राजसु पूज्यते न हि धनं विद्याविहीनः पशुः ॥
విద్యా రాజసు పూజ్యతే న హి ధనం విద్యావిహీనః పశుః॥

Learning is honored by kings, not wealth; one void of learning is a beast.

382. विद्वानेव विजानाति विद्वज्जनपरिश्रमं ।
न हि वंध्या विजानाति गुर्वीं प्रसववेदनां ॥
విద్వానేవ విజానాతి విద్వజ్జనపరిశ్రమం।
న హి వంధ్యా విజానాతి గుర్వీం ప్రసవవేదనాం॥

The learned only know the labour of the learned, the barren woman knows not the great pains of childbirth.

(See TELUGU No. 807.)

383. विधिरहो बलवानिति मे मतिः ॥
విధిరహో బలవానితి మే మతిః॥

Lo! Fate is all powerful, that's my mind.

शशिदिवाकरयोर्ग्रहपीडनं गजभुजंगमयोरपि बंधनं ।
मतिमतां च विलोक्य दरिद्रतां विधिरहो बलवानिति मे मतिः॥
శశిదివాకరయోర్గ్రహపీడనం గజభుజంగమయోరపి బంధనం।
మతిమతాం చ విలోక్య దరిద్రతాం విధిరహో బలవానితి మే మతిః॥

Seeing the seizure of the sun and the moon by Graha, the restraint [exercised] over elephants and serpents, and the poverty of the wise, lo! I am of opinion that Fate is all powerful. (Bhartṛihari.)

Graha is a name of Râhu, the personified ascending node.

384. विधिविहितं बुद्धिरनुसरति ॥
విధివిహితం బుద్ధిరనుసరతి॥

Mind follows what Fate has decreed.

385. विनाशकाले विपरीतबुद्धिः ॥
వినాశకాలే విపరీతబుద్ధిః॥

In the time of calamity, the sense is perverted.

386. विपदस्संतु नश्शश्वत्तासु संस्मर्यते हरिः ॥
విపదస్సంతు నశ్శశ్వద్యాసు సంస్మర్యతే హరిః॥

Let misfortunes come upon us often, by which Hari (Vishṇu) is remembered.

387. विपदि धैर्यमथाभ्युदये क्षमा सदसि वाक्पटुता युधि विक्रमः ।
यशसि चाभिरतिर्व्यसनं श्रुतौ प्रकृतिसिद्धमिदं हि महात्मनां ॥

విపది ధైర్యమథాభ్యుదయే క్షమా సదసి వాక్పటుతా యుధి విక్రమః।
యశసి చాభిరతిర్వ్యసనం శ్రుతౌ ప్రకృతిసిద్ధమిదం హి మహాత్మనాం॥

Fortitude in misfortune, forbearance in prosperity, eloquence in the assembly, valour in battle, eagerness in [seeking] fame, attention to the Vedas—these are natural to a great man.

388. विप्राणां ज्ञानतो ज्यैष्ठ्यं क्षत्रियाणां तु वीर्यतः ।
वैश्यानां धान्यधनतश्शूद्राणामेव जन्मतः ॥

విప్రాణాం జ్ఞానతో జ్యైష్ఠ్యం క్షత్రియాణాం తు వీర్యతః।
వైశ్యానాం ధాన్యధనతశ్శూద్రాణామేవ జన్మతః॥

Among Brahmans, seniority is [attained] by knowledge; among Kshatriyas, by valour; among Vaiśyas, by corn and money; and only among Śûdras, by birth.

(See No. 163.)

389. विभूषणं मौनमपंडितानां ॥

విభూషణం మౌనమపండితానాం॥

Silence is the ornament of the ignorant.

(See No. 169.)

390. विषं सभा दरिद्रस्य वृद्धस्य तरुणी विषं ॥

విషం సభా దరిద్రస్య వృద్ధస్య తరుణీ విషం॥

An assembly is poison to a poor man; a young wife is poison to an old man.

(See TELUGU No. 1779.)

Poor men's words have little weight. (Greek.)*

A young wife is an old man's post-horse to the grave. (German.)†

* Τῶν γὰρ πενήτων εἰσιν οἱ λόγοι κενοί.
† Jung Weib ist altem Mann, das Postpferd zum Grabe.

391. विषकुंभं पयोमुखं ॥

విషకుంభం పయోముఖం॥

A vessel of poison, with a face of milk.

(See TELUGU No. 4, &c.)

परोक्षे कार्यहंतारं प्रत्यक्षे प्रियवादिनं ।
वर्जयेत्तादृशं मित्रं विषकुंभं पयोमुखं ॥
పరోక్షే కార్యహంతారం ప్రత్యక్షే ప్రియవాదినం।
వర్జయేత్తాదృశం మిత్రం విషకుంభం పయోముఖం॥

Such a friend as, like a vessel of poison with a face (i. e. covering) of milk, ruins [a man's] business behind his back and speaks soft words to his face, must be shunned.

392. विषक्रिमिन्यायः ॥

విషక్రిమిన్యాయః॥

Like the worm living in poison.

393. विषवृक्षोपि संवर्ध्य स्वयं छेत्तुमसांप्रतं ॥

విషవృక్షోపి సంవర్ధ్య స్వయం ఛేత్తుమసాంప్రతం॥

It is not right for one to cut down even a poisonous tree which he himself has reared.

इतस्सदैत्यः प्राप्तश्रीर्नेत एवार्हति क्षयं ।
विषवृक्षोपि संवर्ध्य स्वयं छेत्तुमसांप्रतं ॥
ఇతస్సదైత్యః ప్రాప్తశ్రీర్నేత ఏవార్హతి క్షయం।
విషవృక్షోపి సంవర్ధ్య స్వయం ఛేత్తుమసాంప్రతం॥

Hence has the Daitya derived his prosperity and for this very reason he does not deserve destruction: it is not right for one to cut down even a poisonous tree which he himself has reared.

394. **विषस्य विषमौषधं ॥**

విషస్య విషమౌషధం॥

Poison is the remedy for poison.

दृष्टिं देहि पुनर्बाले हरिणायतलोचने ।

श्रूयते हि पुरा लोके विषस्य विषमौषधं ॥

దృష్టిం దేహి పునర్బాలే హరిణాయతలోచనే।

శ్రూయతే హి పురా లోకే విషస్య విషమౌషధం॥

Caste your sight, broad fawn-eyed damsel, once more [upon me]—have we not heard from the olden time that poison is the remedy for poison?

Poison quells poison. (Italian.)*

One nail drives out another.

395. **विषादप्यमृतं ग्राह्यं बालादपि सुभाषितं ।**

अमित्रादपि सद्वृत्तममेध्यादपि कांचनं ॥

విషాదప్యమృతం గ్రాహ్యం బాలాదపి సుభాషితం।

అమిత్రాదపి సద్వృత్తమమేధ్యాదపి కాంచనం॥

Nectar should be taken even out of poison; a well spoken word should be received even from a youth; rectitude should be acknowledged even in an enemy, and gold should be taken even out of filth.

396. **वृथा वृष्टिस्समुद्रे च वृथा तृप्ते तु भोजनं ।**

वृथा धनपतौ दानं दरिद्रे यौवनं वृथा ॥

వృథా వృష్టిస్సముద్రే చ వృథా తృప్తే తు భోజనం।

వృథా ధనపతౌ దానం దరిద్రే యౌవనం వృథా॥

Useless is rain to the sea, and useless is food to one satisfied; useless is a gift to a rich man, useless is youth to a poor man.

(cf. Böhtlingk's *Indische Sprüche*, 2890, 5031.)

---

* Il veleno si spegne col veleno.

397. **वृद्धा नारी पतिव्रता ॥**

వృద్ధా నారీ పతివ్రతా॥

An old woman, a chaste wife.

398. **वृद्धा वेश्या तपस्विनी ॥**

వృద్ధా వేశ్యా తపస్వినీ॥

An old harlot, a female devotee.

> **अशक्तस्तस्करस्साधुः कुरूपा चेत्पतिव्रता ।**
> **रोगी च देवताभक्तो वृद्धा वेश्या तपस्विनी ॥**
> అశక్తస్తస్కరస్సాధుః కురూపా చేత్పతివ్రతా।
> రోగీ చ దేవతాభక్తో వృద్ధా వేశ్యా తపస్వినీ॥
>
> A feeble thief, a good man; an ugly woman, a chaste wife; a sick man, a worshipper of the deity; an old harlot, a female devotee.

399. **वृद्धस्य वचनं ग्राह्यमापत्काले ह्युपस्थिते ॥**

వృద్ధస్య వచనం గ్రాహ్యమాపత్కాలే హ్యుపస్థితే॥

An old man's advice should be taken in a time of misfortune.

400. **वृश्चिकस्य विषं पुच्छं मक्षिकाया विषं शिरः ।**
भुजंगस्य विषं दंष्ट्रा सर्वांगं दुर्जने विषं ॥

వృశ్చికస్య విషం పుచ్ఛం మక్షికాయా విషం శిరః।
భుజంగస్య విషం దంష్ట్రా సర్వాంగం దుర్జనే విషం॥

The poison of a scorpion is in his tail; the poison of a fly is in his head; the poison of a serpent is in his fang; the poison of a bad man is in his whole body.

401. **वृषभकलहे वत्सपादभंगः ॥**

వృషభకలహే వత్సపాదభంగః॥

In a fight between bulls, the calf's leg is broken.

(See TELUGU No. 212.)

402. **वैश्यो विश्वासघातकः ॥**

వైశ్యో విశ్వాసఘాతకః॥

A Vaiśya is a betrayer of confidence.

403. **व्यापारं द्रोहचिंतनं ॥**

వ్యాపారం ద్రోహచింతనం॥

Trade is treachery.

An ungrammatical, but common saying, corrupted from "*Vyâpâdo droha chintanam*" in the Amarakośa.

404. **व्यासघट्टः ॥**

వ్యాసఘట్టః॥

Vyâsa's pass.

Said of "any difficult passage in the Mahâbhârata" or of "any puzzle or stumbling block." (Brown.)

श.

405. **शचीपतिर्मघवा वा ॥**

శచీపతిర్మఘవా వా॥

Is not Śachipati Maghavâ ?

Both names of Indra.

406. **शठे शाठ्यं समाचरेत् ॥**

శఠే శాఠ్యం సమాచరేత్॥

Deceit must be practised towards the deceitful.

सारल्यं सरले कुर्याच्छठे शाठ्यं समाचरेत् ॥

సారల్యం సరలే కుర్యాచ్ఛఠే శాఠ్యం సమాచరేత్॥

One must be upright towards an upright man and deceitful towards a deceitful man.

407. शतं विहाय भोक्तव्यं ॥
శతం విహాయ భోక్తవ్యం॥

Leave off a hundred [works] and eat.

Food is the first thing.

408. शतश्लोकेन पंडितः ॥
శతశ్లోకేన పండితః॥

A Paṇḍit by a hundred stanzas.

Said derisively.

409. शतेषु जायते शूरस्सहस्रेषु च पंडितः ॥
శతేషు జాయతే శూరస్సహస్రేషు చ పండితః॥

In a hundred, one hero is found; in a thousand, one Paṇḍit.

410. शनैः पंथाः शनैः कंथा ॥
శనైః పంథాః శనైః కంథా॥

Slowly along the road, slowly through the quilt.

A quilt of patch work is referred to.

शनैः पंथाः शनैः कंथा शनैः पर्वतलंघनं ।
शनैः कर्म च धर्मश्च एते पंच शनैः शनैः ॥
శనైః పంథాః శనైః కంథా శనైః పర్వతలంఘనం।
శనైః కర్మ చ ధర్మశ్చ ఏతే పంచ శనైః శనైః॥

Slowly along the road; slowly through the quilt; slowly over the mountain; slowly through your business; slowly in your charities—slowly, slowly, through these five.

The admonition, nothing rashly, is everywhere useful. (Greek.)*

---

* Τὸ μηδὲν εἰκῇ, πανταχοῦ 'στι χρήσιμον.

411. शनैः पर्वतलंघनं ॥

శనైః పర్వతలంఘనం॥

Slowly over the mountain.

अटनेन महारण्ये सुपंथा जायते शनैः ।
वेदाभ्यासात्तथा ज्ञानं शनैः पर्वतलंघनं ॥
అటనేన మహారణ్యే సుపంథా జాయతే శనైః।
వేదాభ్యాసాత్తథా జ్ఞానం శనైః పర్వతలంఘనం॥

The right path will gradually be found in a forest by wandering in it; so wisdom will be gradually acquired by study of the Vedas, as a mountain is slowly crossed.

412. शनैः शनैः क्षिपेत्पादं ॥

శనైః శనైః క్షిపేత్పాదం॥

Slowly, slowly, place the foot.

Be careful in each step you take in any business.

413. शरीरं व्याधिमंदिरं ॥

శరీరం వ్యాధిమందిరం॥

The body is the abode of diseases.

दुःखोपकारसच्चर्याज्ञानं यत्र न भास्वरं ।
वृथा वहति तज्जीवः शरीरं व्याधिमंदिरं ॥
దుఃఖోపకారసచ్చర్యాజ్ఞానం యత్ర న భాస్వరం।
వృథా వహతి తజ్జీవః శరీరం వ్యాధిమందిరం॥

That soul, in which there is no perception of sorrow, beneficence, or virtue [in others], bears in vain a body, the abode of diseases.

414. शरीरमाद्यं खलु धर्मसाधनं ॥

శరీరమాద్యం ఖలు ధర్మసాధనం॥

Is not the body the chief instrument of doing good?

(See No. 261.)

अपि क्रियार्थं सुलभं समित्कुशं जलान्यपि स्नानविधिक्षमाणि ते।
अपि स्वशक्त्या तपसि प्रवर्तसे शरीरमाद्यं खलु धर्मसाधनं ॥
అపి క్రియార్థం సులభం సమిత్కుశం జలాన్యపి స్నానవిధిక్షమాణి తే।
అపి స్వశక్త్యా తపసి ప్రవర్తసే శరీరమాద్యం ఖలు ధర్మసాధనం॥

Are fuel and Kusa grass easy to get? Is the water fit for your bathing? Are you engaged in penance according to your strength? Is not the body the chief instrument of doing good?

Said by Śiva to Pârvatî—(see the Kumâra-sambhava).—*Kuśa* is the Poa cynosuroides.

415. शाकाय वा स्याल्लवणाय वा स्यात् ॥

శాకాయ వా స్యాల్లవణాయ వా స్యాత్॥

It will do for vegetable, or it will do for salt.

Said by a beggar.

416. शापादपि शरादपि ॥

శాపాదపి శరాదపి॥

By curse, and by arrow.

अग्रतश्चतुरो वेदान् पृष्ठतस्सशरं धनुः ।
उभाभ्यां च समर्थोहं शापादपि शरादपि ॥
అగ్రతశ్చతురో వేదాన్ పృష్ఠతస్సశరం ధనుః।
ఉభాభ్యాం చ సమర్థోహం శాపాదపి శరాదపి॥

With the four Vedas before me, and the bow and arrow behind me, I am powerful both by curse and by arrow.

Said by Paraśurâma.

417. शिरो नास्ति शिरोव्यथा ॥

శిరో నాస్తి శిరోవ్యథా॥

No head, but head-ache.

Applied to irrational argument, &c.—(cf. Morton 861.)

418. शीलं सर्वत्र भूषणं ॥

శీలం సర్వత్ర భూషణం॥

Moral rectitude is everywhere an ornament.

i. e., it is an ornament to a man wherever he goes.

419. शुनि दृष्टे न पाषाणः पाषाणे श्वा न दृश्यते ।
दृष्टे शुनि च पाषाणे राजश्वा किं नु कुर्महे ॥

శుని దృష్టే న పాషాణః పాషాణే శ్వా న దృశ్యతే।
దృష్టే శుని చ పాషాణే రాజశ్వా కిం ను కుర్మహే॥

When a dog is seen, there is no stone; when a stone is found, the dog is not seen; when both the dog and stone are seen, then what can we do to the king's dog?

420. शुभस्य शीघ्रं अशुभस्य कालहरणं ॥

శుభస్య శీఘ్రం అశుభస్య కాలహరణం॥

In an auspicious [business] haste, in an inauspicious [business] delay.

421. शुष्कवैरं विवादं च न कुर्यात्केनचित्सह ॥

శుష్కవైరం వివాదం చ న కుర్యాత్కేనచిత్సహ॥

Entertain not groundless enmity towards, nor quarrel with any one.

422. श्वः कार्यमद्य कर्तव्यं ॥

శ్వః కార్యమద్య కర్తవ్యం॥

Do to-day what must be done to-morrow.

Be beforehand with your business.

Take time by the forelock.

श्वः कार्यमद्य कर्तव्यं पूर्वाह्णे चापराह्णिकं ।
न हि प्रतीक्षते मृत्युः कृतमस्य न वा कृतं ॥

శ్వః కార్యమద్య కర్తవ్యం పూర్వాహ్ణే చాపరాహ్ణికం।
న హి ప్రతీక్షతే మృత్యుః కృతమస్య న వా కృతం॥

The business of to-morrow should be done to-day, and that of the after-noon in the forenoon : Death waits not, whether the thing be done or not done.

423. श्वशुरगृहं परमसुखं त्रिरात्राच्छुनकसमानः ॥

శ్వశురగృహం పరమసుఖం త్రిరాత్రాచ్ఛునకసమానః॥

In the father-in-law's house is the greatest happiness, but after the third night [the son-in-law is treated] like a dog.

424. श्वानारोहे कुतस्सौख्यं ॥

శ్వానారోహే కుతస్సౌఖ్యం॥

Where is the pleasure in mounting a dog ?

ष.

425. षट्कर्णो भिद्यते मंत्रः ॥

షట్కర్ణో భిద్యతే మంత్రః॥

The six-eared counsel is split.

i. e., nothing remains secret which is known to three persons.

षट्कर्णो भिद्यते मंत्रस्तथा प्राप्तश्च वार्तया ।
इतिमंत्रिद्वितीयेन मंत्रः कार्यो महीभुजा ॥

షట్కర్ణో భిద్యతే మంత్రస్తథా ప్రాప్తశ్చ వార్తయా।
ఇతిమంత్రిద్వితీయేన మంత్రః కార్యో మహీభుజా॥

[Knowing] that counsel is divulged by six ears and spread by report, a king should take counsel [only] with a second, his minister.

(cf. Hitopadesa, Book III.)

426. **षड्भिः कर्णो निपातितः ॥**

షడ్భిః కర్ణో నిపాతితః॥

By six, was Karṇa made to fall.

> **त्वया मया च कुंत्या च धरण्या वासवेन च ।**
> **जामदग्न्येन रामेण षड्भिः कर्णो निपातितः ॥**
> త్వయా మయా చ కుంత్యా చ ధరణ్యా వాసవేన చ।
> జామదగ్న్యేన రామేణ షడ్భిః కర్ణో నిపాతితః॥

By you, by me, by Kuntî, by the Earth, by Vâsava, and by Râma, the son of Jamadagni—by six was Karṇa ruined.

427. **षण्णां रसानां लवणं प्रधानं ॥**

షణ్ణాం రసానాం లవణం ప్రధానం॥

Of the six flavours, salt is the chief.

The others are sweet, pungent, bitter, sour, and astringent.

स.

428. **संतस्स्वयं परहिते विहिताभियोगाः ॥**

సంతస్స్వయం పరహితే విహితాభియోగాః॥

Good men are energetic in seeking the good of others.

429. **संतोषो नंदने वने ॥**

సంతోషో నందనే వనే॥

Happiness is in the Nandana garden.

***Nandana* is Indra's pleasure ground.**

430. संप्रीतिभोज्यान्यन्नानि ॥

సంప్రీతిభోజ్యాన్యన్నాని॥

Food should be eaten with affection.

(See TELUGU No. 1581, &c.)

431. संसर्गजा दोषगुणा भवंति ॥

సంసర్గజా దోషగుణా భవంతి॥

Vice and virtue spring from association.

माताप्येका पिताप्येको मम तस्य च पक्षिणः ।
अहं मुनिभिरानीतस्स चानीतो गवाशनैः ॥
अहं मुनीनां वचनं शृणोमि गवाशनानां स वचश्शृणोति ।
न तस्य दोषा न गुणा ममापि संसर्गजा दोषगुणा भवंति॥

మాతాప్యేకా పితాప్యేకో మమ తస్య చ పక్షిణః।
అహం మునిభిరానీతస్స చానీతో గవాశనైః॥
అహం మునీనాం వచనం శృణోమి గవాశనానాం స వచశ్శృణోతి।
న తస్య దోషా న గుణా మమాపి సంసర్గజా దోషగుణా భవంతి॥

The mother and the father of me and of that bird are one; I was brought by Munis and he was taken by Gavâśanas; I hear the Munis' speech and he hears that of the Gavâśanas; neither are his defects nor are mine good qualities—vice and virtue spring from association.

Gavâśanas [*lit.* "beef-eaters"] are outcastes.

432. संसारसागरे दुःखं ॥

సంసారసాగరే దుఃఖం॥

In the world's ocean is grief.

433. संसारी दुःखी सन्न्यासी सुखी ॥

సంసారీ దుఃఖీ సన్న్యాసీ సుఖీ॥

The worldly man is a man of sorrows, the Sannyâsî is a man of joys.

434. सकलं शीलेन कुर्याद्वशं ॥
సకలం శీలేన కుర్యాద్వశం॥

A good disposition gains all.

मित्रं स्वच्छतया रिपुं नयबलैर्लुब्धं धनैरीश्वरं
कार्येण द्विजमादरेण युवतिं प्रेम्णा शमैर्बांधवान् ।
अत्युग्रंस्तुतिभिर्गुरुं प्रणतिभिर्मूर्खं कथाभिर्बुधं
विद्याभीरसिकं रसेन सकलं शीलेन कुर्याद्वशं ॥

మిత్రం స్వచ్ఛతయా రిపుం నయబలైర్లుబ్ధం ధనైరీశ్వరం
కార్యేణ ద్విజమాదరేణ యువతిం ప్రేమ్ణా శమైర్బాంధవాన్।
అత్యుగ్రంస్తుతిభిర్గురుం ప్రణతిభిర్మూర్ఖం కథాభిర్బుధం
విద్యాభీరసికం రసేన సకలం శీలేన కుర్యాద్వశం॥

A friend can be gained by transparency [of conduct]; an enemy, by prudence and power; a miser, by money; a master, by service; a brahman, by kindness; a young wife, by tenderness; relatives, by patience; a passionate man, by praise; a priest, by reverence; a fool, by stories; a wise man, by learning; a man with a taste, by humouring him; and all, by good conduct.

435. सति कुड्ये चित्रकर्म ॥
సతి కుడ్యే చిత్రకర్మ॥

Where there's a wall, you can draw on it.

(See TELUGU No. 824.)

436. सत्पुत्रः कुलदीपकः ॥
సత్పుత్రః కులదీపకః॥

A good son is the light of his family.

शर्वरीदीपकश्चंद्रः प्रभाते दीपको रविः ।
त्रैलोक्यदीपको धर्मस्सत्पुत्रः कुलदीपकः ॥

శర్వరీదీపకశ్చంద్రః ప్రభాతే దీపకో రవిః।
త్రైలోక్యదీపకో ధర్మస్సత్పుత్రః కులదీపకః॥

The moon is the light of the night, the sun is the light of the day; virtue is the light of the three worlds; a good son is the light of his family.

(cf. Böhtlingk's *Indische Sprüche* 2968.)

437. सत्यं ब्रूयात्प्रियं ब्रूयान्न ब्रूयात्सत्यमप्रियं ।
प्रियं च नानृतं ब्रूयादेष धर्मस्सनातनः ॥
సత్యం బ్రూయాత్ప్రియం బ్రూయాన్న బ్రూయాత్సత్యమప్రియం।
ప్రియం చ నానృతం బ్రూయాదేష ధర్మస్సనాతనః॥

Speak the truth, and speak to please; speak not the truth, to displease; speak not untruth, to please; this is eternal virtue.

438. सत्येन लोकाञ्जयति ॥
సత్యేన లోకాఞ్జయతి॥

By truth, he conquers the worlds.

439. सत्रे भुक्तिर्मठे निद्रा ॥
సత్రే భుక్తిర్మఠే నిద్రా॥

Eating in a Satram, sleeping in a Matha.

Satram (Chuttrum) is a travellers' rest-house ; *Matha* is a convent.

Said of one who leads a wandering life.

440. सत्संगतिः कथय किं न करोति पुंसां ॥
సత్సంగతిః కథయ కిం న కరోతి పుంసాం॥

Say, what does not good association do for men?

जाड्यं धियो हरति सिंचति वाचि सत्यं ।
मानोन्नतिं दिशति पापमपाकरोति ॥
चेतः प्रसादयति दिक्षु तनोति कीर्तिं ।
सत्संगतिः कथय किं न करोति पुंसां ॥
జాడ్యం ధియో హరతి సించతి వాచి సత్యం।
మానోన్నతిం దిశతి పాపమపాకరోతి॥
చేతః ప్రసాదయతి దిక్షు తనోతి కీర్తిం।
సత్సంగతిః కథయ కిం న కరోతి పుంసాం॥

Say, what does not good association do for men? It removes the dulness of their intellects ; it sprinkles truth in their speech ; it gains the highest honors for them ; expels sin from them ; it purifies their mind ; and spreads their fame towards all quarters.

441. सद्यः फलं तु संगीतं ॥

సద్యః ఫలం తు సంగీతం॥

The effect of music is immediate.

442. सद्यो ददातिचतुरः सद्यो नास्तीति चतुरतमः ॥

సద్యో దదాతిచతురః సద్యో నాస్తీతి చతురతమః॥

A wise man gives at once, a wiser man at once refuses.

443. सद्विद्या यदि किं धनैरपयशो यद्यस्ति किं मृत्युना ॥

సద్విద్యా యది కిం ధనైరపయశో యద్యస్తి కిం మృత్యునా॥

If there be great learning, what of money? If there be an ill name, what of death?

444. स बंधुर्यो हितेषु स्यात् स पिता यस्तु पोषकः ।

स सखा यत्र विश्वासस्सा भार्या यत्र निर्वृतिः ॥

స బంధుర్యో హితేషు స్యాత్ స పితా యస్తు పోషకః।

స సఖా యత్ర విశ్వాసస్సా భార్యా యత్ర నిర్వృతిః॥

Who befriends, he is a relation; who supports, he is a father; he is a friend, in whom there is confidence; she is a wife, in whom there is pleasure.

445. सभा वा न प्रवेष्टव्या वक्तव्यं वा समंजसं ।

अब्रुवन्विब्रुवन्वापि नरो भवति किल्बिषी ॥

సభా వా న ప్రవేష్టవ్యా వక్తవ్యం వా సమంజసం।

అబ్రువన్విబ్రువన్వాపి నరో భవతి కిల్బిషీ॥

Either go not into an assembly, or if you go, speak well; if a man speak not, or speak badly, he becomes a sinner.

446. समाश्रयबलादेव गरुडं यांतमध्वनि ।
पिनाकपाणिपाणिस्थः कुशलं पृष्टवानहिः ॥

సమాశ్రయబలాదేవ గరుడం యాంతమధ్వని।
పినాకపాణిపాణిస్థః కుశలం పృష్టవానహిః॥

On the strength of his position, the serpent dwelling on the wrist of Pinâkapâṇi (Śiva) asked Garuḍa when going along the road, whether he was well.

(See TELUGU No. 751.)

447. सर्वं परवशं दुःखं सर्वमात्मवशं सुखं ॥

సర్వం పరవశం దుఃఖం సర్వమాత్మవశం సుఖం॥

All entrusted to another is grief, all undertaken by one's self is joy.

यद्यत्परवशं कर्म तत्तद्यत्नेन वर्जयेत् ।
यद्यदात्मवशं तु स्यात्तत्तत्सेवेत यत्नतः ॥
सर्वं परवशं दुःखं सर्वमात्मवशं सुखं ।
एतद्विद्यात्समासेन लक्षणं सुखदुःखयोः ॥

యద్యత్పరవశం కర్మ తత్తద్యత్నేన వర్జయేత్।
యద్యదాత్మవశం తు స్యాత్తత్తత్సేవేత యత్నతః॥
సర్వం పరవశం దుఃఖం సర్వమాత్మవశం సుఖం।
ఏతద్విద్యాత్సమాసేన లక్షణం సుఖదుఃఖయోః॥

Endeavour should be made to relinquish whatever business is in another's hands; that which is in one's own hands should be done earnestly: all entrusted to another is grief; all undertaken by one's self is joy; these should be known, in short, as the characteristics of joy and sorrow.

Self do, self have.

If you would have a thing well done, do it yourself.

The master orders the man, the man orders the cat, and the cat orders her tail. (Portuguese.)*

---

* Manda o amo ao moço, o moço ao gato, e o gato ao rabo.

448. सर्वमेकं जगन्नाथे ॥

సర్వమేకం జగన్నాథే॥

At Jagannâtha, all are one.

No caste distinctions in eating.

449. सर्वस्य गात्रस्य शिरः प्रधानं ॥

సర్వస్య గాత్రస్య శిరః ప్రధానం॥

In the whole body, the head is chief.

450. सर्वस्स्वार्थं समीहते ॥

సర్వస్స్వార్థం సమీహతే॥

All seek their own object

यजतां पांडवस्स्वर्गमवत्विंद्रस्तपत्विनः ।
वयं हनाम द्विषतस्सर्वस्स्वार्थं समीहते ॥

యజతాం పాండవస్స్వర్గమవత్వింద్రస్తపత్వినః।
వయం హనామ ద్విషతస్సర్వస్స్వార్థం సమీహతే॥

Let the Pâṇḍava sacrifice; let Indra protect Svarga; let the sun shine; we will kill our enemies—all seek their own object.

451. सर्वैरुपायैः फलमेव साध्यं ॥

సర్వైరుపాయైః ఫలమేవ సాధ్యం॥

By every means, one's object must be accomplished.

त्रिविक्रमोभूदपि वामनोसौ स सूकरश्चेति स वै नृसिंहः ।
नीचैरनीचैरतिनीचनीचैस्सर्वैरुपायैः फलमेव साध्यं ॥

త్రివిక్రమోభూదపి వామనోసౌ స సూకరశ్చేతి స వై నృసింహః।
నీచైరనీచైరతినీచనీచైస్సర్వైరుపాయైః ఫలమేవ సాధ్యం॥

Though a dwarf, he (Vishṇu) became Trivikrama and Sûkara and Nṛisimha; by all means, whether base or not base, or the basest of the base, one's object must be accomplished.

452. सर्वेंद्रियाणां नयनं प्रधानं ॥
సర్వేంద్రియాణాం నయనం ప్రధానం॥
Of all the senses, sight is the chief.

453. सर्वे जनाः कांचनमाश्रयंति ॥
సర్వే జనాః కాంచనమాశ్రయంతి॥
All people seek gold.

(See No. 345.)

454. सर्वे जनास्सुखिनो भवंतु ॥
సర్వే జనాస్సుఖినో భవంతు॥
May all people be happy!

Said on auspicious occasions.

455. सहवासतः पुण्यगुणा भवंति सहवासतो दोषगुणा भवंति ॥
సహవాసతః పుణ్యగుణా భవంతి సహవాసతో దోషగుణా భవంతి॥
By association good qualities are acquired, by association bad qualities are acquired.

(See No. 431.)

456. सहसा विदधीत न क्रियां ॥
సహసా విదధీత న క్రియాం॥
No business should be done rashly.

(See No. 410.)

457. सहायो बलवत्तरः ॥
సహాయో బలవత్తరః॥
A companion is an additional strength.

(See TELUGU No. 480.)

सगुणो निर्गुणो वापि सहायो बलवत्तरः ।
तुषेणापि परिभ्रष्टस्तंडुलो नांकुरायते ॥
సగుణో నిర్గుణో వాపి సహాయో బలవత్తరః।
తుషేణాపి పరిభ్రష్టస్తండులో నాంకురాయతే॥

Whether he have talent or be without it, a companion is an additional strength; if deprived of husk the rice will not sprout.

458. साहसाद्भजते लक्ष्मीः ॥

సాహసాద్భజతే లక్ష్మీః॥

Fortune is secured by boldness.

Fortune favors the bold. (Latin.)*

459. साहसे लक्ष्मीः ॥

సాహసే లక్ష్మీః॥

Fortune is in boldness.

460. सिकतालवालं ॥

సికతాలవాలం॥

A flower-bed of sand.

461. सिद्धमन्नं परित्यज्य भिक्षामटति दुर्मतिः ॥

సిద్ధమన్నం పరిత్యజ్య భిక్షామటతి దుర్మతిః॥

A foolish man leaves the food which is ready for him and goes to beg.

462. सुखस्यानंतरं दुःखं दुःखस्यानंतरं सुखं ।
चक्रवत्परिवर्तंते दुःखानि च सुखानि च ॥

సుఖస్యానంతరం దుఃఖం దుఃఖస్యానంతరం సుఖం।
చక్రవత్పరివర్తంతే దుఃఖాని చ సుఖాని చ॥

After happiness, sorrow; after sorrow, happiness; happiness and sorrow revolve like a discus.

(See TELUGU Nos. 561, 568.)

Joy and sorrow are next-door neighbours. (German.)†

463. सूचीकटाहन्यायः ॥

సూచీకటాహన్యాయః॥

A needle and a boiler.

The first takes a short time to make, it should therefore be made first.

---

*Fortes fortuna adjuvat.
†Freud' und Leid sind nahe Nachbarn.

464. सेवकान्नं पुरातनं ॥

సేవకాన్నం పురాతనం॥

A servant and food [are good] old.

नवं वस्त्रं नवं छत्रं नव्या स्त्री नूतनं गृहं ।
सर्वत्र नूतनं शस्तं सेवकान्नं पुरातनं ॥

నవం వస్త్రం నవం ఛత్రం నవ్యా స్త్రీ నూతనం గృహం।
సర్వత్ర నూతనం శస్తం సేవకాన్నం పురాతనం॥

A new cloth, a new umbrella, a new wife, a new house are everywhere good new; a servant and food are good old.

465. स्यालको गृहनाशाय सर्वनाशाय मातुलः ॥

స్యాలకో గృహనాశాయ సర్వనాశాయ మాతులః॥

A brother-in-law is the ruin of the house, a maternal uncle is the ruin of everything.

466. स्त्रियाश्चरित्रं पुरुषस्य भाग्यं देवा न जानंति कुतो मनुष्याः ॥

స్త్రియాశ్చరిత్రం పురుషస్య భాగ్యం దేవా న జానంతి కుతో మనుష్యాః॥

The gods know not a woman's conduct and a man's fortune, how then can men?

467. स्त्रियो मूलमनर्थानां ॥

స్త్రియో మూలమనర్థానాం॥

Women are the cause of mischief.

468. स्त्रीणां द्विगुण आहारो बुद्धिश्चापि चतुर्गुणा ।
साहसं षड्गुणं चैव कामोऽष्टगुण उच्यते ॥

స్త్రీణాం ద్విగుణ ఆహారో బుద్ధిశ్చాపి చతుర్గుణా।
సాహసం షడ్గుణం చైవ కామోష్టగుణ ఉచ్యతే॥

Women are said to eat twice as much [as men], to have four times as much sense, six times as much pluck, and eight times as much desire.

(Cf. Böhtlingk's *Indische Sprüche* 412, 5306.)

469. स्त्रीणामालोचनं विना ॥

స్త్రీణామాలోచనం వినా॥

Without the advice of women.

i. e. Admit not women into your counsels.

470. स्त्रीरत्नं दुष्कुलादपि ॥

స్త్రీరత్నం దుష్కులాదపి॥

Take an excellent woman even from a bad caste.

श्रद्दधानः शुभां विद्यामाददीतावरादपि ।
अंत्यादपि परं धर्मं स्त्रीरत्नं दुष्कुलादपि ॥

శ్రద్దధానః శుభాం విద్యామాదదీతావరాదపి।
అంత్యాదపి పరం ధర్మం స్త్రీరత్నం దుష్కులాదపి॥

An assiduous man should receive good learning even from a low fellow; excellent virtue even from an outcaste, and an excellent woman [*lit.* a woman-gem] even from a bad caste.

471. स्थानस्थितः कापुरुषोपि सिंहः ॥

స్థానస్థితః కాపురుషోపి సింహః॥

In a strong position, even a coward is a lion.

(See TELUGU No. 2124.)

जानामि रे सर्प तव प्रभावं कंठस्थितो गर्जसि शंकरस्य ।
स्थानं प्रधानं न बलं प्रधानं स्थानस्थितः कापुरुषोपि सिंहः ॥

జానామి రే సర్ప తవ ప్రభావం కంఠస్థితో గర్జసి శంకరస్య।
స్థానం ప్రధానం న బలం ప్రధానం స్థానస్థితః కాపురుషోపి సింహః॥

O Serpent! I know thy power; dwelling on the neck of Śankara (Śiva), thou dost hiss: position is the chief thing, not strength;—even a coward is a lion in a strong position.

472. स्थालीपुलाकन्यायः ॥
స్థాలీపులాకన్యాయః॥

The pot and a grain of boiled rice.

(See TELUGU No. 1921.)

473. स्थितस्य गतिश्चिंतनीया ॥
స్థితస్య గతిశ్చింతనీయా॥

The disposal of what remains should be thought of.

Without vain regrets for what has gone.

474. स्नेहे च बंधुर्न कदापि दूरः ॥
స్నేహే చ బంధుర్న కదాపి దూరః॥

Where there is friendship, the friend is never far off.

(See TELUGU No. 186.)

475. स्वकार्यधुरंधरास्स्वामिकार्यवंचकाः ॥
స్వకార్యధురంధరాస్స్వామికార్యవంచకాః॥

Hard working men in their own business, but rogues in their master's business.

(See TELUGU No. 2652.)

476. स्वकार्यमुद्धरेत्प्राज्ञः कार्यध्वंसे च मूर्खता ॥
స్వకార్యముద్ధరేత్ప్రాజ్ఞః కార్యధ్వంసే చ మూర్ఖతా॥

A wise man gains his object; in failure is foolishness.

अवमानं पुरस्कृत्य मानं कृत्वा च पृष्ठतः ।
स्वकार्यमुद्धरेत्प्राज्ञः कार्यध्वंसे च मूर्खता ॥
అవమానం పురస్కృత్య మానం కృత్వా చ పృష్ఠతః।
స్వకార్యముద్ధరేత్ప్రాజ్ఞః కార్యధ్వంసే చ మూర్ఖతా॥

Disregarding honor and even courting dishonor, a wise man gains his object; in failure is foolishness.

477. स्वगृहे को विचारोऽस्ति ॥

స్వగృహే కో విచారో౽స్తి॥

What deliberation is there in one's own house?

Said by very intimate friends, meaning that no formality is required to be observed by them in each other's houses.

478. स्वगृहे पूज्यते मूर्खः स्वग्रामे पूज्यते प्रभुः ।
स्वदेशे पूज्यते राजा विद्वान्सर्वत्र पूज्यते ॥

స్వగృహే పూజ్యతే మూర్ఖః స్వగ్రామే పూజ్యతే ప్రభుః।
స్వదేశే పూజ్యతే రాజా విద్వాన్సర్వత్ర పూజ్యతే॥

A fool is honored in his own house; a proprietor is honored in his own village; a king is honored in his own country; a learned man is honored everywhere.

479. स्वभावो मूर्ध्नि वर्तते ॥

స్వభావో మూర్ధ్ని వర్తతే॥

The natural disposition stands at the head.

सर्वस्य हि परीक्ष्यंते स्वभावा नेतरे गुणाः ।
अतीत्य हि गुणान् सर्वान्स्वभावो मूर्ध्नि वर्तते ॥

సర్వస్య హి పరీక్ష్యంతే స్వభావా నేతరే గుణాః।
అతీత్య హి గుణాన్ సర్వాన్స్వభావో మూర్ధ్ని వర్తతే॥

The natural disposition of every one is investigated, not the other qualities; the natural disposition excelling all other qualities, stands at the head of them.

480. स्वयं तीर्त्वा परान् तारयेत् ॥

స్వయం తీర్త్వా పరాన్ తారయేత్॥

Having crossed yourself, get others across.

Help yourself first and then others.

Self's the man. (Dutch.)*

* Zelf is de Man.

481. स्वानुष्ठानस्य समये मुनयोपि न पंडिताः ॥
స్వానుష్ఠానస్య సమయే మునయోపి న పండితాః॥

In their own actions even Munis are not wise.

परोपदेशसमये सर्व एव हि पंडिताः ।
स्वानुष्ठानस्य समये मुनयोपि न पंडिताः ॥
పరోపదేశసమయే సర్వ ఏవ హి పండితాః।
స్వానుష్ఠానస్య సమయే మునయోపి న పండితాః॥

In teaching others, all are wise; but in their own actions even Munis are not wise.

ह.

482. हलांतं ब्रह्मवर्चसं ॥
హలాంతం బ్రహ్మవర్చసం॥

Sanctity as far as the plough.

If a Brahman commence to till the ground, he loses his sanctity.

483. हसद्भिः क्रियते कर्म रुदद्भिरनुभूयते ॥
హసద్భిః క్రియతే కర్మ రుదద్భిరనుభూయతే॥

Laughing, a thing is done; weeping, the fruit of it is suffered.

(See TELUGU No. 2485.)

484. हस्तिमशकांतरं ॥
హస్తిమశకాంతరం॥

The difference between an elephant and a muskito.

क्ष.

485. क्षणं वित्तं क्षणं चित्तं क्षणं जीवितमावयोः ॥
క్షణం విత్తం క్షణం చిత్తం క్షణం జీవితమావయోః॥

Wealth for a moment, the mind for a moment, our life for a moment.

क्षणं वित्तं क्षणं चित्तं क्षणं जीवितमावयोः ।
यमस्य करुणा नास्ति धर्मस्य त्वरिता गतिः ॥
క్షణం విత్తం క్షణం చిత్తం క్షణం జీవితమావయోః।
యమస్య కరుణా నాస్తి ధర్మస్య త్వరితా గతిః॥

Wealth for a moment, mind for a moment, our life for a moment; Yama has no pity, [therefore] do good works quickly.

(See No. 24.)

486. क्षीणे कस्यास्ति गौरवं ॥

క్షీణే కస్యాస్తి గౌరవం॥

Who is honored in adversity?

वनानि दहते वह्निस्सखा भवति मारुतः ।
स एव दीपनाशाय क्षीणे कस्यास्ति गौरवं ॥
వనాని దహతే వహ్నిస్సఖా భవతి మారుతః।
స ఏవ దీపనాశాయ క్షీణే కస్యాస్తి గౌరవం॥

Fire burns forests and Wind is a friend [assists] ; but that very Wind proves destructive to the lamp. Who is honored when reduced [in circumstances?]

487. क्षीणे पुण्ये मर्त्यलोकं विशंति ॥

క్షీణే పుణ్యే మర్త్యలోకం విశంతి॥

When the reward of good deeds is ended, [souls] come back to the world of men.

488. क्षीरोदकन्यायः ॥

క్షీరోదకన్యాయః॥

Like milk and water.

(See TELUGU No. 1283, &c.)

Close friendship.

ఆంధ్రలోకోక్తిచంద్రికాశేషము.

A

SUPPLEMENT

TO THE

COLLECTION

OF

TELUGU PROVERBS:

CONTAINING

ADDITIONAL PROVERBS, AN INDEX VERBORUM, AND AN INDEX TO THE EUROPEAN PROVERBS QUOTED IN ILLUSTRATION.

BY

CAPTAIN M. W. CARR,
Madras Staff Corps.

MADRAS:

PRINTED AND SOLD AT THE CHRISTIAN KNOWLEDGE SOCIETY'S PRESS,
18, CHURCH STREET, VEPERY.

LONDON:
SOLD BY TRÜBNER AND CO. 60, PATERNOSTER ROW.
1868.

CONTENTS.

ఆంధ్రలోకోక్తిచంద్రికాశేషము.

TELUGU PROVERBS,

SUPPLEMENT.

అ.

2135. అంగటి వీథిలో ఆలిని పడుకోబెట్టి వచ్చేవారు పొయ్యేవారు దాటిపోయినారు అన్నట్టు.

Having put his wife to bed in the Bazaar street, he complained that the comers and goers stepped over her.

2136. అంటక ముట్టక దేవరకు పెట్టుతున్నాను, ఆశపడకండి బిడ్డలారా అవతలికి పొండి అన్నదట.

Without touching or handling I offer it to the deity, don't wish for it O children! Be off!

(See No. 420.)

2137. అంతమాత్రం వుంటే, దొంతులతో కాపరం చెయ్యనా.

If I had so much, would I not live with piles of pots?

2138. అందని పూలు దేవునికి అర్పణ.

An offering to the deity of the flowers which cannot be reached.

(See No. 766.)

2139. అందరికీ శకునము చెప్పే బల్లి కుడితితొట్టిలో పడ్డట్టు.

The lizard which tells the fortunes of all fell itself into the tub of rice-washings.

The sound of the lizard is believed to be auspicious or ominous according to the quarter from whence it is heard, the hour, &c.

2140. అందరూ అందలము యెక్కితే, మోశేవారు యెవరు.

If all get into the palankin, who will be the bearers?

You a lady, I a lady, who is to drive out the sow? (Galician.)*

2141. అందానకు పెట్టిన సొమ్ము, ఆపదకు అడ్డం వస్తుంది.

Ornaments worn for beauty will be useful in the time of want.

2142. అంబటికీ ఆశ, మీసాలకూ ఆశ.

Wishing for porridge and also for mustaches.

(See No. 147.)

The two don't go well together.

2143. అక్క మనది అయితే, బావ మనవాడా.

The sister is ours, but is the sisters's husband ours also?

(See No. 82.)

2144. అగ్నికి వాయువు సహాయమయినట్టు.

Like wind assisting fire.

2145. అద్దా గోడా మీద ఆదీ రోటీ వుండాది, అతడూ వస్తే ఖావు కనా, ముంగిట్లో యేమో మూలుగుతూ వుండాది, మూలా వున్నా మునగా కర్రా లావు కనా.

There's half a loaf on the cross wall, when he comes tell him to eat it; something is groaning in the yard, tell him to bring the Moringa stick that's in the corner.

The language of the above is barbarous and partly Hindustani. It is supposed to have been said by a Mussalman and is used in ridicule.

---

* Vos dona, yo dona, quien botara á porca fora?

2146. అత్త చచ్చిన ఆరు మాసములకు కోడలి కంట నీరు వచ్చినదట.

Six months after the death of the mother-in-law, tears came into the eyes of the daughter-in-law.

(See No. 1196.)

2147. అత్తిపండు పగలకొట్టితే, అన్నీ పురుగులే.

If you break a fig, it is all worms.

(For *Atti*, see No. 59.—See No. 230, &c.)

2148. అదృష్టం కలిశివస్తే, ఆలు పెండ్లామవుతుంది.

When good fortune comes, your wife will become your spouse.

Said in joke to a man who fancied that he had been very fortunate.

2149. అదే వూరు అయితే, కోళ్లు కుయ్యవా.

If that be a village, will the cocks not crow?

Applied to the evidence of a fact.

2150. అనువు కానిచోట అధికులమనరాదు.

In an unsuitable place we should not assert our superiority.

2151. అన్నదేవర సన్నగిస్తే, అన్నీ అణుగుతవి.

If the food is reduced, all will sink with it.

A man's bad qualities will disappear if he is put on short commons.

2152. అన్నమదమువల్ల అన్ని మదములు కలుగుతవి.

Food is the source of all vices.

2153. అన్నమయం ప్రాణమయం.

Sustained by food, dependent on life.

Said of the body.

ఆంధ్రలోకోక్తిచంద్రికా శేషము.

2154. అన్నము పెట్టినవారిల్లు కన్నము పెట్టవచ్చునా.

May you break into the house of him who has fed you ?

(See No. 1077, &c.)

Kannam is a hole made by burglars in the wall of a house.

2155. అన్నాలన్నీ సున్నాలు, అప్పాలన్నీ కప్పలు.

Let all your rice be chunam and all your cakes frogs !

A certain sage was, on account of his eccentricities, treated as a crazy fellow and not received into society. On one occasion, irritated by being refused admittance to an entertainment, he uttered the above imprecation which to the consternation of the assembled company took effect. They begged his pardon, whereupon he restored in the same miraculous manner the chunam into rice and the frogs into cakes !

The power acquired by austerities.

2156. అన్ని రుచులూ సరేగాని, అందులో వుప్పు లేదు.

All the flavours are right, but there is no salt in it.

Said of badly prepared food.

2157. అన్నీ తెలిశినవాడూ లేడు, యేమీ తెలియనివాడూ లేడు.

There is no one who knows everything, there is no one who knows nothing.

2158. అబద్ధమాడినా గోడ పెట్టినట్టు వుండవలెను.

If you do tell a lie, let it be like a wall.

(See No. 171.)

2159. అభిషేకం చేశిన అగ్నివలె వున్నాడు.

Like fire inaugurated with water.

Abhisheka is the term used for bathing or anointing an idol.

2160. అమావాస్య కూడు నిత్యం దొరుకునా.

Can you get new-moon food every day ?

The Hindu Law prescribes one meal only on the day of the new-moon, and it is in consequence a good one.

2161. అయితే ఆదివారం, కాకుంటే సోమవారం.

If it's not Sunday it's Monday.

If to-day will not, to-morrow may.

2162. అయిన పనికి చింతించేవాడు అల్పబుద్ధిగలవాడు.

He who grieves over that which is past is a man of little sense.

2163. అయ్య కదురువలె, అమ్మ కుదురువలె.

The husband like a spindle, the wife like a mortar.

Kuduru is the upper and larger part of a stone mortar.

2164. అయ్యవారయ్యవారు అటికకంత, అయ్యవారి పెండ్లాము పుటికంత, పుటిక తీసుకొని పోయి మూల యింట్లో పెట్టితే, నక్కయెత్తుకొని పోయినది నారాయణా.

The priest, the priest is like a pot with a large mouth, the priest's wife is like a small basket—when the basket was put in the corner a jackal walked off with it, O Nârâyaṇa!

2165. అయ్యోరా బోకేతూ, వస్తాబో శింగామా.

"Come father and eat" [said the daughter] "I'm coming directly Śingâma" [replied the father.]

The daughter waved her hand to display her new gold bangles, the father nodded his head to show his new gold earings.

Said of people "showing off."

2166. అయ్యో అంటే, ఆరు నెలల పాపం వస్తున్నది.

If you say "Alas!" it will equal six months' sin.

Applied to pitying an atrocious sinner.

2167. అర్జున భర్జున పడెర పిడుగు అన్నాడట.

"Arjuna, Bharjuna—Ah! the thunder bolt has fallen," he cried.

The man in a fright tried to utter the spell given under No. 1444, but lost his head and broke down at the second word.

2168. అర్థము లేనివాడు నిరర్థకుడు.

A man without money is useless.

(See No. 1876.)

A man without money is like a ship without sails. (Dutch.)*

2169. అర్థము లేనివాడు వ్యర్థుడు.

A man without money is vain.

2170. అల్లికాయల సందడిని పెండ్లి మరిచినాడు.

In his haste about the Alli kâyas he forgot the marriage.

Alli kâya is the fruit of the Memecylon Capitellatum.

2171. అవ్వా గుర్రమూ వకటి అయినట్టు.

The grandmother and the horse were one.

A man and his grandmother started on a journey, the former riding, the latter on foot; the grandson rested frequently on the road and eventually only reached his destination just as his grandmother had completed her journey.

The tortoise and the hare.

2172. అశ్వత్థ ప్రదక్షిణము చేసి, కడుపు పట్టి చూచుకొన్నదట.

While she was going round the holy fig tree, she felt for signs of pregnancy.

Pradakshaṇa is "reverential salutation, by circumambulating a person or object, keeping the right side towards them." (Wilson). *Asvattha* is the Ficus Religiosa.

Expecting the result to be obtained at the very commencement of an enterprize.

---

* Een man zonder geld is een schip zonder zeilen.

ఆ.

2173. ఆకలి కాకుండా నీకు ఔషధము యిస్తాను, నీ యింట్లో చద్ది నాకు పెట్టు అన్నాడట.

I'll give you medicine to keep away hunger, give me your cold breakfast.

Said by a quack.

2174. ఆకలిగొన్నవాడు యెంగిటికి యేవగించడు.

The hungry man will not refuse leavings.

2175. ఆకాశం గద్ద తన్నుకొని పోయినది.

The sky was kicked away by the kite.

Said in answer to an impertinent question.

2176. ఆకాశానికి నిచ్చెన వేశేవాడు.

A man who plants a ladder on the sky.

Ambitious.

2177. ఆచారం ముందర, అనాచారం వెనక.

Purity first and impurity after.

Impurity always attends purity.

2178. ఆచార్యునికి ద్రోహము చేసినా, ఆత్మకు ద్రోహం చెయ్యరాదు.

Though you cheat your priest you should not cheat your own life.

Take good care of yourself, even though you treat your priest badly.

Said by a selfish, greedy man.

2179. ఆడదాని బుద్ధి అపర బుద్ధి.

A woman's sense is wrong sense.

(See No. 436.)

Lit. in the back of the head.

2180. ఆడపిల్లను కన్నవారు అయిదు బిరుదులు తెగకోసుకోవలెను.

They who beget female children must cut off five of their badges of honor.

A man though raised to a distinguished position in the world has yet to humble himself before his sons-in-law for the sake of his daughters, who might otherwise not be well treated.

2181. ఆడే కాలూ పాడే నోరూ వూరకుండవు.

A dancing foot and a singing mouth are never quiet.

(See Nos. 255, 1085, 1639.)

2182. ఆత్మకు ద్రోహం చేస్తే, అప్పుడే అడుగుతుంది.

If you cheat your life, it will then and there ask [for food].

2183. ఆ మంట యీా మంట, బ్రాహ్మణార్థం కడుపు మంట.

[Talk of] that burning and this burning, this Brâhmaṇârtha is belly burning.

Said by a greedy Vaidika Brahman.

Brâhmaṇârtha is an invitation issued to two or three Brahmans on the anniversary of the death of a relative.

2184. ఆమాట అనిపింతామా మామగారా.

Shall we have that word said ? O father-in-law !

When a Kômaṭi was dying and the word "Nârâyaṇa" had to be pronounced in his ears, all his relations tried to shirk this disagreeable duty. The allusion in the proverb is to a proposal made by one of them that the task should be imposed upon the oldest man present.

2185. ఆముదపు విత్తులు, ఆణి ముత్యాలు అవునా.

Will castor oil seeds become fine pearls ?

2186. ఆయన వుంటే, విస్తరి అయినా కుట్టును.

If he were here, he would at least stitch the leaf platter.

(See No. 46.)

2187. ఆరంభ శూరత్వము.

Valour in the beginning.

Dash, but not steady unflinching courage.

2188. ఆర్భాటానకు ఆరు కుంపట్లు వక దుంపదాలి.

Six chafing dishes and a fire of roots were the cause of the uproar.

2189. ఆలు గుణవంతురాలు అయితే, మేలు కలుగును.

If the wife is of good disposition, good will accrue.

2190. ఆళ్లు కొత్తవి అయితే, తిరగండ్లు కొత్తవా.

Though the Âḷḷu be new, are the mill stones new ?

(For *Âḷḷu* see No. 86.)

An answer to a lame excuse.

2191. ఆవగింజ అట్టె దాచి గుమ్మడి కాయ గుల్లకానుగా యెంచేవాడు.

A man who saves a mustard seed and thinks a pumpkin worth a shell-coin.

(For *Gummaḍi kâya* see No. 517.)

Penny wise and pound foolish.

They drink their water by measure, but eat their cake without. (Greek.)*

2192. ఆవుల సాధుత్వమూ, బ్రాహ్మణుల పేదరికమూ లేదు.

There is no meekness in cows, nor poverty in Brahmans.

---

* Μέτρῳ ὕδωρ πίνοντες ἀμέτρως μάζαν ἔδοντες.

2193. ఆశ ఆలి మీద, ఆధారం చాప మీద.

His desire is on his wife and his support on his mat.

Nothing for it but resignation.

2194. ఆశలేనివానికి దేశమెందుకు.

Why should a man without desire be in the world ?

ఇ.

2195. ఇంటి పిల్లికి పొరుగింటి పిల్లి తోడు.

The neighbour's cat is the ally of the house cat.

Both join in mischief.

2196. ఇచ్చకాలవారు బుచ్చకాలవారు పొట్ట కొరకు పొక్కులు గోకుతారు.

Sycophants scratch pimples for a livelihood.

2197. ఇచ్చేటప్పుడు కాముని పండగ, పుచ్చుకొనేటప్పుడు దీపావళి పండగ.

Giving is like Kâma's festival, taking is like the feast of Dîpâvali.

Kâmadahana is the mournful commemoration of the burning of *Kandarpa* or *Kâmadeva* (the god of love) by the fire from Śiva's eye, when he interrupted the god in his devotions. *Dîpâvali* or *Dîpâli* is a joyous festival with nocturnal illuminations in honour of *Kârtikeya.* The name signifies " a row of lamps."

2198. ఇత్యపులు కూయగా కోనంగు డేయగా।
అప్యేకదంతుండు పున్నపుంసకమెక్కి ఆడెనమ్మా॥

When the Ityapis cried, and Konanga shot [his darts,] Apyekadanta mounted the Punnapumsakam and danced O lady!

An absurd couplet composed by a would-be poet. He attempted to make use of the synonyms given in the Amara Kosha; in his ignorance he mistook *Ityapi* (" so also") for a name of the cuckoo, divided the words *Darpakonañga* (names of Kâmadeva) wrongly, taking *Konañga*, used *Apyekadanta* (" also Ekadanta") as a name of Gaṇeśa and read *Punnapumsakam* (" masculine and neuter") as a synonym of *Valmîka* ("an anthill.")—(See Colebrooke's *Amara Kosha* 2nd edn., pp. 5,7,76,131.)

2199. ఇరుగింటమ్మా పొరుగింటమ్మా మా యింటిఆయన గోడు చూడండి.

O lady neighbours! see the conduct of my husband.

Inviting the sympathy of those who cannot interfere.

2200. ఇరుసుకు కందెన పెట్టక, పరమేశ్వరుని బండి అయినా పారదు.

Without grease to the axle, even Paramesvara's car will not run.

2201. ఇల్లు కాలినా యిల్లాలు చచ్చినా గోల్లు మానదు.

If the house be burnt or the goodwife die, there will certainly be lamentations.

ఈ.

2202. ఈ అంబటికేనా యిరువైనాలుగు నామములు.

Are twenty-four Nâmams for this porridge only?

Said by a formalist who had put on twenty-four sectarial marks instead of twelve (the prescribed number) and was disappointed at not being treated accordingly.

2203. ఈ నెలలో వడ్డీ లేదు, వచ్చే నెలలో మొదలూ లేదు.

There is no interest for you this month, and no principal for you next month.

Said by a cheat to his creditor.

2204. ఈ పిల్లి ఆ పాలు తాగునా.

Would this cat have drunk that milk?

(See No. [illegible].)

A demure humbug.

ఉ.

2205. ఉండలేక పోతే, బొండను వెయ్యమన్నాడట.

If he can't keep quiet, put him in the stocks.

(See No. [illegible].)

2206. ఉట్టిమీద వెన్న వుండగా, వూరెల్లా నేతికి దేవులాడనేల.

While there is butter in the net why hunt through the whole village for ghî?

(For *Uṭṭi* see No. 304.—See Nos. 118, 2002.)

2207. ఉడికిన మెతుకులు తిని వూళ్లో వుండే వాణ్ని, నాకు యెవరితో యేమి పని వున్నది.

I am a man who eats boiled rice and lives in the village, what have I to do with others?

(See No. 755.)

2208. ఉతికేవానికిగాని చాకలి వుతకడు.

A washerman will only wash for one who thrashes him.

There is a pun here on the word *Utuku*: it is the term used for beating clothes—the Indian washerman's mode of cleansing them—and it also signifies in jocular language to "drub" or "thrash."

2209. ఉన్నది వక కూతురు, వూరెల్లా అల్లుండ్లు.

He has but one daughter, but the whole village is [full of] sons-in-law.

i. e. they all wish to marry her.

(See No. 349.)

2210. ఉపనయనమునాటి మాట వుండక పోదు.

The word [taught] on the day of Upanayana will not be forgotten.

At the *Upanayana* or investiture of the sacerdotal thread the novice is taught to repeat the words భవతి భిక్షాం దేహి (*Bhavati bhikshâm dehi*) "Madam, give alms."

Said by a lazy fellow.

2211. ఉప్పుతో ముప్ఫయి ఆరు వుంటే, వుత్తముండయినా వండుతుంది.

If you have with salt the thirty-six a stupid woman even can cook.

There are thirty-six requisites, it is said, for cooking, salt included.

(See No. [illegible].)

ఊ.

2212. ఊర పిచ్చుక మీాద తాటికాయ వుంచినట్టు.

Like putting a palmyra fruit on a sparrow.

(For *Palmyra* see No. 290.)

Expecting a person to do what is beyond his power.

2213. ఊర పిచ్చుక మీాద వాడి వజ్రాయుధమూ.

Is a sharp Vajrâyudha [to be used] on a sparrow ?

(See No. 14[illegible].)

Vajra or *Vajrâyudha* is the mythological thunderbolt of Indra.

2214. ఊరి జబ్బు చాకలి యెరుగును, వుద్యోగపు జబ్బు బంట్రౌతు యెరుగును.

The washerman knows the reduced state of the village; the peon knows the reduction [of his superiors] in office.

2215. ఊరి ముందరికి వచ్చి నా పెండ్లామూ పిల్లలూ యెట్లా వున్నారని అడిగినాడట.

He came to the outskirts of the village and asked "How are my wife and children ?"

A few yards more would have enabled the man to judge for himself.

Said of impatience.

2216. ఊరు వున్నది, చిప్ప వున్నది.

There is the village and here is my cup.

Said by a beggar.

ఎ.

2217. ఎండు మామిడి టెంకలు వ్రెల్లో పెట్టుకొని యెవరి తాడు తెంప వచ్చినావోయి వీరన్నా అన్నదట.

Whom have you come to cheat with dried mango stones in your skirt? O Vîranna!

A glutton attempted to get more food from a cateress after he had eaten the ordinary meal at the fixed rate; she refused, adding—by way of excuse—that she had no more condiments and could only give him plain rice and buttermilk. Not to be done in this way, he came again with dried pickled mangos hidden in his cloth. *Tâḍu tempu* means literally to break the cord, i. e. to make a widow (See No. 878.)

2218. ఎక్కడ కొట్టినా, కుక్కకు కాలు కుంటు.

Wherever you strike a dog, he will limp.

(See Nos. 580, 1307, 1401.)

2219. ఎక్కుమంటే యెద్దుకు కోపం, దిగుమంటే కుంటివానికి కోపం.

If you say "Mount," the bullock is angry; if you say "Get off" the lame man is angry.

(See No. 1976.)

It is hard to please every one. (Dutch.)*

2220. ఎద్దును అడిగా గంత కట్టడము.

Are you to ask the bullock before putting on the packsaddle?

2221. ఎద్దును యెక్కినవాడే లింగడు, గద్దను యెక్కినవాడే రంగడు.

He who rides on a bullock is Lingaḍu (Śiva), he who rides on a kite is Rangaḍu (Vishṇu).

i. e. the two are but one under different forms.

Said by Smârtas.

2222. ఎద్దు మోశినంత, గోనె పట్టినంత.

As much as the bullock can carry, as much as the bag will hold.

No more can be taken.

---

* Effen is kwaad passen.

2223. ఎద్దువలె తిని మొద్దువలె నిద్రపోయినట్టు.

He eats like a bullock, and sleeps like a log.

2224. ఎనుము యీనినది రెడ్డీ అంటే, నీకేమి కద్దే బొడ్డీ అన్నాడట.

When she said "O Reḍḍi! your buffalo has calved," he replied "O Boḍḍi! what 's that to you?"

The woman wanted some milk.

2225. ఎప్పటి అమ్మకు నిప్పటే గతి.

The woman who always comes gets only a plain cake.

Nippaṭi is a kind of damper.

2226. ఎముకలేని నాలుక యెట్లా తిప్పినా తిరుగుతుంది.

The boneless tongue turns in any way.

(See No. 1237.)

Said of a liar.

He lies as fast as a dog can trot.

2227. ఎరువుల సొమ్ములు యెరువుల వారు యెత్తుకొని పోతే, పెండ్లికొడుకు ముఖాన పేడనీళ్లు చల్లినట్టే వుంటుంది.

When the lenders take back the ornaments lent, it is like sprinkling cowdung water on the face of a bridegroom.

(See No. 1507.)

2228. ఎరువు సతము కాదు, వాక్కు తోడు కాదు.

Lent property is not lasting, speech is not help.

You cannot always depend upon getting a livelihood by your plausibility.

2229. ఎలుక యెంత యేడ్చినా, పిల్లి తన పట్టు వదలదు.

However much the rat may cry, the cat will not let go her hold.

(See Nos. 406, 1437.)

2230. ఎలుక యేట్లో పోతేనేమి, పులి బోనున పోతేనేమి.

What if the rat is carried down the river? What if the tiger is caught in the trap?

Who cares?

2231. ఎవరి కొంప తియ్యడానకు యీ జంగం వేషం వేశినావు.

To ruin whom are you disguised as a Jangam?

(For *Jangam* see No. 943).

Said to an impostor.

2232. ఎవరి జానతో వారు యెనిమిది జానలే.

[Measured] with his own span, every man is eight spans high.

2233. ఎవరివల్ల చెడ్డావోయి వీరన్నా అంటే, నోటివల్ల చెడ్డానోయి కాటమరాజా అన్నాడట.

When Kâṭamarâzu said " O Viranna! by whom have you been ruined?" he replied " I have been ruined by my own mouth O Kâṭamarâzu"!

(See Nos. 1970, 1947.)

2234. ఎవరు యిచ్చినది యీ మాన్యము అంటే, నేనే యిచ్చుకొన్నాను అన్నాడట.

When asked " Who gave you the freehold?" he said " I gave it to myself."

Said of one who helps himself without regard to the law of *meum* and *tuum*.

ఏ.

2235. ఏకముండం గృహచ్ఛిద్రం ద్విముండం గృహనాశనం।
త్రిముండం గ్రామనాశంచ చాతుర్ముండంచ పట్టణం।
అథవా పంచముండంచ బ్రహ్మ పట్నం వినశ్యతి॥

One widow and household broils, two widows and ruin to a family, three widows and ruin to a village, four widows and ruin to a city, five widows and ruin to Brahma-paṭṭaṇa.

2236. ఏకాదశినాడు తల అంటుకొంటావేమి అంటే, అది నిత్యవ్రతము నేడే ఆరంభము అన్నాడట; మర్నాడు తల యెందుకు అంటుకోలేదంటే, నిన్నటితో వ్రతసమాప్తి అన్నాడట.

"What! are you anointing your head on the Êkâdaśi?" said one, "That is a daily task, which I have commenced to-day," replied the other. When asked next day "Why have you not anointed your head?" he said "Yesterday completed my task."

Said in joke of a man who does not observe the ceremonial laws.

2237. ఏట్లో కలిపిన చింతపండు.

Tamarinds mixed in the river.

(See No. 1147.)

2238. ఏట్లో పారే నీళ్లు యెవరు తాగితే యేమి.

What matters it who drinks the water flowing in the river?

(See No. 580.)

A right common to all.

2239. ఏట్లో వుదకము వున్నది సూర్యదేవా.

There is water in the river, O Sûryadeva!

Said by an irreligious fellow, too lazy to bring water as an oblation to the Sun.

2240. ఏతాంపాటకు యెదురు పాట లేదు.

There is no rival song to the Êtâm song.

(For *Êtâm* See No. 2096.)

The song of drawers of water is not composed according to the rules of music and cannot be compared with any other.

2241. ఏనుగ మదిస్తే నెత్తిన మన్ను వేసుకొంటున్నది.

When the elephant is in rut, he throws earth on his head.

Pride goes before and shame follows after.

2242. ఏనుగ మీద దోమ వాలితే యెంత బరువు.

If a musquito light on an elephant, what weight?

2243. ఏనుగల పోట్లాటకు యేట్రింత రాయభారము.

In the quarrels of elephants, a king-crow the ambassador.

Said of an insignificant person, who has no influence.

2244. ఏరు అయినా మూడు నేరములు కాస్తుంది.

Even a river will forgive three offences.

Referring to the three times which a man is said to sink before drowning.

The duty of forgiveness.

2245. ఏరు యెన్నివంకలు పోయినా, సముద్రములోనే పడవలెను.

However many twists the river take, it must fall into the sea at last.

2246. ఏవూరే యేతామా అంటే, దువ్వూరే దూలామా అన్నదట.

"What village [do you come from]? O Êtâm!" [said the beam] "From Duvvûru, O beam!" [replied the swape.]

An answer given to a foolish question.—Duvvûru is in the Cuddapah District.

ఒ.

2247. ఒక అబద్ధము కప్పడానకు వెయ్యి అబద్ధాలు కావలెను.

To hide one lie a thousand lies are wanted.

One lie makes many.

One lie draws ten after it. (Italian.)*

2248. ఒక చెంప కొట్టితే పాలు, వక చెంప కొట్టితే నీళ్లు.

If you slap one cheek, milk [comes]; if you slap the other cheek, water [comes].

Said of a very tender, delicate boy.

2249. ఒక చేత పసుపు, వక చేత ముసుకు.

In one hand turmeric, in the other hand a hood.

Turmeric is much used on auspicious occasions such as marriages. Every woman, except she be a widow, also rubs it daily on her body before bathing. *Musuku* is the skirt of a woman's cloth thrown over the head (by widows) as a hood.

2250. ఒక వరలో రెండు కత్తులు యిమడవు.

Two swords cannot be contained in one scabbard.

Said of two masters in a house, &c.

Two cats and a mouse, two wives in one house, two dogs and a bone, never agree in one.

2251. ఒక్కడి సంపాద్యము పది మంది పాలు.

One man's gains are shared by ten.

A man's relations live on him.

2252. ఒక్కపొద్దు మాట కుక్క యెరుగునా.

Does a dog know what a fast means?

---

* Una bugia ne tira dieci.

ఓ.

2253. ఓలో నగం చెప్పు నాయనా అన్నాడట.

In O teach me half, O father!

Said by a spoilt child who wished his father to teach him half a letter at a time.

2254. ఓహో బాబూ కనుక్కొన్నారు అన్నాడట.

O father! they have discovered us.

(See Nos. 996, 958.)

Two *Tambaḷis* (No. 173), father and son, went to a Brahman feast disguised as Brahmans. When the sandal was handed round for making the horizontal Sectarial mark on the forehead, the son took it with his right hand instead of with his left. The server thereupon called him a *Tambaḷi* when he stupidly cried out to his father that they had been discovered and brought him too into trouble.

క.

2255. కంటికి రెప్ప, కాలికి చెప్పు.

A lid to the eye, a shoe to the foot.

The protection necessary.

2256. కండ్లకు గంతకట్టి అడవిలో వదిలిపెట్టబడ్డ వానివలె.

Like blindfolding [and pinioning] a man and leaving him in the jungle.

Putting a man into great difficulties.

2257. కండ్లు ఆర్చినమ్మ యిండ్లు ఆర్చినది.

The winking woman ruined families.

A pun on the word *Ârçu*.

2258. కంసాలిమాయ కంసాలికి గాని తెలియదు.

A goldsmith's fraud is only known to a goldsmith.

A story is told of a young goldsmith who disguised himself as a Brahman and married a Brahman's daughter. He perceived and disclosed on one occasion the fraud of another goldsmith who had cheated his father-in-law ; this man in revenge exposed the young impostor.

2259. కంసాలి వద్ద వుండవలె, కుంపట్లో వుండవలె.

It must be with the goldsmith, or in the chafing-dish.

Said of gold made away with by a swindling goldsmith.

2260. కట్టినవారు వకరు అయితే, కాపురం చేసేవారు వకరు.

The builder [of a house] is one and he who lives in it is another.

" *He that buildeth, [let him be] as he that shall not dwell therein.*" 2 Esdras xvi. 42.

2261. కట్టెయస్వాహా కంపాయస్వాహా, నీకూ నాకూ చెరిసగాయస్వాహా.

Svâhâ to the wood, svâhâ to the twigs—svâhâ to the shares of you and me.

Svâhâ is "an exclamation used in making an oblation to the gods" (Wilson). When an ignorant impostor was heard repeating the pretended formulæ contained in the first part of the above, he added to it the second to shut the mouth of the man who had found him out, by promising him half his fees. (For the first part of this story see No. 2282.)

2262. కట్టె లేదు, పిడకా లేదు, కాచీ పోయా నీళ్లూ లేవు, పదవోయి అల్లుడా బావిగట్టుకు అన్నట్టు.

There is no firewood, there is no dry cowdung, there is no water to boil—come away to the well O son-in-law !

The son-in-law should have been provided with a warm bath, but his wife's parents were too poor.

2263. కద్దు అనడానకూ లేదు అనడానకూ దీనికే అధికారమా.

Has she a right to say "there is" or "there is not"?

A beggar once asked alms from a daughter-in-law when her mother-in-law was out. She told him there was nothing for him. As he went he met the mother-in-law who enquired whether he had received alms at the house. On being told by the beggar that he had been sent away, she brought him back to the house and after chastising her daughter-in-law said to the man "Now you may go, has she any authority to say there are alms for you or there are not?"

Told as an illustration of the fact that a daughter-in-law has no anthority whatever in the house.

2264. కన్న తల్లిని కాళ్లు పట్టి యీడ్చి పినతల్లికి పెట్టరా పిండప్రదానము అన్నట్లు.

Like pulling away your own mother by the legs and saying "Offer the rice-ball for the maternal aunt."

2265. కన్ను మూస్తే కల.

If you shut your eyes, a dream.

After death the unreality of things temporal appears.

2266. కమ్మర వీధిలో సూదులు అమ్మినట్లు.

Like selling needles in the blacksmiths' street.

(See No. 2286.)

To carry coals to Newcastle.

2267. కరువున కడుపు కాల్చినమ్మను యెన్నటికీ మరవను.

I shall never forget the lady who burnt my stomach [i. e. who fed me insufficiently] in the famine time.

2268. కరువులో బిడ్డను అమ్ముకొన్నట్లు.

Like selling a child in a famine.

Selling in a bad market.

2269. కర్మకు అంతమూ లేదు, కాలముకు నిశ్చయమూ లేదు.

There is no end to religious ceremonies, and there is no finding the times [fixed for the observance of them].

2270. కలిగిన వారికి అందరూ చుట్టాలే.

All are relatives of the rich man.

(See No. 1557.)

A full purse never lacked friends.

2271. కాచిన చెట్టుకు రాళ్ల దెబ్బలు.

Blows with stones to the bearing tree.

The liberal only meet with ingratitude.

The best bearing trees are the most beaten. (Italian.)*

It is only at the tree laden with fruit that people throw stones. (French.)†

2272. కానికాలముకు పయిబట్ట పక్షులు యెత్తుకొని పోయినవి.

In an evil time birds flew away with the cloth off his body.

Alluding to the story of Nala.—See the *Nalopâkhyânam* Book ix.

2273. కానివాని కొంప కాచి చెరచవలెను.

One must watch and ruin an enemy.

Wait time and place to take your revenge, for it is never done well in a hurry. (Italian.)‡

2274. కాలమందు చేస్తే దేవతలకు ప్రీతి, అకాలమందు చేస్తే అసురులకు ప్రీతి, యిద్దరి వాతా మన్ను కొట్టుతాను అన్నాడట.

"If done at the right time it is pleasing to the gods, if done at the wrong time it is pleasing to the Asuras—I'll disappoint them both" said he.

Said by an irreligious Brahman on being asked why he neglected his daily prayers *(Sandhyâvandanam.)* The *Asuras* are 'demons of the first order and in perpetual hostility with the gods' (Wilson.)

---

* I migliori alberi sono i più battuti.

† On ne jette des pierres qu'à l'arbre chargé de fruits.

‡ Aspetta tempo e loco à far la tua vendetta, che la non si fa mai ben in fretta.

2275. కాలము పోను, మాట నిలుచును.

Time will go, an accusation will remain.

(See Nos. 1896, 1898.)

2276. కాలితో నడిస్తే కాశికి పోవచ్చునేగాని, తలతో నడిస్తే తలవాకిలి అయినా దాట వచ్చునా.

If you walk on your feet you may go to Kâśi, but if you walk on your head can you even pass over the threshold?

2277. కిమాలస్యం—ఆలస్య, అరసస్య, పుంగస్య, పులియస్య, వేపస్య.

When one said "Kimâlasyam?" the other replied "Âlasya, Arasasya, Pungasya, Puḷiyasya, Vêpasya."

A learned Paṇḍit once asked, in Sanscrit, an ignorant but witty Village priest who had named an unlucky day for an auspicious ceremony "Why this delay? [in explaining the matter]"; the other replied, punning upon the word *Âlasya*, "Banyan tree, holy fig tree, Punga tree, Tamarind tree, and Margosa tree." (The words used are Tamil.) The Village priest had previously to the disputation agreed with his fellow villagers that the man who spoke most words should be considered the more learned of the two; they therefore thrashed the Paṇḍit and turned him out of their village.

2278. కుంచెడు బియ్యము గుమ్మడి కాయ.

A Kunçam of raw-rice and a gourd.

(For *Kunçam*, See No. 619.)

A modest request.

A thousand Brahmans went on an auspicious occasion to bless the king and on being asked how much rice and vegetable they would each have for their meal, replied as above. The king angry and disgusted at their greediness ordered that each should be forced, with the penalty of his life, to eat the whole quantity demanded. The Brahmans however cheated the king at the suggestion of a cunning Kômaṭi, by distributing one *Kunçam* of rice and one pumpkin at a time among the whole number of men.

2279. కుక్క ఆశ గుండ్రాతితో తీరెను.

A dog's greed will be satisfied with a grinding stone.

(For *Gunḍrâyi*.—See No. 770.)

2280. కుక్కకు నెయ్యి యెక్కడనయినా యిందునా.

Can a dog ever retain ghî?

He always throws it up.

2281. కుక్క వస్తే రాయి దొరకదు, రాయి దొరికితే కుక్క రాదు.

When the dog comes, a stone cannot be found; when a stone is found, the dog does not come.

A thing can never be found when it is most wanted.

2282. కుక్కశ్చ పచ్చిగోడశ్చ దాటితే మళ్లిదాటితే రెడ్డిశ్చ రెడ్డిసానిశ్చ
సహామూలం వినశ్యతః॥

If a dog crosses a wet wall and recrosses, the Reḍḍi and his lady with all the family perish.

There was a certain stingy Reḍḍi who paid nothing to the village priest (Grâma Purohita). On one occasion when the Reḍḍi was making some additions to his house a dog jumped over a freshly built wall. The village priest, who happened to be present, determined to take advantage of this circumstance, simulated great consternation, and repeated the above sham Mantra. The Reḍḍi was successfully taken in, and at his expense the priest performed expiatory burnt offerings, &c. (For the continuation of this story see No. 2261.)

2283. కుట్టితే తేలు, కుట్టకుంటే కుమ్మర పురుగు.

If it stings it is a scorpion, if it does not sting it is a mole cricket.

A man's character is known by his acts.

2284. కుడవమంటే పొడవ వస్తాడు.

When asked to dine he comes to stab.

2285. కుమ్మరవారింటి పెండ్లికూతురు ఆవకట్టుకు రాక యెక్కడికి పోతుంది.

How can the potter's bride help coming to the kiln ?

She must appear in public, however bashful.

2286. కుమ్మర వీధిలో కుండలు అమ్మినట్టు.

Like selling pots in potters' street.

(See No. 2266.)

2287. కుళ్లి కుళ్లి కాయనష్టి, కాలి కాలి కట్టెనష్టి.

By decaying and decaying the fruit is destroyed, by burning and burning the wood is destroyed.

(See No. 2044.)

2288. కూర్చుండి తింటూవుంటే, కొండ కూడా సమిసిపోతుంది.

If you sit still and eat, even a mountain will be consumed.

If you spend your principal, it will soon disappear, however large.

2289. కొండమీదినుంచి బండ దొర్లించినట్టు.

Like rolling a boulder down a hill.

It is easy to bowl down hill.

2290. కొత్త అప్పుకు పోతే, పాత అప్పు పయిన పడ్డది.

When he went to raise a new loan, the old debt fell upon him.

i. e. His creditor reminded him of the old score.

2291. కొద్ది కొద్దిగా తీస్తే, కొండ కూడా సమిసి పోతుంది.

If you take it away by degrees even a mountain will be removed.

(See No. 461.)

2292. కొన్నది వంకాయ, కొసరినది గుమ్మడికాయ.

What he bought was a brinjal, what he got to boot was a gourd.

(For *Brinjal* see No. 97.—For *Gummaḍi Kâya* see No. 517.)

2293. కొల్లేటి బ్రహ్మహత్య క్రాపు మీదుగా కొట్టుకొని పోయినది.

The crime of Brahman slaying at Kollêru fell on Krâpa.

(See No. 353.)

Kollêru and Krâpa are adjacent villages in the Kṛishṇa District.

2294. కోడలు నలుపు అయితే, కులమంతా నలుపు.

If the daughter-in-law be black, the whole family will be blackened.

i. e. a bad daughter-in-law will bring disgrace on her husband's family.

2295. కోడిని గద్ద తన్నుకొని పోయినది.

The fowl was carried off by the kite.

(See No. 2175.)

2296. కోతి చావు, కోమటి రంకు.

A monkey's death, a Kômaṭi's adultery.

Both are concealed from the eye of the world.

2297. కోపం పాపకారణం.

Anger is a cause of sin.

Anger is a sworn enemy.

Anger is the fever and frenzy of the soul.

2298. కోల ఆడితే, కోతి ఆడును.

If you shake the stick the monkey will dance.

It is the raised stick that makes the dog obey. (Danish.)*

---

* Holder man el Kieppen til, agter Hunden intet Bud.

గ.

2299. గంగలో మునిగినా కాకి హంస అవుతుందా.

Though it bathe in the Ganges, will a crow become a swan?

(See Nos. 609, 1086.)

2300. గంధపొడి మోశే గాడిదవలె.

Like a donkey carrying sandal powder.

2301. గంధము అమ్మిన చోట కట్టెలు అమ్మినట్టు.

Like selling firewood where sandal had been sold.

Said of the ruin of what once was beautiful.

2302. గడిచి బ్రతికినాము అని గంతులు వెయ్యరాదు.

Don't jump about saying you have got through [your difficulties.]

Don't halloo till you are out of the wood.

2303. గడ్డింత లేక ముడ్డంత యెండీ, వేంచేశెనే గుర్రము దేవలోకం.

The horse without grass, dried up and went to Devaloka.

Devaloka is heaven, the 'gods' world.'

2304. గతుకులకు పోతే, బతుకులు పోయినవి.

When he went to lap, his livelihood went.

When a greedy man went to spoon upon another for his breakfast he was kept waiting so long that he lost his situation.

2305. గరుత్మంతుణ్ని చూచిన పాము వలె.

Like a snake seeing Garutmat.

Garutmat or *Garuḍa* (No. 751) was "the king of the feathered tribes, and the remorseless enemy of the serpent race." (Vishṇu Purāṇa—Wilson's trans.)*

---

* विनतायाश्च पुत्रौ द्वौ विख्यातौ गरुडारुणौ।
सुपर्णः पततां श्रेष्ठो दारुणः पन्नगाशनः॥

2306. గాజుపూసల గనిలో ఘనమయిన మణి కలుగునా.

Will a large gem be found in a crystal bead mine?

2307. గాడిద గాడిదే, గుర్రము గుర్రమే.

An ass is an ass, a horse is a horse.

(See No. 1494.)

2308. గాలి వచ్చినప్పుడుగదా తూర్పార పట్టుకోవలెను.

Is it not when the wind blows that you must winnow?

(See Nos. 316, 508, 1189.)

Strike while the iron is hot.

Take time while time is, for time will away.

2309. గుడ్డివాడికి గుడ్డివాడు దారి చూపితే, యిద్దరూ గోతిలో పడుతారు.

If a blind man lead a blind man, both will fall into the pit.

2310. గుడ్డివాడు కన్ను రాగోరునా, పోగోరునా.

Will a blind man wish to have an eye or not to have one?

2311. గుద్దులాడిన యింట్లో గుప్పెడు గింజలు నిలవవు.

In a quarrelsome family not a handful of grain will be left.

2312. గురికి జానెడు యెచ్చు తక్కువగా కాల్చే వాడు.

A man who misses the mark by a span.

A bad shot.

2313. గురువుకు తగ్గ శిష్యుడు.

A disciple worthy of his Guru.

Both blockheads.

2314. గురువు నిలుచుండి తాగితే, శిష్యుడు పరుగెత్తుతూ తాగుతాడు.

If the Guru drink standing, the disciple will drink running.

According to Hindu practice, water should always be drunk sitting.

2315. గుర్రము తోకకు కళ్లెము పెట్టినట్టు.

Like putting the bridle on the horse's tail.

To put the cart before the horse.

2316. గుర్రము పేరు గోడ అయితే, జీని పేరు మదురు—ఇకను నాకు అంతా తెలుసును అన్నాడట.

If a horse is Gôḍa, then a saddle is Maduru—I don't want to be told more.

Said by a Kômaṭi who was learning Hindustani from a Mussalman at so much per word. He mistook *Ghoṛâ* (Hind.) " a horse" for *Gôḍa* (Tel.) " a wall," and with the stinginess common to his caste said he did not want to be told what a saddle was as it must be *Maduru* " coping."

2317. గుర్రానికి ముడ్డి మొండితే, ఆరిక కసువయినా తింటున్నది.

If a horse be starving it will eat even Ârika grass.

(For *Ârika* or *Âruga* see No. 92.—See No. 606.)

2318. గుసగుస యోచనలు గుడిశెలు తియ్యడానకు కారణము.

Whispered counsels are a cause of ruin [to others].

2319. గూట్లో దీపం, కుక్షిలో అన్నం.

[As soon as] the light [is] in the niche, [he puts his] food into his belly.

To save the oil.

2320. గొంతమ్మ కోరికలు.

Gontamma's wishes.

2321. గొడ్డుపోతును బిడ్డ కనమంటే, కంటుందా.

Will a barren woman bring forth a child at your bidding?

2322. గొఱ్ఱె యేడిస్తే తోడేలుకు విచారమా.

When the sheep cries will the wolf be grieved?

(See Nos. 389, 1333.)

2323. గోరు వాస్తే వేలంత, వేలు వాస్తే కాలంత, కాలు వాస్తే రోలంత, రోలు వాస్తే యెంత.

If the nail swell, [it will be] as big as the finger; if the finger swell, [it will be] as big as the leg; if the leg swell, [it will be] as big as a mortar; if the mortar swell, how big [will it be?]

Said in ridicule of a logician.

చ.

2324. చంద్రుణ్ని చూచి కుక్కలు మొరిగినట్టు.

Like dogs barking at the moon.

(See Nos. 40, 441, 682.)

2325. చక్కెర పందిట్లో తేనెవాన కురిశినట్టు.

Like honey raining on a sugar Pandili.

(For *Pandili* see No. 61—See Nos. 195, 1362, 1425, 1430, 1866.)

2326. చచ్చిన తర్వాత తెలుస్తుంది శెట్టిగారి బండాలము.

After his death the state of the Śeṭṭi's affairs will be known.

He is very close in his lifetime.

2327. చచ్చిన వాని తల తూర్పున వుంటేనేమి, పడమట వుంటేనేమి.

What does it matter whether a dead man's head lie towards the east or towards the west?

2328. చచ్చేటప్పుడు శంకరా శంకరా అన్నాడట.

When he was at the point of death he cried "Śankara! Śankara!" (Śiva.)

Deathbed repentance.

2329. చదువులలో మర్మమంతా చదివినాను అన్నాడట.

I have become acquainted with all the secret mysteries of learning.

The allusion is to the story of Prahlâda son of Hiraṇyakaśipa. The words of the Proverb are found in the Telugu translation of the Bhâgavata Purâṇa, (but not in the Sanscrit original,) as having been used by Prahlâda to his father.—(See Vishṇu Purâṇa Book I, Chapters 17—20.)

Said of a man who pretends to be learned.

2330. చదువూ లేదు, సంధ్యా లేదు, సంతానం మెండు.

[He has] no learning and [says] no prayers but [has] numerous issue.

Said of an ignorant, irreligious, sensual man.

2331. చవి మెరిగిన కుక్క చావగొట్టినా పోదు.

A dog attached [to his master] will not leave him though he be beaten [almost] to death.

2332. చింత లేదు, చింత లేకపోతే పులుసు లేదు.

"No matter" said one, "Then if there's no tamarind, there's no acid" said the other.

There is here a pun upon the word *Chinta* which means both "thought, sorrow" and also "tamarinds."

2333. చిదిగి పొదిగి చిన్నవానికి పెండ్లి చేశే వరకు పెద్దవాని పెండ్లాము పెద్దలలోకి పోయినదట.

When by saving and saving they married the younger son, the elder son's wife went to her ancestors.

2334. చినుకులకు చెరువులు నిండుతవా.

Will the tanks be filled by drizzling rain?

2335. చిన్నక్కను పెద్దక్కను, పెద్దక్కను చిన్నక్కను చేశే వాడు.

He makes the younger sister the elder, and the elder sister the younger.

(See No. 1082.)

Said of an unprincipled, untruthful man.

2336. చిన్న యిల్లు కట్టుకొని పెద్ద కాపురము చెయ్య వలెను.

Build a small house, and become great.

The Hindus consider it unlucky to commence housekeeping in a large house.

2337. చిన్నవాడి తండ్రి విద్వాంసుడు, చిన్నవాడు చదువుకొంటే అక్కర లోకి వస్తాడు.

The boy's father is a learned man, if the boy acquire learning he will be of use.

2338. చీకటి కొన్నాళ్లు, వెన్నెల కొన్నాళ్లు.

Darkness for some days, moonlight for some days.

(See Nos. 561, 568.)

Joy and sorrow are equally divided.

2339. చీమలు పెట్టిన పుట్టలు పాములకు యిరవు అవుతున్నవి.

Anthills raised by ants become the dwelling of snakes.

One enjoys what another has acquired.

2340. చూడక తిరగక చూస్తూ చెయ్య వలశినది.

Before seeing him, before he turns, and looking at him, you must do it.

i. e. Before you see the sun in the morning, before it passes the meridian, and at sunset you must perform *Sandhyâvandanam* (daily prayers).

2341. చూస్తే నీది, చూడకుంటే నాది.

If seen it's yours, if not seen it's mine.

The trick of a thief or a shoplifter who, if noticed, pretends that his intentions were not dishonest.

2342. చెడి చెన్నాపట్నం చేరు.

Ruined, go to Chennâpaṭṭaṇam.

To recover your fortune.

2343. చెప్పితే శిగ్గు, దాస్తే దుఃఖం.

If you tell it—shame; if you hide it—sorrow.

The allusion is to adultery.

2344. చెప్పులు చిన్నవి అని కాళ్లు తెగకోసుకో వచ్చునా.

Are you to cut your feet because your shoes are too small?

2345. చెరుకు వుండే చోటికి చీమలు తామే వస్తవి.

Ants come of themselves to the place where there is sugar-cane.

Where the carcase is, the ravens will gather.

2346. చెరువు నిండితే కప్పలు చేరుతవి.

When the tank fills, the frogs assemble.

2347. చెల్లని కాసు యెన్నడూ చెల్లదు, వల్లని మొగుడు యెన్నడూ వల్లడు.

Non-current cash will never pass [in currency]; an unloving husband will never love [his wife].

(For *Cash* [కాసు] See No. 613.)

2348. చోద్యాల సోమిదేవమ్మకు వాధ్యారి మొగుడు.

The fastidious Somidevi has a Veda-teacher for a husband.

(For *Somidevi* see No. 28.)

A pair of hypocrites.

జ.

2349. జరిగేమట్టుకు జయభేరి, జరగకపోతే రణభేరి.

As long as successful, the drum of victory; when unsuccessful, the war drum.

By smooth means if possible, if not, by force.

2350. జిల్లేడు చెట్టున పారిజాతములు పుట్టునా.

Will Pârijâta flowers grow on a Jillêḍu tree?

Pârijâta is the Nyctanthes Arbor Tristis, a very celebrated tree said to grow in Svarga, Indra's paradise (W. Elliot). *Jillêḍu* is the Calotropes Gigantea.

2351. జెముడుకు కాయలు వున్నవా నీడ వున్నదా.

Has the Jemuḍu fruit or shade?

Jemuḍu is the Euphorbia Tirucalli.

డ.

2352. డబ్బుకు వచ్చిన చెయ్యి వరహాకు వస్తుంది.

The hand which touches a Ḍabb, will touch a pagoda.

(For *Ḍabbu* see No. 1913.—See No. 2269.)

A man who is dishonest in trifles will not be scrupulous in greater matters.

He that will steal an egg will steal an ox.

2353. డబ్బుకూ ప్రాణానకూ లంకె.

There is a link between money and life.

2354. డబ్బా యివ్వను, డబ్బుమీది దుమ్మూ యివ్వను.

I won't give a Ḍabb, I won't give the dust on a Ḍabb.

(For *Ḍabbu* see No. 1913.)

ఢ.

2355. ఢిల్లీకి ఢిల్లి, పల్లెకు పల్లె.

Delhi to Delhi, village to village.

Great people with great, little with little.

త.

2356. తంగేటి జున్ను.

Honey in the Tangêḍu tree.

(For *Tangêḍu* see No. 1120.)

Easy to get at because the tree is small.

2357. తండ్రిని చంపపోయిన పాపము అత్తవారింటికి పోయి అంబటికట్ట తెగేవరకు వుంటే పోను.

The sin of intending to kill your father will be effaced if you go to your mother-in-law's house and stay there till the porridge dish is burst.

A man was in the habit of telling his friends when they enquired how his son progressed with his studies that he was very stupid and idle. This he did from a superstitious dread of his son being struck by the evil eye of an envious person if he praised him. The son, not understanding his father's motive and being greatly irritated, determined to kill him. He got upon a beam over his father's couch and was about to drop a large stone on his head when he fortunately overheard him explaining to his mother the reason of his strange conduct. The boy then came down and fell at his father's feet confessing his murderous intentions and begging for forgiveness and to be shown a way of expiating his sin. The father replied to him in the words of the Proverb, telling him he was to remain in his mother-in-law's house until the porridge dish was broken. He went, and after having been paid the usual attentions for a day or two was afterwards treated with rudeness and fed with poor fare. At last the butter milk was one day poured so roughly into his porridge that the side of it gave way. He was then released from his expiatory ordeal and returned home rejoicing!

2358. తద్దినము నాటి జంధ్యము.

The sacerdotal thread given on the day of obsequial rites.

(For *Taddinam* see No. 271.)

It is worn temporarily by Śûdras on such occasions.

Said of any temporary honor.

2359. తన నీడే తన పిశాచము.

His shadow is his devil.

Afraid of his own shadow.

2360. తన బంగారము కాకపోతే వన్నే లేదు, వురపూ లేదు.

If it is not his own gold, it has no colour and no touch (fineness.)

The purchaser depreciates the value of an article brought for sale.

2361. తనయుని పుట్టుక తల్లి యెరుగును.

The mother knows the birth of the son.

i. e. she knows who is his father.

2362. తన వారిని యెరగని మొర్రి తెడ్డు వున్నదా.

Is there a broken ladle which knows not its own people ?

(See No. 1937.)

A man serves his friends well.

2363. తప్పెట కొట్టిన వాడు దాసరి, శంఖం వూదినవాడు జంగము.

He who beats a drum is a Dâsari, he who sounds a conch is a Jangam.

(For *Dâsari* and *Jangam* see No. 111.)

2364. తల గట్టి, కడుపు గుల్ల.

Head solid, belly hollow.

(See No. 740.)

2365. తల తిరిగి అయినా కబళము నోటికి రావలెను.

Although it goes round the head yet the mouthful must come to the mouth.

2366. తల్లి చేసినది తనయులకు.

What a mother does, [falls] on her children.

(See No. 1047.)

If she sin, her children are disgraced.

2367. తల్లి బంగారు అయినా కంసలవాడు దొంగిలక మానడు.

Though the gold were his mother's, the goldsmith would not stick at stealing it.

2368. తల్లీ బిడ్డా వకటి అయినా, నోరూ కడుపూ వేరు.

Although the mother and child are one, the mouth and belly are separate.

Two men may be great friends, still their wants must be separately provided for.

2369. తవిటికి వచ్చిన చెయ్యే ధనముకు వస్తుంది.

The hand which touches bran, will touch money.

(See No. 2362.)

He that will steal a pin will steal a better thing.

2370. తాటోటుగానికి దధ్యన్నము, విశ్వాసముకలవానికి వేణ్ణీళ్ల అన్నము.

The knave gets rice and curds, the honest man gets rice and warm water.

The more rogue the more luck.

The devil's children have the devil's luck.

2371. తాడు అని యెత్తి పారవెయ్యనూ కూడదు, పాము అని దాటనూ కూడదు.

Thinking it a rope, you should not take it up and throw it away; thinking it a snake you should not step over it.

(See Nos. 6, 1553.)

A very difficult person to deal with.

2372. తాతా సంధ్యవచ్చునా అంటే, యిప్పుడు చదువుకొన్న నీకే రాకపోతే అరవైయేండ్లకు ముందు చదువుకొన్న నాకు వచ్చునా అన్నాడట.

" O grandfather! do you know your Sandhyâ," [asked a boy]; "If you who have just learnt it don't know it, can I who learnt it sixty years ago remember it?" [replied the old man.]

2373. తాను అనుభవించని అర్థము ధరణిపాలు.

Wealth unenjoyed returns to the earth.

2374. తాను పతివ్రత అయితే, బోగమింట కాపురము వుంటే యేమి.

If she herself be virtuous, what though she dwell in the house of a harlot?

If a man be upright it matters not if he be among bad men.

2375. తానే మాగని కాయ తన్నితే మాగునా.

Will a fruit which ripens not of itself ripen if you kick it?

Advice is thrown away upon the headstrong.

2376. తామసం తామసీ.

By anger a man is burnt up.

Anger punishes itself.

2377. తిట్టే నోరు కుట్టినా వూరకుండదు.

An abusive mouth will not be quiet though you sew it up.

(See No. 1066.)

2378. తిరిపెము యెత్తేవానికి పెరుగు అన్నముకు కరువా.

Will one who receives alms lack rice and curds?

2379. తిరునాళ్లకు పోతావా, తిండికి పోతావా.

Are you going for the festival (lit. holy days) or for the feast?

(See No. 1961.)

2380. తుపాకీ కడుపున ఫిరంగీ పుట్టినట్టు.

Like a cannon being born in the belly of a musket.

Great things from small.

2381. తురక వీధిలో సన్న్యాసి భిక్ష.

A Sannyâsî's alms in Mussulman street.

Not the place for him to go to.

2382. తెంపుల తాళ్లు, చిల్లుల కడవ.

A rope in pieces, a pot with holes.

Useless instruments.

2383. తెగించిన వానికి తెడ్డే ఆయుధము.

To the bold man his ladle is a weapon.

(See No. 1107.)

2384. తెలిశిన వారికి ముందరనే వున్నది మోక్షము.

Salvation awaits the wise.

2385. తెల్లగా వుంటే పాలు, నల్లగా వుంటే నీళ్లు.

If it's white it's milk, if it's dark it's water.

Said of a simple minded, guileless man.

2386. తేనె వున్న చోట యీగలు పోగవుతవి.

Flies collect in the place where there is honey.

2387. తోడేటిని గొర్రెల కాయపెట్టినట్టు.

Like putting a wolf to watch the sheep.

You give the wolf the wether to keep.

To entrust the sheep to the wolf. (Latin.)*

He sets the wolf to guard the sheep. (Italian.)†

2388. తోలు తియ్యకనే తొనలు మింగేవాడు.

One who swallows fruit without taking off the skin.

A glutton.

ద.

2389. దయలేని అత్తకు దండం పెట్టినా తప్పే.

If [the daughter-in-law] even salute her unkind mother-in-law, it's a fault.

(See No. 151.)

2390. దాగబోయి తలారి యింట్లో దూరినాడట.

He went to hide and entered the house of the village watchman.

To run into the Lion's mouth.

To break the Constable's head and take refuge with the Sheriff. (Spanish.)‡

---

* Ovem lupo committere.
† Egli dà le pecore in guardia al lupo.
‡ Descalabrar el alguacil, y accogerse al corregidor.

2391. దీపము వుండగా నిప్పుకు దేవులాడనేల.

When there is a lamp, why should you search for fire?

2392. దీపాన వెలిగించిన దివిటీ.

A torch lighted from a lamp.

Said of a great man sprung from a humble family.

2393. దున్నపోతు యీనినదంటే, చెంబు తేరా పాలు పితుకుదామన్నట్టు.

"The male buffalo has calved" cried one, "Then bring the pot and we'll milk him" replied the other.

(See Nos. 380, 1172.)

2394. దున్నలాగున కష్టపడి దొరలాగున తినవలెను.

One must work like a buffalo, and eat like a gentleman.

2395. దున్నిన పొలానకూ తాగిన గంజికీ సరి.

The rice water which he drank was equivalent to the field which he ploughed.

Pay proportionate to labor.

2396. దున్నే రోజులలో దేశం మీద పోయి కోత రోజులలో కొడవలి పట్టుకొని వచ్చినాడట.

In the ploughing season he went about the country, and at harvest time he came with his sickle.

(See No. 1171.)

2397. దున్నేవాడు లెక్క చూస్తే నాగలి కూడా మిగలదు.

If the plougher look into his accounts [he will find] that the plough even does not remain [as profit].

The expenses of cultivation.

2398. దుమ్ము పోశి అంబలి కాచినట్టు.

Like making porridge of dust.

Labour wasted in a hopeless scheme.

2399. దుర్మార్గముకు తండ్రి బద్ధకము.

Idleness is the father of vice.

Idleness is the root of all evil.

Idleness is hunger's mother, and of theft it is first brother. (Dutch.)*

2400. దూడ చస్తే కమ్మలం, గేదె చస్తే నిమ్మళం.

If the calf dies there will be Kammalam, if the she buffalo dies there will be quiet.

Kammalam, corrupted from the Tamil *Kaimûlam* (கைமூலம்) is a name given to milk drawn from a cow or buffalo which has lost its calf.

2401. దేవుడు యిస్తాడుగాని, వండి వార్చి వాత కొట్టుతాడా.

God gives [food] but does He cook and strain it and put in the mouth ?

(See No. 1153.)

God gives every bird its food, but does not throw it into the nest. (Danish.)†

2402. దేహము నీరుబుగ్గ వంటిది.

The body is like a water bubble.

Frail and transitory.

2403. దేహి అంటే నాస్తి అన రాదు.

If one say "Dehi" (give) you should not reply "Nâsti" (there is not).

Alms should never be refused.

---

* Ledigheid is hongers moeder, en van diefte volle broeder.

† Gud giver hver Fugl Sin Föde, men kaster den ei i Reden til ham.

2404. దొంగకు అందరిమీఁద అనుమానమే.

The thief suspects every one.

A thief thinks every man steals. (Danish.)*

2405. దొంగకు దొంగ బుద్ధి, దొరకు దొర బుద్ధి.

A thief has a thief's thoughts, a gentleman has a gentleman's thoughts.

2406. దొంగను దొంగ యెరుగును.

A thief is known by a thief.

A thief knows a thief, as a wolf knows a wolf.

2407. దొంగ వస్తానని ముందు చెప్పి వుంటే, సాక్షులను సంపాదించి వుందును.

If the thief had said before that he was coming, I would have obtained witnesses.

2408. దొంగవాడి దృష్టి మూట మీఁదనే.

The thief's eye is upon the bundle.

2409. దొంగిలించేటంత దొరతనము వుండగా, అడిగేటంత అన్యాయముకు లోబడుతానా.

When I have such power of stealing shall I submit to the injustice of asking?

Said by a thief.

2410. దొరలేని మూకలు.

Troops without a leader.

---

* Tyv taenker Hvermand stiaeler.

2411. ద్రావిడానాం ఘృతం నాస్తి, మిళ్లే మిళ్లే నిరంతరం.

There is no ghî among the Drâviḍas, [they serve it] always in spoonfuls.

Said by a Telugu man of the Tamilians who eat very little *ghî* with their food. *Miḷḷi* is a very small spoon used in offerings, &c., called in Sanscrit *Darvvi*.

ధ.

2412. ధర్మము తల కాచును.

Virtue protects the head.

The reward of virtue in this life is protection from evil.

2413. ధర్మమే జయము, దైవమే గతి.

Virtue alone is success, God alone is a refuge.

2414. ధూపం వేస్తే పాపం పోతున్నది.

If you offer incense, sin will be removed.

న.

2415. నక్కవాత మన్ను కొట్టినాడు.

He threw mud into the mouth of the jackal.

i. e. he cheated him.

Said of the surprising recovery of a sick man who had been given up, and whose body it was expected might provide food for the jackals.

2416. నక్కా నక్కా నా నామం చూడు, తిరిగి చూస్తే తిరుమణి చూడు.

O Jackal ! Jackal ! look at my Nâmam, if you look again see my Tirumani.

(For *Nâmam* see No. 789).—*Tirumaṇi* (lit. sacred earth) is the name given to the outer lines, made with white clay, of the *Nâmam*.

2417. నమ్మి నడివీధిలో వేశినవారు యెవరు.

Who throws [his property] into the middle of the street and trusts it there?

(See No. 2135.)

2418. నమ్మినాను రామన్నా అంటే, నట్టేట్లో ముంచుతాను లక్ష్మన్నా అన్నాడట.

"I trusted you O Râmanna!" said one "Then I'll drown you in the middle of the river O Lakshmanna!" replied his friend.

Misplaced confidence.

Trust makes way for treachery.

Trust, beware whom! (German.)*

Trust was a good man, Trust-not was a better. (Italian.)†

2419. నయము నష్టకారి, భయము భాగ్యకారి.

Leniency is injurious, severity is profitable.

Applied to children.

Spare the rod and spoil the child.

2420. నయానా భయానా.

By mildness or severity.

If one does not answer, the other must be tried.

2421. నల్ల పూసకు తెల్ల పూసా లేదు, తెల్ల పూసకు నల్ల పూసా లేదు.

For the black bead there is no white bead, and for the white bead there is no black bead.

Said by a wretchedly poor woman who could not afford to buy white beads when she had black, or black when she had white. The beads are strung alternately and used as a necklace by poor women who have not the means of getting gold or silver ornaments.—Hindu married women are not permitted to appear without some neck ornament however trifling the value of it may be.

---

* Traue, schaue Wem!

† Fidati era un buon uomo, Nonfidare era meglio.

2422. నల్లి నలిగి పోయినది, చెత్త కానము.

The bug is crushed but the remains are not to be seen.

Robbers' slang, referring to a murdered man.—*Chetta* means literally 'rubbish,' 'sweepings.'

2423. నవగ్రహాలు వక్రించి వున్నట్టు.

As if the nine planets were out of their course.

Said of a family at sixes and sevens.

2424. నవాబంత దరిద్రుడు, పులి అంత సాధువు.

As poor as a Nawâb, as mild as a tiger.

2425. నవ్వుతూ చేస్తున్నారు, యేడుస్తూ అనుభవిస్తున్నారు.

Laughing, they do it; weeping, they suffer for it.

(See No. 1947.)

Said of criminals.

2426. నాకు సొగసెందుకు, బాగుంటే సరి.

What do I care for beauty? If it is good it is enough.

2427. నాకూ బెబ్బేనా అంటే, నీకూ బెబ్బే నీ అబ్బకూ బెబ్బే అన్నాడట.

When he said "What! Bebbe to me?" "Yes, Bebbe to you and Bebbe to your father" was the reply.

A great man pressed by his creditors was advised by a friend, himself also a creditor, to escape from their importunities by feigning madness. He accordingly did so, replying to them all like an idiot "*Bebbe*." The plan was successful, and the friend then asked that *his* debt should be paid, but he himself received the treatment he had prescribed for others.

Trickery comes back to its master. (French.)*

---

* Tricherie revient à son maître.

2428. నాడు కట్టా లేదు, నేడు చించా లేదు.

Neither on that day did I put it on, nor on this day have I torn it.

(See No. 2429.)

Said by a poor fellow who had never had the pleasure of putting on a good cloth or the annoyance of tearing it.

2429. నాడు నిలువబడా లేదు, నేడు యెత్తుబడా లేదు.

I was never rich one day and poor another.

(See No. 2428.)

Said by a man who had not experienced the ups and downs of fortune, but had remained in a mediocre state throughout his life.

2430. నాడు వుంటే నవాబు సాయెబు, అన్నము వుంటే అమీరు సాయెబు, బీద పడితే ఫకీరు సాయెబు, చస్తే పీరు సాయెబు.

If he has a country, Nawâb Ṣâḥib; if he has food, Amîr Ṣâḥib; if he becomes poor, Faḳîr Ṣâḥib; when he dies Pîr Ṣâḥib.

The Mussulman sticks to his title of *Ṣâḥib* under all circumstances.

2431. నాడు వ్రాశినవాడు నేడు చెరిపి మళ్లీ వ్రాస్తాడా.

Will he who wrote at that time, now cancel it and write again?

(See Nos. 1344, 1837.)

2432. నాభిలో పుట్టిన పురుగు వంటివాడు.

One like a worm born in the Nâbhi.

Nâbhi (Sans. *Vatsanâbha*) is an active vegetable poison, 'the root of the Aconite ferox brought from Nepâl' (Wilson).

Said of a treacherous villain.

2433. నా ముందర నీవేమి బ్రతక గలవు అన్నట్టు.

How can you live before me?

What are you when compared with me?

Said by a conceited Paṇḍit.

2434. నారిగాడు—నారడు—నారాయడు—నారాయ—నారయ్య—నారాయణయ్య—నారాయణరావు—నారాయణరావుపంతులు—నారాయణరావుపంతులవారు.

Nârigâḍu—Nâraḍu—Nârâyaḍu—Nârâya—Nârayya—Nârâyaṇayya—Nârâyaṇa Râu—Nârâyaṇa Râu Pantulu—Nârâyaṇa Râu Pantulavâru.

When a person is in a very indigent state he is called by the first name (Nârigâḍu) and he receives the other names—each form being more respectful than the last—as he advances in social position. The highest position he could possibly attain to would give him the last and most honorific form (Nârâyaṇa Râu Pantulavâru).

2435. నిన్న వున్నవారు నేడు లేరు.

They who yesterday were to-day are not.

The uncertainty of life.

To-day stately and brave, to-morrow in the grave. (Danish.)*

2436. నిప్పున కాలడు, నీళ్లను తడియడు.

He won't be burnt with fire, he won't be wet with water.

Said of an obstinate blockhead.

2437. నిలకడ లేనివాని మాట నీళ్లమూట.

The word of an unstable man is a bundle of water.

(See No. 170.)

A fool's speech is a bubble of air.

2438. నీకు యెక్కడ సంశయమో నాకు అక్కడ సందేహము.

Where you are doubtful, there I am dubious.

A joke among Paṇḍits when one is not able to help another through difficult passages.

2439. నీ పెండ్లాము ముండమోస్తే, నీకు యెవరు అన్నము వండిపెట్టుతారు అన్నాడట.

If your wife becomes a widow, who will cook for you?

(See No. 1603.)

---

* Heden in figuur, morgen in het graf.

2440. నీ బఱ్ఱె గొడ్డును యెవరు కాస్తారు చూతాము అంటే, నా తిత్తి లోని డబ్బే కాస్తున్నది అన్నాడట.

"Who will watch your buffalo?" said [a herdsman]—"The money in my purse will do it" replied [the master].

A fit answer to an impertinent servant.

2441. నీళ్లమీద వ్రాసిన మాట.

A word written on water.

2442. నీవు తలిచినప్పుడు బిడ్డ కనవలెను.

When you wish for it, I must bring forth a child.

Said by a wife to an unreasonable, exacting husband.

2443. నువ్వులకు తగిన నూనె.

Oil according to the [quantity of] Sesamum.

(For *Nuvvu* see No. 1819—see No. 1486.)

2444. నూటికి పెట్టి కోటికి గొరిగించేవాడు.

One who feeds a hundred and shaves (i. e. plunders) a crore.

2445. నూటికి పొడిచి శెలగో అనే వాడు.

He kills a hundred and cries "Śelaga !"

Śelaga **is a term used in counting or measuring, signifying the completion of a lot of one hundred.**

Said of a great hero.

2446. నూరు అయ్యేవరకు నన్ను కాపాడితే, నూరు అయిన వెనక నిన్ను కాపాడుతాను.

Save me up to a hundred, and after that I will support you.

Money's advice.

Take care of the pence, the pounds will take care of themselves.

2447. నెయ్యి అని తాగా కూడదు, నూనె అని తలకు పూసుకోనూ కూడదు.

Thinking it to be Ghî you must not drink it, thinking it to be oil you must not rub it on your head.

(See Nos. 6, 1553, 2871.)

2448. నేర్పుగల అమ్మ నేతితో అతిరసములు కాలిస్తే, ఓర్పుగల అమ్మ ఒళ్లో కట్టుకొని పోయినదట.

When the clever lady had fried the cakes in Ghî, the patient lady walked off with them in her lap.

Atirasam is a sweet cake made of rice meal and syrup and fried, or rather boiled, in *ghî*.

A cool trick.

2449. నొచ్చిపోయిన వాడా నువ్వులు చల్లుము అన్నట్టు.

O unfortunate man! sow Sesamum.

Advice given to a farmer very unfortunate in his crops. The Sesamum crop is generally profitable.

2450. నొసట వ్రాసిన వ్రాలకన్నా, నూరేండ్లు చింతించినా యేమీ లేదు.

Though you think for a hundred years you will get no more than has been written on your forehead.

(See Nos. 1344, 1687.)

2451. నోరు వుంటే పోరు గెలుస్తాడు.

If he has a mouth he'll win the fight.

(See No. 1850.)

ప.

2452. పండగనాడూ పాత మొగుడేనా.

What! my old husband on the feast day?

When everything else is new.

A joke.

ఆంధ్రలోకోక్తిచంద్రికాశేషము.

2453. పందికి పెడతలబుద్ధి.

A pig's sense is in its occiput.

(See No. 436.)

2454. పంది యెంత బలిసినా నందితో సమమవునా.

However fat the pig may grow will it ever be equal to Nandi?

(For *Nandi* see No. 1364—see Nos. 609, 1066.)

2455. పగలు తల్లి, రాత్రి భార్య, అనే వాడు.

He calls her a mother in the day time and a wife at night.

An unprincipled rascal.

2456. పగలు పక్కచూచి మాట్లాడు, రాత్రి అదీ మాట్లాడ వద్దు.

When you speak in the day time, look around; at night don't speak at all.

Hills see, walls hear. (Spanish.)*

2457. పగలు రేజీకటి, రాత్రి హుటాహుటి.

Night blindness in the day time, running about at night.

(See Nos. 304, 486, 2021.)

2458. పట్టు కత్తిరించినట్టు మాట్లాడ వలెను.

You should speak as silk is cut.

i. e. give a decided answer, as unmistakable as the cut of silk is clean.

2459. పడవ వొడ్డు చేరితే, పడవ వాని మీద వక సొడ్డు.

When the boat reached the shore the ferry-man was made a fool of.

(See No. 1953.)

2460. పడుకోవడము పాడుగోడల్లో, కలవరింతలు మిద్దెటిండ్లల్లో.

Sleeping within ruined walls, but talking in his sleep of upper storied houses.

---

* Montes veen, paredes oyen.

2461. పరుల సొమ్ము పేలపిండి, తన సొమ్ము దేవుడి సొమ్ము.

The property of others is Pêlapindi, his own property is the property of God.

It is kept as sacred as that which has been offered to the deity.—*Pêlapindi* is flour made of fried grain.

(See Nos. 8, 910, 1121, 1396, 1580, 1740.)

2462. పాడి ఆవును దానము చేసి పాలు మాత్రము పితుకుకొన్నట్టు.

Like making a present of a milch cow and merely milking her for himself afterwards.

2463. పాత దొంగ వొక్క రోజున దొరకక మానడు.

The old thief will be one day caught.

(See No. 551.)

2464. పాపము వుంటే భయము, పల్లము వుంటే నీళ్లు.

Where there is sin there will be fear, where there is low ground there will be water.

2465. పాముకు బదనిక చూపినట్టు.

Like showing Badanika to a snake.

Badanika is the Loranthus Longiflorus; the term is also applied generally to all plants of the order. (W. Elliot.) It is said to be used as an antidote for snake bites.

2466. పాముకు విషము పండ్లలోనే వున్నది.

A snake's poison is in its fangs.

Said of a man ready for any villainy.

2467. పాము చిన్నది అయినా వకటే, పెద్దది అయినా వకటే.

A snake is the same whether small or big.

2468. పాముతో చెలిమి రాజుతో చెలిమి వొక్కటే.

Friendship with a snake and friendship with a king are one.

Both treacherous.

2469. పిండికి తగ్గ పిడచ.

A lump according to the flour.

(See No. 1436.)

2470. పిడుగుకు గొడుగు అడ్డమా.

Will an umbrella stop a thunderbolt?

2471. పిడుగు పడడానకు వారశూలా.

Is there a bad day of the week for the falling of the thunderbolt?

Does the thunderbolt observe auspicious and inauspicious days?

(See No. 2536.)

2472. పిల్లకు సొమ్ము పెట్టి చూడు, గోడకు సున్నము పెట్టి చూడు.

Adorn the child and look at it, whitewash the wall and look at it.

2473. పిల్లకోసరం గడ్డి తింటారు.

They make themselves fools for a child.

Lit. They eat grass.

Foolish vows are made and silly ceremonies performed to propitiate the gods and obtain children.

2474. పుంజం పెట్టినది బట్ట, లంచం పెట్టినది మాట.

That is a cloth into which Punjam has been put, that is the word into which a bribe has been put.

A *Punjam* is a skein of 60 threads; the word is here used to signify the proper quantity of thread required for good cloth.

The only way of obtaining a good recommendation is to purchase it with a bribe.

2475. పుట్టు వాసనా, పెట్టు వాసనా.

Is this natural fragrance, or borrowed perfume?

Said of a man of great pretensions but of no real learning.

2476. పుట్టు శాస్త్రులా, పెట్టు శాస్త్రులా.

Is he a born Śâstrî or a deplomated Śâstrî ?

Said also of a *Somayâjî* (No. 2053).

2477. పుణ్యానికి పోతే, పాపము యెదురుగా వచ్చినది.

When he went to do good, evil met him.

(See No. 323.)

2478. పులికి ఆకలి అయితే, గడ్డి తింటున్నదా.

Though the tiger be hungry will it eat grass ?

2479. పూలు అమ్మిన చోట పుడకలు అమ్మినట్టు.

Like selling firewood where flowers were sold.

(See No. 2301.)

2480. పూచిన పూలెల్లా కాయలయితే, భూమి పట్టడానకు స్థలము వుండదు.

If all the flowers which blossom should become fruit, there would be no room for the earth to hold them.

2481. పెండ్లి సందట్లో బొట్టుకట్ట మరిచినాడట.

In the bustle of the marriage he forgot to tie on the Boṭṭu.

(For *Boṭṭu* or *Tâliboṭṭu* see No. 878.)

2482. పెట్ట కూస్తే పుంజు కేరుతున్నది.

When the hen clucks, the cock chucks.

2483. పెన్న రావడం వెన్న కరిగేలోపల.

The coming down of the Penna is quicker than butter melts.

(For *Penna* see No. 1538.)

2484. పెరగగా పెరగగా పెదబావగారు కోతి అయినాడు.

Growing and growing the big brother-in-law became a monkey.

2485. పొమ్మనలేక పొగ పెట్టినట్టు.

Not being able to tell him to go he smoked him out.

2486. పొయ్యి వూదినమ్మకు బొక్కెడయినా దక్కదా.

Will she who blows the fire not even get a mouthful?

(See No. 1965.)

He is a very bad manager of honey who leaves nothing to lick off his fingers. (French.)*

He who manages other people's wealth does not go supperless to bed. (Italian.)†

2487. పొర్లించి పొర్లించి కొట్టుతూ వుండగా, మీసాలకు మన్ను తగల లేదు అన్నట్టు.

When he was being rolled over and over and beaten, he said that earth had not stuck to his mustaches.

Said by a defeated coward.

2488. ప్రాణము వుండే వరకు భయము లేదు.

As long as life remains, there is no fear.

Until the destined period of life has come to a close death need not be feared.

While there is life there is hope.

2489. ప్రాతస్సంధ్యావందన అర్ధ హృదయపాఠ అర్ధ పుస్తకపాఠ, మధ్యాహ్నసంధ్యావందన నమగూ తెలియదు నమ్మ ఆచారరిగూ తెలియదు, సాయంసంధ్యావందన యథోచిత.

Of the morning Sandhyâ, half is known in my heart, and half is known by the book; the noon Sandhyâ is neither known to me nor to my priest; as for the evening Sandhyâ I don't know it very well.

i. e. He did not know a word of it.

---

* Celui gouverne bien mal le miel, qui n'en taste et ses doightz n'en lèche.

† Chi maneggia quel degli altri, non va a letto senza cena.

2490. ప్రొద్దున వచ్చిన బంధువూ వానా నిలవవు.

A relation and rain coming in the morning don't stay.

బ.

2491. బంగారు ముచ్చెలు అయినా కాళ్లనే తొడగ వలెను.

Though the slippers be of gold they can only be worn on the feet.

2492. బంగీ తిన్న కోతివలె తిరుగుతాడు.

He runs about like a Bhanged monkey.

(For *Bhang* see No. 1034.)

2493. బంధువుడవు సరే గాని, పయిరులో చెయ్యి పెట్ట వద్దు.

It is true you are a relative, but don't put your hand into the corn.

i. e. I won't allow you even to pluck the ears.

(See No. 874.)

2494. బట్ట తలకు పేలు పట్టినట్టు.

Like lice infesting a bald head.

2495. బయిట తన్ని యింట్లో కాళ్లు పట్టుకొన్నట్టు.

Kicking [a man] when out of doors and falling at his feet in the house.

Disgracing him in public and cringing to him in private.

2496. బఱ్ఱె అమేధ్యము తింటే, పాలు చెడుతున్నవా.

Though the she-buffalo eat filth, will the milk be spoilt ?

2497. బలవంతాన పిల్లను యిస్తానంటే, కులమేమి గోత్రమేమి అని అడిగినాడట.

When one offered his daughter unasked to another, he was answered "What is your caste and what is your Gotra ?"

When a man goes out of his way to make an unusual offer, his intentions are apt to be suspected.

2498. బహునాయకం, బాలనాయకం, స్త్రీనాయకం.

Having many leaders, having a youthful leader, having a female leader.

Said of people, an army, &c.

2499. బాధకు వక కాలము, భాగ్యానికి వక కాలము.

A time for misfortune, a time for fortune.

(See Nos. 561, 568.)

2500. బాపడికి పప్పాశ, అత్తకు అల్లుడాశ.

The Brahman is fond of Dâl, the mother-in-law is fond of her son-in-law.

(For *Dâl* see No. 189.)

2501. బాపన వావి బండ వావి.

The Brahmans' rule for intermarrying is a disgusting rule.

(For *Vâvi* see No. 1947.)

2502. బిచ్చపు కూటికి పేదరికమా.

Is there any poverty in a beggar's food ?

Does he feel any want ?

2503. బుట్టలో పాము వలె అణిగినాడు.

He sank down like a snake in a basket.

i. e. his pride was humbled.

A snake charmer's covered basket is here referred to.

2504. బురద గుంటలో పడ్డ పేడ పురుగు వత్తు.

Like a beetle (*lit.* a cowdung worm) fallen into a mire pit.

Said of a man being in an harassing service from which he cannot escape, &c.

2505. బూరుగ పంటికి చిలుక కాచి వున్నట్టు.

Like a parrot waiting [to eat] a Bûrugu pod.

Bûrugu or *Bûraga* is the silk cotton tree (Eriodendron Anfractuosum).

Vain expectations.

2506. బెల్లము పారవేసి ఆకు నాకినట్టు.

Like throwing away the molasses and licking the leaf.

2507. బెల్లము వుండే చోట యీగలు ముసురుతున్నవి.

In the place where there is molasses flies swarm.

(See No. 2345.)

Daub yourself with honey, and you'll be covered with flies.

2508. బొజ్జను నమ్మి యేట పడ్డట్టు.

Trusting to his corpulency and throwing himself into the river.

2509. బొట్టు కట్టితేనేగాని, ముండ మొయ్యదు.

Unless the Boṭṭu be tied, she cannot become a widow.

(For *Boṭṭu* or *Tâliboṭṭu* see No. 878.)

Fortune must come before misfortune.

2510. బోడితలకూ మోకాటికీ ముడి పెట్టినట్టు.

Like tying a bald head and the knee in a knot.

2511. బోశి నోటి వానికి పేలపిండిమీద ప్రీతి.

A toothless fellow likes Pêlapiṇḍi.

(For *Pêlapiṇḍi* see No. 2461.)

2512. బ్రహ్మ వ్రాశిన వ్రాలకు యేడవనా, రాగల సంకటికి యేడవనా.

Am I to weep on account of the writing written by Brahmâ? Am I to weep on account of the coming Sankaṭi? *

Sankaṭi is a coarse porridge generally made with *Çôḷḷu* (Eleusine Coracana) commonly called *Râgi*.

భ.

2513. భయమెంతో అంత కోట కట్టుకో వలశినది.

According to your fear, so you must build your fort.

2514. భార్య చేతి పంచభక్ష్యపరమాన్నములకన్నా తల్లి చేతి తవిటి రొట్టె నయము.

Bran-bread from the hand of a mother is better than the five cakes and rich food from the hand of a wife.

Pañchabhakshyam are five kinds of cakes.—*Paramânnam* is a rich dish of rice boiled with milk, sugar, spices, &c.

2515. భిక్షాధికారి అయినా కావలె, లక్షాధికారి అయినా కావలె.

One must be a master of alms or a master of lakhs.

i. e. either a beggar or a very rich man.

మ.

2516. మంచి చేసిన ముంగికి మరణము సంభవించినట్టు.

Although it did a good act, death overtook the Mongoose.

The Mongoose tore in pieces a snake which approached a sleeping child. The mother, who had been out, met the little animal covered with the blood of the snake and killed it, thinking it had killed her son.—(See *Telugu Selections* 20th story.)

2517. మంచివానికి వక మాట, మూర్ఖునికి వక చేట.

A word to a good man, [a blow with] a sieve for an obstinate blockhead.

(See No. 1661.)

A blow with a sieve, a broom, or a slipper is very degrading.

2518. మందూ లేదు గుండూ లేదు, తుపాకీ పట్టి కాల్చుము అన్నట్టు.

Like saying "Take the gun and shoot" when there is no powder and no ball.

2519. మడ్డి ముండకు మల్లెపూలు యిస్తే, మడిచి ముడ్డికింద పెట్టుకొన్నదట.

When Jasmine flowers were given to a boorish woman, she folded them up and sat on them.

Instead of putting the garland round her neck.—*Malle* (prop. Jasminum Sambac) is a general name given to all common jasmines (W. Elliot.)

2520. మణి మణితో కొయ్య వలెను.

You must cut a gem with a gem.

2521. మతులు యెన్ని చెప్పినా మంకుబుద్ధి మానదు.

However much advice you give her, she will not mend her stubbornness.

(See No. 784.)

2522. మన బంగారము మంచిదయితే, కంసాలి యేమి చెయ్యగలడు.

If our gold be good, what can the goldsmith do?

The purest gold is the most easily tested, and a goldsmith cannot easily cheat with it.

A good character is proof against slander.

2523. మనసెరుగని అబద్ధము వున్నదా.

Is there a lie unknown to the heart?

(See No. 465.)

2524. మనస్సుకు మనస్సే సాక్షి.

The mind is witness to the mind.

i. e. A man is judged by his own conscience.

2525. మనువు చెడి ముండ బుద్ధిమంతురాలయినది.

When the good match was broken off, the jade became wise.

2526. మనువును నమ్మి, బొంత బోర్లవేసుకొన్నదట.

Trusting to the good match, she turned every thing topsy turvy.

But she was disappointed after all.

2527. మనుష్యులు వుండరుగాని, మాటలు వుంటున్నవి.

Men remain not, but words last.

2528. మన్ను పెట్టితే బంగారము, బంగారము పెట్టితే మన్ను.

You get gold out of earth and earth out of gold.

i. e. you buy land with money.

2529. మరిచిపోయి చచ్చినాను ప్రాణమా రమ్మంటే, తిరిగీ వచ్చునా.

If one says "O life! I died by mistake, come back," will the life return?

2530. మాటకు మాట శృంగారము, పేటకు కోట శృంగారము.

A word is the ornament of a word, a fort is the ornament of a town.

2531. మాటలు యెన్నిచెప్పినా, మామగారి పొత్తు వదలను అన్నదట.

However much you talk, I won't give up eating with my maternal uncle.

Said by a woman who had been brought up from childhood by her uncle.

Force of habit.

Continuance becomes usage. (Italian.)*

2532. మాదిగవాడి ఆలు అయినా మాడే కాలికి చెప్పు లేదు.

Though a shoemaker's wife, she has no shoes for her burning feet.

A shoemaker's wife and a smith's mare are always the worst shod.

2533. మాధుకరి వాని యింటికి వుపాదానం వాడు పోయినట్టు.

Like the raw rice beggar going to the house of the boiled rice beggar.

Some beggars will only receive raw rice which they cook for themselves, others receive boiled rice.

2534. మా పిల్లవానికి ముప్ఫయిరెండు గుణములు వున్నవిగాని, రెండు మాత్రము తక్కువ.

My boy has the thirty-two qualities, only he is two short.

---

* Continuanza diventa usanza.

2535. మామతోకూడా మంచము అల్లి తాతతోకూడా తడిక కట్టడానకు వచ్చినదట.

Having woven the cot with her maternal uncle, she came to put up the mat with her grandfather.

2536. మారికి వారశూలా.

Will Mâri care for a 'bad day'?

(For *Mâri* see No. 1672.—See No. 2471.)

2537. మాలిస్తు చేశినట్టే వుండవలె, కాపు చెడ్డట్టే వుండవలె.

One must be threshing, and the master must be cheated.

Said by a dishonest servant.

2538. మాశిమీద మాశి ఎక్కి కూర్చుంటే, మోశి మోశి చచ్చినాను అన్నాడట.

"When a man gets up and sits on a man, the weight kills me" said he.

A stupid lout was persuaded by his wife to go and hear the Râmâyaṇa read as she thought it might improve his mind. While standing leaning his head on his stick, a scamp got upon his shoulders and sat there. The blockhead thought this was a necessary part of the performance. When he returned home he was asked how he liked the Râmâyaṇa and replied as above.

2539. మాశీ పెద్దా మాశీ వుండావు, బుద్ధీ గాడ్దె బుద్ధీ వుండాది.

To look at you are a great man, but you are a mean fellow at heart.

Lit. You have the sense of an ass.

2540. మా సేన బొమణి నక్కలు గూసెఁ.

Bomaṇi jackals cried in our army.

A reader complained that he received less pay than an expounder. He was told that much less learning was required. On the next occasion he read the Ândhrabhârata in such a manner that the expounder was completely puzzled. The passage, correctly written, is as follows :—

క॥ మాసె నభోమణి నక్కలు। గూసెఁ.

The sun *(Nabhomaṇi)* turned dark ; the jackals cried.

Which was interpreted in the above ridiculous manner.

2541. మా సొమ్ము మాకిచ్చుట మడి మాన్యములిచ్చుట.

Giving me back my own money will be giving me glebe land.

Said by a creditor.

2542. మిగిలిన సున్నాన్ని మెగిలిన రాజునూ వదల రాదు.

You must not desert the leavings of chunam or a deposed king.

The chunam will be wanted again to eat with betel leaf (See No. 823). The king, if restored to power, will reward those who were faithful to him in adversity.

2543. మితము తప్పితే అమృతమయినా విషమే.

If you exceed the bounds of moderation nectar too is poison.

2544. మీ గురువులు మా శిష్యులవద్దనే చదువుకొన్నారు.

Your Guru learnt from my pupils.

Said in a disputation between two rival Paṇḍits.

2545. ముండ్లమీద పడ్డ గుడ్డ మెల్లగా తీసుకో వలెను.

The cloth which has fallen upon thorns must be taken off slowly.

2546. ముందరి కాళ్లకు బందాలువేశి ముండల తాళ్లు తెంపేవాడు.

A man who ties the fore legs together and breaks the widows' cords.

Said of a crafty swindler, who having made his victim as helpless as an animal whose fore feet have been tied together proceeds to plunder. Widows wear no cords (See No. 1415) ; the expression signifies a state of helplessness.

2547. ముందు చూస్తే అయ్యవారి గుర్రముగా వున్నది, వెనక చూస్తే సాయెబు గుర్రముగా వున్నది.

Looking from the front it seems to be the Brahman's horse, looking from behind it seems to be the Ṣâḥib's.

The Kômaṭi's evidence (See No. 729). The words are ambiguous and bear another meaning viz. " Before, this was the Brahman's horse—now, it is the Ṣâḥib's" (i. e. the Ṣâḥib has taken possession of it).

2548. ముందు వచ్చినందుకు మున్నూరు వరహాలు దండుగ, మళ్లీ యేల వచ్చినావే మాయధారి తొత్తా.

When you came before you cost me three hundred pagodas, why have you come again, you deceitful jade ?

A man married a bad wife. After getting 300 pagodas' worth of jewels frôm him she went off to her mother's house and left her husband to shift for himself. After some time, the jewels having been sold and the proceeds spent, she returned to try her old trick, whereupon the husband accosted her as above.

2549. ముక్కు పట్టుకొంటే ప్రాణము పోనా.

If I touch your nose will you lose your life ?

A Guru was endeavouring to initiate his disciple into the mysteries of *Prâṇâyâma* (see Wilson) and touched his nose which the unwilling disciple pretended caused him intense pain. " This ceremony is performed in the following manner : 1st he [the Brahman] presses in the right nostril with the fourth finger of his left hand, repeating the name of each Deity ; and counting them nine times over upon the joints of the fingers of his right hand with great rapidity, half closing his eyes the while, and drawing in his breath : then gently pressing in the left nostril with the thumb, he breathes out, repeating the same name as many times over. Then releasing the right nostril, and still pressing in the left with the thumb, he terminates the Prunayama [*Prâṇâyâma.*]" (*The Sundhya* by Mrs. S. C. Belnos.)

Said of a lazy sculk.

2550. ముగ్గురు ఆడవారు కూడితే, పట్టపగలే చుక్కలు పొడుస్తవి.

When three women join together the stars come out in broad daylight.

The above is taken from the following verse :—

క॥ జగములు వణకవె యొకతెకు।
నగణితముగ నిద్దరయిన నంబుధులింకున్।
ముగురాడ వారు గూడిన।
సుగుణాకర పట్టపగలు చుక్కలు పొడుచున్॥

[At the sight] of one woman, will not the worlds tremble? When there are two the oceans will greatly sink ; when three women join together the stars will appear in broad daylight, O Possessor of good qualities !

2551. ముదికొమ్మ వంగదు.

The old bough will not bend.

(See No. 901.)

It is not easy to straighten in the oak the crook that grew in the sapling. (Gaelic.)

2552. ముదిరి చచ్చినా, తొండి యిడిశినా వగపు లేదు.

If [a man] ripens and dies, if [the grain] goes into pieces there is no grief.

When a man dies at a good old age, his relations do not greatly grieve for him; and if grain goes into pieces when pounded on account of overdryness, people do not care much, as the grit is nearly as good as the whole grain.

2553. ముద్దున పేరు చెడె, మురిపాన నడుపు చెడె.

The name is spoilt by affection, the gait is spoilt by strutting.

A child's proper name is corrupted into a familiar name as *Śinayya* for Śrînivâsayya, *Kakkâi* for Kanakamma, &c.

2554. ముప్ఫయి మూడు కోట్ల దేవతలూ కూడి ముక్కు పట్టించగలరు గాని, నారాయణా అనిపించ గలరా.

Thirty-three crores of gods joined together can make me hold my nose, but can they make me say Nârâyaṇa?

(See No. 1835.)

You cannot make an ass drink if he is not thirsty. (French.)*

You may force a man to shut his eyes but not to sleep. (Danish.)†

2555. ముప్ఫయి యేండ్లు కష్టము అనుభవించినవాడూ లేదు, ముప్ఫయి యేండ్లు సుఖము అనుభవించినవాడూ లేదు.

There is no one who has suffered thirty years of trouble, there is no one who has enjoyed thirty years of happiness.

2556. ముసలివాడికి ముండ ముద్దు.

An old man is fond of women.

---

* On ne saurait faire boire un âne s'il n'a pas soif.

† Man kan nöde en Mand til at blunde, men ikke til at sove.

2557. మూడు జన్మాల సంగతి చెప్పగలను; పూర్వ జన్మమునందు యిచ్చి పెట్టుకో లేదు గనుక యీ జన్మమునందు దేవుడు నాకు యివ్వ లేదు, యీ జన్మాన వకరికి యివ్వలేను గనుక ముందు జన్మా నకు నాకు యేమీా లేదు.

I can tell my state in three births—in the last I laid up nothing by generosity, in this God has given me nothing, and as I can give to no one here there is nothing for me in the next birth.

2558. మెతుకులు చల్లితే కాకులకు తక్కువా.

If you scatter grains [of boiled rice] will there be any lack of crows ?

(See Nos. 2345, 2507.)

2559. మెత్తనాళ్లు పోయినవి, చెత్తనాళ్లు వచ్చినది.

The days of bedding are gone, the days of straw have come.

The reverses of fortune.

2560. మేకును పెరికిన కోతి వలె.

Like the monkey that drew out the wedge.

" ' You know the story of the Monkey, don't you ?' [said Karaṭaka].

" The Monkey drew the sawyer's wedge, and died :
Let meddlers mark it, and be edified."

' No !' said Damanaka. ' How was it ?

' In this way,' answered Karataka :—

' In south Behar, close by the retreat of Dhurmma, there was an open plot of ground, upon which a temple was in course of erection, under the management of a man of the Kayeth caste named Subhadatta. A carpenter upon the works had partly sawed through a long beam of wood, and wedged it open, and was gone away, leaving the wedge fixed. Shortly afterwards a large herd of Monkeys came frolicking that way, and one of their number, directed doubtless by the Angel of death, got astride the beam, and grasped the wedge, with his tail and lower parts dangling down between the pieces of the wood. Not content with this, in the mischief natural to monkeys, he began to tug at the wedge ; till at last it yielded to a great effort and came out ; when the wood closed upon him, and jammed him all fast. So perished the monkey, miserably crushed ; and I say again,—

" Let meddlers mark it and be edified." "

(Arnold's *Book of Good Counsels from the Hitopadesa* pp. 49, 50.)

2561. మొండికి తగ్గ మిండడు.

A master fit for a skulk.

2562. మొగుడు చచ్చిన వెనక ముండకు బుద్ధి వచ్చినది.

After her husband's death, the jade came to her senses.

(See No. 2525.)

2563. మొగుడు లేని దానికి మంత్రసాని యెందుకు.

What does a woman without a husband want with a midwife ?

2564. మొదట మానెడు, దూడ చస్తే దుత్తెడు.

At first one Mânika, after the calf's death a potful [of milk].

(For *Mânika* see No. 1704.)

2565. మొదలు మోదుగ పూస్తే, కొన సంపెంగ పూచునా.

Will [a branch] bear Môduga flowers at one end and Sampenga at the other ?

Môduga is the Butea Frondosa, the flowers of which have no perfume. *Sampenga* is the Michelia Champaca.

2566. మోకాల్లో మెడ నరం పట్టినది.

A neck-sprain in the knee.

Like saying " He has a head-ache in his big toe."

2567. మోకాలు మునిగినది అని ముక్కు ముంచుకొంటారా.

Because the water is up to the knee are we to plunge above the nose ?

Because we experience a little difficulty, are we to give way to despair ?

2568. మోటకు కోపము ముక్కుమీద.

The rough man's anger is on his nose.

Said of a very bad tempered man.

2569. మోహము లేకపోతే, మోదము లేదు.

Where there is no love, there is no delight.

య.

2570. యథాయథలందరూ వెల్లువను పోగా, పుల్లాకు నా పని యేమి అన్నదట.

After all the great men had been carried away by the flood, the leaf dish said "What is to become of me ?"

(See No. 745.)

2571. యథార్థమునకు యేడు చుట్లు అక్కర లేదు.

For the truth seven twists are not required.

When you tell the truth you can be outspoken.

Truth seeks no corners. (Latin.)*

2572. యుగాలనాటి యుధిష్ఠిరుడు.

A Yudhishṭhira of the olden days.

Applied, ironically, to a great liar.

He shall have the king's horse.

2573. యోగికీ రోగికీ భోగికీ నిద్రలేదు.

There is no sleep for an ascetic, a sick man, or a rake.

ర.

2574. రాగము రానివాడూ రోగము లేనివాడూ లేదు.

There is no one who cannot hum a tune, there is no one free from disease.

(See No. 843.)

---

* Veritas non quaerit angulos.

2575. రాజాం కాయ పిచ్చికొండ, యా మన్నగారికి భసా పంకం.

"O king! accept this cocoanut" [said one,] "My elder brother is agitated at [the sight of] the Royal Court" [said the other.]

There were two clerical Brahman brothers who were very poor, but well versed in the Vedas. Vexed at their poverty, they proposed to go to the king, present him with a cocoanut and obtain a present in return. Having arrived at Court, the elder brother held out the cocoanut to the king and attempted to say రాజా టెంకాయ పుచ్చుకోండి *(Râjâ ṭenkâya puççukonḍi)* "O king! accept the cocoanut" but being quite confused, mumbled nonsensically రాజాం కాయ పిచ్చికొండ *(Râjân kâya pichchikonḍa)*. The younger brother attempted to apologize but was equally flurried and stammered out యా మన్నగారికి భసాపంకం *(Yâ mannagâriki bhasâpankam)* instead of saying మా అన్నగారికి సభాకంపం *(Mâ annagâriki sabhâkampam)* "my elder brother is agitated at [the sight of] the Royal Court." The king was greatly amused and gave them each a present.

2576. రాజీకా సౌదా.

A bargain with the consent [of both parties.] (Hind.)

i. e. the purchaser and the seller.

In the days of Muhammadan Government free trade was unknown and the poor were forced to sell at the prices fixed by their oppressive Rulers.

2577. రాజు కూతురయినా వకని ఆలే.

Even the king's daughter must be some one's wife.

2578. రాజుల సొమ్ము రాళ్ల పాలూ, లంజల పాలూ.

The wealth of kings goes to stones and harlots.

Kings addicted to debauchery spent their wealth in constructing houses, temples, &c. and also lavished much on their concubines instead of spending their Revenue for the good of people they governed.

2579. రామాయణమంటే యేమో అనుకొన్నానుగాని, మాశి బరువు వున్నది అన్నాడట.

When I heard of the Râmâyaṇa I did not know what it was, but [I find] it is the weight of a man.

(See No. 2538.)

2580. రాముని తోక.

Râma's tail.

A joke.—A bad reader instead of reading రామునితో కపివరుండిట్లనియె *(Râmunitô Kapivaruṇḍiṭlaniye)* (' The Monkey-Chief said thus to Râma') read రాముని తోక పివరుండు, &c. *(Râmuni tôka Pivaruṇḍu, &c.)*

(See No. 2540.)

Used to a blundering reader.

2581. రామునివంటి రాజు వుంటే, హనుమంతుని వంటి బంటు అప్పుడే వుంటాడు.

When there is a king like Râma, a servant like Hanumân will at once be found.

(See Nos. 1662, 2606.)

2582. రామో లక్ష్మణ మబ్ర వీత్.

Râmo, Lakshmaṇa, Mabra, and—his tail !

The interpretation of an ignoramus of the sentence *Râmo Lakshmaṇam-abravît* (" Râma said to Lakshmaṇa.")

(See No. 2540.)

2583. రాళ్లు గుండ్లు దొర్లించినట్టు మాట్లాడుతాడు.

He speaks like one rolling stones and boulders.

Said of a man who speaks boldly whether right or wrong.

2584. రెండు ఆవుల పాలు తాగిన దూడ.

A calf which has drunk the milk of two cows.

It is common among Hindus for childless persons to adopt children of their friends and treat them as their own. Such children are petted both by their real and by their adoptive parents, and are in consequence often spoilt.

2585. రోగము వకటి, మందు వకటి.

The disease is one, the medicine is another.

i. e. the one is not fitted to remove the other.

Said of unsuitable remedies.

ల.

2586. లంక కాల్చినవాడు హనుమంతుడు.

The man who burnt Lankâ is Hanumân.

(See No. 211.)

2587. లంజకొడుకు తండ్రికి తద్దినం పెట్టినట్టు.

Like a bastard performing his father's annual ceremonies.

(For *Taddinam* See No. 271.)

2588. లంజ పితాళ్లకు పెట్టి ఆకాశము చూచినదట.

A harlot made an offering to the manes of her ancestors and looked towards heaven.

2589. లంజలు లేకపోతే గుడీ రంజిల్లదు ప్రజల మనసూ రంజిల్లదు.

If there were no harlots the temple would not shine and men's minds would not be fascinated.

An apology for the impure accompaniments of the Hindu's religion!

2590. లబ్ధుడికి పని నిండా, లుబ్ధుడికి ఖర్చు నిండా.

A man got [for nothing] has much work, a miser has great expenses.

(See Nos. 1912, 2595.)

Labdhudu is applied to a prisoner taken in war and made a slave.—The false economy of misers costs them much in the end.

2591. లక్షణం చెడితే అవలక్షణం.

If Lakshaṇam is neglected it becomes Avalakshaṇam.

There is a pun here on the word *Lakshaṇam* which as a noun signifies the 'rules of classic composition,' and as an adjective 'handsome.'—*Avalakshanam* means 'ugly,' 'deformed.'

(See No. 142.)

2592. లక్ష నక్షత్రములయినా ఒక చంద్రుడు కాడు.

A lakh of stars won't make one moon.

" Better one virtuous son than even a hundred fools; the one moon dispels darkness and not hosts of stars." (Hitopadeśa Book I. 17.)*

2593. లింగము మీద ఎలుక.

A rat on the Lingam.

One is afraid to knock the rat off lest he should strike the Lingam, and at the same time he cannot bear to see the emblem so insulted.

A difficult dilemma.

2594. లేనివాడు పుడమి లేనివాడు.

One who has not is as one who is not in the world.

i. e. A penniless man has nothing in the world.

2595. లోభికి రెంట నష్టి.

A miser loses both ways.

(See Nos. 1912, 2590.)

वरमेको गुणी पुत्रो न च मूर्खशतैरपि।
एकश्चन्द्रस्तमो हन्ति न च तारागणैरपि॥

వ.

2596. వంగసములో పుట్టినది పొంగలి పెట్టితే పోతుందా.

Will [the evil] born in the family go by offering Pongali ?

(For *Pongali* see No. 912.)

2597. వంశమో, వాడి ఆలి తోకో.

[I don't know] whether it comes from his family or from his wife's tail.

i. e. whether the man's mean actions are the fruit of his low birth or whether he is instigated to such conduct by his wife.

2598. వచ్చే వారికి స్వాగతం, వెళ్లే వారికి ఆసీమాంతం.

Welcome the coming, speed the parting guests.

Svâgatam signifies literally "well come."—*Âsîmântam* is an abbreviation of *Âsîmântamanuvrajeyam*, "I follow you to the boundary," used to Brahman guests at the conclusion of a *Śrâddha*.

2599. వట్టి చెయ్యి మూర వేస్తే, యేమి ఫలము.

If you measure cubits with an empty hand, what is the use of it ?

i. e. what is the use of measuring the air.

(See No. 313.)

Vain hopes.

2600. వడ్ల గింజలోది బియ్యపు గింజ.

That which is in the paddy is rice.

Said to an inquisitive person.

2601. వడ్లు ముత్తుం, పిచ్చికలు ఆర్తుం.

Three Tûms of paddy and six Tûms of sparrows.

Losses keeping pace with gains.

(For *Tûms* see No. 1104.)

2602. వాడి తండ్రీ మా తండ్రీ సయాం మొగవాండ్లు.

His father and my father are real males.

An answer given to an impertinent question regarding relationship.

2603. వాడు చెడ్డాడు తాగుబోతు, నాకు వక ముంతెడు కల్లు పొయ్యి అన్నాడట.

Hang the drunkard! Pour me out a potful of toddy.

2604. వాశిరెడ్డి వెంకటాద్రినాయుడు తులాభారం తూగితే, కరెడ్ల కామక్క వంకాయల భారం తూగినదట.

When Vâśi Reḍḍi Venkaṭâdri Nâyuḍu was weighed in gold Kareḍla Kâmakka was weighed in brinjals.

It was an old custom for Indian princes and wealthy landowners to give their weight in gold to the Brahmans.

(For *Brinjal* see No. 97—See Nos. 22, 1857.)

2605. విందూ మందూ మూడు పూటలు.

For feasting or for medicine, three times.

A man will not be treated as a guest for more than three meals and he is not expected to stay longer.—The effect of medicine should be tried by three doses after which, if it fail, it should be given up.

2606. విక్రమార్కునివంటి రాజు వుంటే, భట్టివంటి మంత్రి అప్పుడే వుంటాడు.

When there is a prince like Vikramârka, a minister like Bhaṭṭi will at once be found.

(See Nos. 1652, 2581.)

2607. విగ్రహా పుష్టి, నైవేద్య నష్టి.

Stoutness of body, consumption of food.

The only advantage of obesity is expensive living.

2608. విత్తము కొద్దీ విభవము, విద్య కొద్దీ వినయము.

In proportion to the wealth there will be enjoyment, in proportion to the learning there will be humility.

(See Nos. 454, 1974.)

2609. వినయము లోకవశ్యము, విద్య రాజవశ్యము.

Humility subjects the world, learning subjects kings.

Humility often gains more than pride. (Italian.)

2610. విన్నవి అన్నీ విశ్వసించ వద్దు, విశ్వసించినవి అన్నీ వెలిబుచ్చ వద్దు.

Don't believe all you hear, don't divulge all you believe.

Do not all you can ; spend not all you have ; believe not all you hear ; and tell not all you know.

2611. విశ్వమేలే నకులుడు అశ్వశిక్షకుడు అయినాడు.

The world-governing Nakula became a horsebreaker.

(See Virâṭaparva of the Mahâbhârata.)

The will of Providence.

2612. వీసము యిచ్చి వాసానికి ఒడ్డే వాడు.

One who gives a Visam and expects a Vâsam.

(See No. 290.)

For *Visam* see No. 876 ; the word here means of $\frac{1}{16}$ of a Rupee (anna).—*Vâsam* is a rafter ; (the original word has been retained to preserve the jingle .)

2613. వీసానికి వాసన్నర అయితే, దూలన్నర యెంత.

If a rafter and half goes for a Vîsam, how much for a beam and a half?

(For *Vîsam* see No. 2612—See No. 2321.)

Chaffing an arithmetician.

2614. వెట్టికి కని వెలుగులో పారవేశినారా.

Did [my parents] beget me for nothing and throw me into the hedge?

Said by a disciple illtreated by his Guru, or by an apprentice illtreated by his master, &c.

2615. వెన్న పెట్టితే మింగలేడు, వేలు పెట్టితే కరవలేడు.

If you give him butter he cannot swallow it, if you give him your finger he cannot bite it.

(See No. 233.)

As demure as if butter would not melt in his mouth, and yet cheese will not choke him.

2616. వెయ్యి ఆవులు గలవానికి వకటి తన్నుకొనిపోతే యేమి.

What is it to him who has a thousand cows, if one will not be milked?

(See Nos. 243, 284, 1510, 1512.)

Said by an impertinent beggar, when refused alms.

2617. వెయ్యి పుట్ల వడ్లకు వక్క చిలకపురుగు చాలును.

One Chilakapurugu is enough for a thousand Puṭṭis of Paddy.

(For *Puṭṭi* see No. 876.)

Chilakapurugu (*lit.* parrot-worm) is a small worm found in stored grain.

2618. వెయ్యి వరహాలు పెట్టి యేనుగను కొనుక్కొని అరవీసం అంకుశానకు పాలుమాలనా.

Should one buy an elephant for a thousand pagodas, and grudge half a Vîsam for a hook to drive him with ?

Vîsam (No. 876) is here used for an anna.

(See No. 2191.)

2619. వెఱ్ఱివాని విందు పెట్టేవరకూ నిశ్చయం లేదు.

A madman's feast is never certain till he gives it.

2620. వెలగల జీవరత్నము వక్కటే చాలును, చిలిపిరాళ్లు తట్టెడు వున్నా ఫలము యేమి.

One valuable gem of the first water is sufficient—though of pebbles there be a basketful, of what use are they ?

(See Vâmana Book I. 4.)

One grain of pepper is worth a cart-load of hail.

2621. వెలలేని మాణిక్యము.

A ruby without price.

Said of anything of inestimable value.

2622. వెల్లకిత్తలా పరుండి వుమ్మివేస్తే, ముఖముమీాద పడుతుంది.

If you spit when lying on your back it will fall on your face.

Who spits against heaven, it falls on his head. (French.)*

He who spits against heaven will have it fall on his face. (Spanish.)†

" *Whoso casteth a stone on high casteth it on his own head.*" Ecclesiasticus xxvii. 25.

---

* Qui crache contre le ciel, il lui tombe sur la tête.
† Quien al cielo escupe, en la cara le cae.

2623. వేరు తవ్వి వేణ్నీళ్లు పోశినట్టు.

To dig out the roots and pour in hot water.

To ruin a man utterly.

2624. వేషగాని అడుగులు వేట్లాటకు అక్కరకు వచ్చునా.

Will the postures of an actor be of use in war?

2625. వైద్యుడా నీ సంచిలో వేణ్నీళ్లు వున్నవా అన్నదట.

O Physician! have you hot water in your bag?

A lazy woman consulted a doctor: he gave her a prescription—she said that she had no one to send for the medicines; he then gave her a powder which he told her to mix with honey—she could get no honey; at last he gave her some medicine which only required to be mixed in hot water—thereupon she asked whether he had any hot water in his bag!

Said of a helpless, feckless creature.

2626. వ్యాధికి మందు వున్నదిగాని, విధికి మందు వున్నదా.

There is a remedy for disease, but is there a remedy for fate?

(See Nos. 1344, 1637, 1960, 1984.)

2627. వ్రాత రాజ్యమేలవలెనని వుంటే, గ్రహచారం గాడిదెలు మేప వలెనని వున్నదట.

When his fortune would have him govern a kingdom, his misfortune would have him graze asses.

The man was so unlucky that even the decrees of Brahmâ were overruled by his evil stars.—(See Nos. 1344, 1637.) *Grahachâra* literally signifies the rotation of the planets.

శ.

2628. శంఖులో పోస్తే తీర్థము, పెంకులో పోస్తే నీళ్లు.

If you pour it into the conch shell it is holy water, if you pour it into a potsherd it is common water.

(See No. 2047.)

2629. శేఖుభాయీకి గోకులాష్టమి వకటా.

Has Shai*kh* Bhâî a Gokulâshṭamî?

Gokulâshṭamî is a festival observed in commemoration of the birth of Kṛishṇa; it falls on the eighth day of the dark fortnight of the month Śrâvaṇa.

2630. శ్మశానమునకు పోయిన శవము తిరగదు.

The corpse which has gone to the cemetery does not return.

2631. శ్రీరామరక్ష.

The protection of the great Râma.

(See Nos. 168, 278, 1644, 1867.)

Said in cases of absolute want, &c.

2632. శ్వాసం వుండేవరకు ఆశ వుంటుంది.

As long as there is breath there is hope.

(See No. 2488.)

స.

2633. సంతకు దొంగనయితే చీల్లు యెక్కడ అమ్ముకోను.

If I were a smuggler in the fair, where could I sell my thread?

2634. సంతలో కొట్టినందుకు సాక్షులెవరు.

Who are witnesses to the [blow] struck in the fair?

In a crowd, no one can tell by whom a blow was struck.

2635. సంధ్యావందనం చేస్తే పుణ్యంలేదుగాని చెయ్యకపోతే పాపము.

If you perform Sandhyâvandanam there is no merit, but if you neglect it there is sin.

2636. సంధ్యావందన హృదయపాఠ, వాయుస్తుతి పుస్తకపాఠ.

The Sandhyâvandanam is known to my heart, the praise of Vâyu is known to the book.

(See No. 2489.)

2637. సత్రపు కూటికి సర్కారు శెలవు యెందుకు.

Why an order of Government for [eating] the food [given] in an alms-house ?

2638. సభలో నమస్కారం.

A salutation in an assembly.

A general compliment.

2639. సముద్రపు అల నిలిచేదెప్పుడు, స్నానము చేశేదెప్పుడు.

When will the waves of the sea cease [to roll] ? When will you bathe ?

i. e. Will you wait to bathe until the sea is motionless ?

2640. సాతానిజుట్టుకూ సన్న్యాసిజంధ్యానకూ ముడిపెట్టినట్టు.

Like tying a Sâtâni's top-lock and a Sannyâsî's sacerdotal thread in a knot.

A joke—Sâtânis (Râmânujas) do not wear the lock of hair common to other castes,* and Sannyâsîs wear no thread.

Said of a ridiculous scheme.

---

* निष्कच्छो मुण्डितश्चैव शंखचक्रांकितस्तथा ।
ऊर्ध्वपुण्ड्रसमायुक्तो वैष्णवः परिकीर्त्यते ॥

Without a top-lock, with shaven head, marked with the shell and discus, and having the upright streak [on the forehead]—he is called a Vaishṇava. (cf. note 1 p. 41 Wilson's *Essays and Lectures* vol. 1.)

2641. సాక్షికాళ్లు పట్టుకోవడముకన్నా వాదికాళ్లు పట్టుకోవచ్చును.

Better fall at the feet of the prosecutor than at the feet of the witnesses.

2642. సీతపుట్టడం లంకచేటుకే.

Sîtâ was born for Lankâ's ruin.

2643. సుఖవాసిదేహము మెత్తనిచెప్పుతో కొట్టవలెను.

You must beat his delicate body with a soft slipper.

Said in joke of a person who affects to be very delicate.

2644. సుగ్రీవాజ్ఞ.

The command of Sugrîva.

Strictly enforced and disobedience to it cruelly punished.

See *Kishkindhâkânda* of the Râmâyana.

2645. సుపుత్రః కొంపచెరపకః.

The best son is the ruin of the house.

All the sons were bad.

2646. సూదికిగాను సోదికి పోతే, పాత రంకులు బయిటపడ్డవి.

When he went to the oracle to find the needle, his old sins came out.

2647. సూదేటువాణ్ని, సుత్తేటువాణ్ని, కండేటువాణ్ని నమ్మరాదు.

You should not trust a needle-worker, a hammer-wielder or a bottom-thrower.

i. e. a tailor, a blacksmith, or a weaver.

(See Nos. 1759, 2045.)

A hundred tailors, a hundred millers, and a hundred weavers are three hundred thieves. (Spanish.)*

---

* Cien sastres, cien molineros, y cien texederos son trecientos ladrones.

2648. సూర్యోదయానకు కూర్చుండి శుక్రోదయానకు లేచినట్లు.

He sits down at sunrise and gets up with Venus.

Said of a glutton who sits long at his meals.

2649. సూర్యోదయానకు మాంగల్యధారణము, శుక్రోదయానకు మాంగల్య విసర్జనము.

Putting on the wedding cord at sunrise, and taking it off when Venus rises.

In the morning a bride, at night a widow.

(See Nos. 99, 711.)

2650. సొమ్మేమి లక్ష్యము, మనిషేమి పావనము.

What good is there in money ? what purity is there in man ?

2651. సోమార్లకు స్వయంపాకం చేశిపెట్టి, పందలకు పక్కవేశేవాడు.

One who cooks rice for lazy fellows and makes beds for idle scamps.

Said of a good-for-nothing fellow.

2652. స్వకార్యధురంధరుడు, స్వామికార్యవంచకుడు.

In his own business a great worker, in his master's business a great cheat.

2653. స్వపక్షపరపక్షనిర్ధూమధాముడు.

A ruiner of himself and of others.

Nirdhûmadhâma signifies literally " one who has flame without smoke."

2654. స్వర్గారోహణపర్వం చదువుతున్నాడు.

He is reading the Svargârohaṇaparva.

Svargârohaṇaparva is the last or 18th Chapter of the Mahâbhârata which contains the story of the Pâṇḍavas ascending to the heavens.

The saying is applied to a person on his death-bed.

2655. హనుమంతునిమెదట కుప్పిగంతులా

What! will you jump before Hanumân?

i. e. Who can jump like the monkey-chief?

Applied to a ridiculous attempt.

ADDITIONAL.

2656. అండలేనివూళ్లో వుండదోషం, ఆశలేనిపుట్టింట అడగదోషం.

It is wrong to live in a village that has no protection; it is wrong [for a woman] to ask [for any thing] in the house where she was born if there is no love [for her].

2657. అంపబోయిన అల్లీసాయెబూ, పిలవబోయిన పీరుసాయెబూ, మాయమ్మయినారు.

'Alî Ṣâḥib who went to set out [the departing guests], and Pîr Ṣâḥib who went to call him, both disappeared.

2658. అత్త యెత్తుకొని తింటూ వుంటే, అల్లుడికి మనుగుడుపా.

If the mother-in-law live by begging will the son-in-law have a feast?

Manuguḍupu is "a final entertainment given by the bride's parents to the bridegroom, after the conclusion of the whole marriage ceremonies." (Brown.)

2659. అయితే ఆడబిడ్డ, కాకుంటే మొగబిడ్డ, అదీ యిదీ తప్పితే అంతా అబద్ధం.

Perhaps a female child, if not, a male child ; if neither this nor that, it is all a lie.

Said by an astrologer when consulted regarding a pregnant woman.

2660. అయిసరబొజ్జ, తోప తోప.

Bravo! Bravo!—Wale! Wale!

A man was once fed with porridge (*tôpa*) in his mother-in-law's house. Never having tasted it before and wishing to have some at home he enquired its name—on his way home he had to jump over a nullah; on his clearing it, a bystander cried out *Aisarabozza* " Bravo! Bravo!" The man in his excitement forgot the word *tôpa* and substituted for it *Aisarabozza* and beat his wife because she could not make the dish until wales rose on her body. There is a pun here on the word *tôpa.*

2661. అరే గడ్డితినే కోమటీ అంటే, యేమోయి బెల్లంతినే సాయెబూ అన్నాడట; అట్లా అంటివేమి కోమటీ అంటే, అతనికి అది వాడుక నాకు యిదివాడుక అన్నాడట.

"Hollow! grass-eating Kômaṭi," said [a Mussulman], "Well! molasses-eating Ṣâhib," replied [the shopkeeper]: "How is it you speak in this way?" asked [a bystander], "He is accustomed to that and I to this," said [the Kômaṭi.]

i. e. He meant to say that the Mussulman was accustomed to grass and he to molasses.

2662. ఇంట్లో లింగాకారం, దోవలో చక్రాకారం, యిక్కడ జడలాకారం, యెక్కడా అన్నాకారం లేదు అన్నాడట.

At home the form of the Lingam, in the road the form of the Chakra, here the form of matted hair, but no where is there the form of rice.

Said by a disappointed man. At home he was too poor to eat any thing but *Sankaṭi* (No. 2512) which being coarse food stands up in the dish like a Lingam. When travelling to visit a relative he could only get in the road common round cakes (*Dôsc*) in shape like the *Chakra* (Vishṇu's discus) and when he arrived at his kinsman's house instead of being treated with good fare he was only given *Zantikalu* (country Vermicelli).

2663. ఉన్నవూరా, మన్నప్రజా.

Is it a village that I have lived in? Are the people those with whom I have been intimate?

Said of a strange place.

2664. ఉన్నశాంతం వూడ్చుకొని పోయినదిగాని కోపమే లేదు.

All my patience is swept away, but I am not at all angry.

An ironical speech used by a man boiling with indignation.

2665. ఎవరి పయిగుడ్డ వారికి బరువే.

Every man feels his own upper cloth heavy.

(See No. 414.)

Every one has his care.

Every one feels his own burden heavy. (French.)*

2666. ఏట్లో పడ్డవానికి యెన్నో యెన్నికలు.

To him who has fallen into a river how many thoughts [do not arise?]

Said of one in utter despair.

2667. ఏపట్లా చావకపోతే బాపట్లకు పంపండి.

If he does not die in any way, send him to Bâpaṭla.

i. e. If you can't get rid of him in any other way, send him to that place. *Bâpaṭla* is a village in the Guntoor District, once notorious for the rascality of its inhabitants. The Revenue officers sent there to collect the land tax are said to have been killed one after the other by being accomodated on the day of their arrival with a dwelling infested by hornets, which came out in the night and disposed of the obnoxious visitor!

---

* A chacun son fardeau pèse.

2668. ఒళ్లంతా తడిశినవెనక ప్రాపలేనివానికయినా చలిలేదు.

After the whole body is wet even an invalid does not feel the cold.

(See Nos. 1501 and 2673.)

2669. కక్కిన కూటికి ఆశించరాదు.

You should not wish for food thrown up.

Don't wish to get back what you have given away.

(See No. 81.)

2670. కలిగినవారింటి కడగొట్టుకోడలు అయ్యేటంతకన్నా పేదవారింటి పెద్దకోడలు అయితే మేలు.

Better be the eldest daughter-in-law in a poor man's house, than the youngest daughter-in-law in a rich man's house.

The eldest son's wife has authority in a household next to a mother-in-law and in the case of the latter's death she becomes mistress of the establishment. The youngest son's daughter, though generally petted, is allowed no voice in the management of the household affairs.

2671. కూడు వుడికినవెనక పొయ్యి మండుతుంది, కులం చెడ్డవెనక బుద్ధి వస్తుంది.

After the food has boiled the fire burns well, after the caste has been lost [a man's] sense comes.

i. e. He comes to his senses after losing his caste.

2672. కేశవా నారాయణా అవ్వా బువ్వ పెట్టు.

O Keśava! O Nârâyaṇa !—O grandmother! give me food.

A boy began his Sandhyâ but soon broke off to ask for his food.

2673. కొంగు తడిస్తే చలిగాని కోకంతా తడిస్తే యేమిచలి.

If the hem be wet, cold [is felt], but if the whole garment be wet, what cold [is felt ?].

(See Nos. 1501 and 2668.)

2674. గంగాధరుడు చచ్చినాడు అమ్మా.

O Madam! Gangâdhara is dead.

The story is as follows :—The washerwoman of a certain Queen had a female donkey which was pregnant. The woman vowed to Śiva that if the donkey was safely delivered she would call the young one *Gangâdhara* (one of the names of Śiva, signifying " the receiver of the Ganges"). The birth took place and the vow was fulfilled, but after a short time the young donkey died. The washerwoman was in great grief, neglected to bring the Queen's clothes, and weeping cried out " Gangâdhara is dead !" The servant sent from the palace, thinking that Gangâdhara must be some important person, went crying to the Queen. The Queen believing that a relation of the king had died commenced to weep, her whole household joining in her lamentations—the king on enquiring the cause of his consort's grief received the same information that Gangâdhara was dead, whereupon, imagining that he was a relation of the Queen's, he joined in the general howling, in which he was assisted by all his court! When the truth was at last known, all were ashamed.

2675. ఘోరకలి.

The horrible Kali.

Referring to the *Kaliyuga* " the Iron Age."

Applied to crimes of great enormity.

2676. చచ్చినా పయికం తప్పదచ్చమ్మ యిక తిట్టకు.

Though you die the money must be forthcoming—O Achchamma! Don't abuse me any more.

A Brahman after eating is bound by the ceremonial law to repeat the following :

అమృతాపిధానమసి।
రౌరవే పుణ్యనిలయే పద్మార్బుదనివాసినాం।
అర్థినాముదకం దత్తమక్షయ్యముపతిష్ఠతు॥

O Amṛita! thou art a covering. May the water given to the hundreds and thousands of [thirsty] askers in hell, the habitation of the wicked, endure without diminution.

The above is a parody, the allusion being to a hard-hearted creditor and hypocritical formalist.

2677. చిన్ననాడూ లేవు, పెద్దనాడూ లేవు, చంద్రశేఖరుడినాడు చెవుల పోగులా.

I had them not in childhood, nor in age, am I now to have earrings in Chandraśekhara's time ?

Said by a father to whom earrings were offered when, in his old age, a son had been born to him.

2678. చుక్కలూళ్లో చక్కిలాలు తేబోయినాడు.

He has gone to fetch Çakkilams from star-town.

i. e. He has died. For *Çakkilam* see No. 1609.

2679. చూస్తే సుంకం, చూడకపోతే బింకం.

If seen—duty ; if not seen—bragging.

The allusion is to a person attempting to smuggle goods through a custom house—If caught, double duty was exacted.

2680. చెడ్డా పడ్డా చేబ్రోలే గతి.

If one is unfortunate, Chêbrôlu is a refuge.

Chêbrôlu is a village in the Guntoor District.

2681. తప్పతిని కులం మరిచినట్టు.

Eating to excess, he forgets his caste.

Said of a man who, being sumptuously entertained, forgets his low origin.

2682. తప్పులేనివాణ్ని ఉప్పులో వెయ్యమన్నాడట.

Put the faultless man into the salt.

If you cannot ruin him in any other way, put him into the Salt Department—there, you can easily bring a charge of dishonesty against him and get rid of him.

2683. తింతలు తూతినవే, తూతే తాతే తాలంతత్తే తూతకతాతకతోనా దొందుదొందే.

"The tamarinds have flowered," [said one]. "When the time of blossoming and bearing fruit comes, will flowers and fruit be wanting?" [said another] "You are both alike," [said the third].

Three sisters suffered from an impediment in their speech—each thought she spoke better than either of the other two. The first instead of "*Chintalu pûchinavê,*" said "*Tintalu tûtinavê*" the second pronounced "*Pûchê kâchê kâlam vastê, pûyaka kâyaka pônâ?*" as "*Tûtê tâtê tâlam tattê, tûtaka tâtaka tônâ?*" and the third, taunting both her sisters, said of their speech "*Dondu dondê*" for "*Reṇḍu reṇḍê*" (literally, "the two are two").

2684. తిట్టితే కోపం, కొట్టితే నొప్పి.

If you abuse—anger; if you beat—pain.

2685. తిప్పులాడీ మా అప్పను చూచినావా, తీర్థంలో మా బావను చూచినావా.

Well, you affected creature, did you see my sister? Did you see my brother-in-law at the festival?

An affected woman sees no one but herself.

2686. తిమ్మన్న బంతికి రమ్మంటారు కాబోలు.

Perhaps they'll ask you to dine with Timmanna.

Timmanna is a jocose term for a monkey. The boisterous fun at the time of investing a Brahmachârî with the sacerdotal thread is called in joke *Timmannabanti,* the monkey feast.

2687. తిమ్మన్నా తిమ్మన్నా నమస్కారము అన్నాడట; నా పేరు నీకు యెట్లా తెలిసినది అంటే, నీ ముఖం చూడగానే తెలిసినది అన్నాడట.

"Timmanna! Timmanna! I salute you" cried one—"How do you know my name?" said the other. "I knew it directly I saw your face" replied the first.

2688. తుడుముకాడినుంచి దేవతార్చనదాకా వకటే మాట.

From the tom-tom to the worship of the idols, he has but one word.

(For *Tuḍum* see No. 1094.)

Said of an ignorant man, who has but one idea in his noddle.

2689. తొత్తువలె పాటుపడి, దొరవలె తినవలెను.

One must work like a slut and eat like a gentleman.

(See No. 2394.)

2690. నా నెత్తురు నావాత కొట్టుతాడు.

He casts my blood into my mouth.

i. e. He harasses and annoys me exceedingly.

2691. నీలకంఠాయ విద్మహే కొలుకులూరాయ ధీమహి।
తన్నో గుడ్లూరుః ప్రచోదయాత్॥

We think on blue-throat, we meditate on eye-corners; may the eyeball-village stimulate us.

A parody on the *Durgâ-gâyatrî* :—

కాత్యాయనాయ విద్మహే కన్యకుమారి ధీమహి।
తన్నో దుర్గిః ప్రచోదయాత్॥

We think on Kâtyâyanî, we meditate on Kanyâkumârî; may Durgâ stimulate us.

Said in joke to a boy about to cry.

2692. పాడు అయిపోయిన కూరలు బాపడికి.

The rotten vegetables to the Brahman.

(See No. 2694.)

Spurious benevolence.

When Tom's pitcher is broken I shall get the sherds.

2693. పిలిచేవారు వుంటే, బిగిశేవారు శానామంది వున్నారు.

When sought after, many become proud.

(See No. 1947.)

2694. పుచ్చిన వంకాయలు బాపనయ్యలకు.

The rotten brinjals to the Brahmans.

(For *Brinjal* see No. 97—See No. 2692.)

2695. పెక్కు రేగుల్లో వక జిల్లేడు బ్రతుకునా.

Can a Jillêḍu live in the midst of Rêgu bushes?

(For *Jillêḍu* see No. 2350.—For *Rêgu* see No. 119.)

How can a good man live in the midst of the wicked?

2696. బ్రహ్మచారి శతమర్కటం.

A Brahmachârî [is equal to] a hundred monkeys.

2697. ముక్కులో వెంట్రుక కొప్పులోకి వచ్చి మూగవాడు అమ్మా అన్న నాటికి చూతాము.

We will see about it when the hair in the nose comes into the top-lock and the dumb man calls out "Mother!"

2698. రేగుచెట్టుకింది చెవిటి గుడ్డివాని వత్తు.

Like the deaf blind man under the Rêgu tree.

(For *Rêgu* see No. 119.)

The story runs as follows:—A deaf blind man insisted on being taken to a comedy, and begged his friends to nudge him when anything very amusing was acted so that he might laugh. They pretended to agree to this, but left him half way under a *Rêgu* tree, telling him that the performance was going on there. He sat there all night laughing whenever the slender branches of the tree, moved by the wind, touched him.

2699. వండవే పెండ్లికూతురా అంటే, కుండ తీసుకొని నీళ్లకు వెళ్లుతాను అన్నదట.

When the bride was asked to cook, she said she would take a pot and go for water.

2700. శుభాలుముంచి దీపాలు ఆర్పేవాడు.

One who drowns fortune and extinguishes lamps.

Said of a man who causes the ruin of others.

INDEX TO THE TELUGU PROVERBS.

*** The Proverbs being alphabetically arranged, the initial words have not been repeated in this Index.

అ.

ధ.

న.

ప.

య.

శ.

INDEX I.

హ.

క్ష.

INDEX TO EUROPEAN PROVERBS QUOTED IN ILLUSTRATION OF TELUGU PROVERBS.

A

B

C

P

R

S

T

* Omitted to be entered under No. 984.

OTHERS, TO BE FOUND AMONG THE SANSCRIT PROVERBS.

CORRIGENDA, &c.

TELUGU.

Proverb 55, for *As long I was*, read *As long as I was*.—Pro. 87, transpose the * and †.—Pro. 105, *for* Aithampûḍi, *read* Aitampûḍi.—Pro. 150, for *large*, read *lazy*.—Pro. 160, for *gain*, read *game*.—Pro. 172, for *a hook*, read *a good hook*.—Pro. 252, *for* Rivaling, *read* Rivalling.—Pro. 226, for *his weel*, read *his house weel*.—Pro. 330, *for* Sanyâsi, *read* Sannyâsî.—Pro. 515, for *inclination*, read *inclinations*.—Pro. 536 & 1918, గడ్డు in these sayings is a vulgarism coined to rhyme with చెప్పుడు.—Pro. 560†, *for* Lente, *read* Leute.—Pro. 610, for *Great labour, &c.*, *read* Great labour, &c.—Pro. 823, *for* విడయము, *read* విడియము.—Pro. 849, *for* Sandhya, *read* Sandhyâ.—Pro. 1341, *Nêti bira* is the Luffa pentandra.—Pro. 1343, *for* loose, *read* lose.—Pro. 1790, *for* three pairs, *read* six pairs.—Pro. 1864, for *kust*, read *knot*.—Pro. 1921, for *Herles*, read *Hercules*.—Pro. 2293, *for* తాళ్వు, *read* తాళ్వ.

SANSCRIT.

Proverb 44, *for* मा भुक्तं, మా భుక్తం, *read* माभुक्तं, మాభుక్తం.—Pro. 165, टूका is a mere expletive.—Pro. 204 & 247, *for* Kunti, *read* Kuntî.—Pro. 337, *for* 111, *read* III.—Pro. 343, *for* जायत जायत, *read* जाग्रत जाग्रत, and *for* జాగృత జాగృత, *read* జాగ్రత జాగ్రత.—Pro. 390, *for* Germau, *read* German.—Pro. 414, *for* Kusa, *read* Kuśa.